MONEY

****

MONEY

EVERYTHING YOU NEVER KNEW
ABOUT YOUR FAVORITE THING
TO COVET, SAVE & SPEND

SANDRA & HARRY CHORON

CHRONICLE BOOKS

SAN FRANCISCO

ACKNOWLEDGMENTS

Worth their weight in gold: Chronicle Books, for their enthusiasm and creativity, especially Emily Haynes, our editor; Emilie Sandoz; Becca Cohen; and Christine Carswell; Jay Schaefer, who acquired the book and helped shape it; Mark Burstein, the kind of copy editor that most writers only dream about; Rochelle Diogenes, who worked on our original proposal and who nurtured it all along; Andrew Friedman of AFJ Financial, who provided professional insight and ideas about abundance and the true importance of money that were nothing less than inspirational; Dave Marsh, who somehow manages to put his two cents into everything we do, whether he knows it or not; our loving, supportive family: Shirley Glickman, Casey Choron, and Libby Hai-Choron, who enrich our lives every day; the many professionals who took the time to collaborate on both text and illustrations: Alan Halprin of WalletPop.com; Daniel J. Goevert of US-Coin-Values-Advisor.com; Shell Harris of TopTenz.net; Mitch Hight of ProfitSystems.net; John Pack of Stacks.com; Audrius Tomonis of Banknotes.com; Brian Wagoner of CoinAltar.com; Lyn Knight Auctions; and Heritage Auction Galleries.

Library of Congress Cataloging-in-Publication Data:
Choron, Sandra.
    Money : everything you never knew about your favorite thing to covet, save & spend / Sandra and Harry Choron.
        p. cm.
    Includes bibliographical references and index.
    ISBN 978-0-8118-7036-8 (pbk.)
    1. Money. 2. Money—Miscellanea. I. Choron, Harry. II. Title.

    HG221.C496 2011
    332.4--dc22

    2010031493

Manufactured in China

Designed by Allison Weiner

10 9 8 7 6 5 4 3 2 1

Chronicle Books LLC
680 Second Street
San Francisco, CA 94107
www.chroniclebooks.com

For our parents,
Kalman & Fay Samelson and
Morris & Sonia Choron,
who taught us values

TABLE OF CONTENTS

INTRODUCTION
11

CHAPTER 1: OLD MONEY   13

CHAPTER 2: NEW MONEY   105

CHAPTER 3: OTHER PEOPLE'S MONEY   215

INTRODUCTION

he love of it is the root of all evil, yet it makes the world go 'round. Most of us never seem to have enough of it, and we disdain those who do. ("If you want to know what God thinks of money," quipped Dorothy Parker, "just look at who he gave it to.") It permeates every aspect of our existence, yet it's considered an inappropriate subject in polite conversation. We claim that it can't buy happiness, but Donald Trump's perpetual smirk belies the point, and of the 685,000 books available on the subject, just about all of them pretty much focus on how to get your hands on more of it. This book is the exception.

Instead, we're looking at money from all of its angles—the historical, the cultural, the personal, and the off-the-wall. Money is at the center of our lives. We spend more time pursuing money than we spend on any other activity. It keeps us up at night, busy during the day, and (too) often accounts for how we define ourselves. Yet the fact is that most of us fear money for the simple reason that we don't understand it.

"Money is . . . a hugely emotional, psychological, and symbolic entity in our lives," says psychotherapist Kate Levinson, Ph.D., in her "Emotional Currency" workshops. "We each bring our own meanings, emotions, and experiences to our relationship with it." Yet facing our fears of it and learning how it works can reveal more to us than the mechanics of money. "It's an incredibly good vehicle for seeing our issues and vulnerabilities because it touches on almost all aspects of life and it reveals deep parts of our psyches, including our needs, fears, and desires," says Levinson. Thus, in learning about money, we learn about ourselves.

The lessons come not a moment too soon. At the time of this writing, the world has been plunged into an economic recession that has affected every aspect of our society. As faith in the workings of the government are eroded, now more than ever we each need to take responsibility for our well-being and for our futures. At the very least, we need to make peace with money. Learning about how it came to be, what it means, how it works, and what happens when it doesn't is a good first step in that direction.

"Information about money has become almost as important as money itself."—Walter Wriston, former chair and CEO of Citicorp/Citibank

Before there was money, there was chocolate—and corn kernels and knives and even pigs' feet. It was from these early forms that money as we know it was born, and it was from these humble beginnings that money changed the world—by making commerce, wars, religion, and even civilization possible. The centerpiece of this chapter is a timeline that follows money from the lumps of metal that were once used as currency to the sophisticated works of art produced by so many countries today. The economists who created theories that are still useful today, the first bankers, and the scoundrels who spawned the counterfeiting industry are just some of the characters we will meet along the way. The body of art and literature, as well as proverbs and superstitions, that grew up around the subject of money, is represented here as well.

What's notable is that despite the trouble that money has caused—the wars, the greed, the class struggles, and human suffering—we nonetheless pursue it at all costs. "Humans have found many ways to bring order to the . . . flow of our existence," says Jack Weatherford in his classic work *The History of Money*, "and money is one of the most important."

This chapter proves, beyond a shadow of doubt, that money does indeed change everything.

BEYOND BARTER: A MONEY TIMELINE

We can only imagine the origins of a barter system and the problems it presented. At its best, someone with more chickens than he knew what to do with could make a trade with someone down the road who had too many cows. Before money was created, the system was useful. But what if the whole county was overrun with chickens and you found that you couldn't even give the damn things away? Even if you did manage to locate a buyer, how did you go about making change if all he had was one measly blanket to trade? Our entire system of money was invented to solve these and other problems. This timeline shows how these were solved—and how many other difficulties were created by the development of money.

C. 3000–C. 2000 B.C.
Even before money is invented, banking originates in Babylonia out of the activities of temples and palaces, which provide safe places for the storage of valuables. Initially, deposits of grain are accepted and later other goods, including cattle, agricultural implements, and precious metals, are stored in banks.

1792–1750 B.C.
A code of law is issued by Hammurabi, who rules Babylon during this period. For the first time, specific values are ascribed to property, as the code addresses the subjects of loans, theft, land-leasing, and debt.

1200 B.C.
The earliest record of cowrie shells being used as money. The practice began in China, where the shells were found in the Pacific and Indian Oceans. Their use spreads as the Chinese begin to trade with other countries. Cowries were still in use in Nigeria until World War II.

1000 B.C.
China points the way to metal money by instituting the use of metal knives and spades as money. They also begin to make metal copies of the cowrie shells but soon discover that lumps of metal are easier to produce than the faux shells. Thus the first "coins" are produced. They are round, with holes in the middle so that they can be strung and easily carried to market.

600 B.C.
As people begin to travel more widely and trade with other countries, the idea of money begins to spread. The earliest coins, found in Lydia, part of present-day Turkey, are round pieces of metal that are stamped with the faces of gods and emperors. By 550 B.C., they are made of gold and silver. Greeks and Romans, who also use bronze for minting, soon follow suit, and coins appear in different values.

390 B.C.
The Gauls attack Rome, but the cackling of geese in the capitol, where the city's reserves of money are kept, alerts the Romans, who later build a shrine to Juno Moneta, the protector of funds. The words *money* and *mint* are derived from her name.

269 B.C.
The Romans finally adopt coinage to replace the cumbersome bronze bars (called *aes signatum*) that have been commonly used as currency.

218–201 B.C.
To fund the Second Punic War between Rome and Carthage, Roman rulers

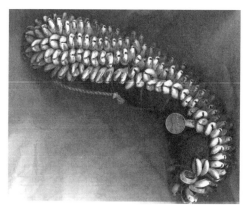

ABOVE: A bracelet of cowrie shells

By A.D. 250, the silver in Roman coins is down to 40 percent of its original silver content; by 270, it has fallen to 4 percent.

A.D. 300

The Roman denarius has been devalued by 50 percent.

A.D. 313

Constantine adopts Christianity and confiscates the treasures that lie within pagan temples throughout the empire, but nevertheless produces debased coins, leaving most of the population with inflated currency.

A.D. 400

The Roman Empire collapses, taking Western Europe's banking system with it. Banking will not develop again until the Crusades.

A.D. 435

The Anglo-Saxons invade Britain, and the use of coins there disappears for some two hundred years, during which time precious metals and other commodities are used as money. Although some coins are manufactured, they are used only as ornaments. By A.D. 630, they are back in fashion due to the influences of French and Spanish traders, and coins remain in circulation until the present day.

A.D. 650

Paper money is in popular use in China. When Marco Polo returns from his trip there in 1275, he will tell all his friends back home about this odd "paper money": "I tell you that people are glad to take these tokens, because wherever they go in the empire of the great Khan, they can use them to buy and sell as if they were pure gold."

BELOW: Cowrie shells

reduce the weight and purity of their coins, and one of the earliest periods of inflation ensues.

118 B.C.

China is the first to use paper money, in the form of a 30-centimeter square of white deerskin. Society soon learns that the value of money depends on how much of it is available, as those in financial need simply "manufacture" more by killing more deer. This lesson in inflation leads to the greater popularity of gold and silver coins.

30 B.C.–A.D. 14

Augustus Caesar reforms the Roman monetary system by introducing coins made of almost-pure gold, silver, copper, and brass.

A.D. 54–68

Nero copies the practice of other emperors by debasing gold and silver coinage, and prolonged inflation results.

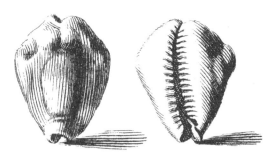

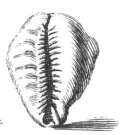

A.D. 925–940

King Athelstan of England establishes a single national currency and decrees that the amount of silver in a coin must be uniform for that denomination.

A.D. 959–975

King Edgar of England further refines the law by designating exact sizes for coins. Recognizing that coins passed from hand to hand become grubby and worn, he introduces the idea of recycling money.

1095–1270

The large sum of money needed to fund the Crusades leads to the re-emergence of banking in Western Europe.

1124

The mint masters of Winchester, England, accused of producing substandard coinage, are punished by having their right hands cut off. The quality of coins immediately improves.

1149

Hung Tsun's *Chhuan Chih (A Treatise on Coinage)*, the first book on numismatics in any language, is published.

ABOVE: Early Japanese coins; these could be strung together for convenience

1232–1253

Gold coins are issued by several Italian states, and the florin, made in Florence, is copied throughout Europe.

"In prehistoric times, there was no such thing as money. When people needed to buy something, they had to charge it. And then when the bills came, nobody could understand them, because there was also no such thing as reading. This led to a lot of misunderstandings and hitting with rocks."
—Dave Barry

1319–1331

Paper currency appears in parts of India and Japan.

1360

The French franc is first issued, as a gold coin. Prior to this date, Greek and Roman coins were in use. In 1577, a silver franc will be introduced, but the franc won't become the main unit of French currency until 1795.

1452–1519

In Italy, one of Leonardo da Vinci's many inventions is a water-powered press that can produce nearly identical coins.

1492

Christopher Columbus and, six years later, Vasco da Gama, sail from Portugal and dramatically change the course of history by discovering new trade routes, along which vast amounts of gold and silver may now be transported from one continent to another. Pooling resources to fund trade expeditions will evolve into the concept of joint-stock companies. A global economy is born.

1601

England establishes laws for dealing with the problems of the destitute. These are the first "poor laws."

1619

Tobacco is first used as currency in Virginia, and will remain in use for the next two hundred years.

1637–1638

Holland is gripped by "tulipmania," a period during which prices for the newly introduced tulip bulb reach a peak level and then suddenly collapse. This is generally considered to be the first speculative bubble, and when it bursts, it takes an entire economy with it. At the peak of tulipmania, a single tulip could be traded for an entire estate; at the bottom, a tulip costs the same as a common onion.

Alexandre Dumas (père)'s 1850 tale of financial corruption, *Black Tulip*, is based on the story of Johan de Witt and his brother Cornelis, who were executed in 1672 for their role in the event. Little is learned from the debacle, and it

BELOW: The belt of wampum that was delivered to William Penn by the Indians upon the signing of the Great Treaty of 1682

will serve as a template for similar commodity disasters throughout history.

Copyright, 1905, by John D. Morris & Company

THE BELT OF WAMPUM DELIVERED BY THE INDIANS TO WILLIAM PENN AT THE "GREAT TREATY" UNDER THE ELM TREE AT SHACKAMAXON, IN 1682

1637

Wampum—strings of beads or disks made from shells—becomes legal tender in Massachusetts. Although it will be declared illegal in 1661, wampum will remain in use in parts of America for the next two hundred years.

1652

The General Court of England passes the Massachusetts Bay Mint Act, establishing the only colonial mint. It is denied reestablishment by King James II on October 27, 1686.

1690

The Massachusetts Bay Colony issues the first paper money to replace the English, Spanish, and French currencies that have been in use in colonial America.

1694

The Bank of England is founded, and it establishes what is being called the

"interest rate" on borrowed money. The first banknotes are issued. They are printed in black on one side only and are very easy to copy. Special watermarked paper from Sweden is imported to curb counterfeiting.

1715

Suffering from a shortage of British coinage, the colonists use various substitutes, including tobacco, and Spanish and Portuguese coins. At this time, seventeen different forms of money are legal tender here.

1719–1720

The Mississippi Company had been set up by a businessman named John Law to exploit the wealth of French colonies, especially in Louisiana. In 1719, it is also given a monopoly on trade with the East Indies and China, and a speculative boom in the value of its shares ensues. The boom, combined with the over-issue of notes by the Banque Royale, leads to a drain of precious metals

from France to London. Law's enemies persuade the Regent to dismiss him from his post, the bank stops payment, and the boom collapses. The debacle sets back the development of banking in France by about a hundred years.

1720

In London, speculators invest in the South Sea Company, which has an exclusive trading monopoly with South America and the Pacific. This artificially inflates prices of stock, and the "South Sea Bubble" bursts. It takes more than a hundred years for the market to recover from the fiasco.

1764

Britain forbids the colonies to issue paper money.

1769

The Rhode Island Militia sinks the British ship *HMS Liberty* off the coast of Newport, Rhode Island, in the first major act of defiance by colonists against British taxation, which eventually sparks the American Revolution.

1775–1783

The colonists issue paper money to finance the Revolutionary War. (The paper

money issued by the state of Maryland depicts George III trampling the Magna Carta.) The notes are backed by anticipated tax revenues that never materialize, and they quickly lose their value. Hyperinflation renders the *continentals*, as they are called, worthless.

1780–1810

Banking has flourished throughout England and Wales. By the end of this period, there are more than eight hundred banks. Most of these have ties to specific trades, and it is these bankers who make the Industrial Revolution possible.

1781

The first real bank on this side of the Atlantic—the Bank of North America, in Philadelphia—is established by the Continental Congress and the dollar is adopted as the national unit of currency. At this time, private banking companies as well as the individual states are still issuing their own currencies, called State Bank Notes.

1785

A decimal coinage system is adopted, although this does not have any practical meaning until the passage of the

Mint Act of 1792, when coins are first produced.

1789
Upon adoption of the Constitution, Congress charters the First Bank of the United States, which is headed by Alexander Hamilton and serves as the fiscal agent of the U.S. Treasury. Henceforth, the individual states will not be allowed to coin money or designate anything other than gold or silver as legal tender.

"Gold is too heavy to be constantly lugged around. So, to make it easier for everybody, governments began to issue pieces of paper to represent gold. The deal was, whenever you wanted, you could redeem the paper for gold. The government was just holding your gold for you. But it was YOUR gold! You could get it anytime! That was the sacred promise that the government made to the people. That's why the people trusted paper money. And that's why, to this very day, if you—an ordinary citizen—go to Fort Knox and ask to exchange your U.S. dollars for gold, you will be used as a human chew toy by large federal dogs."
—Dave Barry

1792
The Federal Monetary System is established with the creation of the U.S. Mint in Philadelphia, and the first coins are struck the following year. Within three years, all foreign coins will lose their status as American legal tender.

1792
An American merchant ship arrives in Sydney Cove, Australia, with a new form of currency: rum. It is used as money in New South Wales until 1813.

1797
The Bank of England issues the first £1 note.

1800
There are now twenty banks in the United States, up from four in 1790. Fears that the Bank of the United States would have monopoly powers, and therefore discourage the founding of more banks, subside.

1800–1860
Cowrie shells, still in use in Uganda, suffer from inflation. At the end of the eighteenth century, it costs only two cowries to purchase a woman. After 1860, a woman will cost more than a thousand.

1801
The London Stock Exchange is established.

1825
Gregor MacGregor, a Scottish soldier and adventurer, convinces British investors to fork over money to fund the economy of the Republic of Poyais in South America. So attractive are the prospects that even the colonists clamor to get in on the action. But Poyais is a figment of MacGregor's imagination, and when the scam is uncovered, almost seventy banks fail.

1832
While the drachma has been applied to various forms of Greek currency as far back as 1100 B.C., it is not until now that the modern drachma, subdivisible into 100 lepta, is adopted as the official monetary unit of Greece.

1834
An Act of Congress redefines the amount of gold in a dollar, making coins minted prior to July 31, 1834, worth 5.2 percent less than their stated value.

1837
The Panic of 1837 begins when all the banks in New York City suspend specie payments. The panic is the second worst depression in the history of the United States and lasts until 1843.

1857
A financial panic is sparked by the failure of the Ohio Life Insurance and Trust Company, fed also by over-speculation in real estate and railroad securities. The market recovers in less than a year.

1861
To finance the Civil War, Congress authorizes the U.S. Treasury to issue paper money called Demand Notes, which are not redeemable for gold or silver but still are used for legal tender. Called "greenbacks" for their green hue, they are also referred to as Treasury Notes. In addition, the individual Confederate states, as well as railway and insurance companies, issue notes; the Confederate States of America authorizes the printing of $50, $100, $500, and $1,000 notes. Hyperinflation results and Confederate paper notes become worthless.

The first U.S. income tax is imposed: Everyone who

BELOW: Property owners suffer while ministers of finance vomit taxes into a bag labeled "budget." From the nineteenth century.

Sick of the PROPERTY TAX or ministerial Influnza

is subdivided into 100 *céntimos* or 4 *reales*.

1872

The yen becomes the official monetary unit of Japan, replacing a complex system of coinage. It can be subdivided into 100 *sen* or 1,000 *rin*, but these are taken out of circulation in 1953.

1879

To deter dishonest bartenders, the cash register is invented. James Ritty and John Birch eventually sell their patent to the National Cash Register Company.

1890

The Sherman Silver Purchase Act is enacted, requiring the government to purchase 4.5 million ounces of silver bullion

earns more than $800 must pay a 3 percent tax.

1862

The first U.S. paper money is issued in denominations of $5, $10, $20, $50, $100, and $500.

1863

The design of U.S. currency now incorporates a Treasury seal, fine-line engraving necessary for intaglio printing, intricate lathe-work patterns, and distinctive cotton and linen paper embedded with red and blue fibers. Counterfeiters respond with better equipment and more sophisticated materials.

1864

Congress first authorizes the use of the phrase "In God We Trust," on a two-cent coin.

1865

The Secret Service is established specifically to control counterfeiting. At this time, it is estimated that approximately one-third of all circulating currency is counterfeit. The Treasury issues Gold Certificates against gold coin and bullion deposits, and these are circulated until 1933.

RIGHT: A bulletin board from the New York Stock Exchange photographed on September 24, 1870, during a gold panic

1869

An attempt to corner the gold market causes the Black Friday financial panic.

1869

Spain adopts the peseta as its official unit of currency. It

"Money speaks sense in a language all nations understand." —Aphra Behn (1640–1689), English dramatist

every month with currency that is backed by both gold and silver. This causes people to sell their silver and then demand gold for the notes they receive, depleting the U.S. gold reserves.

1891
The first traveler's checks are issued by American Express.

1893
A worldwide financial panic occurs after a series of economic setbacks: the Reading Railroad, a major Eastern line, goes bankrupt, and the hundreds of banks and businesses dependent on the railroad suffer. European investors fearing the worst pull their funds out of the United States, but it's too late, and the depression reaches across the Atlantic.

1900
The Gold Standard Act officially places the United States on the gold standard.

1907
A financial crisis follows when the New York Stock Exchange falls close to 50 percent from its peak the previous year. Numerous banks and trust companies enter into bankruptcy when a nervous public rushes to withdraw funds after a failed speculation causes the fall of two major brokerage firms. J. P. Morgan saves the day by loaning the government enough money to shore up the banks.

1909
The first Lincoln pennies are minted—the first coins to bear the likeness of a president.

ABOVE: A $20 gold certificate from 1905

1910
In Central Asia, the Kirghiz people continue to use horses as money. Sheep are used as smaller units of currency, and change is made in sheepskins.

1913
To deter future economic disasters, the Federal Reserve Act is passed and creates the Federal Reserve System, which will be the nation's central bank through which all money and credit will flow. Federal Reserve Notes are issued, and are now the only currency produced.

1913
The first buffalo-head, also known as Indian-head, nickels, are circulated.

1917
The U.S. enters World War I, and the national debt rises from about $1 billion in 1916 to $25 billion in 1920.

1921
In the United States, the number of banks has reached 30,000.

1927
The first image ever to be transmitted via television is a dollar sign.

1928–1929
The U.S. stock market enjoys a boom that goes unchecked by government, until the market crashes in October of 1929. Widespread bank failures result and businesses fail. The Great Depression, as it is called, finds thousands of investors flooding the stock market with some 13 million shares. Banks that have invested in the market fail when they are unable to produce enough money for angry depositors. Some $30 billion in paper money becomes worthless overnight.

1932
The Reconstruction Finance Corporation is established and distributes $9.465 billion in loans from 1932 to 1941.

1933
Franklin Roosevelt institutes the New Deal program, restoring the failed banking

system and confidence in the country's financial system. The U.S. Federal Deposit Insurance Corporation (FDIC) is established and will insure bank deposits up to $2,500 (by 2009, this limit will have been raised to $100,000). The United States is taken off the gold standard, and all but ten of the 445,000 newly minted $20 "Double Eagle" coins are destroyed (in 2002, one of these coins will be sold for $7.59 million). It is now illegal to hoard gold coin, gold bullion, or gold certificates. Eventually, gold coins from 1933 and earlier are exempted from this rule so that coin collectors can avoid prosecution.

"We don't have the gold standard anymore. Nobody does. Over the years, all the governments in the world, having discovered that gold is, like, rare, decided that it would be more convenient to back their money with something that is easier to come by, namely: nothing. So even though the U.S. government still allegedly holds tons of gold in "reserve," you can no longer exchange your dollars for it. You can't even see it, because visitors are not allowed. For all you know, Fort Knox is filled with Cheez Whiz." –Dave Barry

1934

The U.S. Gold Reserve Act is passed, withdrawing gold coins from circulation and raising the official price of gold from $20.67 to $35 per ounce, a substantial devaluation of the dollar.

1937

The first deposit of gold bullion is shipped to the United States Bullion Depository at Fort Knox.

1938

The Federal National Mortgage Association (Fannie Mae) is created to expand the flow of money to mortgage lenders.

1939–1945

The U.S. national debt, which was only $16 billion in 1930, reaches a peak of $269 billion in 1946 but because the money was borrowed at very low interest rates, the U.S. economy thrives while those of European countries are devastated.

1944

Delegates from forty-four countries attend a meeting at Bretton Woods, New Hampshire, where they agree to establish the International Monetary Fund and what is now the World Bank to promote international trade. The countries all agree on a gold standard, and only the United States is required to convert its currency into gold at a fixed rate.

1950

A businessman named Frank McNamara pays for his meal at Major's Cabin Grill in New York City using the newly invented Diner's Club card. It is made of cardboard and is the first such device to be usable at multiple establishments.

1955

In September, following President Dwight Eisenhower's heart attack, the New York Stock Exchange suffers a $44 million loss, its most devastating setback since 1929.

1957

"In God We Trust" appears on paper currency for the first time.

1958

American Express begins issuing credit cards.

1964

Secretary C. Douglas Dillon announces that Silver Certificates will be redeemable only for silver dollars.

1965

Because older silver quarters are worth more than face value and are being melted down for profit, the Coinage Act of 1965 is passed, authorizing the removal of silver from circulating coins and providing that cupronickel-clad coins, made of copper and nickel, be used instead for the half-dollar, quarter, and dime.

1967

The first modern automatic teller machine (ATM) is installed in London outside a Barclays bank.

1968

President Lyndon Johnson signs a bill removing gold backing from U.S. paper money.

1969

The export ban on U.S. silver coins ends, allowing the export of silver coins for the first time since 1967.

> "Birth and lineage mean nothing; money is the only family tree for a townman.... Though mothers and fathers give us life, it is money alone which preserves it." —Saikaku Ihara (1642–1693), Japanese writer

1970
The U.S. government creates the Federal Home Loan Mortgage Corporation (FHLMC or Freddie Mac), to give borrowers further access to mortgages.

1972
President Richard Nixon raises the official U.S. gold price from $35 an ounce to $38 an ounce. The change in gold price is the first made since an Executive Order by President Roosevelt in 1934.

1974
President Gerald Ford lifts the ban, enacted in 1933, on gold ownership by U.S. citizens.

1976
A typical American CEO now earns 36 times as much as the average worker. By 2008, the CEO will be paid 369 times more than his working-stiff counterpart.

EARLY 1980s
Kuwait's Souk al-Manakh Stock Bubble bursts after Kuwait allows investors to pay for oil stock using post-dated checks. Billions of dollars worth of stock are purchased with unsecured checks, and the market pops just as quickly as it was inflated. The debacle represents one of the most speculative eras of all time.

Meanwhile, under America's Reagan Administration, the outsourcing of jobs to foreign countries begins on a large scale; massive numbers of jobs are lost in the United States. Over the next decades, this practice will weaken the American economy.

Also at this time, the idea of Internet banking is evolving along with the Internet. Online shopping with the use of credit cards is being promoted. Banks have already started creating databases that will be crucial to the development of the ATM system. In 1983, the Nottingham Building Society in the United Kingdom will launch the first Internet banking service, and it will form the basis for most of the Internet banking facilities that follow.

1990s
What goes up must come down. In the early 1990s, the computer revolution changes the world when each day, it seems, another geek becomes a millionaire overnight by inventing a "dot-com." The industry booms, as "dot-com"s spring up around hardware, software, and everything in between, and American cities compete for the title of "the next Silicon Valley." The bubble bursts in March of 2000, when the NASDAQ Composite Index, which tracks all the securities traded on the NASDAQ Stock Market, rises to an all-time high and the speculative nature of these investments becomes apparent.

1990
The U.S. federal minimum wage is set at $3.80 an hour.

1993
Lending institutions begin to offer low-interest "subprime mortgages" to buyers with poor credit histories. But, as interest rates begin to climb over the next few years, so do the "balloon" payments, and many of these homeowners are forced to sell.

1995
Britain's Barings Bank, the nation's oldest merchant bank, which had financed the Napoleonic wars, the Louisiana purchase, and the Erie Canal, goes from apparent strength to bankruptcy in the course of just a few days, all due to the actions of a single trader—Nick Leeson—who, after working his way up to top banking positions, took unauthorized speculative positions primarily in futures linked to the Nikkei 225 (the Tokyo stock exchange)

and Japanese government bonds, as well as options on the Nikkei. He hid his activities in a phony account, and when he finally fled the country, he left behind an £827 million ($1.4 billion) hole in the Barings balance sheet. He was eventually captured and sentenced to prison.

Meanwhile, electronic banking has replaced the use of money; by this time, 90 percent of all U.S. bank transactions are made over the Internet. In addition to saving on the cost of minting money, this development puts banking—and therefore spending—literally at the fingertips of anyone with a computer. While "digital cash" provides convenience and efficiency, privacy issues give rise to more sophisticated and centralized payment systems such as PayPal, which, only three years after its birth in 1999, will be acquired by eBay for $1.5 billion.

1999
On January 1, a single European currency, called the *euro* (€), is created. It is the official currency of Belgium, Germany, Spain, France, Ireland, Italy, Luxembourg, the Netherlands, Austria, Portugal, and Finland. The first euros will go into circulation in 2002.

2001
Under the leadership of chairman Alan Greenspan, the Federal Reserve reduces interest rates to stimulate the economy, which has become weakened by the World Trade Center tragedy. By the end of the year, interest rates will be lowered ten times.

The average American CEO now earns 282 times as much as the average worker.

2003
In January, the Bush administration predicts that the 2003 budget deficit will exceed $200 billion. The White House announces that the year's deficit will reach $445 billion. Still, the U.S. House of Representatives agrees to a 2.2 percent pay raise for themselves.

2004
Homeowners who were given loans at subprime interest rates begin defaulting on their loans as interest rates continue to rise. This will result in an annual increase in the number of foreclosures in the United States.

The U.S. national debt now exceeds the $7 trillion mark. This indicates a severe economic decline and warns that a financial collapse may be imminent.

2005
At the World Economic Forum held in Davos, Switzerland, China states that it has lost faith in the U.S. dollar and wishes to use other world currencies to establish the exchange rate for their yuan. Meanwhile, the World Bank warns that the severity of the coming slowdown in the global economy is based on the fear that foreign investors have about the strength of the U.S. dollar.

2008
In March, the U.S. Treasury announces the highest budget deficit ever posted for a single month; a staggering $175.56 billion. Later on that month, U.S. investment giant Bear Stearns and its bailout by the Federal Reserve is the first sign of a spreading global credit crunch.

It is now evident that the U.S. economy is failing and that a general slowdown in economic activity, known as a "recession," is causing record-breaking job losses, business failures, and mortgage foreclosures.

At the end of 2009, the national debt was $12,311,350,000,000.

"The only thing that differentiates man from animals is money." —Gertrude Stein

"Commodity money" is money whose value is based on that of which the money is made. It differs from "representative money," which is a token that can be exchanged for a commodity.

Using commodity money is different from bartering in that each item that is used as commodity money has a fixed value. The advantage of a commodity economy is that if all else fails, you can always use commodity money for that which it was originally intended. Grains can be consumed, and tools can be put to use. The disadvantages have mostly to do with making change and having to transport unwieldy "cash."

The commodities that societies have designated as money are those things around which their culture is based. Guatemalans used corn, which was plentiful in their country and central to their economy. The Aztecs used cacao beans, which were abundant throughout Mexico. Even cattle, which play an important role in the economies of ancient Europe, have been used as money. Here is a list of other items that we don't normally think of as mediums of exchange but which have been used as commodity money in one society or another.

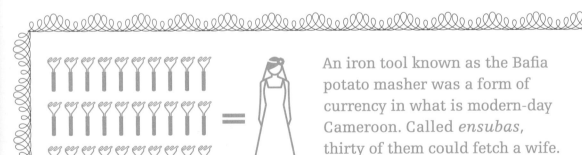

An iron tool known as the Bafia potato masher was a form of currency in what is modern-day Cameroon. Called *ensubas*, thirty of them could fetch a wife.

1   Alcohol

2   Almonds

3   Barley

4   Beads, copper

5   Belts

6   Butter

7   Cacao beans

In 2009, fourteen branches of the Tangbunia Bank on Vanuatu's Pentecost Island were accepting pig tusks as currency.

8   Candy

9   Cattle

10   Chewing gum

11   Cigarettes

12   Clay

13   Cloaks

14   Cloth

15   Coconuts

16   Corn

17   Fish

18   Furs

19   Glass

20   Gold

21   Logs

22   Marijuana

23   Olive oil

24   Peppercorns

25   Porcelain

The Yap islands, part of Micronesia, were once famous for their money—not the amount of it, but rather the size. Enormous stone disks up to twelve feet in diameter were used for money and are still in use there today, although mostly for ceremonial or traditional exchanges. Most of the stone used for these was quarried from Palau, almost 250 miles away. Stones as small as 2.8 inches in diameter were also in use.

26   Rice

27   Rubber

28   Rum

29   Salt

30   Shells

31   Silver

32   Wood

ABOVE, LEFT: Tools such as this, a spade from the middle Zaire basin, were often used as money.

ABOVE: A collection of bells, all of which were once used as currency

14 WAYS IN WHICH MONEY CHANGED THE WORLD

"Humans have found many ways to bring order to the . . . flow of existence, and money is one of the most important. . . . It allows humans to structure life in incredibly complex ways. . . . Money represents an infinitely expandable way of structuring value and social relationships—personal, political, and religious, as well as commercial and economic."
—Jack Weatherford, *The History of Money*

Once the Lydians put coinage in motion, the business of accumulating wealth became a lot easier, and with wealth came new lifestyles. The Greeks were the first society to be transformed by money, but it wasn't long before the idea spread. Here are just a few of the ways in which the commercialization of societies changed the world.

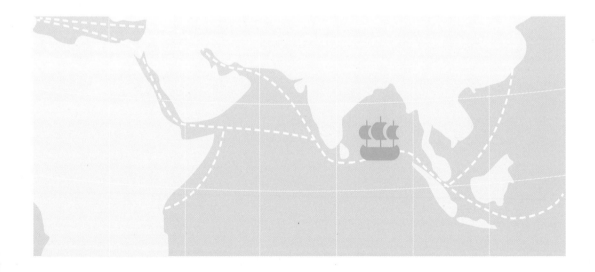

1

The ability to exchange goods for fixed prices encouraged people to widen their horizons. New trade routes to faraway towns—as well as to faraway continents—were all fueled by a hunger for wealth.

2

Kings could now afford armies; more wars became possible.

3

The modern marketplace came into being, bringing with it the ability to acquire more, and more varied, goods. It also became a social and cultural center around which towns and cities grew.

4

Kinship-based communities gave way to societies organized around commerce and financial interests. Wealth created social and financial ties that fostered more social and financial relationships than ever before.

5

In some societies, money made political elections a lot easier: The guy with the most money was simply appointed to public office.

6

In cities like Athens, which had a strong currency, democracy flourished.

7

Wealth led to more leisure time, which gave rise to the social luxuries of fine food and entertainment.

8

Temples, civic buildings, theaters, and schools could be produced, and they would soon be filled with bodies of art, philosophy, poetry, and science.

9

Now everyone needed to learn to count; a new interest in numbers gave people a new way to think, a new way to equate things with one another. The first economists emerged.

10

With the ability to offer their own dowries, women had more choices where their marriages were concerned. (In Sardis, women were allowed to work in brothels to earn larger dowries.)

11

Marriage became a business; dowries, bride prices, and payments made upon divorce or death were now taken into account when matches were made.

12

More families could now afford elaborate burials; tombs decorated with gold, silver, ivory, and marble became the new way to keep up with the Joneses.

13

The value of human work could now be fixed—good news for everyone from stable boys to prostitutes.

14

United in a common culture, people could now imagine a common religion as well; Christianity, the first religion to cross social and cultural lines, flourished in this new world.

7 ANCIENT ECONOMISTS

Their theories and observations on religious and metaphysical principles can't be discounted. In fact, they are the basis of modern day economic thought.

1 **CHANAKYA** (c. 350–283 B.C.) is known as the "Pioneer Economist of India." His classic work *Arthashastra*, a treatise on the principles of politics and the inner workings of the state, are read in Europe even today. As a professor at Takshashila University in the state of Gandhar, India, Chanakya imparted his wisdom in the fields of commerce, warfare, and economics. He also served as an advisor and Prime Minister to Emperor Chandragupta.

2 **CTESIAS FROM CNIDUS** (c. 400–300 B.C.) was a physician and historian as well as an advisor to Artaxerxes II of Persia. Ctesias is known for his treatise on Persian and Indian wealth, called *Tax in Asia*.

3 Greek philosopher **ARISTOTLE** (382–322 B.C.) was the first person to use the words "economist" and "economics," and wrote many theories on economic planning and growth. According to Aristotle, "A State . . . arises, as I conceive, out of the needs of mankind; no one is self-sufficing, but all of us have many wants. . . . Then, as we have many wants, and many persons are needed to supply them, one takes a helper for one purpose and another for another; and when these partners and helpers are gathered together in one habitation the body of inhabitants is termed a State." These thoughts are considered an important step in the development of economic analysis.

4 Greek historian **XENOPHON** (c. 430–354 B.C.) wrote about money matters in his work *Oeconomicus*, which describes the management of agricultural land and the concept of division of labor. His book *Way and Means* advocated laws regulating the activities of foreign merchants.

5 **QIN SHI HUANG** (259–210 B.C.) unified China's warring states and thus became the first emperor of a unified China in 221 B.C. Although his reign was short, he established an effective economic policy by standardizing coin currency, weights, and measures throughout China and creating the strong central bureaucracy that China had always lacked. Qin Shi Huang had the greatest and longest lasting influence among all rulers in Chinese history; it was he who ordered the building of the Great Wall of China.

6 **WANG ANSHI** (A.D. 1021–1086), a Chinese economist during the Song Dynasty, believed that government should play an active role in stimulating economic growth, and that putting more money into circulation would benefit both the government and its people. Though successful for a while, he eventually fell out of favor with the emperor, and his reforms were reversed.

7 **AL-GHAZALI** (1058–1111), a Persian philosopher and economist, based his theories of economics on the laws of the Koran that govern religion, life, family, property, and intellect. He distinguished the difference between necessities, comforts, and luxuries, maintaining that subsistence living was as dangerous as was excessive wealth. He taught that extravagance and miserliness were to be avoided and that one should seek a middle ground in all money matters.

12 GODS OF MONEY

Ever since people realized that money could be exchanged for the goods they needed, they have prayed for prosperity. Here are some of the forerunners of money worship in society today.

1. ABUNDANTIA

A minor Roman goddess of abundance, prosperity, and good fortune, she is often depicted with a cornucopia ("horn of plenty") from which she distributes grain and money. She sometimes shows up in French folklore as a character named Lady Hobunde.

2. COCHIMETL

The Aztec god of merchants and commerce is known as an excellent negotiator who never pays the asking price for anything. Shifty and thrifty, he disdains the trading of slaves.

3. DAIKOKU

The Japanese god of wealth and protector of the soil and patron of farmers is portrayed as a fat, prosperous man with two bags of rice and a bag of jewels on his shoulder. Also known as the Great Black One, his activities included granting the wishes of mortals.

4. EVENTUS BONUS

Eventus Bonus, whose name means, literally, "good ending," was a minor Roman goddess of success in business, which usually meant a good harvest, with which she is also associated.

5. HERMES

The Greek god of riches, trade, and good fortune is also the messenger of the gods. The son of Zeus and Maia, he is also associated with thievery; he is said to have stolen cattle from none other than Apollo himself when he was just two days old.

6. MERCURY

The Roman god of trade, profit, merchants, and travelers had a temple in Rome dedicated to him near the Circus Maximus where trade fairs were held. Each year on May 15, during Mercury's festival, the Mercuralia, merchants sprinkled their heads and their merchandise with water from Mercury's well near the Porta Capena. Mercury is often depicted carrying a purse, a symbol of his connection to commerce.

7. MINERVA

The goddess of wisdom, medicine, the arts, dying, and science also headed up the craft and trade division of Roman mythology, giving her a strong association with money.

ABOVE: Mosaic depicting the goddess Minerva, who had many associations with money

8. FORTUNA

Daughter of Jupiter, the veiled and blind Fortuna (Greek: Tyche), goddess of fortune, was the personification of luck in Roman religion. The luck she brought might be good or bad: she came to represent life's unpredictability.

9. OSHUN

The African goddess of love, pleasure, beauty, and diplomacy with origins in Yoruba is often associated with money, as she is known for her generosity. A goddess with a temper, she is a champion of negotiation.

10. PLUTUS

The Greek god and personification of wealth is said to have been blinded by Zeus so that he might dispense his gifts without regard to merit. He is often depicted with a cornucopia or a basket filled with ears of corn.

11. TEUTATES

Teutates (or Toutatis), ancient god of Celts and Gauls, oversaw war, prosperity, fertility, and wealth. Humans sacrificed to Teutates were killed by being plunged headfirst into a vat of ale.

12. VELES

The Slavic god of cattle and horned livestock is also associated with commerce, wealth, and prosperity; merchants often sealed their agreements by swearing upon his name, and legal documents often included oaths to him. Whether or not it stems from his connection to money, Veles is often depicted as a devil.

ABOVE, clockwise: Early drawing of Japanese god Ebisu depicted with an abacus; Relief depiction of Hermes; the goddess Oshun reigns over wealth, among other things; a statue of Mercury, the Roman god of trade and profit and merchants and travelers

The teachings of ancient Greek philosophers are still basic to modern economic thought. The fact that they are relevant today says much about how money has changed over the course of history—and how it hasn't.

EURIPIDES

"Whoever does not regard what he has as most ample wealth is unhappy, though he be master of the world."

PLATO

"He who steals a little steals with the same wish as he who steals much, but with less power."

"Honesty is for the most part less profitable than dishonesty."

"The community which has neither poverty nor riches will always have the noblest principles."

"The greatest wealth is to live content with little."

"Wealth is well known to be a great comforter."

PUBLILIUS SYRUS

"Money alone sets all the world in motion."

SOCRATES

"Are you not ashamed of caring so much for the making of money and for fame and prestige, when you neither think nor care about wisdom and truth and the improvement of your soul?"

"He who is not contented with what he has would not be contented with what he would like to have."

SOPHOCLES

"There's nothing in the world so demoralizing as money."

THEMISTOCLES

"I choose the likely man in preference to the rich man; I want a man without money rather than money without a man."

THEOPHRASTUS

"Time is the most valuable thing a man can spend."

ARISTOTLE

"All paid jobs absorb and degrade the mind."

"Gold. Get you some."

CATO

"Those who steal from private individuals spend their lives in stocks and chains; those who steal from the public treasure go dressed in gold and purple."

CICERO

"Endless money forms the sinews of war."

DIOGENES

"In a rich man's house there is no place to spit but in his face."

EPICTETUS

"Wealth consists not in having great possessions, but in having few wants."

EPICURUS

"Riches do not exhilarate us so much with their possession as they torment us with their loss."

LYDIA, OH LYDIA (WHAT WE OWE THE LYDIANS)

The ancient country of Lydia, situated in what is now Turkey, was known for its soil, rich with deposits of gold and silver. Lydia reached its peak in power at around 685 B.C. By the sixth century B.C., Lydian conquests had transformed the kingdom into an empire, its borders reaching to Greece. The empire came to a nasty end in about 546 B.C. when the Persians captured it. The Lydians may be gone, but they are not forgotten—thanks to these contributions.

» Under the rule of King Croesus, who ruled from 560 to 546 B.C, Lydians were the first to invent coins of uniform weight and value, making commerce a snap.

» The phrase "as rich as Croesus" comes from this region.

» They invented permanent retail stores, replacing "market days."

» They initiated the biggest step humankind has ever taken by creating "Ionian science," in which nature was first studied without the effects of religious beliefs and superstition. Such thought served as the foundation for modern-day mathematics, geometry, astronomy, philosophy, and most of the other sciences.

It was here that the philosopher Thales demonstrated the power of modern science to humankind by calculating the solar eclipse, for the first time in history, *before* the event took place.

» They invented the touchstone, a device for testing the true content of a coin. When metal was rubbed against the stone, a small amount of the metal was ground off into the stone, forming a stripe, which could then be examined for its true content. By enabling merchants to test for forgeries, the touchstone revolutionized commerce and eventually led to the use of gold and silver as standard equivalents of value.

» Their liberal sexual attitudes enabled women to become entrepreneurs: Prostitution was an acceptable means through which a girl could obtain a dowry.

THE EARLIEST COINS

The first "metallic money" was produced by the Chinese around 500 B.C. Although technically not coins, they were a form of coin-like money made out of base metals, such as bronze. These "coins" weren't standardized or guaranteed by a reigning monarch or governing authority; the first true coins were struck under the Lydian reign of King Croesus.

1

King Ardys of Lydia (652–615 B.C.) established a mint in the Lydian capital of Sardis, located in modern-day Turkey. Coins were produced from a naturally occurring alloy of gold and silver known as electrum, lumps of which were readily found in the mountains and streams close by. These lumps were softened by heat and placed on a plate that had a roughened face. They were then struck with a hammer and punch. These first coins were quite random as to size, weight, and purity; nevertheless, they served an important role in that period.

2

Two major advances were made in the production of coinage during the reign of King Alyattes (610–561 B.C.), the son of King Ardys. First, an established weight of 168 grains was set as the standard for a coin they called the *stater*–fractional coins of the stater were produced as well. Secondly, a reverse design was now employed on most coins, replacing the plain or blank side. The coins struck during Alyattes's reign were produced using an anvil and hammer die, allowing for a design to be simultaneously struck on both sides of the coin, pretty much the way it is still done today.

3

Lydian King Croesus (560–546 B.C.) created the first official coins in the true sense of the word. These coins were issued by a state authority and guaranteed by the monarch. They bore the official symbol of the empire, a lion's head, and the coinage metal content was pure. Croesus even went so far as to prohibit the use of electrum, allowing only pure silver and gold coins to circulate freely. He is also credited with establishing the first bimetallic standard, in which thirteen pieces of silver were the equivalent of one piece of gold.

4

The Kingdom of Lydia came to an end in 546 B.C. when it was conquered by the Persian King, Cyrus the Great. Cyrus' successor, Darius the Great (521–486 B.C.), began striking a new coin known as the *daric*. Darius introduced a small amount of copper in order to overcome the problem of pure gold being too soft for daily use. The daric was comprised of 95 percent gold, 3 percent copper, and 2 percent silver and other impurities. This coin would become the new standard throughout the areas under Persian rule and the Mediterranean for nearly two hundred years to come.

HAMMURABI'S CODE:

PENALTIES AND REWARDS IN ANCIENT MESOPOTAMIA

King Hammurabi (1792–1750 B.C.), who established Babylon as the world's first metropolis, is best known for the set of laws called Hammurabi's Code, a body of laws whose purpose was "to promote the welfare of the people . . . [and] cause justice to prevail in the land by destroying the wicked and the evil, and that the strong might not oppress the weak." These 282 laws, etched into a black stone tablet over six feet in height, were unearthed in 1901.

Where money was concerned, Hammurabi took a very dim view of any form of thievery or fraud and prescribed specific punishments for various transgressions.

FELLING A TREE

30
shekels

CRIMES DESERVING THE DEATH PENALTY

» If you killed or stole an animal and were not able to repay the owner thirty times its value.

» If you were caught breaking into someone's home or committing any robbery, you were executed on the spot.

» If thieves met in the house of a tavern-keeper to plan their crime and were not captured or reported to the court, the tavern-keeper was put to death.

» If a tavern-keeper cheated a customer by overcharging for a drink, he was thrown into a river. (At the time, most people did not know how to swim.)

» If you looted someone's home while his house was on fire, you were thrown into the fire.

» A home builder would be put to death if the house he built killed the owner or his son.

FINES FOR:

» Felling a tree: 30 shekels

» Demanding a false claim by force: 2 shekels

» Allowing a slave prisoner to die: 20 shekels

» Divorce for upper class: 60 shekels

» Divorce for middle class: 20 shekels

» Seducing a daughter-in-law to be: 30 shekels

» Injuring someone's eye or breaking a bone (middle class): 60 shekels

» Injuring a middle-class person's teeth: 20 shekels

» Assault on someone of upper class or equal rank: 60 shekels

» Assault on a middle-class person: 10 shekels

» Accidental death from wounding in a quarrel of an upper-class person: 30 shekels

» Accidental death from wounding in a quarrel of a middle-class person: 20 shekels

» Striking an upper-class woman who lost her child: 10 shekels

» Striking a middle-class woman who lost her child: 5 shekels

» Striking a maidservant who lost her child: 2 shekels

» Striking a woman, causing her to lose her child (upper-class): 30 shekels

» Accidentally goring an ox of an upper-class person: 30 shekels

» Stealing a waterwheel: 5 shekels

» Stealing a plow: 3 shekels

STEALING A PLOW

3 SHEKELS

REWARDS AND PAYMENTS FOR:

» Retrieving a runaway slave: 2 shekels

» Payment to a physician for an operation on an upper-class person: 10 shekels

» Payment to a physician for an operation on a middle-class person: 5 shekels

» Payment to a physician for an operation on a slave patient: 2 shekels

» Payment to a physician for healing a fracture of an upper-class patient: 5 shekels

» Payment to a physician for healing a fracture of a middle-class patient: 3 shekels

» Payment to a physician for healing a fracture of a slave: 2 shekels

» Payment to a veterinarian for operating on an ox or ass: ⅙ shekel

BIBLE VERSES ABOUT MONEY AND FINANCES

To believers, the Bible is as relevant and helpful today as it was when it was written; for all of us, it has plenty to say about money. In fact, money is mentioned in the Bible more than eight hundred times, and of Jesus's thirty-nine parables, more than half of them use money or work as a teaching tool. Here are some representative verses, organized by subject:

CONTENTMENT

For we brought nothing into the world, and we can take nothing out of it. But if we have food and clothing, we will be content with that. People who want to get rich fall into temptation and a trap and into many foolish and harmful desires that plunge men into ruin and destruction. For the love of money is a root of all kinds of evil. Some people, eager for money, have wandered from the faith and pierced themselves with many griefs. –Hebrews 13:5

Keep your life free from the love of money, and be content with what you have. –Philippians 4:11–13

Then He said to them, Beware, and be on your guard against every form of greed; for not even when one has an abundance does his life consist of his possessions. –Ecclesiastes 5:10

Whoever loves money never has money enough; whoever loves wealth is never satisfied with his income. –Colossians 3:15

DEBT

Open thy mouth, judge righteously, and plead the cause of the poor and needy. –Proverbs 31:9

For the LORD your God will bless you as He has promised you, and you will lend to many nations, but you will not borrow; and you will rule over many nations, but they will not rule over you. –Psalm 37:21

The wicked borrows and does not pay back, but the righteous is gracious and gives. –Proverbs 22:7

The rich rules over the poor, and the borrower becomes the lender's slave. –Romans 13:8

Owe nothing to anyone except to love one another; for he who loves his neighbor has fulfilled the law. –Proverbs 22:26–27

LENDING AND USURY

It is better that you should not vow than that you should vow and not pay. –Matthew 5:42

Give to him who asks of you, and do not turn away from him who wants to borrow from you. –Proverbs 3:27–28

Do not withhold good from those to whom it is due, when it is in your power to do it. Do not say to your neighbor, "Go, and come back, and tomorrow I will give it," when you have it with you. –Exodus 22:25

If you lend money to My people, to the poor among you, you are not to act as a creditor to him; you shall not charge him interest. –Leviticus 25:35–37

He that . . . hath given forth usury, and hath taken interest: Shall he live? He shall not live: He hath done all these abominations; he shall surely die. –Ezekiel 18:13

You shall not charge interest to your countrymen: interest on money, food, or anything that may be loaned at interest. You may charge interest to a foreigner, but to your countrymen you shall not charge interest, so that the Lord your God may bless you in all that you undertake in the land which you are about to enter to possess. –Proverbs 28:8

Poor is he who works with a negligent hand, but the hand of the diligent makes rich. —Proverbs 12:24

He who tills his land will have plenty of food, but he who follows empty pursuits will have poverty in plenty.
—Proverbs 24:27

The sleep of the working man is pleasant, whether he eats little or much; but the full stomach of the rich man does not allow him to sleep.
—Matthew 5:41

In the *Anguttara Nikaya*, a collection of Buddhist teachings, the Buddha names four kinds of happiness that stem from wealth:

ATTHISUKHA
the happiness of ownership

ANAVAJJASUKHA
the happiness that comes from earning a just livelihood

ANANASUKHA
the happiness that comes from not being in debt

BHOGASUKHA
the happiness of sharing one's wealth with others

SAVING

On the first day of every week each one of you is to put aside and save, as he may prosper, so that no collections be made when I come.
—Proverbs 27:12

Four things are small on the earth, but they are exceedingly wise: The ants are not a strong people, but they prepare their food in the summer. —Proverbs 21:5

The plans of the diligent lead surely to advantage, but everyone who is hasty comes surely to poverty.
—Proverbs 21:20

The wise man saves for the future but the foolish man spends whatever he gets.
—Matthew 19:29

Go to the ant, sluggard, consider her ways and be wise, who, having no guide, overseer, or ruler, provides her food in the summer and gathers her food in the harvest.
—Proverbs 21:5

TITHING

Honor the Lord from your wealth and from the first of all your produce; so your barns will be filled with plenty and your vats will overflow with new wine. —Exodus 23:19

Sell your possessions and give to charity; make yourselves money belts which do not wear out, an unfailing treasure in heaven, where no thief comes near nor moth destroys. For where your treasure is, there your heart will be also.
—Proverbs 11:24–25

WORK

Do not be deceived, God is not mocked; for whatever a man sows, this he will also reap. —Daniel 6:3

"O money, money, how blindly thou hast been worshipped, and how stupidly abused!"
—Charles Lamb

American bankruptcy law has its roots in Deuteronomy, which requires a forgiveness of debt "every seventh year."

"Sell not gold except for gold in equal quantity . . . Nor silver for silver except in equal quantity."
—The Koran

THE 8 LEVELS OF TZEDAKAH

Tzedakah is the Jewish form of charity, and under Jewish law, it is organized into a list from the most to the least honorable. It's interesting to note that according to some rabbinical opinions, educating your child counts as tzedakah.

ABOVE: A tzedakah box

1 The highest form of charity is to help sustain a person before they become impoverished by offering a substantial gift in a dignified manner, or by extending a suitable loan, or by helping them find employment or establish themselves in business so as to make it unnecessary for them to become dependent on others.

2 When the donor and recipient are unknown to each other.

3 When the donor is aware of the recipient's identity, but the recipient is unaware of the source.

4 When the recipient is aware of the donor's identity, but the donor does not know the identity of the recipient.

5 When one gives directly to the poor without being asked.

6 When one gives directly to the poor upon being asked.

7 When one gives less than he should, but does so cheerfully.

8 When donations are given grudgingly.

A SHORT HISTORY OF BANKING

During the Italian Renaissance, Florentine bankers conducted business in offices and in marketplaces on desks or benches—*bancos* in Italian—and it is from here that the word *bank* derives. Like so many other aspects of money, the idea of banks began simply enough, and then it grew, and grew, and grew.

EIGHTEENTH CENTURY B.C.
In early civilizations, temples, with their thick walls, constant attendance, and sacred nature, are the safest places of refuge, and so it is here that valuables, once in the form of grain and later in the form of gold, are stored. A share of the deposit is given to the temple in exchange for safekeeping. But there the riches lie idle, while monarchs and merchants have need of it; the concept of loans is born. The Babylonian Hammurabi Code includes provisions for loans made by the priests of the temples, and banking as we know it is brought into being.

FOURTH CENTURY B.C.
By the fourth century B.C., Greece has developed a sophisticated banking system in which private entrepreneurs also offer loans, exchange currencies, and some moneylenders will even accept payment in one city and arrange credit in another, eliminating the need to transport funds.

"Not too bright."
—Sgt. James Perez of the Fairfield, Connecticut Police Department on two would-be robbers who, in 2010, called a bank asking that a bag of money be prepared for them ahead of time.

The first known banker was a merchant named Pythias who traded throughout Asia Minor. His records date back to 600 B.C.

"Bankers are just like everybody else, only richer."
—Ogden Nash

TWELFTH AND THIRTEENTH CENTURIES A.D.

Rome adopts and refines banking, but there's little need of it once the Empire falls. With the Christian Church's pronouncement that the charging of interest is morally wrong, the future of banking seems uncertain until Jews, who are barred from most other vocations, take up the practice but perform transactions largely among merchants and tradesmen. Similarly, the Knights Templar, an order that was first founded in Jerusalem around A.D. 1118 by the Crusaders to serve the Church and help liberate the Holy Land from the infidels, become bankers to the rich. By the early 1300s, the Templars are condemned for their private rituals and are accused of heresy, and money-lending, for a time, is almost solely the province of Jews.

ABOVE: The illustrations on this chart represent the values and vows of the Knights Templar.

THIRTEENTH AND FOURTEENTH CENTURIES

Italy becomes the world's banking center as the florin, its gold coin, becomes recognized and trusted everywhere. Italians further refine the system by inventing double-entry bookkeeping and openly charging interest on loans, although these are considered to be "gifts" from the borrower; by creating a distinction between a loan and a contract, Italian families are able to become bankers. Two banking families in particular, the Bardi and the Peruzzi, with offices throughout the country, emerge as the most powerful, arranging the transfer of monies for the public in general and the papacy in particular. Most notably, they issue bills of exchange, a written order that allows a bank client to direct his bank to pay money to another party. These are the first checks, and they are commonly used until paper money becomes popular.

FIFTEENTH AND SIXTEENTH CENTURIES

The powerful Medici family, which controls banking during this period, is challenged and replaced by the German Fuggers, another family of great wealth who are as involved in banking as they are in politics, providing most of the bribery money that was used to elect Holy Roman Emperor Charles V. They amass vast fortunes, as they fund expensive wars at an interest rate of anywhere from 12 percent a year to 45 percent (in the case of a loan that must be arranged quickly).

In 394 B.C., a Greek slave named Pasion became the wealthiest banker in Athens.

SIXTEENTH CENTURY

In 1587, the Banco della Piazza di Rialto is opened in Venice, and although it performs the same functions as the moneylenders, it is among the first such ventures backed by the state as opposed to private interests. The complex contracts called bills of exchange are replaced with a simpler form known as a cheque.

SEVENTEENTH AND EIGHTEENTH CENTURIES

Eying the vast profits made by bankers, governments begin to open banks, using profits to finance the state. The first state-sponsored bank is Venice's Banco Giro, which opens in 1617. The Bank of Sweden is founded in 1668 and is the first national bank. Before the end of the eighteenth century, the Bank of England becomes one of the most powerful ever, with almost all of the nation's gold stored there. By this time, banking has been taken from the hands of the moneylenders and placed squarely into those of private banks. Banking is now part and parcel of commercial life.

NINETEENTH AND TWENTIETH CENTURIES

Modern banking emerges as many small banks merge to form large ones, and cheques, or checks, become a common method of transferring money. But when the cost of World War II devastates banks throughout the world, measures are taken. In 1944, delegates from forty-four countries meet in Bretton Woods, New Hampshire, to create a truly global system of banking. The International Monetary Fund and the International Bank for Reconstruction and Development (now part of the World Bank) are established. Exchange rates become fixed (though subject to change), and all currencies are required to be convertible for trade. This period will see an emphasis on protecting investments, as bank failures abound, usually around wartime. Corporations (such as the Federal Deposit Insurance Corporation in the United States) are developed solely for this purpose. In some countries, banks add other financial functions to their list of services. In Germany, the banks are the primary owners of industrial corporations, and in France, banks offer insurance services. In the United States, banks are prohibited from owning non-financial companies.

Today, banks serve both industry and private citizens throughout the world, and although they vary in levels of government regulation from country to country, an international network has made banks a truly global pursuit. Indeed, the economy of any given country is directly dependent on the security of its banking system.

THE RISE OF THE HOUSE OF ROTHSCHILD

Strict family control, total black-box operation, precision, rational thinking, a hunger for money, and an amazing ability to predict: These traits have made the Rothschild family invincible for the past two hundred years, through all the turmoil of war, politics, and finances. They built the largest financial empire known to the world, with total assets estimated at $30 trillion today.

In Hebrew, the name Rothschild is synonymous with wealth. In fact, the title line to the song "If I Were a Rich Man" (from the musical *Fiddler on the Roof*) translates in Hebrew literally as "If I were a Rothschild."

> "Give me control of a nation's money and I care not who makes the laws." —Mayer Amschel Rothschild

It began with Nathan Rothschild, the third son of Mayer Rothschild, a Jew of German origin, who was sent by his father from Frankfurt to England in 1798 to begin building the Rothschild banking empire there. Using his amazing financial talent and unpredictable methods, by 1815 he had become the largest banking power in London.

Meanwhile, first son Amschel Rothschild remained in Frankfurt to manage the Rothschild headquarters there, while second son Salomon Rothschild was sent to Vienna, to start the family banking empire in Austria. Fourth son Calmann Rothschild set out for Naples, Italy, and fifth son James represented the family in Paris. Thus the Rothschild family established the first international banking system in the world.

According to a long-standing legend, the Rothschild family owed the first millions of their fortune to Nathan Rothschild's successful speculation (or inside information, according to another theory) about the effect of the outcome of the Battle of Waterloo on the price of British bonds.

A series of carefully arranged marriages for his sons ensured that Mayer Rothschild's fortune would remain within the family. His last will and testament, disclosed in 1812 upon his death, contained strict stipulations for the management of his company:

1. Only male members of the family can participate in the family business. All top management positions would be given to family members only.
2. Marriage could only occur within the family to prevent the dilution or loss of wealth.
3. Never disclose the details of the family assets; they should never be exposed.
4. Attorneys must never interfere in inheritance issues.
5. The first son of each sub-family would become the head of the household.
6. Anyone who disobeyed these rules would automatically lose all inheritance rights.

By the mid-nineteenth century, England, France, Germany, Austria, Italy, and most other European countries' currency supply was controlled by the Rothschild family, the most powerful bankers on the planet, and their economic might was the foundation of the American banking system. Andrew Jackson viewed the Rothschilds as archenemies to a democratic banking system, ordering "I Killed the Bank," to be inscribed on his headstone, a reference to the fact that he banished the Rothschilds from the U.S. banking system in 1837.

It is estimated that the Rothschild family controls half the world's wealth at the present time, yet their power appears invisible, as they apply their name only to a small number of the companies they control. "We have had 250 years or so of family involvement in the finance business," said Baron David de Rothschild in 2008. "We provide advice on both sides of the balance sheet, and we do it globally." Today there are only five nations on the world left without a Rothschild-controlled central bank: Iran, North Korea, Sudan, Cuba, and Libya. His advice for aspiring banking families? "Don't be complacent about giving the family jobs."

A MEDIEVAL PRICE GUIDE

Here are some prices of commodities and the centuries during which they were recorded.

COW
14th century
10
shillings

CANDLES,
1 pound
12th century
1.5
pence*

*Not really all that cheap when you consider that a large house could use over 100 pounds of candles in a single night.

CERAMIC COOKING POT
12th century
.5
pence

ARMOR,
complete set, for knight
14th century
£16

PILLOWS, 4
15th century
4
pence

FOR REFERENCE:
1 pound = 20 shillings
1 shilling = 12 pence

SWORD,
cheap
12th century
6
pence

ARMOR,
complete set, for ordinary soldier
14th century
£4

GOWN,
woman's fashionable
14th century
£10–50

HORSE,
high grade
13th century
£10

ALE, cheap, 1 gallon
12th century
.75
pence

CHICKENS, 2
14th century
1
shilling

SPINNING WHEEL
13th century
10
pence

SHOES,
cheap
14th century
6
shillings

THE HIGH COST OF MEDIEVAL LIFE

12TH CENTURY

Tuition for one year of monastery school	£3
Rent for one year for three taverns and the right to sell wine	£200

14TH CENTURY

Rental of a two-story cottage outside London for one year	£3
Rental of a large house with courtyard outside London for one year	£90
Wedding party for a wealthy peasant	£3–4

15TH CENTURY

Feeding a knight's household for one year	£30–60
Dowry for a baron's daughter	£1000
Funeral for a gentleman	£7

ABOVE: "The Moneylender and His Wife," painted by Quentin Massys, 1514

WEIRD TAXES IN HISTORY

"In levying taxes and in shearing sheep, it is well to stop when you get down to the skin."
—Austin O'Malley (1858–1932), American humorist

"The income tax has made more liars out of the American people than gold has."
—Will Rogers

Lady Godiva was an Anglo-Saxon woman who lived in England during the eleventh century. According to legend, she rode naked on a horse through the streets of Coventry in protest of high taxes that had been levied by her husband, the Earl of Mercia.

And that is called asking for Dane-geld,
And the people who ask it explain
That you've only to pay 'em the Dane-geld
And then you'll get rid of the Dane!
It is always a temptation for a rich and lazy nation,
To puff and look important and to say:
"Though we know we should defeat you,
we have not the time to meet you.
We will therefore pay you cash to go away."
And that is called paying the Dane-geld;
But we've proved it again and again,
That if once you have paid him the Dane-geld
You never get rid of the Dane.

–from "Danegeld"
by Rudyard Kipling, 1911

Tax his land, tax his wage,
Tax his bed in which he lays.
Tax his tractor, tax his mule,
Teach him taxes is the rule.
Tax his cow, tax his goat,
Tax his pants, tax his coat.
Tax his ties, tax his shirts,
Tax his work, tax his dirt.
Tax his chew, tax his smoke,
Teach him taxes are no joke.
Tax his car, tax his ass,
Tax the roads he must pass.
Tax his tobacco, tax his drink,
Tax him if he tries to think.
Tax his booze, tax his beers,
If he cries, tax his tears.
Tax his bills, tax his gas,
Tax his notes, tax his cash.
Tax him good and let him know
That after taxes, he has no dough.
If he hollers, tax him more,
Tax him until he's good and sore.
Tax his coffin, tax his grave,
Tax the sod in which he lays.
Put these words upon his tomb,
"Taxes drove me to my doom!"
And when he's gone, we won't relax,
We'll still be after the inheritance TAX!
–Anonymous

"It's income tax time again, Americans: time to gather up those receipts, get out those tax forms, sharpen up that pencil, and stab yourself in the aorta." —Dave Barry

URINE TAX

This is actually how pay toilets got started: In the first century A.D., Nero, who was considered insane (he killed his wife and mother and is said to have played his lyre while Rome burned), imposed a urine tax that was collected when peasants urinated into public pots. Not only did he make money on the tax, but he then sold the urine, which was used by tanners, cloth dyers, and launderers. The tax was eventually removed, but it was reintroduced by Nero's successor, Vespasian, and applied to all public toilets. When criticized for the tax, the emperor responded, "Money doesn't stink." The tax—and our modern-day pay toilets—was the inspiration for the satire *Urinetown*, which ran on Broadway from 2001 until 2004.

COOKING OIL TAX

In ancient Egypt, a tax was placed on cooking oil, and to make sure that households weren't avoiding the tax by reusing oil, special agents were employed to audit oil consumption.

FREEDOM TAX

In ancient Rome, a slave who had purchased his own freedom had to pay an extra 10 percent tax to the government for the privilege of not being a slave anymore.

SCUTAGE

In feudal England, those who chose not to serve in the king's army were invited to pay a tax instead. Henry I came up with the idea at the beginning of the twelfth century, and it proved useful as a fund-raiser. The money collected was used to hire mercenaries. Richard I often refused payment of the *scutage*, as it was called, until a higher price was offered. Edward III was the last king to charge scutage.

DANEGELD

The *Danegeld* was a tax raised in Anglo-Saxon England in order to pay off the Vikings, in the hopes that they would be more interested in money than they would be in raping their women and pillaging their country. The first payment of 3,300 kilograms of silver was paid in A.D. 991 after the Vikings beat the Saxons at the Battle of Maldon in Essex. The Vikings were so enamored of this system that they came back for more—in 1002, 1007, 1012, and 1016.

Future kings raised Danegeld for future wars.

BEARD TAX

In 1535, Henry VIII, King of England, decided to levy a tax on beards despite the fact that he sported one. Elizabeth I, his daughter, reintroduced the tax under her rule. Tsar Peter I of Russia issued a beard tax in 1705; Orthodox clergy (who were obliged to wear beards) were exempt.

WINDOW TAX

When an income tax was originally proposed in England, people for the most part voiced the opinion that their salaries were none of the government's business. Instead, in 1696 King William III placed a two-shilling tax on each house; if you had more than ten windows, you paid more. Before the tax was abolished in 1851, citizens avoided the tax by boarding or bricking up their windows.

HEARTH TAX

King Charles II introduced a hearth tax in 1662 after deciding that it was easier to count hearths than it was people, who could move or hide. People resented both the tax and its collectors, who were free to enter any home to count hearths and who confiscated household items if the tax was not paid. Typically, people stopped up hearths to avoid the two-shilling-a-year tax.

HAT AND WIG TAX

In the late eighteenth century, when men of means were known for their wigs and fancy hats, a "progressive" form of tax was instituted in England that targeted these well-to-do individuals. To show that the tax had been paid, each legal hat and wig was so labeled. But did a scarf constitute a hat? What about caps—did they count? In 1804, the government was forced to pass an act that defined hats.

ILLEGAL DRUGS TAX

Several U.S. states actually have this one in the books. In North Carolina, for instance, if you buy illegal drugs, you must go to a tax revenue office and pay a tax so that your illegal drugs can be declared legally taxed. In Tennessee, those who bought illegal drugs in 2005 had 48 hours to pay the taxes, which varied from $3.50 for cannabis up to $200 for crack. A judge declared the tax illegal the following year.

CATCH ME IF YOU CAN:

THE 10 MOST FAMOUS COUNTERFEITING SCANDALS

The crime of counterfeiting is probably as old as money itself, and kings have often dealt very harshly with its perpetrators. The counterfeiting of coins, or "coining," was once considered a form of treason. As a result, in England, gruesome punishments for the crime have included being hanged, being drawn and quartered, and being burned at the stake. In America, too, counterfeiting was once punishable by death; banknotes printed by Benjamin Franklin often bore the phrase "To Counterfeit is Death." Here are the ten most famous counterfeiting scandals throughout history, in chronological order:

1 Mary Butterworth was a counterfeiter in colonial America. She started her operation in 1716 and organized it into a cottage industry, sternly overseeing the work of her entire family. Authorities became suspicious of Butterworth when they noticed unexpected changes in the colonial economy and, amid a flurry of rumors about the family, her husband John purchased an expensive new home.

2 The unfortunate Georgian counterfeiter Catherine Murphy was convicted of coining in 1789 and was the last woman to suffer execution by burning in England. Her co-defendants, including her husband, were executed at the same time by hanging, but as a woman the law provided that she be burned at the stake. Burning as a method of execution was abolished the following year.

3 At the start of the American Civil War, Samuel C. Upham began marketing patriotic items to support the Union and novelty items mocking the Confederacy. In February 1862, he acquired a Confederate banknote and quickly started producing novelty copies. Cotton smugglers in the South quickly bought up the bogus bills and flooded the Confederate economy with them. Since his death, many of Upham's counterfeit bills have become valuable collector's items.

4 During World War II, the Nazis forced Jewish artists in the Sachsenhausen concentration camp to forge British pounds and American dollars. The quality of the counterfeiting was very good, but the Germans were unable to circulate the bogus bills and wound up dumping them into a lake.

5 Frank William Abagnale, Jr., worked under eight identities during the 1960s, including his first as Pan American World Airways pilot Frank Williams. Over the course of five years, he passed more than $2.5 million in counterfeit checks in more than twenty-six countries and all fifty states. He was arrested in France at an Air France ticket counter when an agent recognized his face from a wanted poster. In the movie based on his life, *Catch Me If You Can* (2002), Abagnale made a cameo appearance as a French policeman.

6 Stephen Jory, known as a lovable rogue, is Great Britain's most renowned counterfeiter. Born in 1949 and brought up in North London, Jory left his grammar school and entered the criminal fraternity, he said, through his own choice. Jory started off selling cheap perfume in designer bottles and later established his own illegal printing operation, producing and distributing an estimated £5 billion in counterfeit money throughout the United Kingdom. His counterfeit notes were so convincing that they fooled counterfeit detectors. Jory died in 2006.

7 In 2004, French police seized fake €10 and €20 banknotes worth around $1.8 million from two laboratories, and estimated that 145,000 counterfeit notes had already entered circulation.

8 Anatasios Arnaouti a criminal from Manchester, U.K., led one of the most ambitious forgery operations in history before he and his accomplices were jailed in 2005. The total amount of counterfeit money they produced was never determined; their printing operation may very well have produced tens of thousands of counterfeit notes each day. The crime was considered so severe that unchecked, it could have compromised both the U.K. and U.S. economies.

9 In 2006, a Pakistani government printing press in the city of Quetta was accused of churning out large quantities of counterfeit Indian banknotes. The *Times of India* reported this scandal, revealed by a Central Bureau of Intelligence investigation. The money was allegedly used to fund terrorist activities inside India.

10 Today the finest counterfeit notes are said to be U.S. hundred-dollar bills produced in North Korea, called "Superdollars" because of their high quality. The U.S. government believes they have been circulating since the late 1980s with the dual purpose of providing a source of income and undermining the U.S. economy.

During the Civil War, one-third to one-half of the currency in circulation was counterfeit. At that time, approximately 1,600 state banks designed and printed their own bills. Each bill carried a different design, making it difficult to detect counterfeit bills from the seven thousand varieties of real bills.

"THIS IS A STICKUP!": 8 BANK ROBBERY FIRSTS

John Dillinger, "Baby Face" Nelson, the James Gang, the Newton Boys, Bonnie and Clyde—these names have made history, inspiring books, movies, and tall stories about their bank-robbing exploits. Yet while we tend to view them through sepia-colored glasses, bank robberies are still a reality today (there were almost fifteen hundred in the United States in 2007). According to the FBI, "Bank robberies may seem old-fashioned in this age of high-tech heists, but they continue to take a serious, sometimes deadly toll on local communities and businesses." Economists suggest a relationship between the rise of bank robberies and the increase in the number of mortgage foreclosures. Here are some of the daring individuals who left their mark not only on the banks they robbed, but on history as well:

1. FIRST BANK ROBBERY

Like so many others that came after it, the first bank robbery was an inside job. The then enormous sum of $162,821 was taken from the vaults of the Bank of Pennsylvania at Carpenters' Hall during the night of Saturday, August 31, or in the morning hours of Sunday, September 1, 1798. The heist occurred while Philadelphia was ravaged by yellow fever. Patrick Lyon, a blacksmith who had worked on the bank's keys, was accused and spent three months in prison for the crime before the real culprits—Isaac Davis and Thomas Cunningham, who also had access to the keys—were identified. Davis got off easy—he just lost his membership in the carpenters union. Cunningham was punished by dying of yellow fever shortly after the arrest. In fact, only Lyon benefited from the robbery: He won $9,000 in a lawsuit for wrongful prosecution and wrote a book about his ordeal titled *Narrative of Patrick Lyon Who Suffered Three Months Severe Imprisonment in Philadelphia Gaol on Merely a Vague Suspicion of Being Concerned in a Robbery of the Bank of Pennsylvania with His Remarks Thereon.*

2. FIRST MAN TO BE INDICTED FOR BANK ROBBERY

Edward Smith got away with $245,000 in cash and Spanish doubloons when he robbed the City Bank on Wall Street in New York City in 1831. As an employee at the bank, he had access to a duplicate set of keys to the vault. He was caught after a spending spree aroused suspicion and was sentenced to five years hard labor at Sing Sing.

3. FIRST ROBBER TO HOLD A PISTOL ON A BANK EMPLOYEE

Edward Green, a Massachusetts postmaster, didn't exactly plan his moves. In fact, it was only when he caught sight of Frank Converse, the son of the bank president, minding the joint all on his own one night in 1863, that Green hatched his scheme. He soon returned with a pistol, shot Converse, and walked away with more than $5,000. Green may have been the first to pull a gun on an employee, but he's on a long list of bank robbers who made the fatal error of embarking on a spending spree once the loot was in hand. Green was sentenced to death and executed in 1866.

4. FIRST BANK ROBBER TO USE A GETAWAY CAR

During his thirty-two years in crime, Henry "Bearcat" Starr claims to have robbed more banks than anyone. He began his career as a horse thief around 1879 and eventually found his way to prison. He was paroled by FDR himself for his role in helping to quell a prison riot. After more robberies and more time behind bars, he was paroled again in 1914. He remained a reformed man—for sixteen days, after which he robbed fourteen banks over the next five months. He spent fifteen years in prison and was killed during a robbery shortly thereafter. Sadly, Starr never actually got to ride the Stutz Bearcat in which he had hoped to escape and for which history awarded him his nickname.

5. FIRST HEIRESS TO BECOME A BANK ROBBER

Patty Hearst, granddaughter of publishing magnate William Randolph Hearst, made headlines when she was kidnapped by the Symbionese Liberation Army, an American self-styled urban guerrilla warfare group, in 1973. But the public turned from sad to astounded when the heiress was caught on camera during a bank robbery conducted by the SLA. While it was assumed that Hearst had been coerced into participating in the robbery, it soon became evident that she had joined her captors in their cause. She spent almost two years in prison before her sentence was commuted by President Jimmy Carter.

6. FIRST AND LARGEST ELECTRONIC BANK HEIST

Stanley Rifkin didn't need a disguise, a getaway car, or even a demand note to pull off the largest electronic bank heist in history. As a consultant to the Security Pacific National Bank in Los Angeles, Rifkin noticed that while valuables were stored in steel vaults with electronic security systems, the wire transfer room at the bank was pretty much accessible to anyone who worked there. Cleverly obtaining the right codes and identification numbers, Rifkin didn't even have to enter the bank to execute the heist. One day in 1978 he transferred $10.2 million into a bogus bank account over the phone and arranged to have the money exchanged for diamonds, which he would then sell. Rifkin was betrayed by his attorney, who turned him into the FBI. He was released after spending only three and a half years in prison; he spent the remainder of his career helping companies develop security systems that would thwart guys like him.

7. FIRST COMPUTER BANK HEIST

Bank managers learned their lesson after Stanley Rifkin made his famous phone transfer. Thereafter, wire transfers were handled by computers. This worked out just fine—until 1994, when Vladimir Levin, a biochemistry grad student in St. Petersburg, Russia, managed to hack into the Citibank computers using only a modem and a laptop and transfer $10 million to bank accounts he had opened with the help of accomplices in the United States

and across Europe. The phony transfers were discovered, but not before Levin et al. had already collected some $400,000 of the loot. Levin was rewarded for his cleverness with three years in prison, an order to repay $240,015, and immortalization on the Web in various hacker halls of fame.

8. SINGLE LARGEST BANK ROBBERY

Ray Bowman and Billy Kirkpatrick, known together as the Trench Coat Robbers, pulled off twenty-six bank heists with both precision and subtlety before entering the Seafirst Bank in Lakewood, Washington, one day in 1997. There was no violence and no resistance. There was, however, surprise on the faces of Bowman and Kirkpatrick when they opened the vault to find the largest amount of money ever taken from a single bank: $4,461,681. The two were captured after a number of uncharacteristic mistakes. Although by the time of their arrest in 1999 twenty of their robberies were past the statute of limitations, they each were sentenced to thirty-five years in prison.

"Part of the loot went for gambling, part for horses, and part for women. The rest I spent foolishly."

—George Raft, film actor, when asked how he disposed of some $10 million in the course of his career

WANTED: THE HIGHEST REWARDS POSTED

FOR OUTLAWS OF THE WILD WEST

In November 1880, Pat Garrett, sheriff of Lincoln County, New Mexico, got a posse together and set out to capture legendary gunman Henry McCarty, a.k.a. Billy the Kid. Wanted posters offered a reward of $500 for Billy's capture or death. Although this was a great deal of money at the time it was by no means the highest reward posted for an outlaw. Here are some of America's most notorious criminals and the price tags that were placed on their heads.

José Doroteo Arango, a.k.a. Francisco "Pancho" Villa (1878–1923)	100,000 pesos
Sam Bass (1851–1878)	$10,000
Mary Katherine Horony Cummings, a.k.a. Big Nose Kate (1850–1940)	$5,000
The Dalton Gang, Frank Dalton (1859–1887), Grattan Dalton (1861–1892), Emmett Dalton (1871–1937), Bob Dalton (unknown)	$15,000
William "Bill" Doolin (1858–1896)	$5,000
John Wesley Hardin (1853–1895)	$5,000
Frank James (1843–1915)	$10,000
Jesse James (1847–1882)	$15,000
Harry Alonzo Longabaugh, a.k.a. The Sundance Kid (1867–1908)	$6,500
William Preston Longley, a.k.a. Bill Longley (1851–1878)	$500
Henry McCarty, a.k.a. Billy the Kid and William H. Bonney (1859–1881)	$500
Haskay-bay-nay-natyl, a.k.a. The Apache Kid (unknown)	$500
Robert LeRoy Parker, a.k.a. Butch Cassidy (1866–1908)	$4,000
Myra Belle Shirley, a.k.a. Belle Star (1848–1889)	$10,000
Chief Sitting Bull (c.1831–1890)	$1,000
The Younger Brothers, Cole (1844–1916), Jim (1848–1902), John (1851–1874), and Bob (1853–1889)	$15,000

JESSE JAMES

BILLY THE KID

"A criminal is a person with predatory instincts who has not sufficient capital to form a corporation."
—Howard Scott

MONEY TALKS: 94 MONEY IDIOMS

ANTE UP pay an amount of money

ARM AND A LEG a great deal of money

AT ALL COSTS at any expense

BACK ON YOUR FEET returned to good financial health

BET ON THE WRONG HORSE to guess wrong

BET YOUR BOTTOM DOLLAR bet all one has on something

BORN WITH A SILVER SPOON IN ONE'S MOUTH born to wealth and comfort

BOTTOM LINE the line in a financial statement that shows net loss or gain; *also*, the last word or main point

BREAK EVEN have income equal to expenses

BREAK THE BANK win all the money at a gambling table

BRING HOME THE BACON earn the family living

BUBKES (YIDDISH) a paltry amount of money

BUNDLE a large amount of money

BURN A HOLE IN YOUR POCKET money that one wishes or intends to spend quickly (usually for something frivolous)

BUY OFF bribe

CASH-AND-CARRY selling something for cash only with no delivery

CASH IN ON make money from an opportunity

CASH IN YOUR CHIPS exchange or sell something to get some money

CASH ON THE BARRELHEAD money paid in cash immediately when something is purchased

CAUGHT SHORT not have enough money

CHEAPSKATE a stingy person

CHICKEN FEED a small amount of money

CHIP IN contribute money or pay jointly

CLEAN UP make a lot of money

COLD, HARD CASH cash, coins, and bills

COOK THE BOOKS illegally change information in accounting books

CUT-RATE discounted

DEADBEAT one who doesn't pay money that is owed

DIME A DOZEN easy to obtain; of little value

DOWN AND OUT have no money

DUTCH TREAT a plan in which each person pays their own share

FACE VALUE the worth or price printed on a stamp, bond, note, or paper money

FAST BUCK money earned quickly and easily

FEEL LIKE A MILLION DOLLARS/ BUCKS feel wonderful

FLAT BROKE penniless

FOOT THE BILL pay for something

FOR A SONG at a low price, cheaply

FORK OVER (OR OUT) pay, pay out

FOR LOVE OR MONEY for anything, for any price

GO BROKE lose all one's money

GRAVY TRAIN a situation in which one is paid more money than one would expect, as in the case of getting paid more than a job is worth

GREASE A PALM give a tip, pay for a special favor, bribe

HAND-OUT a gift of money, usually for someone in need

HARD UP not have much money

HAVE STICKY FINGERS be a thief

HIGHWAY ROBBERY charge an unconscionably high price for something

HIT THE JACKPOT make a lot of money suddenly

> "They say money talks. All it ever said to me was 'Good-bye.'" —Cary Grant

IN THE BLACK profitable, making money

IN THE HOLE in debt, owing money

IN THE RED unprofitable, losing money

KEEP BOOKS keep records of money earned and spent

KICKBACK money paid illegally for favorable treatment

LAY AWAY save

LAY OUT spend, pay money, sometimes on behalf of another individual

LIVE FROM HAND TO MOUTH live on little money

LIVE HIGH OFF (OR ON) THE HOG live in great comfort

LOADED having lots of money

LOSE ONE'S SHIRT lose all or most of one's money

MAKE A KILLING make a large amount of money

MAKE A LIVING earn enough money to live on

MAKE ENDS MEET have enough money to pay bills

MAKE MONEY HAND OVER FIST make money fast and in large amounts

MONEY TO BURN more money than is needed

NEST EGG money that has been saved for a special purpose

NOT WORTH TWO CENTS having almost no value

ON A DIME abruptly

ON A SHOESTRING on a very low budget

ON THE HOUSE paid for by the owner

PAD THE BILL add false expenses to a bill

PASS THE BUCK pass the blame

PAY DIRT a useful discovery or object

PAYOFF a bribe; a final reward

PAY THROUGH THE NOSE pay a very high price

PENNY FOR YOUR THOUGHTS asking someone what they are thinking about

PENNY-WISE AND POUND FOOL-ISH wise or careful in small things to the costly neglect of important things

PICK UP THE TAB pay the bill

PINCH PENNIES be thrifty

PONY UP pay

PUT IN ONE'S TWO CENTS give one's opinion

QUICK BUCK money earned quickly and easily, sometimes dishonestly

RAIN CHECK a promise to repeat an invitation at a later date

RAKE IN THE MONEY make a lot of money

RED CENT the smallest coin, a trivial sum of money, a penny

SALT AWAY save money

SCRAPE TOGETHER gather small amounts of money with difficulty

SHELL OUT pay

SPLURGE spend a lot of money, usually on a luxury

STONE BROKE having no money

STRAPPED have no money available

STRIKE IT RICH suddenly become rich or successful

TAKE A BEATING lose a lot of money

TIGHTEN ONE'S BELT live on less money

TWO BITS twenty-five cents, a quarter of a dollar

WORTH ONE'S SALT worth what one is paid

38 PROVERBS ABOUT MONEY

Look at a culture's proverbs and you learn about the essence of their values. Most of these proverbs about money have become part of universal wisdom.

1 A penny saved is a penny earned. –Benjamin Franklin

2 Many a pupil has gained more wealth than his master. –Greek

3 If a person has a hundred dollars and makes a million, that is incredible; but if a person has a hundred million dollars and makes a million, that is inevitable. –American

4 Misers amass wealth for those who wish them dead. –Polish

5 Deceive the rich and powerful if you will, but don't insult them. –Japanese

6 He who borrows gets sorrows. –Turkish

7 When gold speaks, every tongue is silent. –Italian

8 The saving man becomes the free man. –Chinese

9 When money speaks, the truth keeps silent. –Russian

10 Public money is like holy water; everyone helps himself to it. –Italian

11 Money makes a bastard legitimate. –Yiddish

12 Money is money, wherever it comes from. –French

13 If you have money, you have wisdom; if none, you are a fool. –Turkish

14 He who borrows gets sorrows. –Turkish

15 If wherever you go you're tight with money, you'll find your welcome will not be sunny. –Chinese

16 Who pays his debts gets rich. –French

17 Eat and drink with your friends but do not trade with them. –Turkish

18 Under capitalism, man exploits man; under socialism, the reverse is true. –Polish

19 Losing comes of winning money. –Chinese

20 A money worry isn't a mortal wound. –French

21 When you are poor, neighbors close by will not come; once you become rich, you'll be surprised by visits from (alleged) relatives afar. –Chinese

22 Getting money is like digging with a needle. Spending it is like water soaking into the sand. –Japanese

23 When you have only two pennies left in the world, buy a loaf of bread with one and a lily with the other. –Chinese

24 If small money does not go out, big money will not come in. –Chinese

25 A penny is a lot of money if you haven't got a penny. –Yiddish

26 It's as difficult to be rich without bragging as it is to be poor without complaining. –Chinese

27 Those who despise money will eventually sponge on their friends. –Chinese

28 A happy heart is better than a full purse. –Italian

29 After a rich man gets rich, his next ambition is to get richer. –American

30 No amount of money can make others speak well of you behind your back. –Chinese

31 Money cannot purchase what the heart desires. –Chinese

32 When your fortune increases, the columns of your house appear to be crooked. –Armenian

33 It's not money that brings happiness, it's lots of money. –Russian

34 Want a thing long enough and you don't. –Chinese

35 The foolish sayings of a rich man pass for wise ones. –Spanish

36 If you have money, you can make the ghosts and devils turn your grindstone. –Chinese

37 The shortest road to wealth lies in the contempt of wealth. –Seneca

38 With money in your pocket, you are wise and you are handsome and you sing well, too. –Yiddish

With money you can buy a house, but not a home.

With money you can buy a clock, but not time.

With money you can buy a bed, but not sleep.

With money you can buy a book, but not knowledge.

With money you can buy a doctor, but not good health.

With money you can buy a position, but not respect.

With money you can buy blood, but not life.

With money you can buy sex, but not love.

–Chinese Proverb

CLASSICAL WRITERS AND MONEY

Given that economics is part and parcel of the human experience, at least in modern times, it's hard to find writers who didn't touch on the subject of money in one form or another at some point. But some writers had a penchant for the subject; some would say an ax to grind. Geoffrey Chaucer's experiences as a customs officer and an accountant are reflected in *The Canterbury Tales*.

In the General Prologue, for instance, the host points out that time is money and poetry is idleness. In fact, all of the pilgrims in the stories are linked to money by virtue of their professions. Here are some other classic writers who were inspired by their personal experiences with and philosophies about money.

HONORÉ DE BALZAC
(1799–1850)

Money figures largely in *The Human Comedy*, Balzac's collection of novels and plays depicting French society in the first half of the nineteenth century. One of these, *The Rise and Fall of César Birotteau*, deals with the process of bankruptcy, with which the writer had had his own run-in. The book is also noteworthy for its discussion of branding as a marketing ploy. The short story "The House of Nucingen" depicts the details of financial manipulation in the early days of private, unrestricted banking. The work is said to have been a comment on the financial activities of the Rothschilds, who greatly benefited from early news of the Battle of Waterloo.

DANIEL DEFOE
(1660–1731)

While best known as the author of *Robinson Crusoe* and *Moll Flanders*, Daniel Defoe's connections to money were plenty: He worked as an economist, and he was a friend and supporter of William Paterson, the founder of the Bank of England.

Defoe dabbled in speculation himself but was not above attacking such investors in his writings. Karl Marx referred to Robinson Crusoe's lifestyle in the course of explaining the theory of value: Crusoe finds money and takes it back to his cave, only to discover that it is worthless and that the value of things depends solely on their usefulness. Despite his contributions, Defoe spent his last years hiding from his debtors, and he died penniless.

> "If dishonesty can live in a gorgeous palace with pictures on all its walls, and gems in all its cupboards, with marble and ivory in all its corners . . .

CHARLES DICKENS
(1812–1870)

Dickens's early life pretty much set the stage for the books that would make him famous. His father was thrown into debtors' prison after living an extravagant lifestyle that was well beyond his means, and his mother sent her children to work, despite an income of her own. Dickens began working at the age of twelve and eventually poured his feelings about his situation into some of the most memorable books ever written. The relationship between the rich and the poor became the defining theme of his work, including *A Christmas Carol*, *The Adventures of Oliver Twist*, *Great Expectations*, *David Copperfield*, and others. Unlike so many authors, Dickens was able to realize a fortune during his lifetime, as his books sold well in both Britain and the United States.

THEODORE DREISER
(1871–1945)

Dreiser, like so many of his ilk, also found inspiration in the greed and avarice of the times in which he lived. In *The Financier*, the main character, Henry Worthington Cowperwood, is based on Charles Tyson Yerkes, who, after being jailed for embezzlement, made a fortune from dealing in street railway (tram) stock in Chicago, using bribery and prostitutes to seduce lawmakers. Dreiser's most famous work, *Sister Carrie*, is about a woman who is completely driven by her financial circumstances.

AYN RAND
(1905–1982)

Russian-born Ayn Rand came to America at the age of twenty-one, where she eventually earned her reputation as a novelist and as a philosopher. Her best-known work, *Atlas Shrugged*, is a celebration of capitalism, which she admired and supported, and in it, she suggests a world in which capitalists, like Atlas, become tired of holding up the world. In 1991, the book was listed by the Library of Congress as being second only to the Bible in terms of its influence in America. She describes America's special relationship with money in this passage from *Atlas Shrugged*: "If you ask me to name the proudest distinction of Americans, I would choose—because it contains all the others—the fact that they were the people who created the phrase 'to MAKE money.' No other language or nation had ever used these words before; men had always thought of wealth as a static quantity—to be seized, begged, inherited, shared, looted, or obtained as a favor. Americans were the first to understand that wealth has to be created. The words 'to make money' hold the essence of human morality."

SIR WALTER SCOTT
(1771–1832)

The Scottish banking system owes the author of *Ivanhoe* plenty. When more than sixty English banks failed during the period 1825–1826, the crisis was blamed on the small denomination notes that small banks were issuing, so Parliament proposed to ban notes of less than £5. Under the pseudonym of Malchi Malagrowther, Scott wrote an impassioned series of letters for the *Edinburgh Weekly Journal* warning of the consequences of the move. Parliament got the message, and the ban was limited to England and Wales. Today, Scottish banks still have the right to issue banknotes even though only the Bank of England may do so in England and Wales.

WILLIAM MAKEPEACE THACKERAY
(1811–1863)

The author best known for his novel *Vanity Fair* lived a riches-to-rags existence: Although he inherited a large fortune from his father, who died when Thackeray was only five, it had all been placed in a bank in India, where the writer had been born, and it was lost in that country's financial crisis of 1833. Thackeray was forced to write in order

then dishonesty is not disgraceful, and the man dishonest after such a fashion is not a low scoundrel." —Anthony Trollope

to earn a living, and his financial frustrations show up in his work. In *Samuel Titmarsh and the Great Hoggarty Diamond*, a seemingly honest insurance salesman flees with the firm's money, leaving behind an honest clerk who must shoulder the blame. There's a similar theme in *The Newcomes* (1854), in which bank directors ravage a bank's assets, leaving it to crash. In *Vanity Fair*, he refers to his own experience: "the great Calcutta house of Fogle, Fake, and Cracksman," which "failed for a million, and plunged half the Indian public into misery and ruin." Yet Thackeray did not remain embittered. "I would rather make my name than inherit it," he was known to have said. More infamous is a quote for which young people through the ages will damn him: "Remember, it's as easy to marry a rich woman as a poor woman."

ANTHONY TROLLOPE
(1815–1882)

Trollope's work is best appreciated by those with a detailed understanding of London's economic atmosphere in the 1870s. He derived much of his inspiration from the failure of the Tipperary Bank in 1856, and based the character of Melmotte, chief villain in his novel *The Way We Live Now*, on one John Sadleir, a member of the British House of Commons who was held responsible for the debacle. It's been suggested that Trollope may have based the character on some other scoundrels of the time: George Hudson, "the railway king" who was accused of bribery and embezzling shareholders' money but was never prosecuted; Charles Lefevre, a Frenchman who had been involved in railway schemes in Central America; and Albert Gottheimer, who bought Leicester Square and then promptly lost £20 million out of £24 million that he had raised from taxpayers.

EMILE ZOLA
(1840–1902)

Zola never had much money and never worked in finances; he never even had a bank account. Yet he studied the subject voraciously by reading the work of economists, bankers, and Karl Marx before writing his scathing satire of financiers and politicians, *Money*, which was published in 1891. The main character, Aristide Saccard, working toward power and wealth, is brought to ruin at the hands of a Jewish financier, a character modeled on Baron James de Rothschild. Among Zola's most important works is his Rougon-Macquart cycle (1871–1893), which included the novel *L'Assommoir* (1877), about the suffering of the Parisian working class. He wrote of this period: "I want to portray, at the outset of a century of liberty and truth, a family that cannot restrain itself in its rush to possess all the good things that progress is making available and is derailed by its own momentum, the fatal convulsions that accompany the birth of a new world."

These classic works of literature illuminate the world of investing:

1. "THE BUBBLE"
(1720)

Jonathan Swift

After the bull market (or "bubble") in shares of the South Sea Co. burst, Britain's most caustic poet eviscerated the promoters who lined their own pockets with the investing public's money. Swift could feel their pain; he had, like most of the British intelligentsia, invested in the mania himself. (In fact, he had even written fawning articles about the South Sea Co. in the popular press, helping—temporarily!—to drive up the value of his own shares.) His bitter words ring as true today as they did nearly three hundred years ago.

2. RISE AND FALL OF CÉSAR BIROTTEAU
(1837)

Honoré de Balzac

Based on the real-estate bubble that swept Paris in 1828, this is the saga of an ordinary owner of a perfume shop who deludes himself into thinking he is a genius at property speculation. A few quick flips of lots around the Madeleine, and César is hooked. Told with the narrative sweep and obsession with detail that are Balzac's hallmarks, it all ends as badly as the real-estate bubble that burst in the United States 179 years later. César should have listened to his wife; Mimi saw it coming as clear as day.

3. THE GAMBLER
(1867)

Fyodor Dostoyevsky

In this novella, Dostoyevsky captures the obsessions of a pathological gambler—the tantalizing hope of hitting the jackpot, the automatic perception of patterns in the random spins of a roulette wheel, the giddy thrill of a hot streak, and the humiliation of unexpected losses. There may be no better description anywhere in literature of the emotional roller-coaster of financial gains and losses. Meanwhile, Dostoyevsky also skewers the hypocrisy and snobbery of aristocrats who claim not to care about money but grub for gains at the casino and wheedle cash out of each other.

4. THE GILDED AGE
(1873)

Mark Twain and Charles Dudley Warner

In this scathing satire, Twain and Warner (the editor of *The Hartford Courant*) create an elegantly networked snarl of phony stock promoters, politicians lining their own pockets, naïve investors, and journalists either too stupid or corrupt to warn the public. For the railroads, substitute dot-com stocks; for the coal mines, substitute telecom stocks. For the politicians, no substitutes are necessary. Twain and Warner's novel is as old as the hills and yet as new as Pets.com, Enron, and WorldCom.

5. "THE NECKLACE"
(1884)

Guy de Maupassant

Read this famous short story only if you do not already know how it turns out. Struggling on the fringes of high society in Paris, Mathilde Loisel and her husband want to make something more of themselves. After a glorious night on the town leads to trouble, Mathilde discovers things about herself, her husband, and the nature of work and friendship that she never could have imagined.

6. "HOW MUCH LAND DOES A MAN NEED?"
(1886)

Leo Tolstoy

James Joyce is said to have called this the greatest short story ever written. It is more a parable or a fable than a short story, but it will never leave you once you read it. Tolstoy tells a deceptively simple tale of a man whose greed is circumscribed only by time. How rich can he make himself before the sun sets?

"He who has money has in his pocket those who have none."
—Leo Tolstoy

7. "THE BOTTLE-IMP"
(1893)

Robert Louis Stevenson

In this beautiful little masterpiece, told from the point of view of a Hawaiian fisherman, Stevenson immortalizes the central problem of momentum investing: No matter how many times it seems possible to sell something to someone else who will take it off your hands for the right price, eventually you will run out of such people . . . and then you will have a really big problem on your hands.

8. "ROTHSCHILD'S FIDDLE"
(1894)

Anton Chekhov

No one but Chekhov could have written a story so short and so rich. At once highly empathetic and gently mocking, this tale of poverty, loss, and regret is one of the saddest and yet funniest short stories ever written. It also offers a memorable lesson about the importance of knowing when to stop counting what economists call your "opportunity costs." (Hint: the financial return on your own death is not infinite.)

9. "THE $30,000 BEQUEST"
(1906)

Mark Twain

Twain's short story (from which his volume of stories takes its name) chronicles the way an imaginary fortune changes the lives of a young couple. With keen psychological insight, Twain shows that the anticipation of striking it rich can often be more intense—and more satisfying—than the actual arrival of cash. And when castles in the air collapse, the wreckage is everywhere.

10. "THE HONOUR OF ISRAEL GOW"
(1911)

G. K. Chesterton, from *The Innocence of Father Brown*

Is it possible to be a "just miser"? Can someone crave wealth without being greedy? In one of the most surprising detective stories you will ever read, G. K. Chesterton shows that the answer to both questions can be yes. And, as usual, he tells the tale in dazzlingly beautiful prose.

11. "MONEY"
(1973)

Philip Larkin

In one of the chilliest poems ever written about money, we hear the amazingly detached voice of a man who understands nothing about material wealth other than the fact that other people rather seem to enjoy it. What is the point of all that striving and getting, asks Larkin, when it ends in the grave for rich and poor alike? The closest shave of all comes not from an expensive barber, but from the mortician.

28 FICTIONAL MISERS

The word "miser" derives from the Latin *miser*, meaning "poor" or "wretched." As if the world was not already filled with enough real versions, here are some famous fictional penny-pinchers.

EBENEZER BALFOUR
Scottish antagonist from *Kidnapped* (1886) by Robert Louis Stevenson

PHILLIP BANKS
From *The Fresh Prince of Bel-Air* film and TV series

THE BARON
A character from Alexander Pushkin's drama *The Miserly Knight* (1830; also known as *The Covetous Knight*), which, with music by Sergei Rachmaninoff, comprised a one-act opera (1906)

MR. BRIGGS
The guardian of the title character in *Cecilia* (1782) by Frances Burney

CHARLES MONTGOMERY BURNS
Usually referred to as "Mr. Burns," the owner of the Springfield Nuclear Power Plant in *The Simpsons* cartoon series

NORBERT COLON
British cartoon character from the adult British comic "Viz"

MILBURN DRYSDALE
Banker played by Raymond Bailey in *The Beverly Hillbillies* TV sitcom

HENRY EARLFORWARD
English bookseller in Arnold Bennett's novel *Riceyman Steps* (1923)

FAGIN
Jewish Londoner from Charles Dickens's novel *Oliver Twist* (1838)

GRANDET
Father of Eugénie Grandet in the novel of the same name (1833) by Balzac

HARPAGON
The money-lender from Molière's play *The Miser* (1668)

HEAT MISER
The controller of hot weather in the 1974 animated film *The Year Without Santa Claus*

KAZ
The money-grubbing manager of the duo Puffy Ami Yumi in the Japanese animated series, based on Kaz Harada, the group's real manager

EUGENE H. KRABS (A.K.A. MR. KRABS)
Penny-pinching owner and founder of the Krusty Krab restaurant in *Sponge-Bob SquarePants* animations

THE LADY OF STAVOREN
A character in Dutch legend whose greed caused the ruination of the city in which she lived. Today a statue of her stands in Stavoren, Netherlands, as a reminder of her foolish ways.

LEROY LOCKHORN
Penny-pinching husband of Loretta Lockhorn from the syndicated single-panel comic called "The Lockhorns," created in 1968 by William Hoest

SILAS MARNER
The penurious weaver who raises the child Eppie in *Silas Marner* (1861) by George Eliot

SCROOGE McDUCK
Walt Disney comics character named after Ebenezer Scrooge

TRINA McTEAGUE

The parsimonious wife in Frank Norris's novel *McTeague* (1899) who dies for her fortune

MEAN MR. MUSTARD

Title character in the Beatles' song who "keeps a ten-bob note up his nose," once described by John Lennon as "a bit of crap I wrote in India," from the album *Abbey Road* (1969)

FRED MERTZ

The lovable tightwad in TV's *I Love Lucy*, played by William Frawley

PLYUSHKIN

The pack rat landowner from Nikolai Gogol's novel *Dead Souls* (1842)

POP

A bear from the *Happy Tree Friends* animated Internet phenomenon

HENRY F. POTTER

The character played by Lionel Barrymore in the Frank Capra film *It's a Wonderful Life* (1946), who sets it all in motion

EBENEZER SCROOGE

The man whose last name has become synonymous with the word *miser* from Charles Dickens's *A Christmas Carol* (1843) and who is thus described: "The cold within him froze his old features, nipped his pointed nose, made his eyes red, his thin lips blue, and he spoke out shrewdly in his grating voice."

SHYLOCK

The Jewish moneylender in Shakespeare's *The Merchant of Venice*, who sets the interest for at least one loan at "a pound of flesh"

SNOW MISER

The controller of cold weather in the 1974 animated film *The Year Without Santa Claus*

VLADEK

A mouse from the graphic novel *Maus* by Art Spiegelman (first published as a complete story in 1986)

"The coward regards himself as cautious, the miser as thrifty."

—Publilius Syrus, Roman author, first century B.C.

"The happiest miser on earth is the man who saves up every friend he can make."

—Robert E. Sherwood

LEFT: "Growing Fat on Ill-Gotten Gains." A political cartoon from the nineteenth century complains about police corruption.

Aesop's fables, dating back to the sixth century B.C., contain timeless lessons as well as many of today's common adages and expressions, and are still taught to thousands of schoolchildren daily as basic lessons in humanity. Here are some of Aesop's lessons on the morality of money and wealth:

1. THE FIR TREE AND THE BRAMBLE

A fir tree boasted to a bramble, "Poor you, no use at all, while I am big and strong, and useful for all sorts, like when men need me to build houses." But the bramble replied, "You wait until they come with their axes to chop you down—you'll wish you were a bramble and not a fir."

Moral: Better poverty without a care than the obligations of the wealthy.

2. THE MILKMAID AND HER PAIL

After milking the farmer's cows, a milkmaid was carrying the pail of milk on her head to the dairy and thinking to herself, "With the cream that I shall get from this milk I can make some butter, which I'll take to market and sell. I'll buy some eggs with the money, and when hatched I'll have some chickens for a poultry yard. I can sell the poultry, and with the money I'll buy a fine gown to wear to the fair. All the young men will admire me and make advances, but I shall toss my head and dismiss them." At which, lost in her ambitious thoughts, she did toss her head, dropping the pail and the milk on the ground, dashing her dreams.

Moral: Don't count on good fortune until it is finally realized.

3. THE DOG AND THE MEAT

A dog with a fine slab of meat in his mouth crossed a bridge over a river and saw his reflection in the water. Thinking it to be another dog with a larger piece of meat, he let go his own and dived at the other dog to take it. He surfaced with nothing, and his dinner washed away in the current.

Moral: Be satisfied with what you have or you may lose it.

4. THE SOLDIER AND THE HORSE

A soldier tended his horse well during the wars and the horse served him well in return. At the end of the wars, the soldier treated the horse badly, with little food, no shelter, and heavy, drudging work. War broke out again and the soldier went to use the horse as before, but the wretched beast collapsed, saying that the poor treatment had turned him into an ass, and he would not be restored to a trusty steed.

Moral: Look after what is of value.

A HISTORY OF THE PIGGY BANK

While the exact origin is a little uncertain, historians speculate that the concept of a piggy bank started in England during the Middle Ages, probably in the mid-1500s. At this point in history, metal was still seldom used and very expensive. So expensive, in fact, that common people did not own any metal cooking pots or utensils. Instead, dishes, jars, and cookware were made from an affordable and easily available orange clay that was called *pygg*.

Families often kept any spare household coins in one of their clay pygg jars, and these containers became commonly known in England as pygg jars and later pygg banks.

By around the eighteenth century, the name had evolved into *piggy bank*. Around this same time, a handful of potters began making clay banks in the shape and likeness of the animal namesake, and the first piggy banks were born.

Children and adults were captivated by these new piggy banks and they quickly spread throughout England and eventually the world. The early models were usually ceramic and had no hole in the bottom: Sadly, in order to retrieve the money, the pig had to be broken open. Eventually, someone thought to add a method of emptying the container so the piggy could be spared for another round of saving.

The piggy bank isn't associated with any holiday and it has no religious ties. It is found in many cultures from North and South America to Europe, Asia, and parts of Africa.

In some European countries, it is common to give piggy banks as gifts to both children and adults because they are thought to bring luck and financial good fortune. In German-speaking countries especially, people give "Lucky Pigs" as gifts to mark the start of the New Year.

LEFT: Early cast-iron piggy bank

"All that glistens is not gold," from *The Merchant of Venice*, is perhaps the most recognizable Shakespearian (mis)quote on the subject of money (he actually said "glisters"), but the Bard's thoughts on wealth are revealed in numerous other works. Shakespeare regarded money as an important test of his characters' moral and ethical actions, and his plays therefore raised serious questions about the corrupting nature of wealth.

> "Money is a kind of poetry."
>
> —Wallace Stevens

> "There's no money in poetry, but there's no poetry in money either."
>
> —W. H. Auden

LEFT: Painted scene from *The Merchant of Venice* showing Jewish moneylender Shylock lending money to his Christian rival, Antonio, in return for a pound of flesh

"He that wants money, means, and content is without three good friends."
—*As You Like It*

"My pride fell with my fortunes"
—*As You Like It*

"There is gold for you. Sell me your good report." —*Cymbeline*

"'Tis gold which makes the true man kill'd and saves the thief; Nay, sometimes hangs both thief and true man." —*Cymbeline*

"Neither a borrower nor a lender be; for loan doth oft lose both itself and friend, and borrowing dulls the edge of husbandry." —*Hamlet*

"Rich gifts wax poor when givers prove unkind."
—*Hamlet*

"How quickly nature falls into revolt, When gold becomes her object!"
—*King Henry the Fourth, Part II*

"Will fortune never come with both hands full, But write her fair words still in foulest letters?"
—*King Henry the Fourth, Part II*

"By Jove, I am not covetous for gold, Nor care I who doth feed upon my cost; It yearns me not if men my garments wear; Such outward things dwell not in my desires: But if it be a sin to covet honor, I am the most offending soul alive." —*King Henry the Fifth*

"Thou that so stoutly hast resisted me, Give me thy gold, if thou hast any gold; For I have bought it with a hundred blows."
—*King Henry the Sixth, Part III*

"Bell, book, and candle, shall not drive me back, When gold and silver becks me to come on." —*King John*

"When fortune means to men most good, She looks upon them with a threatening eye." —*King John*

"Remuneration! O, that's the Latin word for three farthings."
—*Love's Labour's Lost*

"With this there grows, In my most ill-compos'd affection such a stanchless avarice that, were I King, I should cut off the nobles for their lands, desire his jewels, and this other's house, And my more-having would be as a sauce to make me hunger more, that I should forge quarrels unjust against the good and loyal, destroying them for wealth."
—*Macbeth*

"If thou art rich, thou'rt poor, For, like an ass whose back with ingots bows, Thou bear'st thy heavy riches but a journey, And death unloads thee."
—*Measure for Measure*

"He that hath the grace of God, hath wealth enough."
—*The Merchant of Venice*

"Yet gold all is not that doth golden seem." —*The Merchant of Venice*

"O, what a world of vile ill-favored faults, Looks handsome in three hundred pounds a year."
—*The Merry Wives of Windsor*

"Who steals my purse steals trash; 'tis something, nothing; 'twas mine, 'tis his, and has been slave to thousands; but he that filches from me my good name robs me of that which not enriches him and makes me poor indeed." —*Othello*

"There is thy gold—worse poison to men's souls, doing more murder in this loathsome world, than these poor compounds that thou mayst not sell."
—*Romeo and Juliet*

"Nothing comes amiss; so money comes withall."
—*The Taming of the Shrew*

"Gold? Yellow, glittering, precious gold? No, Gods, I am no idle votarist!"
—*Timon of Athens*

"Who would not wish to be from wealth exempt, since riches point to misery and contempt?"
—*Timon of Athens*

"Foul cankering rust the hidden treasure frets, But gold that's put to use more gold begets."
—*Venus and Adonis*

"He seems to be of great authority. Close with him, give him gold; and though authority be a stubborn bear, yet he is oft led by the nose with gold."
—*The Winter's Tale*

10 POSSIBLE ORIGINS OF THE DOLLAR $IGN

Although it is one of the most recognized symbols in the world, few agree on the origins of the dollar sign, although most concur that it had something to do with the Spanish pesos that preceded American money. Here are some theories as to how it came about.

1 The first use of $ in an American context was in a 1784 memorandum from Thomas Jefferson suggesting the dollar as the primary unit of currency. Some have deduced from this that he made it up there and then, either as a monogram somehow based on his own initials or as a kind of doodle.

2 A widely held notion is that it originated as the letters U and S superimposed on each other and that the U eventually disintegrated into unconnected parallel lines. Robert Morris, who helped finance the Revolutionary War, is reputed to be the first U.S. official to show the dollar sign by using a single vertical stroke.

3 Some believe that the dollar sign is a simplified depiction of the Spanish coat of arms engraved on the old silver Spanish pieces of eight—the S-shaped scroll wrapped around the twin Pillars of Hercules.

4 Some maintain that the dollar sign was inspired by the mint mark on Spanish "pieces of eight" minted in Potosi (a city and department of Bolivia) comprised of the letters "PTSI" superimposed on one another.

5 It has been suggested that the dollar sign is derived from a notation for a unit of silver. Before the American Revolution, prices were often quoted in units of the Spanish dollar. According to this theory, when a price was quoted, a capital S was used to indicate silver with a capital U written on top to indicate units. Eventually the U was replaced by double vertical hash marks.

6 According to some, the symbol is derived from the German *Thaler*, a coin that had the crucified Christ on one side and a serpent hanging from a cross on the other.

7 A successful Irish immigrant named Oliver Pollack (1727–1823), who settled in Pennsylvania and amassed great wealth as a trader and as a plantation owner, is often credited as having originated the symbol.

8 The dollar sign may have derived from the *sestertius*, a Roman coin represented by the letters HS which, when superimposed, form a dollar sign with two vertical strokes.

9 Another theory maintains that the dollar sign originated with Hermes, the Greek god of bankers, thieves, messengers, and tricksters. One of Hermes's symbols was the caduceus, a staff from which ribbons or snakes dangled in a sinuous curve. Others believe that it's a version of the letters IHS, the Greek abbreviation for the name Jesus.

10 The Masonic Order maintains that the vertical lines represent the pillars of Boaz and Jachin in the original Temple of Solomon in Jerusalem. This theory is supposedly supported by the appearance of the All Seeing Eye of God on U.S. currency.

ALL THAT GLITTERS: THE LURE OF GOLD

A child found a shiny rock in a creek thousands of years ago, and the human race was introduced to gold for the first time.

Gold was first discovered as gleaming, yellow nuggets in its natural state in streams all over the planet. Because gold is dispersed widely throughout the geologic world, its discovery occurred to many different groups in many different locales; respect for gold was universal. Its association with wealth itself is common to many cultures throughout the globe. No doubt it was the first metal known to early hominids.

Gold is the easiest of the metals to work. It occurs in a virtually pure and workable state. Gold's early uses were no doubt ornamental, and its brilliance and permanence (it neither corrodes nor tarnishes) linked it to deities and royalty in early civilizations. Thus gold in ancient times was made into shrines and idols, plates, cups, vases, vessels of all kinds, and, of course, jewelry.

In the quest for gold by the Phoenicians, Egyptians, Indians, Hittites, Chinese, and others, prisoners of war were sent to work the mines, as were slaves and criminals.

The Incas referred to gold as the "tears of the Sun."

As far back as 3100 B.C., there is evidence of a gold/silver value ratio in the code of Menes, the founder of the first Egyptian dynasty. In this code it is stated that "one part of gold is equal to two and one half parts of silver in value." This is our earliest evidence of a value relationship between gold and silver.

The first use of gold as money occurred around 700 B.C., when Lydian merchants produced the first coins. These were simply stamped lumps of a 63 percent gold and 27 percent silver mixture known as "electrum."

The Greeks knew much about the practicalities of gold mining. By the time of the death of Alexander the Great (323 B.C.), the Greeks had mined gold from the Pillars of Hercules (Gibraltar) all the way eastward to Asia Minor and Egypt. The Romans also furthered the quest for gold, mining it extensively throughout their empire, and advancing mining methods considerably.

The concept of money (i.e., gold and silver in standard weight and fineness coins) allowed the world's economies to expand and prosper. During the Classic period of Greek and Roman rule in the Western world, gold and silver both flowed to India for spices, and to China for silk. At the height of the Empire (A.D. 98–160), Roman gold and silver coins reigned from Britain to North Africa and Egypt.

BELOW: $1,250,000 in gold bullion, 1906

Over Half a Million Pyramid of Gold, Bank of B. N. A.

"Annual income twenty pounds, annual expenditure nineteen six, result happiness. Annual income twenty pounds, annual expenditure twenty pounds ought and six, result misery." —Charles Dickens, *David Copperfield*

"Never run into debt, not if you can find anything else to run into." —Josh Billings

Death, dismemberment, slavery (for the debtor and family members), indentured servitude, exile, and debtors' prison have all been used as punishment for the inability to pay one's debts; Dickens did not use the word "misery" lightly. And yet the first known effort to regulate bankruptcy was surprisingly modern in its approach. Appearing in the Code of Hammurabi, which dates to Babylon around the eighteenth century B.C., the law stipulated that a bankrupt's possessions were to be divided among creditors in proportion to the amount of money each was owed.

By 621 B.C., when Draco ruled Athens, the punishment meted out to "deadbeats" (literally, one who is "completely exhausted") was death. Or they and their families might be sold into slavery, with the proceeds going to creditors.

A generation later, the Athenian statesman and poet Solon decided this was perhaps a bit too severe. Under his legal reforms, the bankrupt and his family had to give up their citizenship, but not their freedom—or their lives.

The Romans, however, soon turned back the sundial. Under the Twelve Tables of Rome, promulgated in 451 B.C., maiming became the appropriate sanction. Instead of getting his money back, the creditor was given a pound of flesh or perhaps more, depending on how much was owed. Debtors were cut up and their parts distributed among creditors on a pro rata basis. The Roman writer Petronius would later satirize this practice in the *Satyricon*, a portion of which describes a plutocrat whose will decrees that any friend, parasite, or hanger-on who wants to collect his inheritance must eat a piece of the dead man's corpse. Shakespeare makes reference to the practice in *The Merchant of Venice*.

"Money is better than poverty, if only for financial reasons." —Woody Allen

In thirteenth-century England, Henry III established the practice of imprisoning debtors. By the time of Henry VIII, in the mid-sixteenth century, the first bankruptcy statute was enacted. It applied only to merchants and traders, since they were considered the only people who had a legitimate reason to borrow money, and provided a way for their debts to be addressed (sans death, torture, or even prison) in the event that a storm at sea sank their boats and thus their fortunes, or similar circumstances beyond their control led to bankruptcy. That statute did not get the common man off the hook, however.

Once someone landed in debtors' prison, or *gaol* (pronounced "jail"), it was often nearly impossible to get out. Family or friends might come forward to pay the prisoner's debts; if not, debtors were left to rot.

The absurdity of debtors' prison—a bankrupt's ability to repay his creditor from prison is precisely nil—soon became apparent. In some countries, creditors were required to pay the costs of incarcerating their debtors. The open-ended prison sentence could be cut short, therefore, should the creditor tire of throwing good money after bad. Lucky debtors could end up as "peons," bankrupt persons condemned to work without pay for a creditor until the debt was paid off. This peonage system still exists in some societies despite the fact that it is prohibited under international law.

Today, bankruptcy still entails pain, if only in the form of many, many meetings with lawyers. And Dickens's lesson still rings true: Having slightly more than you need is infinitely better than having even slightly less.

> "It is vain to continue an institution which experience shows to be ineffectual. We have now imprisoned one generation of debtors after another, but we do not find that their numbers lessen." —Samuel Johnson, 1758

"DON'T RUN IN DEBT"

Friends, don't run in debt,
never mind, never mind,
If your clothes are some
tatter'd and torn;
Fix them up, make them do,
it is better by far
Than to have the heart
weary and worn.

Who will love you the more
for the set of your hat?
Or your ruff, or the tie of
your shoe?
Or the shape of your vest
or your boots, or cravat,
If they know you're in debt
for the new?

Chorus:
Then don't run in debt,
never mind, keep at work,
Let your heart be honest
and true;
You'll find it better to wear
your old clothes,
Than to ruin in debt for
the new.

There's no comfort I tell you,
in walking the streets
In new clothes, if you know
you're in debt,
And feel that perchance you
some tradesman may meet,
Who will sneer, "O, they're
not paid for yet!"

Good friends, let me beg
of you, don't run in debt,
Tho' the chairs and the
sofas are old,
They'll fit your back better
than any new set,
Unless they're all paid for
in gold.

If you've money to spare,
I have nothing to say,
Spend your dollars and
dimes as you please,
But mind you, the man
who has a note to pay,
Is the man who is never
at ease . . .
–George M. Clark, 1880

Charles Goodyear, the inventor, did four days of jail-time in France for not paying his Paris distributors.

Robert Morris, who largely financed the American Revolution, spent four years in the gaol after winding up in debt after a land speculation deal went sour.

BENJAMIN FRANKLIN ON MONEY

The author, printer, satirist, political theorist, politician, scientist, inventor, civic activist, statesman, and diplomat was also, according to biographer Walter Isaacson, "the most accomplished American of his age and the most influential in inventing the type of society America would become." During his lifetime (1706–1790), he invented the lightning rod, bifocals, the Franklin stove, a carriage odometer, and the lending library. As a Founding Father, Franklin championed the right of the Colonies to print paper currency, a fight that won him a permanent spot on the obverse side of the $100 bill. Here are some of his thoughts on money.

1 A penny saved is a penny earned.

2 Early to bed, and early to rise, makes a man healthy, wealthy, and wise.

3 Diligence is the mother of good luck.

4 God helps them that help themselves.

5 Sloth, like rust, consumes faster than labor wears, while the used key is always bright.

6 Drive thy business, let not that drive thee.

7 Industry need not wish.

8 He that lives upon hope will die fasting.

9 There are no gains, without pains.

10 Plough deep, while sluggards sleep, and you shall have corn to sell and to keep.

11 One today is worth two tomorrows.

12 He that hath a trade hath an estate.

13 He that hath a calling hath an office of profit and honor.

14 At the working man's house hunger looks in, but dares not enter.

15 Industry pays debts, while despair encreaseth them.

16 For want of a nail the shoe was lost, for want of a shoe the horse was lost, and for want of a horse the rider was lost.

17 Beware of little expenses; a small leak will sink a great ship.

18 Buy what thou hast no need of, and before long thou shalt sell thy necessaries.

19 A fat kitchen makes a lean will.

20 Think of saving as well as of getting: The Indies have not made Spain rich, because her outgoes are greater than her incomes.

21 When the well's dry, they know the worth of water.

22 If you would know the value of money, go and try to borrow some.

"My old father used to have a saying: If you make a bad bargain, hug it all the tighter." –Abraham Lincoln

23 He that goes a borrowing goes a sorrowing.

24 Fond pride of dress is sure a very curse; e'er fancy you consult, consult your purse.

25 When you have bought one fine thing you must buy ten more, that your appearance may be all of a piece.

26 'Tis easier to suppress the first desire than to satisfy all that follow it.

27 Pride breakfasted with plenty, dined with poverty, and supped with infamy.

28 When you run in debt, you give to another power over your liberty.

29 The second vice is lying, the first is running in debt.

30 Lying rides upon debt's back.

31 Poverty often deprives a man of all spirit and virtue: 'Tis hard for an empty bag to stand upright.

32 Creditors are a superstitious sect, great observers of set days and times.

33 Those have a short Lent who owe money to be paid at Easter.

34 The borrower is a slave to the lender, and the debtor to the creditor.

35 Disdain the chain, preserve your freedom, and maintain your independency: Be industrious and free; be frugal and free.

36 Gain may be temporary and uncertain, but ever while you live, expense is constant and certain.

37 Rather go to bed supperless than rise in debt.

THE GOLD STANDARD

The phrase "gold standard" is defined as the use of gold as the standard value for the money of a country. If a country will redeem any of its money in gold, it is said to be using the gold standard. The United States and many other Western countries adhered to the gold standard during the early 1900s. Today, however, gold's role in the worldwide monetary system is negligible. Britain abandoned the gold standard in 1931; the United States abandoned it in 1971. Holdings of gold are still retained because it is an internationally recognized commodity that cannot be legislated upon or manipulated by interested countries. On August 15, 1971, the world entered the first era in its history in which no circulating paper anywhere was redeemable in gold, by anyone. At one point in time, it was illegal for a U.S. citizen to own gold. President Richard Nixon revoked that, thereby closing the "gold window." This action broke the last tie between gold and circulating currency, resulting in our modern financial system, which is called a "floating currency" system.

Gold rules the world. —German proverb

Since 1976, the U.S. government no longer sets the gold value of a dollar. The price of gold rises and falls in relation to the demand for the metal; gold coins have not been minted as legal currency since 1933. In 1986, the U.S. Mint did begin to issue gold coins for collectors (at far above face value) in four denominations: $50, $20, $10, and $5. And there really is a Fort Knox: Since 1937, most of the nation's gold has been stored there, underground.Even though the world's monetary systems are no longer based on the value of gold, people are still intrigued and impressed with it. It is a valuable metal with many high-tech uses, and a beautiful metal that still adorns the artifacts of kings.

THE BENEFITS OF A GOLD STANDARD

The main benefit of a gold standard is that it insures a relatively low level of inflation. So long as the supply of gold does not change too quickly, the supply of money will stay relatively stable.

The gold standard prevents a country from printing too much money. If the supply of money rises too fast, then people will exchange money (which has become less scarce) for gold (which has not). If this goes on for too long, the treasury will eventually run out of gold.

A gold standard restricts the Federal Reserve from enacting policies that significantly alter the growth of the money supply, which in turn limits the inflation rate of a country.

The gold standard benefits the foreign exchange market. If Canada is on the gold standard and has set the price of gold at $100 an ounce, and Mexico is also on the gold standard and set the price of gold at 5,000 pesos an ounce, then one Canadian dollar must be worth fifty pesos. The extensive use of gold standards implies a system of fixed exchange rates. If all countries are on a gold standard, there is then only one real currency, gold, from which all others derive their value.

A HISTORY OF THE STOCK MARKET

The moneylenders of Europe filled important gaps left by the larger banks: They traded debts between each other. A lender looking to unload a high-risk, high-interest loan might exchange it for a different loan with another lender. These lenders also bought government debt issues, statements guaranteeing repayment. As the natural evolution of their business continued, the lenders began to sell debt issues to customers— the first individual investors.

The origin of stock exchanges lies in France, where in the 1300s banks encouraged the trading of debts in order to regulate the agricultural community. The trades were carried out by brokers. During the middle of the century, Venetians took it a step further, trading the first government-issued securities. Brokers would carry slates with information on the various issues for sale and meet with clients, much like a broker does today.

Belgium boasted a stock exchange as far back as 1531, in Antwerp. Brokers and moneylenders would meet there to deal in business, government, and even individual debt issues. It is odd to think of a stock exchange that dealt exclusively in promissory notes and bonds, but in the 1500s there were no real stocks. There were many flavors of business-financier partnerships that produced income like stocks do, but there was no official share that changed hands.

In the 1600s, the Dutch, British, and French governments all gave charters to companies with East India in their names. But the sea voyages that brought back goods from the East were extremely risky—besides the danger of Muslim pirates, there were the more common risks of weather and poor navigation.

In order to reduce the risk of a lost ship ruining their fortunes, ship owners had long been in the practice of seeking investors who would put up money for the voyage—outfitting the ship and crew in return for a percentage of the proceeds if the trip was successful. These early limited liability companies often lasted for only a single voyage. They were then dissolved, and a new one was created for the next voyage. Investors reduced their risk by investing in several different ventures at the same time, thereby playing the odds against all of them ending in disaster.

When the East India companies formed on December 31, 1600, they changed the way business was done. These companies had stocks that would pay dividends on all the proceeds from all the voyages the companies undertook, rather than paying out voyage by voyage. These were the first modern joint stock companies, and they had the leverage to demand more for their shares and larger fleets. The size of the companies, combined with royal restrictions on competition, meant huge profits for investors.

Because the shares in the various East India companies were issued on paper, investors could sell the papers to other investors. Unfortunately, there was no stock exchange in existence, so the investor would have to track down a broker to carry out a trade. In England, most brokers and investors did their business in the various coffee shops around London. Debt issues and shares for sale were written up and posted on the shops doors or distributed as a newsletter.

The British East India Company had one of the biggest competitive advantages in financial history—a government-backed monopoly dealing solely with the East Indies. When the investors began to receive huge dividends and sell their shares for fortunes, other investors became hungry for a piece of the action. The budding financial boom in England came so quickly that there were no rules or regulations for the issuing of shares.

The South Seas Company (SSC), which traded in South America only, emerged with a similar charter from the king, and its shares, and the numerous re-issues, sold as soon as they were listed. Before the first ship ever left the harbor, the SSC had used its new-found investor fortune to open posh offices in the best parts of London.

Encouraged by the success of the SSC and realizing that the company hadn't done a thing except issue shares, other "businessmen" rushed in to offer new shares in their own ventures. Some of these were as ludicrous as reclaiming the sunshine from vegetables or, better yet, a company promising investors shares in an undertaking of such vast importance that it couldn't be revealed. They all sold.

Inevitably, the bubble burst when the SSC failed to pay any dividends off its meager profits, highlighting the difference between these new share issues and the British East India Company. The subsequent crash caused the government to outlaw the issuing of shares of stocks and the ban held until 1825.

The London Stock Exchange was officially formed in 1773, a scant nineteen years before the New York Stock Exchange. Whereas the London Stock Exchange (LSE) was handcuffed by the law restricting shares, the NYSE has dealt in the trading of stocks, for better or worse, since its inception. The NYSE wasn't the first stock exchange in the United States. That honor goes to the Philadelphia Stock Exchange (1790), but the NYSE quickly became the most powerful.

Alexander Hamilton, the first U.S. Secretary of the Treasury, had studied the stock exchanges in Britain and believed they were essential to building and maintaining a vital and robust economy. During his term, from 1789 to 1795, he promoted the development of American stock exchanges. Today, visitors to New York's Wall Street still admire a statue of him nestled among massive buildings.

In March 1792, twenty-four of New York City's leading merchants met secretly at Corre's Hotel to discuss ways to bring order to the securities business and to wrest it from their competitors, the auctioneers. Two months later, on May 17, 1792, these merchants signed the Buttonwood Agreement, named after their traditional meeting place, a buttonwood tree. The agreement called for the signers to trade securities only among themselves, to set trading fees, and not to participate in other auctions of securities. These twenty-four men had founded what was to become the New York Stock Exchange. The Exchange would later be located at 11 Wall Street.

The New York merchant group sent an observer to Philadelphia in early 1817. Upon his return, bearing news of the thriving Philadelphia exchange,

"October. This is one of the peculiarly dangerous months to speculate in stocks. The others are July, January, September, April, November, May, March, June, December, August, and February."
—Mark Twain

LEFT: Exterior of the New York Stock Exchange, 1908
OPPOSITE: A drawing of Wall Street by Augustus Kollner, 1847

WALL STREET, N.Y.
1847.

the New York Stock and Exchange Board was formally organized on March 8, 1817.

The exchange rented a room at 40 Wall Street and every morning the president, Anthony Stockholm, read the stocks to be traded. The exchange was an exclusive organization: New members were required to be voted in, and a candidate could be blackballed by three negative votes. In 1817, a seat on the exchange cost $25. In 1827, it increased to $100, and in 1848, the price was $400. Members wore top hats and swallowtail coats.

From there, the stock market grew. So did the building. The structure at 40 Wall Street is now a 71-story edifice known as the Trump Building, after financial mogul Donald Trump, who bought it and undertook a renovation of the structure in 1996. The rival New York Curb Exchange was founded in 1842 and later changed its name to the American Stock Exchange (AMEX) as stock trading expanded.

A penny saved is an economic breakthrough.

There were three beggars asking for alms on Wall Street. The first beggar wrote "Beggar" on his broken cup. He received ten dollars that day. The next day, the second beggar wrote "Beggar.com" on his cup. He received hundreds of thousands of dollars and an offer to float an IPO on NASDAQ. The following day, the third beggar wrote "e-Beg" on his cup. Microsoft, IBM, and HP sent corporate vice-presidents to talk to him about strategic alliances and offered him free hardware consultancy. In addition, it was reported on CNBC that e-Beg used 95 percent Oracle technology and that I2 had announced the launch of BegTradeMatrix, a b2b industry portal offering supply chain integration in the beggar community.

WALL STREET TRIVIA

As narrow and short as it is, New York's most well-known street is Wall Street. Best known as home to the New York Stock Exchange, Wall Street is steeped in history.

1 Wall Street got its name because it ran along the wooden plank wall that went from the Hudson to the East River at the very southern tip of New York City.

2 George Washington was inaugurated first president of the United States on April 30, 1789, on Wall Street at City Hall, which served as the first capitol of the United States for a little more than a year and a half.

3 The Bill of Rights was drafted and passed on Wall Street on December 15, 1791.

4 The first Congress of the United States met on Wall Street on March 4, 1789.

5 New York City's slave market was located on Wall Street.

6 Beaver furs were among the first commodities traded on Wall Street.

7 In 1920, a group of men blew up a horse-drawn wagon filled with explosives on Wall Street, killing thirty-eight people. They were never caught or identified.

8 The Wall Street Bull, or Charging Bull as it is sometimes called, is a seven-thousand-pound bronze sculpture by Arturo Di Modica that is associated with Wall Street but is actually located on Broadway.

THE TRUTH ABOUT BLACK THURSDAY

It is commonly believed that on Thursday, October 29, 1929, the day the American stock market crashed, stockbrokers who had lost vast amounts of money were committing suicide in despair. News reporters were even investigating rumors that eleven brokers had actually jumped out of their office windows.

Newspapers abroad, believing this, were reporting that pedestrians on Wall Street had to wend their ways around the bodies of these "fallen" stock traders. Will Rogers, American humorist and social commentator, observed, "When Wall Street took that tail spin, you had to stand in line to get a window to jump out of, and speculators were selling space for bodies in the East River."

But truth be told, none of this ever happened. There were no suicides on Wall Street that day, let alone people jumping to their deaths. According to John Kenneth Galbraith, while the U.S. suicide rate increased steadily between 1925 and 1932, during the months of October and November 1929, the number of suicides was low and the day the crash occurred there wasn't a single suicide on Wall Street.

WHERE CREDIT IS DUE

THE HISTORY OF CREDIT CARDS

ABOVE: A stock certificate for five shares of The Diner's Club, Inc.

Credit has been in use ever since money was invented; indeed, the idea of it led to the invention of money. In 1641, the Pilgrims consolidated their debts to London creditors by banding together and borrowing the money from financiers to make four annual payments. They were backed by financiers who charged anywhere from 30 to 70 percent interest. But that special piece of plastic—the one you won't leave home without—didn't come along until 1730, when Christopher Thompson, a furniture merchant, decided it would be fun to sell things to people who couldn't afford them by offering his customers the option of buying merchandise by making weekly payments.

From this date until the early twentieth century, credit was commonly issued in the form of tally sticks. Using this system, merchants sold items that would be paid for in weekly payments. One side of a wooden stick was marked with notches representing the debt, and the other side showed payments made.

While Christopher Thompson was refining his idea, British bankers introduced the concept of overdraft protection: An instant "loan" would be made if funds in a specific account were unavailable. The first known overdraft was awarded in 1728 to a merchant named William Hog, who was permitted to withdraw £1,000 more than he had in his Royal Bank of Scotland account.

Metal cards, called *metal money*, allowed loyal customers of a particular company to defer payments on goods and services. Western Union introduced the first one in 1914; it was interest-free. Ten years later, General Petroleum Corporation offered employees and select customers metal money that could be used exclusively for gas and automotive services. The system worked well, and metal money was soon made available to the general public.

This period also saw the first car loans, which were issued by small companies for the most part, as well as by American Telephone and Telegraph (AT&T), which created the "Bell System Credit Card." Railroad systems and airlines soon followed suit.

The use of credit cards was prohibited during World War II, but as soon as it was over, credit cards became more popular than ever. This postwar boom period saw the rise of a middle class hungry for all the conveniences that technology had to offer. Credit cards offered immediate gratification, and their advent led to an immediate increase in travel and spending.

The first modern credit card was issued by Diner's Club, Inc., in 1950. It could be used in a variety of stores and businesses and was aimed mostly at traveling businessmen. Cardholders had sixty days to make payment in full.

The correlation between credit cards and spending did not go unnoticed by bankers, who, after all, were in the business of making money. In 1951, the Franklin National Bank in New York issued the Charge-It card to those who were pre-approved for credit. It worked much like today's credit card system: The consumer made a purchase using the card; the merchant obtained authorization from the bank; the bank reimbursed the retailer and then collected the debt from the consumer.

In 1958, American Express introduced the "Don't leave home without it" card. Like all other cards issued up to that point, no interest was charged on purchases at any time.

In 1959, the first "revolving credit" card was issued: Customers could pay the debt in full or make monthly payments while interest was charged on the balance. It was the brainchild of Bank of America, and it was available only in the state of California. In 1967, four California banks formed the Western States Bankcard Association and introduced the MasterCharge card to compete with BankAmericard. By 1969, most credit cards in circulation belonged to one of these programs. Member banks shared card program costs, making the bankcard program viable for even small financial institutions.

In the mid 1970s, when BankAmericard began exploring international opportunities, the program name was changed to Visa; in 1979, MasterCharge changed its name to MasterCard.

In 1979, electronic processing, electronic dial-up terminals, and magnetic security stripes made the credit card system even more accessible to more retailers. Today the industry is booming; credit cards account for more than 90 percent of all e-commerce transactions. The five leaders in the industry include Visa International (with more than a billion cards in circulation and carrying more than 50 percent of all credit card transactions conducted worldwide), MasterCard, American Express, Discover, and Diner's Club. Today the average American holds at least $8,000 in credit card debt.

WATCHDOGS OF THE TREASURY

Various directors and caretakers have been referred to as "Watchdog of the Treasury," but one called Nero perhaps has a better claim than any of them.

Nero was a real, live canine watchdog. Henry Voight, first Superintendent and Chief Coiner of the first United States Mint at Philadelphia, was Nero's sponsor. The expenditure is recorded in a handwritten "Account of Contingent Expenses Incurred in the Mint" for the month of January 1793; the $3 item was "for a Dog for the Yard."

There are records of further expenditures over the course of a quarter of a century for food and license tags for Nero and his successor watchdogs. A night watchman was required to visit all sectors of the Mint premises every hour, and Nero went along with him. Nero supposedly took over full responsibility if the watchman was absent. Rules of the Mint forbade the feeding of Nero by any employee except the night watchman.

An early Treasury seal, the origin of which is a matter of speculation, pays homage to the "Watchdog of the Treasury" title. Within a wreath around the seal's edges is a symbolic strongbox, and lying beside the strongbox is a capable-looking watchdog with his left front paw securely clasping a large key. Just how extensively the seal was used is difficult to determine, but it has long since disappeared from Treasury documents. Today the original plate of the seal is on deposit at the Government Printing Office.

"Money is a poor man's credit card."
—Marshal McLuhan

"The creditor hath a better memory than the debtor."
—James Howell

"No man is so poor that he can't afford to keep one dog, and I've seen them so poor that they could afford to keep three."
—Josh Billings

The vault at Fort Knox, located on a military base in Fort Knox, Kentucky, is said to be the most secure vault in the world and serves as the bullion depository of the United States. It is protected 24 hours a day by army units equipped with tanks, heavy artillery, and Apache helicopters. Given that no visitors are allowed (a policy that is strictly enforced), this list is probably the closest you will ever get to Fort Knox.

ABOVE: The United States Bullion Depository is part of Fort Knox.

1 The Depository was completed in December 1936 at a cost of $560,000. Building materials used included 16,000 cubic feet of granite; 4,200 cubic yards of concrete; 750 tons of reinforcing steel; and 670 tons of structural steel. It is located approximately thirty miles southwest of Louisville, Kentucky, on a site that was formerly a part of the Fort Knox military reservation. The first gold was moved to the Depository by railroad in 1937.

2 A large percent of the United States' gold reserves is stored in the vault of the Fort Knox Bullion Depository. The remaining gold reserves are held in the Philadelphia Mint, the Denver Mint, the West Point Bullion Depository, and the San Francisco Assay Office, all facilities of the United States Mint.

3 The present amount of gold holdings is 147.3 million ounces. The only gold removed has been very small quantities used to test the purity of gold during regularly scheduled audits.

4 The highest gold holdings was 649.6 million ounces, on December 31, 1941.

5 During World War II, the U.S. Bullion Depository continued to operate at Fort Knox, receiving more and more shipments of the country's gold reserves. The facility was also used during this time to store and to safeguard the English crown jewels and the Magna Carta, along with the gold reserves of several of the countries of occupied Europe.

6 Don't even think about it: There are good reasons why "Fort Knox" has become synonymous with safekeeping. Within the Depository building is a two-level steel and concrete vault that is divided into compartments. The vault door weighs more than twenty tons. No one person is entrusted with the combination. Various members of the Depository staff must dial separate combinations known only to them. The vault casing is constructed of steel plates, steel I-beams, and steel cylinders encased in concrete.

7 The Depository is equipped with its own emergency power plant, water system, and other facilities. There is a pistol range for use by the guards in the basement.

8 The gold stored in the Depository is in the form of standard mint bars of almost pure gold or coin gold bars resulting from the melting of gold coins. These bars are about the size of an ordinary building brick, but are somewhat smaller. The approximate dimensions are 7 by 3 ⅝ by 1¾ inches. The fine gold bars contain approximately 400 troy ounces of gold, technically worth $16,888.00 (based on the legally regulated price of $42.22 per ounce) but in fact worth at least twenty times that on the open market. They are stored in the vault compartments without wrappings. When the bars are handled, great care is exercised to avoid abrasion of the soft metal.

THE ART OF MONEY

Because governments tend to adorn their money with designs that reflect their major interests, currency, in a sense, tells the story of its people. The very first coins mostly bore either portraits of leaders or symbols of power—bulls, weapons, and the gods who protected them. Here are some of the most common themes depicted on currency today:

QUEEN ELIZABETH II

She was the first monarch ever to appear on British money; today her portrait adorns no fewer than thirty-seven different currencies. The images vary: While she appears age-defying on Isle of Man and St. Helena money, she appears somewhat grandmotherly on the money of Gibraltar and the Fiji Islands. Similarly, while she is dressed royally in some portraits (the Belize dollar, for instance), she wears a simple dress and a single strand of pearls in Australia.

LOCAL HEROES

Although the people who appear on American money are for the most part presidents, other countries have proved far more creative, featuring artists, writers, explorers, musicians, and anyone who has made a contribution to the culture of the country. Some notes even bear images of people who only enjoyed limited and local acclaim but who seemed to deserve commemoration nonetheless. Some of those who have been so honored include:

» Paul Bogle, leader of the failed Morant Bay Rebellion of 1865 during which poverty-stricken slaves rebelled against their conditions (Jamaica)
» Gustave Eiffel, architect of the Eiffel Tower (France)
» James Joyce, writer (Ireland)
» Le Corbusier, architect (Switzerland)
» Kirsten Flagstad, opera singer (Norway)
» Selma Lagerlöf, novelist (Sweden)
» José Abelardo Quiñones, a little-known 21-year-old aviator who was shot down during World War II (Peru)
» Antoine de Saint-Exupéry, writer, along with his creation, the Little Prince (France)
» Sir Edmund Hillary, explorer (New Zealand)
» Mary Reibey, early settler and once the wealthiest person in the country (Australia)
» Adolphe Sax, inventor of the saxophone (Belgium)
» Kate Sheppard, suffrage leader (New Zealand)
» Sigrid Undset, writer (Norway)

PLAIN FOLKS

While bills bearing the likenesses of real individuals depict far more men than women, bills that celebrate the contributions of generic "plain folks" seem to lean the other way. Some bills, for instance, including some from French Polynesia, Bulgaria, and Laos, depict a lovely local woman holding a basket of flowers or fruit. A 1988 Australian Bicentennial bill pays homage to the aboriginal people who lived there for 75,000 years before the Europeans came along.

SEXY MONEY

Some countries are anything but shy when it comes to depicting nudity on currency. The idea seems to be that people are best portrayed in their native dress—or undress, as the case may be. A topless native girl appears on an old bill from the island of Saint-Pierre-et-Miquelon, and a whole row of them, poised to perform a ritual dance, symbolize the country's unity on a note from Swaziland. Lady Liberty, who appears on a number of currencies

throughout history, was often shown with her gown ripped, ta-tas agape; presumably a wardrobe malfunction resulting from the performance of her duties.

NATIONAL PASTIMES

How people spend their leisure time says a lot about their culture, and so national amusements have found their way to currency. Iceland has honored reading, the perfect way to pass their dark, cold winters; a note from Fiji shows a group of men enjoying their favorite pastime, fishing. A 500-afghanis note, as well as other central Asian currency, shows a picture of Afghanistan's national sport, *buzkashi*–something like polo except that an animal carcass is used instead of a ball.

AGRICULTURE

Countries whose economy depends on farming often show agricultural scenes on their currency: people farming, neat rows of ripe produce, and tractors–plenty of tractors. These appear on some of the most beautiful money in the world: Costa Rica,

Morocco, Senegal, Bolivia, Uganda, and Guinea have all used this motif. Chocolate-lovers everywhere might appreciate the 1000-cedis note from Ghana, which celebrates their main export, cocoa.

INDUSTRY

While industrial scenes are often depicted on currency to represent the main economic pursuit of a people, these are often romanticized images, presenting the idea that workers are happily engaged in their duties. A French bill from 1939 celebrates science by showing a handsome scientist bent over his microscope; a 1956 bill from Luxembourg bears an intricate engraving of a factory, with towers emitting billowing clouds of lovely smoke. Kuwait, South Africa, Zaire, Romania, Bulgaria, Albania, and Gambia are just some of the countries that have honored industry on their currency.

TRANSPORTATION

Transportation symbolizes progress, so it's no surprise that this motif is one of the most widespread throughout

the world. Its appearance on money also helps to tell a story. Railroads were popular on currency in the early nineteenth century, when railways were opening doors to new territories, but today, airplanes and jet liners have become more common. Historical approaches to the motif often employ ships, which celebrate the age of exploration, and some of these are among the most beautiful currencies in the world.

BIRDS

More than two hundred different species of birds have shown up on money, telling us much about indigenous life in the countries of the bills they adorn. The practice dates back to some of the earliest coins, which bore the images of creatures of power. The great blue herons of Madagascar, the birds-of-paradise of Papua New Guinea, the condors of Colombia, and even the lowly house sparrow, beloved in Denmark, have been celebrated on currency. Then, of course, there's the familiar American eagle that we just can't seem to get enough of.

SCIENCE

How better to celebrate the achievements of a country than by putting the mugs of its physicists on money? It's a common practice throughout the world, as some of the most celebrated physicists have appeared on money: Marie and Pierre Curie (the French 500-franc note), Albert Einstein (the Israeli 5-pound note), Michael Faraday (the British 20-pound note) and Isaac Newton (the British 1-pound note), are just a few who have been so honored.

FACE VALUE

PEOPLE WHO HAVE APPEARED ON AMERICAN MONEY

In 1866, Congress passed a law prohibiting the use of living people on coins after the Chief of the Bureau of Printing and Engraving allowed himself to be depicted on a five-cent note.

Most but not all of the faces on American money were those of U.S. presidents. Here are the individuals who have been so honored, and the date of first issue of the currency. Of course, many of these are long out of circulation and are familiar only to collectors.

FIVE MORE WOMEN WHO HAVE APPEARED ON U.S. COINS

All of these were issued as commemorative coins.

Queen Isabella of Spain	Columbian Exposition Quarter Dollar	1893
Virginia Dare* and her mother, Elinor Dare	North Carolina Half-Dollar	1937
Eunice Kennedy Shriver	Special Olympics Silver Dollar	1995
Dolley Madison	Silver Dollar	1999

* The first child born in the Americas to English parents

Susan B. Anthony	one-dollar coin	1979
Salmon P. Chase	ten-thousand-dollar bill	1929
Grover Cleveland	twenty-dollar bill thousand-dollar bill	1914 1934
Dwight D. Eisenhower	one-dollar coin	1971
Benjamin Franklin	hundred-dollar bill	1928
James Garfield	twenty-dollar bill	1882
Ulysses S. Grant	five-dollar bill fifty-dollar bill	1886 1913
Alexander Hamilton	ten-dollar bill	1929
Benjamin Harrison	five-dollar bill	1902
Andrew Jackson	twenty-dollar bill	1929
Thomas Jefferson	two-dollar bill nickel	1869 1938
Helen Keller	Alabama State Quarter	2003
John F. Kennedy	half-dollar	1964

Abraham Lincoln	hundred-dollar bill penny five-dollar bill	1869 1909 1928
James Madison	five-thousand-dollar bill	1929
William McKinley	ten-dollar bill five-hundred-dollar bill	1902 1929
James Monroe	hundred-dollar bill	1891
Franklin D. Roosevelt	dime	1946
Sacagawea	one-dollar coin	1999
George Washington	one-dollar bill twenty-dollar bill quarter	1869 1905 1932
Martha Washington	one-dollar silver certificate	1886
Woodrow Wilson	one-hundred-thousand-dollar bill*	1934

*The $100,000 bill is the highest denomination of paper money the U.S. government has ever printed. It was issued in 1934 and was used mainly for bank transactions.

"IN GOD WE TRUST"

CAME TO APPEAR ON U.S. CURRENCY

The motto "In God We Trust" was placed on United States coins largely because of the increased religious sentiment that existed during the Civil War. Secretary of the Treasury Salmon P. Chase received many appeals from devout people throughout the country urging that the United States recognize the Deity on U.S. coins. From Treasury Department records, it appears that the first such appeal came in a letter dated November 13, 1861. It was written to Secretary Chase by Rev. M. R. Watkinson, Minister of the Gospel from Ridleyville, Pennsylvania, and read in part: "Dear Sir, You are about to submit your annual report to the Congress respecting the affairs of the national finances. One fact touching our currency has hitherto been seriously overlooked. I mean the recognition of the Almighty God in some form on our coins." It took three years for Congress to respond.

1

An Act of Congress, approved on April 11, 1864, authorized the coinage of the two-cent coins on which the motto first appeared.

2

The motto was omitted from the new gold coins issued in 1907, causing a storm of public criticism. As a result, legislation passed in May 1908 made "In God We Trust" mandatory on all coins on which it had previously appeared.

3

Legislation approved in 1955 made the appearance of "In God We Trust" mandatory on all coins and paper currency of the United States. On July 30, 1956, by an Act of Congress, "In God We Trust" became the national motto of the United States.

4

Beginning in 1994, the appearance of "In God We Trust" on money was challenged in the federal courts by the Freedom From Religion Foundation, who felt that it represented a symbolic unity of "God" with government and showed a lack of respect for the constitutional principle of the separation of church and state. The challenge was rejected by the lower federal courts, who stated that "the motto is not a religious phrase." The Supreme Court declined to review the case.

THE HIGH COST OF WAR

The histories of war and money are inextricably entwined. Ultimately, the desire for money and power is at the source of all wars, yet rarely have victors been satisfied. Economies are inevitably affected by wartime activities; some countries have taken decades to recuperate from the devastation. Yet as Albert Einstein predicted: "So long as there are men, there will be wars."

This list addresses only one type of damage caused by wars. It does not take into account the lives and the cultures that represent even greater losses.

At present, the United States is engaged in wars in Iraq and Afghanistan that have cost nearly a trillion dollars as of this writing. It is estimated that by the time they're over, the full cost of the wars may reach $2 trillion. Here, in today's dollars, are the costs of all American wars.

THE REVOLUTIONARY WAR (1775–1783):

$3.6
billion

THE SPANISH-AMERICAN WAR (April–August 1898):

$5
billion

THE KOREAN WAR (1950–1953):

$535
billion

THE "WAR ON POVERTY"

$7
billion

THE WAR OF 1812 (1812–1815):

$1.1
billion

WORLD WAR I (1914–1918):

$290
billion

THE VIETNAM WAR (1959–1975):

$686
billion

THE "WAR ON TERROR" (2001–present):

The expenditures are incalculable.

THE CIVIL WAR (1861–1865):

$62
billion

WORLD WAR II (1939–1945):

$4–$5
trillion

THE PERSIAN GULF WAR (1990–1991):

$7
billion

The financial costs of catastrophes cannot be measured if one takes into account the human lives that are lost or ruined. Nor can we compute the effects of any one disaster on future generations. Damage created by the BP oil spill in 2010 won't be tallied until its effects on communities, humans, and wildlife can be studied in the long term. Still, a look at the expenses incurred by historical disasters is telling. The doomed *Titanic* might be one of the most famous disasters in history, but with damages of only $7 million, its hardly the most expensive.

1. CHERNOBYL

On April 26, 1986, the world witnessed the costliest accident and biggest socio-economic catastrophe in peacetime history. Nearly 50 percent of the area of Ukraine was in some way contaminated. More than 200,000 people had to be evacuated and resettled, while 1.7 million people were directly affected by the disaster. The death toll attributed to Chernobyl, including people who died from cancer years later, is estimated at 125,000. The total costs including cleanup, resettlement, and compensation to victims has been estimated to be roughly $200 billion. The accident was officially attributed to power plant operators who violated plant procedures and were ignorant of the safety requirements.

2. SPACE SHUTTLE *COLUMBIA*

The Space Shuttle *Columbia* was the first space-worthy shuttle in NASA's orbital fleet. It was destroyed during re-entry over Texas on February 1, 2003, because a hole had been punctured in one of the wings during launch sixteen days earlier. The original cost of the shuttle had been $2 billion in 1978. Another $500 million was spent on the investigation, making it the costliest aircraft accident investigation in history. The search and recovery of debris alone cost $300 million. In the end, the total cost of the accident (not including replacement of the shuttle) came to $13 billion, according to the American Institute of Aeronautics and Astronautics.

3. *PRESTIGE* OIL SPILL

On November 13, 2002, the *Prestige* oil tanker was carrying 77,000 tons of heavy fuel oil when one of its twelve tanks burst during a storm off Galicia, Spain. Fearing that the ship would sink, the captain called for help from Spanish rescue workers, expecting them to take the ship into harbor. But pressure from local authorities forced the captain to steer the ship away from the coast. The captain tried to get help from the French and Portuguese authorities, but they too ordered the ship away from their shores. The storm eventually took its toll: The tanker split in half and released twenty million gallons of oil into the sea. According to a report by the Pontevedra Economist Board, the total cleanup cost $12 billion.

4. *CHALLENGER* EXPLOSION

The Space Shuttle *Challenger* was destroyed 73 seconds after takeoff on January 28, 1986, due to a faulty O-ring. It failed to seal one of the joints, allowing pressurized gas to escape. This in turn caused the external tank to dump its payload of liquid hydrogen, causing a massive explosion. The cost of just replacing the Space Shuttle was $2 billion. The cost of investigation, problem correction, and replacement of lost equipment brought the total damages to $5.6 billion.

7. B-2 BOMBER CRASH

A B-2 stealth bomber crashed shortly after taking off from an air base in Guam on February 23, 2008, causing the first billion-dollar airplane accident. Investigators blamed distorted data in the flight control computers caused by moisture in the system. This was one of only twenty-one such bombers ever built, at a cost of some $1.4 billion. Both pilots were able to eject to safety.

8. METROLINK CRASH

On September 12, 2008, in what was one of the worst train crashes in California history, twenty-five people were killed when a Metrolink commuter train crashed head-on into a Union Pacific freight train in Los Angeles. It is believed that the Metrolink train may have run through a red signal while the conductor was busy text messaging. At the time of this writing, wrongful death lawsuits are expected to result in $500 million in losses for Metrolink.

ABOVE: The $7 million in damages caused by the *Titanic* didn't even make the record books.

5. PIPER ALPHA OIL RIG

Piper Alpha was a North Sea oil production platform operated by Occidental Petroleum (Caledonia) Ltd. The platform began production in 1976 and at one time was the world's single largest oil producer, spewing out 317,000 barrels per day. On July 6, 1988, as part of routine maintenance, technicians removed and checked safety valves that were essential in preventing the dangerous build-up of liquid gas. When one such valve was overlooked, the world's most expensive oil rig accident was set in motion. Within hours, the 300-foot platform was engulfed in flames, eventually collapsing and killing 167 workers and resulting in $3.4 billion in damages.

6. *EXXON VALDEZ*

The *Exxon Valdez* oil spill was not a large one in relation to the world's biggest oil spills, but it was a costly one due to the remote location of Prince William Sound (accessible only by helicopter and boat). On March 24, 1989, 10.8 million gallons of oil were spilled when the ship's master, Joseph Hazelwood, left the controls and the ship crashed into a reef. The cleanup cost Exxon $2.5 billion.

AT THE MARKET IN 1930

BANANAS
4 lb.

19
cents

BEEF CHUCK ROAST
1 lb.

15
cents

COCONUT MACAROONS
per lb.

27
cents

HOT DOGS
1 lb.

8
cents

EGGS
1 dozen

18
cents

SOAP
1 bar

6
cents

LAMB SHOULDER
1 lb.

17
cents

SUGAR
25 lb.

$1.25

PEANUT BUTTER
1 quart

23
cents

ORANGES
14

25
cents

TOILET TISSUE
2 rolls

9
cents

PORK AND BEANS
1 can

5
cents

HAM
per lb.

39
cents

The prices listed on the following pages varied from state to state and depending on the specific date of record, subject to fluctuations in the marketplace.

AT THE MARKET IN 1948

BACON
1 lb.

59
cents

BANANAS
1 lb.

11
cents

LAMB CHOPS
1 lb.

65
cents

BEEF CHUCK ROAST
1 lb.

43
cents

BLEACH
½ gallon

21
cents

CHICKEN
per lb.

41
cents

SOAP
2 bars

35
cents

JELL-O
3 packs

23
cents

CAULIFLOWER
1 head

15
cents

SALT
1 lb.

10
cents

HOT DOGS
1 lb.

55
cents

EGGS
1 dozen

64
cents

ONIONS
10 lb.

49
cents

AT THE MARKET IN 1950

APPLES
2 lb.

39
cents

BACON
1 lb.

35
cents

CABBAGE
1 lb.

6
cents

CHEESE
1 lb.

45
cents

CHICKEN
1 lb.

43
cents

COFFEE
1 lb.

37
cents

EGGS
1 dozen

49
cents

ORANGES
12 dozen

69
cents

PORTERHOUSE STEAK
1 lb.

95
cents

LAMB CHOPS
1 lb.

49
cents

ONIONS
5 lb.

15
cents

POTATOES
5 lb.

35
cents

PINEAPPLE
each

25
cents

LIVING IN THE FIFTIES

In 1950, the average cost of a new house was $8,450, the average income per year was $3,210; and the average cost of a new car was $1,510 (by 1959, it was up to $2,200). Here are the prices of some actual homes that sold during this decade:

MANSFIELD, OHIO
Modern home with living room, dining room, kitchen, two bedrooms
$6,500 (1950)

CHICAGO, ILLINOIS
Six-room brick home built by one of Chicago's best builders, modern kitchen, gas heating
$14,500 (1950)

SHEBOYGAN, WISCONSIN
1.5 acres riverfront property on Sheboygan River
$750 (1951)

POTTSTOWN, PENNSYLVANIA
Semi-detached five-room brick home with garage on large lot
$7,000 (1952)

OSHKOSH, WISCONSIN
Lakeside four-bedroom home, ninety feet of frontage on Lake Winnebago
$10,000 (1953)

JOPLIN, MISSOURI
Six-room modern with two-car garage
and other outbuildings on eight acres,
close to new school
$8,500 (1953)

PORTSMOUTH, NEW HAMPSHIRE
New cottage on shaded lot within a
three-minute walk of Hampton Beach
$5,500 (1954)

FORT PIERCE, FLORIDA
Five-room home on fifteen acres with
outbuildings and orange groves
$8,500 (1954)

LOWELL, MASSACHUSETTS
Large Colonial home on thirty-two
secluded country acres with brook
running through property, double living
room, dining room, modern kitchen,
three bedrooms, two-car garage
$14,000 (1955)

PITTSFIELD, MASSACHUSETTS
Three-bedroom ranch home, tiled
bath, full basement, fully fitted kitchen,
two-car garage on large plot
$14,300 (1956)

MANSFIELD, OHIO
New three-bedroom ranch home,
large living room, modern kitchen,
double garage
$15,000 (1957)

APPLETON, WISCONSIN
New brick and frame home; all oak
floors, trim, and cupboards; large
kitchen; full basement; oil heating
$15,500 (1958)

WILLIAMSPORT, PENNSYLVANIA
Five-room bungalow with furnace,
garage, large plot
$7,500 (1958)

SALISBURY, MARYLAND
Five-room bungalow with two bedrooms, living room, dining room,
modern kitchen, full basement,
hot-air heating
$7,000 (1959)

MANSFIELD, OHIO
Four-bedroom brick home, kitchen
built-ins, large family room, outbuildings, on twenty-five acres
$15,500 (1959)

"Our real problems
are . . . concealed
from us by our cur-
rent remarkable
prosperity, which
results in part from
the production of
arms that we do not
expect to use, and
in part from our
new way of getting
rich, which is to buy
things from one
another that we do
not want, at prices
we cannot pay, on
terms we cannot
meet, because of
advertising which
we do not believe."

—Robert Hutchins, president of the
University of Chicago, 1959

AT THE MARKET IN 1960

BANANAS
2 lb.

19
cents

BUTTER
1 lb.

67
cents

CHEWING GUM
1 pack

5
cents

PEACHES, CANNED
1 can

29
cents

FLOUR
5 lb.

49
cents

HAM, SMOKED
1 lb.

49
cents

TURKEY, FRESH
1 lb.

39
cents

PORK CHOPS
1 lb.

59
cents

SIRLOIN STEAK
1 lb.

89
cents

LIVER
1 lb.

79
cents

CORN
6 ears

25
cents

JELL-O
4 packs

35
cents

THE COST OF LIVING IN 1960

Average individual annual income	$3,216
Philco model 1403 TV	$199
12" record	$4.85
10" record	$2.85
Gallon of gas	$.31
Loaf of bread	$.14

INFLATION IN THE SIXTIES

One hundred dollars in 1960 would be equivalent to $718.61 in 2009.

A house that cost $12,700 in 1960 would cost $15,500 at the end of the decade.

In 1960, the median annual household income was $5,315; in 1969, it was $8,540.

A gallon of gas cost 31 cents in 1960; it was up to 35 cents by 1969.

In 1960 the average cost of a new car was $2,600; by 1969, it was $3,270.

CAR PRICES IN THE SIXTIES

1960 Austin Healey 3000	$3,400
1960 Cadillac Eldorado	$7,401
1961 Dodge Dart Pioneer	$2,787
1961 Ford Falcon	$1,974
1962 Dodge Coronet V8 Club Coupe	$2,595
1963 Chevrolet Corvette	$4,589
1963 Buick Riviera	$4,300
1964 Chevrolet Corvair Monza	$2,335
1964 Mercury Monterey 4-door	$2,965
1965 Cadillac DeVille	$5,427
1965 Chevrolet Malibu	$2,156
1966 Buick Skylark GS	$2,596
1966 Chrysler Valiant Barracuda	$2,862
1967 Austin Healey Sprite	$2,050
1967 Chrysler Town and Country Wagon	$4,086
1968 Chevrolet Camero SS	$2,588
1968 Alfa Romeo Duetto Spider	$3,950
1969 BMW 2002	$4,200
1969 Buick Le Sabre	$3,356

> "If advertisers spent the same amount of money on improving their products as they do on advertising, then they wouldn't have to advertise them."
> —Will Rogers

INFLATION IN THE SEVENTIES

In 1970, the average cost of a new house was $23,400; by 1979, it was $58,500.

In 1970, the average annual household income was $9,350; by 1979, it was $17,550.

A gallon of gas, which cost 36 cents in 1970, was up to 86 cents by 1979.

The average cost of a new car in 1970 was $3,900; by 1979, it was $5,770.

INFLATION IN THE EIGHTIES

A new house that cost $68,714 in 1980 was up to $120,000 by 1989.

In 1980, the average annual household income was $19,170; by 1989, it was $27,210.

In 1980, the average cost of a new car was $7,210; by 1989, it was $15,400.

COMPARATIVE PRICES, 1960–1990

	1990	1980	1970	1960
COST OF A NEW HOME	$149,800	$76,400	$26,600	$16,500
MEDIAN HOUSEHOLD INCOME	$29,943	$17,710	$8,734	$5,315
COST OF A FIRST-CLASS STAMP	25 cents	15 cents	6 cents	4 cents
COST OF A GALLON OF REGULAR GAS	$1.16	$1.25	36 cents	31 cents
COST OF A DOZEN EGGS	$1.00	91 cents	62 cents	57 cents
COST OF A GALLON OF MILK	$2.78	$2.16	$1.15	49 cents

A HISTORY OF THE
U.S. FEDERAL HOURLY MINIMUM WAGE

Workers rejoiced in 1938 when they could now be guaranteed the solid wage of twenty-five cents an hour for their honest labor. It's interesting to note that at the time, while the minimum-wage act raised incomes for many, the law was easily sidestepped, and factory workers were still paid *bubkes* for fourteen-hour work days. At the other extreme, U.S. Steel was paying its workers five dollars a day, almost double the minimum wage. Here is a history of the minimum wage for non-farm workers (whose wages were typically below these):

Oct 24, 1938	$0.25		Jan 1, 1981	$3.35
Oct 24, 1939	$0.30		Apr 1, 1990	$3.80
Oct 24, 1945	$0.40		Apr 1, 1991	$4.25
Jan 25, 1950	$0.75		Oct 1, 1996	$4.75
Mar 1, 1956	$1.00		Sep 1, 2005	$5.15
Sep 3, 1961	$1.15		Jul 24, 2007	$5.85
Sep 3, 1963	$1.25		Jul 24, 2008	$6.55
Sep 3, 1964	$1.15		Jul 24, 2009	$7.25
Sep 3, 1965	$1.25			
Feb 1, 1967	$1.40			
Feb 1, 1968	$1.60			
Feb 1, 1969	$1.30			
Feb 1, 1970	$1.45			
Feb 1, 1971	$1.60			
May 1, 1974	$2.00			
Jan. 1, 1975	$2.10			
Jan 1, 1976	$2.30			
Jan 1, 1978	$2.65			
Jan 1, 1979	$2.90			
Jan 1, 1980	$3.10			

Minimum wage legislation is designed to ensure a "living wage" for every worker. But in 2009, a person working forty hours a week at $7.25 an hour was making about $15,000 a year, just $4,000 over the poverty threshold of $10,830 for a single person.

THE STORY OF THE U.S. MINT

The job of the U.S. Mint is to produce enough coins so that the nation can conduct its trade and commerce. In recent times, the Mint has produced somewhere between 11 and 20 billion coins annually. Other responsibilities include distributing U.S. coins to the Federal Reserve banks and branches; maintaining physical custody and protection of the nation's gold and silver assets; producing commemorative coins and medals as well as platinum, gold, and silver bullion coins; and overseeing mint facilities in Denver, Philadelphia, San Francisco, and West Point, as well as the U.S. Bullion Depository at Fort Knox, Kentucky. Here are some historical highlights:

The first branch of the Mint was opened in Philadelphia, the U.S. capital at the time, and it was followed by branches in Louisiana, Georgia, North Carolina, California, Colorado, and Nevada because gold was discovered nearby. The Mint is in its fourth building today, where it still displays the key to the first Mint, the original Mint Deed, a boot scraper, and a wooden chair that may have supported the backsides of George Washington and Thomas Jefferson. They both lived in Philadelphia when it was the nation's capital, and visited the Mint often.

The Mint produced its first circulating coins–all $111.78 worth of them–in March 1793. That first batch consisted of 11,178 copper cents. Soon after, the Mint began issuing gold and silver coins as well. The Mint's first gold and silver coins had no denominations on them. Since their designs were the same, the only way to tell them apart was by their size.

Because of what's called *seigniorage*, the whole country makes money when the Mint makes money. Seigniorage is the difference between the cost of making a coin and its face value. (For example, it costs only a few cents to make a quarter, yet its face value is 25 cents.) This profit runs the Mint and puts extra funds into the country's Treasury–funds then spent on education, healthcare, defense, and other services for the nation.

Apparently, nothing.

"From the eighteenth century onward," wrote Glen W. Bowersock, Professor Emeritus of Ancient History at Princeton University, "we have been obsessed with the fall [of the Roman Empire]: It has been valued as an archetype for every perceived decline, and, hence, as a symbol for our own fears." Hundreds of theories exist as to why Rome fell, and even today the subject is under serious debate. But did it really fall? Perhaps it was pushed—by some of the very same conditions that plague our society today. Here are some of the economic factors that led to the fall of Rome in A.D. 476; does any of this sound familiar?

UNEMPLOYMENT

During its final years, Rome began to develop a large "underclass" of unemployed, undereducated people that depended on the state to support them.

The United States has outsourced millions of jobs overseas and the numbers of the unemployed have risen dramatically in recent years. As a result, many businesses unable to compete with large corporations that have outsourced jobs have had to shut their doors. In 2009, more than five million people were receiving welfare in the United States.

OVEREXTENDED MILITARY

The Romans acquired almost all of their wealth through conquest of other lands. The cost of maintaining their army was staggering.

The United States has military bases all over the world and is engaged in two extremely expensive wars at the time of this writing.

INFLATION

Because Rome was importing more goods than it was exporting, a trade imbalance was created. This meant that more money was flowing out of Rome than in. In order to keep the money supply adequate for its citizens, Rome began devaluating its currency, minting new coins that now contained lead and very little gold. Merchants had to charge more for their wares because these new coins were not worth as much as the old ones. Inflation plagued the empire until its fall.

The United States has been on a money-printing binge and the value of the dollar has declined as a result.

LIFESTYLE

The Romans were extravagant people and spent their money like there was no tomorrow.

The credit card revolution that took place in the middle of the twentieth century encouraged the purchase of expensive homes and over-the-top luxuries that were simply not affordable. The need for immediate gratification, together with the greed of money lenders, continues to chip away at our economy.

DEBT

Roman orator Cicero had this to say about debt: "The budget should be balanced, public debt should be reduced, the treasury should be rebuilt, the arrogance of officialdom should be tempered and controlled, and assistance to foreign lands should be curtailed, lest Rome fall."

America imports more products than it manufactures. It routinely purchases millions of dollars worth of oil from hostile countries, and it provides financial aid to third-world countries throughout the globe. In 2008, the U.S. trade deficit was nearly $670 billion.

DISTRIBUTION OF WEALTH

The rich got richer and the poor got poorer. The Roman aristocracy benefited from Rome's conquests but most of the common people were irreparably damaged by imperial conquest and lived in poverty.

The poverty level in the U.S. has increased every year since its founding in 1776, while the wealthiest Americans get wealthier. In 2007, 7.62 million families lived in poverty.

TAXATION

The per capita tax rate on the citizens of Rome was far less then the rate we experience today, primarily because the wealth of the Roman Empire was based on conquest. Various systems of collecting taxes were devised, some of which fostered a fair amount of corruption, but the tax rate never exceeded 5 percent, and was usually much lower.

THE FINANCES OF THE REBELLION.

ABOVE: Political cartoon depicting Jefferson Davis, president of the Confederate States of America for the four years it existed, from 1861 to 1865, trying to establish a budget in the midst of runaway inflation

In 2007, Warren Buffet, then the third richest man in the world, stated that "the taxation system has tilted toward the rich and away from the middle class." He illustrated this by pointing to the fact that his secretary paid a greater share of her earnings in taxes than he did. A more equitable tax system that reduced the number of ways in which the rich could avoid paying taxes was one of Barack Obama's key campaign issues.

> "Money alone sets all the world in motion."
> —Publilius Syrus

CORRUPTION

Rome did not have a standardized system for selecting its emperor. Toward the end of the Empire, it was the emperor's private army, the Praetorian Guard, that chose a successor, and their criterion was simple: They appointed an emperor who was willing to reward them. Eventually the throne was simply sold to the highest bidder.

Political corruption is rampant in the government today. Money has great influence in politics, and lobbyists bribe lawmakers with money and political favors to ignore their own moral codes.

POOR PUBLIC HEALTH

Many public health and environmental issues led to sickness among the Romans. The poor lived in squalor. The lack of sanitation and the exposure to diseases from the dead that were left unattended contributed to declining public health. Alcoholism was also an ever-increasing problem during the last days of the Empire.

People living in U.S. inner cities, Appalachia, and other depressed areas throughout the country have little access to proper medical care and often live in unsanitary conditions. According to the National Coalition on Health Care, nearly 46 million Americans, or 18 percent of the population under the age of sixty-five, were without health insurance in 2007. In 2009, a loss of jobs caused more millions of Americans to lose their health coverage. Since 1991, America has spent billions of dollars a year fighting the "war on drugs"; as of this writing, there is no sign of a possible victory.

odern money has come a long way from the lumps of metal that were once used as currency. Today hundreds of different kinds of money can be found throughout the world, and each is produced by the most sophisticated printing and minting techniques in existence. Yet while the *takas* of Bangladesh, the *dinars* used in Iraq, and Armenian *drams* all look quite different and carry far different values, they basically accomplish the same thing, and they are all part of a modern international system called global economics. Fifteenth-century explorers spent years transporting riches from one country to another; today it takes just a few keystrokes to transfer funds from one end of the world to the other. The ancient Chinese printed their money on leather; today some of the most beautiful art produced by a country can be found on its legal tender. Once money was revered as the province of the high and wealthy; today we play games with the stuff: Parker Bros. prints more money each year than the U.S. Mint. It infuses our language, the movies we watch, the songs we sing.

This chapter is about how we use money today—how we think about it, how we play with it, how we spend it—and the extent to which it is at the heart of all of our pursuits, regardless of the corner of the globe from which we may hail.

A GLOSSARY OF MONETARY TERMS

When we read the statements of economists and the financial media, we can't help but wonder if they don't sometimes go out of their way to make their thoughts and policies sound far more complicated than they need to be. In truth, the basics of money are accessible to us all, once we understand the body of language that has grown up around it. A familiarity with the terms that follow will be helpful in understanding how money works, where it comes from, and where we might be able to find more of it.

AMERICAN STOCK EXCHANGE: One of three national stock markets in the United States (the others being the National Association of Securities Dealers, known as NASD; and New York Stock Exchange, or NYSE) that trade ownership shares in corporations. In terms of daily stock transactions and the number of stocks listed, the American Stock Exchange is the smallest of these three.

BANK: A financial organization that accepts deposits, makes loans, and directly controls a significant portion of the nation's money supply. The term *bank* also includes other financial institutions such as savings and loan companies (institutions that accept deposits and make loans), credit unions (cooperative institutions that are owned and controlled by their members), and mutual savings banks (banks that are chartered through a state or federal government).

BANK FAILURE: This results when a bank's liabilities exceed assets for an extended period and the bank is forced to go out of business. Because the banking system is controlled by the government, bank failure does not necessarily mean that the bank ceases to operate. In many cases, a failure means the bank is taken over by one of the government entities, or it may be merged with another, healthier bank.

BANK RUN: A situation in which a relatively large number of a bank's customers attempt to withdraw their deposits in a relatively short period of time, usually within a day or two. Historically, a bank run was prompted by fears that the bank was on the verge of collapse. Ironically, a bank run often *caused* the bank to fail. Bank runs were often infectious, leading to economy-wide bank panics and business-cycle contractions.

BARTER ECONOMY: An economy that trades goods and services using barter exchanges rather than money. Barter is still practiced today and enjoys a revival thanks to Internet resources.

BEAR MARKET: A condition of the stock market in which stock prices are generally declining and most of the participants expect this decline to continue for months or even years. In a bear market, investors see a sluggish, stagnant economy with few signs of robust growth. (Compare with *bull market*.)

BOND: The general term for a long-term loan in which a borrower agrees to pay a lender an interest rate (usually fixed) over the length of the loan and then repay the principal at the date of maturity. Bond maturities are usually ten years or more, with thirty years quite common. Bonds are used by corporations and federal, state, and local governments

ABOVE: Uncle Sam pleads poverty in this ad for U.S. bonds.

to raise funds. Most bonds are negotiable, or can be readily traded prior to their maturity date.

BULL MARKET: A condition of the stock market in which stock prices are generally rising and the trend is expected to continue. (Compare with *bear market*.)

CAPITALISM: A type of economy based on private ownership of most resources, goods, and property; freedom to generally use the privately owned resources, goods, and property so as to maximize their worth and receive profit; and a system of relatively competitive markets. (Compare with *communism*; *socialism*.)

CENTRAL BANK: The banking authority of a nation that is in charge of ensuring a sound money supply and conducting the country's monetary policy. It's usually authorized by, and works closely with, the government to achieve full employment, low inflation rates, and economic growth.

CERTIFICATE OF DEPOSIT: A type of savings account, commonly termed a CD, maintained by banks and other depository institutions that pays higher interest rates than normal savings accounts, but requires that the funds not be withdrawn for a specified time period.

COMMODITY EXCHANGE: A financial market that trades the ownership of various commodities, such as wheat, corn, cotton, sugar, crude oil, natural gas, gold, silver, and aluminum. Commodity markets offer two basic sorts of trading: spot (immediate delivery of a commodity) and futures (delivery of a commodity at a future date).

COMMON MARKET: An agreement among two or more nations to eliminate trade restrictions with each other, to adopt a common trade policy with other nations, and to allow free movement of resources among their countries. There is, however, no effort to adopt common monetary or fiscal policies.

COMMUNISM: A system of social organization in which all economic and social activity is controlled by a totalitarian state dominated by a single and self-perpetuating political party. (Compare with *capitalism*; *socialism*.)

CONSUMER PRICE INDEX (CPI): An index of prices of goods and services typically purchased by urban consumers. The CPI is compiled and published monthly by the Bureau of Labor Statistics (BLS), using price data obtained from an elaborate survey of 25,000 retail outlets and other data. The CPI is unquestionably one of the most widely recognized price indexes, running second only to the Dow Jones Industrial Average in the price index popularity contest. It is used not only as an indicator of price levels and inflation, but also to adjust wage and income payments (such as Social Security) for inflation.

CREDIT: The promise of future payment in exchange for money, goods, services, or anything else of value. Car loans, mortgages, credit cards, corporate bonds, commercial paper, and government securities are all forms of credit.

"A cynic is a man who knows the price of everything and the value of nothing." —Oscar Wilde

CREDIT CRUNCH: An economy-wide reduction in the ability of banks to make loans or otherwise issue credit, usually caused by contractionary monetary policies of the Federal Reserve System.

DEFLATION: An extended decline in the average level of prices. This is the exact opposite of inflation, in which prices rise over an extended period.

DEPRESSION: An extended period—a decade or so—of restructuring and institutional change in an economy that is often marked by declining or stagnant growth. During this period, unemployment tends to be higher and inflation lower than they are during a recession. Moreover, a depression usually lasts in the range of ten years, often encompassing two or three separate shorter-run business cycles. The most noted depression in the U.S. economy was the Great Depression of the 1930s.

DOW JONES AVERAGES: These are the most widely used and recognized indexes of stock market prices in our economy. There are separate indexes for industrial stocks, transportation stocks, and utility stocks.

ECONOMIC UNION (EU): In 1992, the EU became the economical and political integration of a dozen European nations. Today there are twenty-seven member nations.

EXCHANGE RATE: The price of one nation's currency measured against another nation's currency. It is the specified amount of one currency that can be traded per unit of another.

FEDERAL RESERVE BANK: One of thirty-seven banks (including twelve district banks and twenty-five branch banks) that comprise the Federal Reserve System. These banks are largely responsible for supervising, regulating, and interacting with commercial banks and carrying out the policies established by the Federal Reserve Board of Governors.

FEDERAL RESERVE NOTE: Paper currency issued by each of the twelve Federal Reserve District Banks in denominations of $1, $5, $10, $20, $50, and $100. Unlike paper currency of the past that was issued by the U.S. Treasury, these notes are backed by the Federal Reserve System.

FEDERAL RESERVE SYSTEM: The central bank of the United States. It includes a board of governors, twelve district banks, twenty-five branch banks, and assorted committees. The Fed, as it is called, was established in 1913 and was modified significantly during the Great Depression of the 1930s. Its duties are to maintain the stability of the banking system, regulate banks, and oversee the nation's money supply.

GOLD CERTIFICATE: Paper currency issued by the U.S. Treasury from the Civil War until 1933 that could be exchanged for an equal value of gold. With the exception of those held by collectors, gold certificates have long been out of circulation.

GOLD STANDARD: A monetary standard under which the basic unit of currency is equal in value to and exchangeable for a specified amount of gold.

GROSS DOMESTIC INCOME (GDI): The total market value of all final goods and services produced within the political boundaries of an economy during a given period of time, usually a year. GDI was introduced during the 1990s, replacing its predecessor, gross domestic product (GDP).

HEDGE FUND: A mutual fund that relies heavily on low-risk practices to protect the value of the financial assets. Such a fund specializes in options, futures, and other financial instruments that provide insurance protection against price

"The playthings of our elders are called business." —St. Augustine

fluctuations, and thus limit the risk of loss.

HYPERINFLATION: Exceptionally high inflation rates. While there are no hard and fast guidelines, an annual inflation rate of 20 percent or more is considered hyperinflation.

INFLATION: A persistent increase in the average price levels in an economy. The percentage change in the price level from one period to the next is referred to as the rate of inflation. The two most common price indices used to measure inflation are the CPI and the GDI.

INVESTMENT BANKING: The process of wholesaling newly issued government securities, corporate stocks, bonds, and similar financial assets by purchasing large blocks and reselling them in smaller units to the public.

LEVERAGE: The use of credit or loans to enhance speculation in the financial markets. Suppose, for example, that you take the $1,000 in your bank account to your stockbroker and purchase $1,000 worth of stocks or bonds. A leveraged purchase would let you use your $1,000 to buy, let's say, $10,000 worth of stocks or bonds. The remaining $9,000 of the purchase price comes from a loan.

MARKET: The organized exchange of commodities (goods, services, or resources) between buyers and sellers within a specific geographic area and during a given period of time. A market is the exchange between buyers who want a good (the demand-side of the market) and the sellers who have it (the supply-side of the market). In order to qualify as a market, the following conditions must exist: The target consumers must have the ability to purchase the goods or services; they must have a need or desire to purchase those goods or services; and they must be willing to exchange something of value for the product. Finally, they must have the authority to make the purchase. If all these variables are present, a market exists.

MINT MARK: A small letter on a coin that identifies in which of the U.S. Mints the coin was produced.

NATIONAL ASSOCIATION OF SECURITIES DEALERS (NASD): Supervised by the Securities and Exchange Commission, the NASD standardizes investment practices, sets ethical standards, develops rules and regulations, and enforces the rules with an industry disciplinary body.

THE NATIONAL ASSOCIATION OF SECURITIES DEALERS AUTOMATED QUOTATION (NASDAQ): The stock price index used to measure the relative value of stocks traded over the NASD. This widely used composite index is based on the prices of five thousand over-the-counter stocks.

NEW YORK STOCK EXCHANGE (NYSE): The largest stock market in the United States, located on Wall Street in New York City. Often referred to as the "big board," it was established in the 1790s to help fledgling corporations in a fledgling country raise the funds needed for capital investment.

NOTAPHILY: The study and collecting of paper and printed money.

NUMISMATICS: The study and collecting of coins.

OBVERSE: The front side of a coin; what's usually called "heads."

PRIME RATE: The interest rate banks charge their best, most creditworthy customers. This is one of the key interest rates in the economy, and it is watched closely by financial types, government policy makers, and businesses. It's also an interest rate that should be watched closely by consumers who have loans with adjustable rates, like credit cards, that are "pegged" to the prime rate. Any movement in the prime rate triggers an automatic change in these adjustable rates.

RECESSION: A general period of declining economic activity that can last anywhere from six to eighteen months, with one year being common. Inflation tends to be low or nonexistent during a recession.

RECOVERY: An early expansionary phase of the business cycle shortly after a contraction has ended, but before a full-blown expansion begins. During a recovery, the unemployment rate remains relatively high but starts to fall.

REVERSE: The back side of the coin, or "tails."

S&P 500: Standard & Poor is the world's foremost provider of independent credit ratings, indices, risk evaluation, investment research, and data. It supplies investors with the independent benchmarks they need to assess their investment and financial decisions.

SCRIPOPHILY: The study and collecting of stock certificates, bonds, and fiscal documents.

SECURITIES AND EXCHANGE COMMIS-SION (SEC): A federal government agency that regulates the trading of corporate stock to protect investors against unscrupulous practices. It was established in 1934 to prevent investors from manipulating the stock market and to prevent other practices that contributed to the 1929 stock market crash. The rules of the SEC affect information disclosure, insider trading, speculation, and use of credit.

SILVER CERTIFICATE: Paper currency issued by the U.S. Treasury from 1878 until the 1960s that could be exchanged for an equal value of silver. An occasional silver certificate will pop up in circulation, but for the most part they have been relegated to the storage vaults of collectors and have been replaced by Federal Reserve notes as the nation's paper money.

SOCIALISM: In theory, an economy that is a transition between capitalism and communism. It is based on government rather than individual ownership of resources; workers' control of the government, capital, and other productive resources; and income allocation based on need rather than on resource ownership or contribution to production.

SPECULATION: Buying an asset with the intent of reselling it later at a higher price. Those who engage in speculation have no reason for buying the asset other than resale at a later time.

STANDARD OF LIVING: The financial health of a population, based on the amount of consumption by the members of that population.

STOCK MARKET: A financial market that trades ownership shares in corporations. The three best known national stock markets in the United States are the New York Stock Exchange, the American Stock Exchange, and the National Association of Securities Dealers. Stock markets play a vital role in our economy, making it possible for businesses to raise the large sums of money needed for investment.

How many stockbrokers does it take to change a lightbulb? Two: one to take out the bulb and drop it, and the other to try to sell it before it crashes.

SUPPLY AND DEMAND: An economic model that maintains that the relationship between the supply and demand of any commodity will determine its price. For instance, if there is a great supply of hot dogs, their price will go down. If pizza suddenly became scarce, everyone would want one, and the prices would go up.

T-BILL: The abbreviation for Treasury bill, a type of government security issued by the U.S. Treasury to raise funds. A T-bill has a maturity length of one year or less; a ninety-day maturity is common.

T-BOND: The abbreviation for Treasury bond, which is one kind of government security issued by the U.S. Treasury. A T-bond has a maturity length of more than ten years, with fifteen and thirty years common maturities.

T-NOTE: The abbreviation for Treasury note, a kind of government security issued by the U.S. Treasury. A T-note has a maturity length of between one and ten years.

THIRD ESTATE: In past centuries, this included the peasants, serfs, or slaves who performed the dirty deeds for the ruling elite. In modern times, this is the workers, taxpayers, and consumers who have limited ownership of and control over resources. The third estate, which forms the backbone of any modern economy, is usually at odds with the business leaders of the second estate. Help may come from the government leaders of the first estate or the journalists of the fourth estate—but don't count on it.

TRADE DEFICIT: Formally termed a *balance of trade deficit*, a condition in which a nation's imports are greater than exports. A trade deficit is usually thought to be bad for a country. For this reason, some countries seek to reduce their trade deficit by establishing trade barriers on imports and by reducing the exchange rate so that exports are less expensive and imports are more expensive.

TRADE SURPLUS: Formally termed a *balance of trade surplus*, a condition in which a nation's exports are greater than imports. A trade surplus is usually thought to be a good thing for a country.

WORLD BANK: An agency of the United Nations that was established in 1945 to promote the economic development of the poorer nations in the world. They pursue this goal by providing low-interest loans to less developed countries and offering technical assistance on the best ways to use these loans. Funds for the loans are obtained by the World Bank selling bonds on the world's financial markets. Its long-run economic development orientation is usually coordinated with the shorter-run efforts of its sister U.N. agency, the International Monetary Fund.

WORLD TRADE ORGANIZATION (WTO): An international organization, consisting of about 150 member countries, which oversees multilateral trade among nations. The World Trade Organization was established in 1995. It administers multilateral trade agreements, provides a forum for trade negotiations, handles trade disputes, monitors national trade policies, and provides technical assistance and training for developing countries.

THE 4 TYPES OF MONEY

Money is a token that is used by a society to settle debts and pay for goods and services. It is the medium of exchange that has become mandated by law. There are four basic types of money:

1. COMMODITY MONEY

Whenever any commodity is used for the purpose of exchange, the commodity becomes equivalent to the money and is called *commodity money*. Everything from shells and animal furs to precious metals like gold and silver have been used as commodity money.

2. FIAT MONEY

The word *fiat* means "the command of the sovereign." It is money that is issued by the sovereign—or a government. This kind of money has been declared legal tender by a given government. It has no intrinsic value. Most of the world's paper money is fiat money.

3. FIDUCIARY MONEY

Checks and banknotes are examples of fiduciary money: It is money that represents a promise to pay in a different type of money when a transfer is made. Fiduciary money acts as a token of money and usually originates with a banking transaction.

4. ELECTRONIC MONEY

Electronic money (also known as *e-money*, *electronic cash*, *electronic currency*, *digital money*, *digital cash*, or *digital currency*) refers to money that is transmitted via the Internet, computer networks, or other electronic systems. In an electronic money system, no money actually changes hands, but rather a system of debits and credits is used to make exchanges.

Almost all government agencies, both federal and state, affect the economy—by spending money, by contributing revenue, and by maintaining the nation's business concerns. The sixteen national agencies described here make up the heart of our economy. Central to them all is the work of the Secretary of the Treasury, who is responsible for managing the current account deficit by selling Treasury notes and bonds. Since this controls the value of the dollar, it impacts the entire global economy.

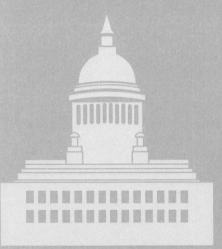

THE TREASURY

Congress established the Department of Treasury in 1789. It employs about 117,000 people, and operates under an annual budget of $11 billion. It controls another $358 billion in tax credits and debt financing. Most of the work of the Treasury is done by the agencies it controls, primarily:

INTERNAL REVENUE SERVICE: Assesses and collects taxes

OFFICE OF THE COMP-TROLLER OF THE CURRENCY: Regulates and supervises national banks

BUREAU OF PRINTING AND ENGRAVING: Manufactures currency

U.S. MINT: Manufactures coins

BUREAU OF PUBLIC DEBT: Borrows money to finance the public debt

FINANCIAL MANAGEMENT SERVICE: Receives and distributes public funds and generally acts as the government's accountant

DEPARTMENT OF COMMERCE

Created in 1903, this agency deals with commercial and industrial issues through their network of smaller bureaus, most significant of which are:

BUREAU OF ECONOMIC ANALYSIS: Compiles and interprets economic data for use by the public and by the government for creating financial policies

CENSUS BUREAU: Compiles and analyzes demographic data every ten years

PATENT AND TRADEMARK OFFICE: Allows inventors to protect their creations

ECONOMIC DEVELOPMENT ADMINISTRATION: Stimulates the job market in economically challenged areas

SMALL BUSINESS ADMINISTRATION: Oversees the creation and management of small businesses

MINORITY BUSINESS DEVELOPMENT AGENCY: Promotes the creation and sound management of minority businesses

INTERNATIONAL TRADE ADMINISTRATION: Encourages and monitors export and import activity

NATIONAL INSTITUTE OF STANDARDS AND TECHNOLOGY: Establishes standards for goods and services that rely on technological measurements—everything from automated teller machines and atomic clocks to mammograms and semiconductors

FEDERAL RESERVE SYSTEM

The Fed, as it is known, maintains the stability of the banking system, regulates banks, and oversees the nation's money supply. Established in 1913, it acts as the central bank of the United States and includes a board of governors, twelve district banks, twenty-five branch banks, and assorted committees, the most important of which is the Federal Open Market Committee, which directs monetary policy.

THE COUNCIL OF ECONOMIC ADVISERS

This agency assists the President with the development and implementation of the nation's economic policy. Led by a chairperson and two members, the Council consists of a team of highly trained economists, forecasters, and statistical experts who draw upon evidence-based research to provide the President with thorough and timely economic analysis.

ABOVE: Engraving the plates for printing money at the Bureau of Engraving, Washington, D.C., 1929

6 MODERN-DAY ECONOMISTS

These individuals each developed economic theories that have affected all of the world's economies. While each offers a unique view, they all draw on the wisdom of the ancient economists.

1. ADAM SMITH
(1723–1790)

In his groundbreaking work *The Wealth of Nations* (1776), Smith promoted a laissez-faire marketplace in which the government had minimal control over the economy and the natural laws of supply and demand were allowed to control growth.

2. KARL MARX
(1818–1883)

The German economist whose thoughts were fundamental in the development of communism and socialism had no faith in Smith's policy, claiming instead that a society left to its own devices would inevitably get rich on the backs of its workers. He disdained the notion of a profit-oriented culture. His most famous works are *The Manifesto of the Communist Party* (1848) and *Das Kapital* (1867).

"The writer must earn money in order to be able to live and to write, but he must by no means live and write for the purpose of making money." –Karl Marx

3. JOHN MAYNARD KEYNES
(1883–1946)

Disagreeing with both Smith and Marx, Keynes, in his work *The General Theory of Employment, Interest, and Money* (1936), expressed what has come to be known as Keynesian Economics, an approach that favors government control only on issues such as taxation, spending, and borrowing in order to maintain a stable and growing economy.

4. JOHN KENNETH GALBRAITH
(1908–2006)

Galbraith was a Keynesian economist who argued that giant firms that were replacing smaller ones had the power to eliminate price competition in the American economy, and that only in a free market would people be able to control the price of goods.

5. MILTON FRIEDMAN
(1912–2006)

An American economist, Friedman challenged the ideas of Keynes, and instead promoted free markets. Claiming that the government could never effectively manage the economy, he argued for, among other things, a volunteer army, freely floating exchange rates, abolition of the licensing of doctors, and a negative income tax.

6. PAUL SAMUELSON
(1915– 2009)

Samuelson's contribution was in teaching the world that the primitive methods they were using to study economics (verbal explanations and diagrams) lacked the element of mathematics, which would allow economists to use various equations to determine the outcome of various economic changes.

"If all economists were laid end to end, they would not reach a conclusion." —George Bernard Shaw

WORLD CURRENCIES

COUNTRY	CURRENCY
AFGHANISTAN	afghani
ALBANIA	lek
ALGERIA	Algerian dinar
ANDORRA	euro*, French franc, Spanish peseta
ANGOLA	kwanza
ANTIGUA AND BARBUDA	East Caribbean dollar
ARGENTINA	Argentinean peso
ARMENIA	dram
AUSTRALIA	Australian dollar
AUSTRIA	euro* and Austrian schilling
AZERBAIJAN	Azerbaijanian manat
BAHAMAS, THE	Bahamian dollar
BAHRAIN	Bahrainian dinar
BANGLADESH	taka
BARBADOS	Barbadian dollar
BELARUS	Belarusian ruble
BELGIUM	euro* and Belgian franc
BELIZE	Belizean dollar
BENIN	Communauté Financière Africaine (CFA) franc
BHUTAN	ngultrum and Indian rupee
BOLIVIA	boliviano
BOSNIA AND HERZEGOVINA	marka

COUNTRY	CURRENCY
BOTSWANA	pula
BRAZIL	real
BRUNEI	Bruneian dollar
BULGARIA	lev
BURKINA FASO	CFA franc
BURUNDI	Burundian franc
CAMBODIA	riel
CAMEROON	CFA franc
CANADA	Canadian dollar
CAPE VERDE	Cape Verdean escudo
CENTRAL AFRICAN REPUBLIC	CFA franc
CHAD	CFA franc
CHILE	Chilean peso
CHINA	yuan
COLOMBIA	Colombian peso
COMOROS	Comoran franc
CONGOKINSHASA	Congolese franc
CONGO-BRAZZAVILLE	CFA franc
COSTA RICA	Costa Rican colón
COTE D'IVOIRE	CFA franc
CROATIA	kuna
CUBA	Cuban peso
CYPRUS	Cypriot pound; Turkish Cypriot area: Turkish lira

*On January 1, 2002, the euro became the sole currency for everyday transactions within these countries, all members of the European Monetary Union.

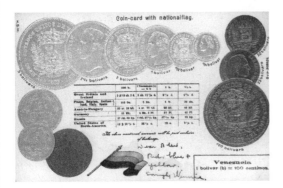

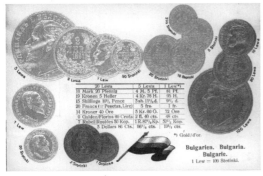

ABOVE: Postcards such as these were frequently issued to announce and define coinage and currency from a particular country. Those shown here are from Venezuela, Bulgaria, and Denmark.

CZECH REPUBLIC	Czech koruna
DENMARK	Danish krone
DJIBOUTI	Djiboutian franc
DOMINICA	East Caribbean dollar
DOMINICAN REPUBLIC	Dominican peso
EAST TIMOR	U.S. dollar
ECUADOR	U.S. dollar
EGYPT	Egyptian pound
EL SALVADOR	Salvadoran colón; U.S. dollar
ERITREA	nakfa
ESTONIA	Estonian kroon
ETHIOPIA	birr
FIJI	Fijian dollar
FINLAND	euro* and markka
FRANCE	euro* and French franc
GABON	CFA franc
GAMBIA	dalasi
GEORGIA, REPUBLIC OF	lari
GERMANY	euro* and deutsche mark
GHANA	cedi
GREECE	euro* and drachma
GRENADA	East Caribbean dollar
GUATEMALA	quetzal and U.S. dollar
GUINEA	Guinean franc
GUINEA-BISSAU	CFA franc
GUYANA	Guyanese dollar
HAITI	gourde
HOLY SEE (VATICAN CITY)	euro* and Italian lira
HONDURAS	lempira
HUNGARY	forint
ICELAND	Icelandic krona

INDIA	Indian rupee
INDONESIA	rupiah
IRAN	Iranian rial
IRAQ	Iraqi dinar
IRELAND	euro* and Irish pound
ISRAEL	new Israeli shekel
ITALY	euro* and Italian lira
JAMAICA	Jamaican dollar
JAPAN	yen
JORDAN	Jordanian dinar
KAZAKHSTAN	tenge

In 2006, the Kazakhstan Central Bank apologized for having misspelled the word *bank* (in the Kazakh language) on the new notes that had just been printed. Nevertheless, they put the misprinted notes—worth 2,000 tenge ($15) and 5,000 tenge—into circulation, then gradually withdrew them to correct the spelling.

KENYA	Kenyan shilling
KIRIBATI	Australian dollar
KOREA, NORTH	North Korean won
KOREA, SOUTH	South Korean won
KUWAIT	Kuwaiti dinar
KYRGYZSTAN	som
LAOS	kip
LATVIA	Latvian lats
LEBANON	Lebanese pound
LESOTHO	loti and South African rand
LIBERIA	Liberian dollar
LIBYA	Libyan dinar
LIECHTENSTEIN	Swiss franc
LITHUANIA	litas

LUXEMBOURG	euro* and Luxembourg franc
MACEDONIA, REPUBLIC OF	Macedonian denar
MADAGASCAR	Malagasy franc
MALAWI	Malawian kwacha
MALAYSIA	ringgit
MALDIVES	rufiyaa
MALI	CFA franc
MALTA	Maltese lira
MARSHALL ISLANDS	U.S. dollar
MAURITANIA	ouguiya
MAURITIUS	Mauritian rupee
MEXICO	Mexican peso
MICRONESIA	U.S. dollar
MOLDOVA	Moldovan leu
MONACO	euro* and French franc
MONGOLIA	togrog/tugrik
MOROCCO	Moroccan dirham
MOZAMBIQUE	metical
NAMIBIA	Namibian dollar and South African rand
NAURU	Australian dollar
NEPAL	Nepalese rupee
NETHERLANDS	euro* and Netherlands guilder
NEW ZEALAND	New Zealand dollar
NICARAGUA	gold córdoba
NIGER	CFA franc
NIGERIA	naira
NORWAY	Norwegian krone
OMAN	Omani rial
PAKISTAN	Pakistani rupee
PALAU	U.S. dollar
PANAMA	balboa and U.S. dollar

PAPUA NEW GUINEA	kina
PARAGUAY	guarani
PERU	nuevo sol
MYANMAR	kyat
PHILIPPINES	Philippine peso
POLAND	zloty
PORTUGAL	euro* and Portuguese escudo
QATAR	Qatari riyal
ROMANIA	Romanian leu
RUSSIA	Russian ruble
RWANDA	Rwandan franc
SAINT KITTS AND NEVIS	East Caribbean dollar
SAINT LUCIA	East Caribbean dollar
SAINT VINCENT AND GRENADINES	East Caribbean dollar
SAMOA	tala
SAN MARINO	euro* and Italian lira
SÃO TOMÉ AND PRÍNCIPE	dobra
SAUDI ARABIA	riyal
SENEGAL	CFA franc
SEYCHELLES	Seychelles rupee
SIERRA LEONE	leone
SINGAPORE	Singapore dollar
SLOVAKIA	Slovak koruna
SLOVENIA	tolar
SOLOMON ISLANDS	Solomon Islands dollar
SOMALIA	Somali shilling
SOUTH AFRICA	rand
SPAIN	euro* and Spanish peseta
SRI LANKA	Sri Lankan rupee
SUDAN	Sudanese dinar
SURINAME	Surinamese guilder
SWAZILAND	lilangeni
SWEDEN	Swedish krona
SWITZERLAND	Swiss franc
SYRIA	Syrian pound
TAJIKISTAN	somoni
TANZANIA	Tanzanian shilling
THAILAND	baht
TOGO	CFA franc
TONGA	pa'anga
TRINIDAD AND TOBAGO	Trinidad and Tobago dollar
TUNISIA	Tunisian dinar
TURKEY	Turkish lira
TURKMENISTAN	Turkmen manat
TUVALU	Australian dollar and Tuvaluan dollar
UGANDA	Ugandan shilling
UKRAINE	hryvnia
UNITED ARAB EMIRATES	Emirati dirham
UNITED KINGDOM	British pound
UNITED STATES	U.S. dollar
URUGUAY	Uruguayan peso
UZBEKISTAN	sum
VANUATU	vatu
VENEZUELA	bolivar
VIETNAM	dong
YEMEN	Yemeni rial
ZAMBIA	Zambian kwacha
ZIMBABWE	Zimbabwean dollar

18 BRITISH SLANG WORDS FOR MONEY

1 **BAR:** £1	**7** **MARIGOLD** sovereign	**13** **PONY:** £25
2 **BOB:** a shilling	**8** **MONKEY:** £500	**14** **QUID:** £1
3 **DOSH:** money	**9** **NICKER:** £1	**15** **SMACKER:** £1
4 **JOEY:** fourpenny piece and later, threepenny piece	**10** **NOTE:** £1	**16** **TANNER:** sixpence
5 **MACARONI:** £25	**11** **ONE-ER:** £100 or £1,000	**17** **TOSHEROON:** half-crown coin
6 **MAGGIE:** gold-colored £1 coin issued in the 1980s	**12** **OXFORD:** old crown coin (five shillings)	**18** **WONGER:** money

23 AMERICAN SLANG TERMS FOR MONEY

1 BACON

2 BOFFO

3 BREAD

4 CABBAGE

5 CLAMS

6 DOUGH

7 FOLDING GREEN

8 GREEN

9 KALE

10 LETTUCE

11 LONG GREEN JACK

12 LOOT

13 MAZUMA

14 MOOLAH

15 OSCAR

16 PAP

17 PLASTER

18 POTATOES

19 RHINO

20 RIVETS

21 SCRATCH

22 SOURDOUGH (counterfeit money)

23 SPONDULICKS

34 SLANG TERMS FOR CURRENCY NOTES

These all refer to the U.S. dollar, unless otherwise indicated.

1 ACE	10 CLAM	19 IRON MAN (dollar coin)	28 SCRIP
2 BEAN	11 COCONUT	20 JACK	29 SIMOLEON
3 BILL ($100)	12 DEAD PRESIDENTS (paper money)	21 JACKSON ($20)	30 SINKER (dollar coin)
4 BOFFO	13 DOUBLE SAWBUCK ($20)	22 LIZARD	31 TWANKIE ($20)
5 BONE	14 FIN ($5)	23 PESO	32 TWO BITS (25 cents)
6 BUCK	15 FISH	24 PLUG (dollar coin)	33 WAGON WHEEL (dollar coin)
7 BULLET	16 FIVER ($5)	25 ROCK	34 YELLOWBACK
8 C-NOTE ($100)	17 FROGSKIN	26 RUTABAGA	
9 CASE NOTE	18 GRAND, OR G ($1,000)	27 SAWBUCK ($10)	

Globalization is the process by which societies and cultures come together to share resources. When we talk about economic globalization, we are referring to the interconnectedness of the U.S. economy, for instance, to that of just about every other country in the world. It's because we live in a global economy that connects virtually all banks to all other banks that you are able to send money to a friend in France, purchase goods from Hong Kong, and enjoy a Big Mac in New Zealand.

Globalization is a process that takes place over the course of time as people begin to share goals and customs. Historians guess that the origins of our global culture may lie in the early trade links between the Roman Empire, the Parthian Empire (what is now northeastern Iran), and China's Han Dynasty. The routes that connected these three entities came to be known as the Silk Road; today it connects East, South, and Western Asia with the Mediterranean world, as well as North and Northeast Africa and Europe. The Muslim traders and explorers of the seventh century A.D. and onward—who roamed the world bringing new crops, knowledge, and technology with them— also played an important role in the ancient world.

Economic globalization was furthered during the fifteenth and sixteenth centuries as the maritime empires of Spain and Portugal initially, and then the British and the Dutch, began trade not only with the New World but also with the countries of Africa and Eurasia. In the seventeenth century, the conquests of the British East India Company and the Dutch East India Company resulted in new resources—such as rubber, diamonds, and coal—that encouraged commerce among all powers great and small throughout the world.

By the twentieth century, global trade had become so integral to the survival of individual economies that world leaders were moved to establish a framework for global commerce and various institutions to oversee it. The World Bank and the International Monetary Fund were formed at this time. Since then, international agreements continue to support international trade through tariffs and laws that enable you to go online, order a dozen beignets from Paris, and have them delivered to your door by breakfast the next morning.

Because globalization connects our economy to that of just about every other country, it is important to constantly gauge the financial well-being of all nations. One of the main indicators of a nation's economy is its gross domestic income, or GDI. This can be calculated in three different ways: by measuring income, expenditures, or goods produced. The latter is the most common and the basis for this list and the one that follows.

25 COUNTRIES WITH THE HIGHEST GDI

The numbers provided represent the total dollar value of all the goods and services provided by that country for the year, according to the International Monetary Fund. These indicate the relative health of the country's economy, and they are listed in order of highest to lowest GDP for the year 2008. The numbers are in millions of U.S. dollars.

#	Country	Value	#	Country	Value	#	Country	Value
1	UNITED STATES	$14,264,600	8	RUSSIA	$1,676,586	17	TURKEY	$729,443
2	JAPAN	$4,923,761	9	SPAIN	$1,611,767	18	POLAND	$525,735
3	PEOPLE'S REPUBLIC OF CHINA	$4,401,614	10	BRAZIL	$1,572,839	19	INDONESIA	$511,765
			11	CANADA	$1,510,957	20	BELGIUM	$506,392
4	GERMANY	$3,667,513	12	INDIA	$1,209,686	21	SWITZERLAND	$492,595
5	FRANCE	$2,865,737	13	MEXICO	$1,088,128	22	SWEDEN	$484,550
6	UNITED KINGDOM	$2,674,085	14	AUSTRALIA	$1,010,699	23	SAUDI ARABIA	$481,631
			15	SOUTH KOREA	$947,010	24	NORWAY	$456,226
7	ITALY	$2,313,893	16	NETHERLANDS	$868,940	25	AUSTRIA	$415,321

25 COUNTRIES WITH THE LOWEST GDI

List from lowest to highest, given in millions of U.S. dollars:

#	Country	Value	#	Country	Value	#	Country	Value
1	KIRIBATI	$137	9	SAMOA	$537	17	DJIBOUTI	$982
2	SÃO TOMÉ AND PRÍNCIPE	$176	10	VANUATU	$573	18	SAINT LUCIA	$1,025
3	TONGA	$258	11	SAINT KITTS AND NEVIS	$555	19	BURUNDI	$1,097
4	DOMINICA	$364	12	SAINT VINCENT AND THE GRENADINES	$601	20	GUYANA	$1,130
5	GUINEA-BISSAU	$461				21	ANTIGUA AND BARBUDA	$1,256
6	SOLOMON ISLANDS	$473	13	GRENADA	$639	22	MALDIVES	$1,259
7	EAST TIMOR	$499	14	GAMBIA	$808	23	BHUTAN	$1,368
8	COMOROS	$532	15	SEYCHELLES	$834	24	BELIZE	$1,381
			16	LIBERIA	$836	25	ERITREA	$1,476

The history of the euro can be traced back as far as World War II, when it was believed that economic ties among nations could promote growth. A single currency would allow for easier payments for consumers, and it would also help businesses protect themselves from losses associated with exchange rates. Trade, therefore, would be beneficial to all.

1951
Belgium, France, West Germany, Italy, Luxembourg, and the Netherlands sign the Paris Treaty, thus forming the European Coal and Steel Community.

1957
The same nations sign the Treaties of Rome and create the European Economic Community (EEC).

1979
The European Monetary System takes effect; its purpose is to keep inflation in check and to stabilize exchange rates.

1986
The six EEC countries agree to the Single European Act, which will further monetary and political cooperation.

1992
Maastrict Treaty is signed, creating a January 1, 1999, deadline for shared currency, one exchange rate policy, and shared economic policies.

1993
Germany becomes the home of the European Monetary Institute.

1994
First meeting of the European Monetary Institute.

1995
It is agreed that the single currency would be the euro, and the 1999 deadline is confirmed.

1998
The European Central Bank is created.

1999
Eleven member countries (Austria, Belgium, Finland, France, Germany, Ireland, Italy, Luxembourg, the Netherlands, Portugal, and Spain) officially tie their currency exchange rates to the euro and stocks begin trading in euros.

2000
The euro loses 30 percent of its value against the dollar. The European Central Bank intervenes.

2001
Euro bills and coins are first distributed in Greece.

2002
Old currency is phased out and euros go into full circulation.

2003
Sweden holds a referendum vote in which the public refuses to adopt the euro.

2004
Cyprus, the Czech Republic, Estonia, Hungary, Latvia, Lithuania, Malta, and Poland join the European Union.

2007
Slovenia joins the European Union.

2008
Cyprus and Malta join the Eurozone.

2009
Slovakia joins the European Union.

ABOVE: Euro note

TOP 10 RICHEST COUNTRIES IN THE WORLD

These countries made the list based on their per capita income in 2008:

1. LUXEMBOURG—$80,800
This tiny country with a total population of less than 500,000 is a true European miracle. By tiny we mean the eighth smallest country in the world in area. From top to bottom it's only about fifty miles and at its widest about thirty miles, yet it tops the list of per capita income. Go, Luxembourg!

2. QATAR—$75,900
This Arabic-speaking country has less than a million people and gained independence from Great Britain only in 1971. Qatar used to be a poor Islamic country but since the discovery of oil and natural gas in the 1940s, it has been completely transformed. With no income tax, it is one of the least taxed countries in the world, while still offering most of its services to the population for free. In 2009, Qatar is also expected to be the fastest-growing economy in the world.

3. NORWAY—$55,600
Norway is one of the few highly developed countries in Europe that are not part of the European Union. This oil and natural gas rich country has living costs more than 30 percent higher than in the United States. In 2006, only Russia and Saudi Arabia exported more oil than Norway.

4. KUWAIT—$55,300
In Arabic, *Kuwait* translates to "fortress built near water." In addition to being on the coast of the Persian Gulf, this country has well-known neighbors like Saudi Arabia and Iraq. Kuwait has the world's fifth-largest proven oil reserves, about 10 percent of the world's total. Being a country without taxes, about 80 percent of the government's revenue comes from exporting oil. Having the second-most free economy in the Middle East, Kuwait has one of the fastest growing economies in the region.

5. UNITED ARAB EMIRATES—$55,200
This oil and natural gas rich country has a highly developed economy which makes it one of the most developed in the world. Having more money than they know what to do with, they have built numerous artificial islands and recently completed the world's highest structure, the 160-story Burj Khalifa; at 818 meters (2,717 feet) tall, it is about twice the height of the Empire State Building in New York. It is estimated that about a quarter of the total construction going on in the world is taking place in Dubai, the largest city in United Arab Emirates.

6. SINGAPORE—$48,900
This tiny country consists of 63 islands and some mainland, with a total area of only 270 square miles (704 sq km). Along with Hong Kong, South Korea, and Taiwan, it is considered one of the Four Asian Tigers. Singapore has the busiest port in the world and is the fourth largest foreign exchange trading center in the world. Singapore is widely believed to be the most business-friendly economy on the planet.

7. UNITED STATES—$46,000
What sets the United States apart from most other countries in this list is its size. Most of the others are among the smallest in the world, while the United States has a population of more than 300 million and a total land area of 3.79 million square miles (9.83 million sq km). It is home to the largest number of billionaires in the world.

8. IRELAND—$45,600
This member of the European Union has been often admired as one of the most modern of all economies, and

is the largest maker of computer software in the world. A 2005 study done by *The Economist* ranked the Celtic Tiger to have the best quality of life in the world.

9. EQUATORIAL GUINEA—$44,100

Most people have never even heard of the Republic of Equatorial Guinea in Central Africa. This country achieved stardom after 1996, when large oil reserves were found in the nation of only half a million people. While being one of the largest producers of oil in Africa, little progress has been made to improve conditions of the people who live there. Corruption is widespread and most people live in poverty. The gap between rich and poor is probably the largest in the world.

10. SWITZERLAND—$39,800

The cheese-making capital is considered to be one of the most neutral countries in the world. During World War II, people from other European countries deposited their money in the banks of Switzerland, knowing that their money would be safer there than in their home countries. Some well-known Swiss companies include the world's largest foods company, Nestlé, along with Logitech, Rolex, and Credit Suisse.

THE MOST EXPENSIVE SHOPPING DISTRICTS IN THE WORLD

The figures below represent the average cost of renting one thousand square feet of commercial space for one year, in U.S. dollars in the year 2008, as reported by CNBC.com.

1. FIFTH AVENUE
New York, New York
$1.50 million

2. CAUSEWAY BAY
Hong Kong, The People's Republic of China
$1.21 million

3. MADISON AVENUE
New York, New York
$1.20 million

4. AVENUE DES CHAMPS-ÉLYSÉES
Paris, France
$922,000

5. EAST 57TH STREET
New York, New York
$900,000

6. NEW BOND STREET
London, England
$813,000

7. GINZA
Tokyo, Japan
$683,000

8. GRAFTON STREET
Dublin, Ireland
$668,000

9. OXFORD STREET
London, England
$631,000

10. RODEO DRIVE
Los Angeles, California
$600,000

"Veni, Vidi, Visa: I came, I saw, I did a little shopping."
—Anonymous

HELIUM WAS UP, FEATHERS WERE DOWN.

PAPER WAS STATIONARY.

FLUORESCENT TUBING WAS DIMMED IN LIGHT TRADING.

KNIVES WERE UP SHARPLY.

COWS STEERED INTO A BULL MARKET.

PENCILS LOST A FEW POINTS.

HIKING EQUIPMENT WAS TRAILING.

ELEVATORS ROSE, WHILE ESCALATORS CONTINUED THEIR SLOW DECLINE.

WEIGHTS WERE UP IN HEAVY TRADING.

LIGHT SWITCHES WERE OFF.

MINING EQUIPMENT HIT ROCK BOTTOM.

DIAPERS REMAIN UNCHANGED.

SHIPPING LINES STAYED AT AN EVEN KEEL.

THE MARKET FOR RAISINS DRIED UP.

COCA-COLA FIZZLED.

CATERPILLAR STOCK INCHED UP A BIT.

SUN PEAKED AT MIDDAY.

BALLOON PRICES WERE INFLATED.

SCOTT TISSUE TOUCHED A NEW BOTTOM.

BATTERIES EXPLODED IN AN ATTEMPT TO RECHARGE THE MARKET.

INVEST YOUR MONEY WITH UNCLE SAM!

LIBERTY BONDS

Join the Crowd - Buy a LIBERTY BOND!

BROKER: Poorer than you were last year

BUDGET: Written proof that you can't afford the things you want

BULL MARKET: A random market movement causing investors to mistake themselves for financial geniuses

CASH FLOW: The movement of money as it disappears down the toilet

CEO: Chief Embezzlement Officer

CFO: Chief Fraud Officer

COMMISSION: The only reliable way to make money on the stock market

CONVENIENCE FEE: Interest charge

DAY TRADER: A socially acceptable gambling addict

ECONOMIST: An expert who will know tomorrow why the things he predicted yesterday didn't happen today

MULTILEVEL-BUSINESS PARTNER: Sucker

SOCIAL SECURITY: A federally mandated pyramid scheme

STOCK ANALYST: The shrink who's treating your depressed financial advisor

201k: What used to be your 401k.

ABOVE: Uncle Sam sells Liberty bonds to a long line of diverse citizens.

WORLD STOCK EXCHANGES

The history of stock exchanges can be traced to twelfth century France, when the first brokers are believed to have appeared, trading in debt and government securities. Unofficial share markets existed across Europe beginning in the mid-1500s, where brokers would meet to make trades.

By the early 1700s, there were fully operational stock exchanges in France and England, and America followed in the later part of the century. Share exchanges became an important way for companies to raise capital for investment, while also offering investors the opportunity to benefit from profits. The early days of the stock exchange experienced many scandals and "share crashes," as there was little to no regulation and almost anyone was allowed to participate in the exchange.

Today, stock exchanges around the world operate as highly regulated institutions. Investors wanting to buy and sell shares must do so through a share broker, who pays to own a seat on the exchange. Companies with shares traded on an exchange are said to be *listed* and they must meet specific criteria, which vary across exchanges. Most stock exchanges began as floor exchanges, where traders made deals face-to-face. The largest stock exchange in the world, the New York Stock Exchange, continues to operate this way (think of that frantic scene in *Trading Places*), but most of the world's exchanges have now become fully electronic.

ABOVE: Stock exchanges in New York, London, Chicago, Hamburg, Frankfurt, Berlin, and Brussels

AFRICAN STOCK EXCHANGES

Ghana Stock Exchange, Ghana
Johannesburg Stock Exchange, South Africa
South African Futures EXchange, South Africa

ASIAN STOCK EXCHANGES

Australian Stock Exchanges, Australia
Sydney Futures Exchange, Australia
Shenzhen Stock Exchange, China
Hong Kong Futures Exchange, Hong Kong
Stock Exchange of Hong Kong, Hong Kong
Bombay Stock Exchange, India
National Stock Exchange of India, India
Indonesia NET Exchange, Indonesia
Jakarta Stock Exchange, Indonesia
Nagoya Stock Exchange, Japan
Osaka Securities Exchange, Japan
Tokyo Grain Exchange, Japan
Tokyo International Financial Futures Exchange, Japan
Tokyo Stock Exchange, Japan
Korea Stock Exchange, Korea
Kuala Lumpur Stock Exchange, Malaysia
New Zealand Stock Exchange, New Zealand
Karachi Stock Exchange, Pakistan
Lahore Stock Exchange, Pakistan
Singapore International Monetary Exchange Ltd., Singapore
Stock Exchange of Singapore, Singapore
Colombo Stock Exchange, Sri Lanka
Sri Lanka Stock Closings, Sri Lanka
Taiwan Stock Exchange, Taiwan
Stock Exchange of Thailand, Thailand

EUROPEAN STOCK EXCHANGES

Vienna Stock Exchange, Austria
Equiduct (formerly European Association of Securities Dealers Automatic Quotation System), Belgium
Zagreb Stock Exchange, Croatia
Prague Stock Exchange, Czech Republic
Copenhagen Stock Exchange, Denmark
Helsinki Stock Exchange, Finland
Les Echos, France
Marché A Terme International de France, France
Nouveau Marché, France
Paris Stock Exchange, France
Frankfurt Stock Exchange, Germany
Athens Stock Exchange, Greece
Budapest Stock Exchange, Hungary
Italian Stock Exchange, Italy
National Stock Exchange of Lithuania, Lithuania
Macedonian Stock Exchange, Macedonia
Amsterdam Stock Exchange, The Netherlands
Oslo Stock Exchange, Norway
Warsaw Stock Exchange, Poland
Lisbon Stock Exchange, Portugal
Bucharest Stock Exchange, Romania
Russian Securities Market News, Russia
Ljubljana Stock Exchange, Inc., Slovenia
Barcelona Stock Exchange, Spain
Madrid Stock Exchange, Spain
Mercado Español de Futuros Financieros, Spain
Stockholm Stock Exchange, Sweden
Swiss Exchange, Switzerland
Istanbul Stock Exchange, Turkey
Electronic Share Information, United Kingdom
Financial Times and the London Stock Exchange, United Kingdom
London International Financial Futures and Options Exchange, United Kingdom
London Metal Exchange, United Kingdom

MIDDLE EASTERN STOCK EXCHANGES

Tel Aviv Stock Exchange, Israel
Amman Financial Market, Jordan
Beirut Stock Exchange, Lebanon
Palestine Securities Exchange, Palestine
Istanbul Stock Exchange, Turkey

NORTH AMERICAN STOCK EXCHANGES

Alberta Stock Exchange, Canada
Montreal Stock Exchange, Canada
Toronto Stock Exchange, Canada
Vancouver Stock Exchange, Canada
Winnipeg Stock Exchange, Canada
Mexican Stock Exchange, Mexico

American Stock Exchange, United States

Arizona Stock Exchange, United States

Chicago Board of Trade, United States

Chicago Board Options Exchange, United States

Chicago Mercantile Exchange, United States

Chicago Stock Exchange, United States

Kansas City Board of Trade, United States

Minneapolis Grain Exchange, United States

National Association of Securities Dealers Automated Quotation, United States

New York Stock Exchange, United States

Pacific Stock Exchange, United States

Philadelphia Stock Exchange, United States

SOUTH AMERICAN STOCK EXCHANGES

Bermuda Stock Exchange, Bermuda

Rio de Janeiro Stock Exchange, Brazil

São Paulo Stock Exchange, Brazil

Cayman Islands Stock Exchange, Cayman Islands

Chile Electronic Stock Exchange, Chile

Santiago Stock Exchange, Chile

Bogota Stock Exchange, Colombia

Occidente Stock Exchange, Colombia

Guayaquil Stock Exchange, Ecuador

Jamaica Stock Exchange, Jamaica

Nicaraguan Stock Exchange, Nicaragua

Lima Stock Exchange, Peru

Trinidad and Tobago Stock Exchange, Trinidad and Tobago

Caracas Stock Exchange, Venezuela

Venezuela Electronic Stock Exchange, Venezuela

ABOVE: The Buenos Aires Stock Exchange, 1908

BURGERNOMICS:
PROFITING FROM THE BIG MAC INDEX

Ever since 1986, *The Economist* has published its famed Big Mac Index, an informal way of measuring the purchasing power parity (PPP) between two currencies. Its purpose is to make complex exchange-rate theory as digestible as, well, a Big Mac.

The theory of purchasing power parity says that a dollar should buy the same amount in all countries. Thus, in the long run, the exchange rate between two countries should move toward the rate that equalizes the prices of an identical basket of goods and services in each country.

By looking at a McDonald's Big Mac— a good that is produced in about 120 countries—*The Economist*'s tongue-in-cheek index illustrates how market exchange rates can result in identical goods having different prices in different countries. By comparing the cost of Big Macs across countries, the Big Mac Index calculates the Big Mac PPP, the exchange rate that would mean hamburgers cost the same in the United States as abroad. Compare the Big Mac PPP to the market exchange rates, and— *voilà!*—you see which currencies are under- or overvalued.

The Big Mac Index does have its shortcomings. A Big Mac's price reflects more than just the cost of bread and meat and vegetables. It also reflects non-tradable elements such as rent and labor. For that reason, the Big Mac Index probably is best when comparing countries at roughly the same stage of development. In any case, there is no theoretical reason why non-tradable goods and services should be equal in different countries.

Furthermore, eating a Big Mac means different things in different countries. Indians eat fewer Big Macs than Americans. In some countries, eating at McDonald's is a relative luxury. Whereas low-income Americans may eat at McDonald's a few times a week, low-income Malaysians rarely eat Big Macs. Finally, local taxes, levels of competition, and import duties on Big Mac components may not be representative of the country's economy as a whole.

For all its weaknesses, the Big Mac Index has caught on even among economists as a shorthanded way of looking at PPP across the world's economies. The table here, reproduced from *The Economist*, shows by how much a Big Mac costs relative to the U.S. dollar at the end of January 2007.

If you had purchased $1,000 of Nortel stock one year ago, it would now be worth $49.00. With Enron, you would have $16.50 left of the original $1,000. With WorldCom, you would have less than $5.00 left. If you had purchased $1,000 of Delta Air Lines stock, you would have $49.00 left. If you had purchased United Airlines, you would have nothing left. But, if you had purchased $1,000 worth of beer one year ago, drank all the beer, and then turned in the cans for recycling, you would have $214.00. Thus the best current investment advice is to drink heavily and recycle. This is called the 401-Keg Plan.

BIG MAC PRICES

	in local currency	in dollars		in local currency	in dollars
United States	$3.22	$3.22	Phillippines	Peso 85	1.74
Argentina	Peso 8.25	2.65	Poland	Zloty 6.90	2.29
Australia	A$3.45	2.67	Russia	Rouble 49	1.85
Brazil	Real 6.4	3.01	Saudi Arabia	Riyal 9	2.40
Britain	£1.99	3.90	Singapore	S$3.60	2.34
Canada	C$3.63	3.08	Slovakia	Crown 57.98	2.13
Chile	Peso 1,670	3.07	South Africa	Rand 15.5	2.14
China	Yuan 11	1.41	South Korea	Won 2,900	3.08
Colombia	Peso 6,900	3.06	Sri Lanka	Rupee 190	1.75
Costa Rica	Colones 1,130	2.18	Sweden	SKr32	4.59
Czech Republic	Koruna 52.1	2.41	Switzerland	SFr6.30	5.05
Denmark	DKr27.75	4.84	Taiwan	NT$75	2.28
Egypt	Pound 9.09	1.60	Thailand	Baht 62	1.78
Estonia	Kroon 30	2.49	Turkey	Lire 4.55	3.22
Euro areas	€ 2.94	3.82	UAE	Dirhams 10	2.72
Hong Kong	HK$12	1.54	Ukraine	Hryvnia 9	1.71
Hungary	Forint 590	3.00	Uruguay	Peso 55	2.17
Iceland	Kronur 509	7.44	Venezuela	Bolivar 6,800	1.58
Indonesia	Rupiah 15,900	1.75			
Japan	¥280	2.31			
Latvia	Lats 1.35	2.52			
Lithuania	Litas 6.50	2.45			
Malaysia	Ringgit 5.50	1.57			
Mexico	Peso 29	2.66			
New Zealand	NZ$4.60	3.16			
Norway	Kroner 41.5	6.63			
Pakistan	Rupee 140	2.31			
Paraguay	Guarani 10,000	1.90			
Peru	New Sol 9.50	2.97			

ECONOMIC AND CORPORATE STRUCTURES

AROUND THE WORLD

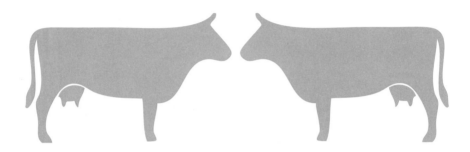

1. SOCIALISM
You have two cows.
You give one to your neighbor.

2. COMMUNISM
You have two cows.
The State takes both and gives you some milk.

3. FASCISM
You have two cows.
The State takes both and sells you some milk.

4. NAZISM
You have two cows.
The State takes both and shoots you.

5. BUREAUCRATISM
You have two cows.
The State takes both, shoots one, milks the other, and then throws the milk away.

6. TRADITIONAL CAPITALISM
You have two cows.
You sell one and buy a bull.
Your herd multiplies, and the economy grows.
You sell them and retire on the income.

7. SURREALISM
You have two giraffes.
The government requires you to take harmonica lessons.

8. AN AMERICAN CORPORATION
You have two cows.
You sell one, and force the other to produce the milk of four cows.
Later, you hire a consultant to analyze why the cow has dropped dead.

9. VENTURE CAPITALISM
You have two cows.
You sell three of them to your publicly listed company, using letters of credit opened by your brother-in-law at the bank, then execute a debt/equity swap with an associated general offer so that you get all four cows back, with a tax exemption for five cows. The milk rights of the six cows are transferred via an intermediary to a Cayman Island company secretly owned by the majority shareholder who sells the rights to all seven cows back to your listed company. The annual report says the company owns eight cows, with an option on one more. You sell one cow to buy a new president of the United States, leaving you with nine cows, and no balance sheet provided with the release. The public then buys your bull.

10. A FRENCH CORPORATION

You have two cows.
You go on strike, organize a riot, and block the roads–because you are demanding three cows.

11. A JAPANESE CORPORATION

You have two cows.
You redesign them so they are one-tenth the size of an ordinary cow and produce twenty times the milk. You then create a clever cow cartoon image called "Cowkimon" and market it worldwide.

12. A GERMAN CORPORATION

You have two cows.
You re-engineer them so they live for a hundred years, eat once a month, and milk themselves.

13. AN ITALIAN CORPORATION

You have two cows, but you don't know where they are.
You decide to have lunch.

14. A SWISS CORPORATION

You have five thousand cows. None of them belong to you.
You charge the owners for storing them.

15. A CHINESE CORPORATION

You have two cows.
You have three hundred people milking them.

You claim that you have full employ-ment, and high bovine productivity. You arrest the newsman who reported the real situation.

16. AN INDIAN CORPORATION

You have two cows.
You worship them.

17. A BRITISH CORPORATION

You have two cows.
Both are mad.

18. AN IRAQI CORPORATION

Everyone thinks you have lots of cows. You tell them that you have none. No one believes you, so they bomb the **** out of you and invade your country. You still have no cows, but at least now you are part of Democracy.

19. AN AUSTRALIAN CORPORATION

You have two cows.
Business seems pretty good.
You close the office and go for a few beers to celebrate.

20. A NEW ZEALAND CORPORATION

You have two cows.
A hobbit grabs one and takes it home.

9 PROPOSED CORPORATE MERGERS

1 Hale Business Systems, Mary Kay Cosmetics, Fuller Brush, and W. R. Grace Co. will merge and become Hale, Mary, Fuller, Grace.

2 Polygram Records, Warner Bros., and Zesta Crackers join forces to become Polly, Warner Cracker.

3 Goodyear will merge with 3M and issue forth as MMMGood.

4 Zippo Mfg., Audi, Dofasco, and Dakota Mining will merge to become, of course, ZipAudiDoDa.

5 Federal Express is expected to join its major competitor, UPS, and consolidate as FedUP.

6 Fairchild Electronics and Honey-well Computers will become Fair-well Honeychild.

7 Grey Poupon and Docker Pants are expected to become Poupon Pants.

8 Knotts Berry Farm and the National Organization of Women will become Knott NOW.

9 A&P is merging with Stop & Shop and will be Stop & P.

THE 10 MOST EXPENSIVE CITIES IN THE WORLD

OverseasPropertyMall.com is an investment blog that has been featuring international property research since 2005. Their recommendations are based on constant monitoring of foreign real estate. The prices given are based on the average price of an apartment within the city center and in good condition. In total, more than 110 cities around the world were surveyed for this purpose; data was collected during 2008.

1. MONTE CARLO
With average prices of $47,578 per square meter, it's no wonder that Monte Carlo ranks as the most expensive city in the world. Long known as the playground for party-friendly billionaires, starlets, and everything in between, Monte Carlo does offer something for everyone: casinos, stunning scenery, the Formula 1 Grand Prix, and plenty of sunshine all year round, not to mention the fact that Monaco, with one of the best yacht harbors in the world, is just around the corner.

2. MOSCOW
It's odd to note that Moscow is even more expensive to live in than London, but the city's real estate will set you back $20,853 per square meter. The vodka may be cheap, but a luxury two-bedroom in Moscow rents for $4,000 a month; a CD costs $24.83; and an international newspaper will set you back $6.30.

3. LONDON
London is only a fraction behind Moscow, with real estate selling for $20,756 per square meter, but has so much more to offer (if you don't mind the weather) in terms of culture, entertainment, and history.

4. TOKYO
If you love the idea of eternal supplies of sushi, sashimi, and Kirin beer, you might not mind living here—at a cost of $17,998 per square meter. The glitz, the neon, and the crowds come with the territory.

5. HONG KONG
Victoria Peak, harbor junks, quick access to mainland China, and a sophisticated mix of ethnic races share Hong Kong, a former British colony, as their home—at a price of $16,125 per square meter.

6. NEW YORK
The Big Apple is the only city in the United States included in this list. From Central Park to Manhattan's skyscraper jungle, you can find just about anything you want in this city—but it will cost you $14,898 per square meter to live here.

7. PARIS
The city of romance has plenty to boast about—the Eiffel Tower, the Louvre, the Arc de Triomphe—and real estate selling at $12,122 per square meter.

8. SINGAPORE
Cosmopolitan Singapore is one of the most pleasant cities in Asia, with strict laws about littering and plenty of green in and around the city. It will set you back some $9,701 per square meter.

9. ROME
If you're depressed by the $9,166 per-square-meter price tag, you can find solace on the Spanish Steps, the Circus Maximus, or in any one of the city's many ancient temples.

10. MUMBAI
Finding Mumbai on this list at all is astounding, considering the fact that until recently, India was viewed as a third-world country. Real estate here sells for around $9,163 per square meter.

It is said that up to 50 percent of businesses fail within five years of inception. Most of these start and end in obscurity. A few of them, however, start up with the verve of a cannonball, only to crash with equal fanfare. Some of the companies listed below, like Enron and DeLorean, exemplify this cataclysmic appeal. Others just tug at our heartstrings. Here, according to Businesspundit.com, are some of the most spectacular failures:

ABOVE: The ill-fated Edsel

1. THE EDSEL

In 1958, Ford's newest vehicle, launched on "E-Day," flailed, flopped, and imploded. Ford had kept the Edsel under wraps as a new kind of futuristic, experimental car. One fateful day in 1958, the Edsel was revealed—and immediately tanked. By November 1959, when Ford finally mercy-killed the Edsel, it had lost an estimated $250 million, nearly two billion in today's dollars. Edsel is now synonymous with a marketing business failure.

2. FLOOZ

Flooz.com spent some fifty million dollars trying to create a currency unique to Internet merchants, similar in concept to frequent flier programs. Users would accumulate *flooz* credits that could be redeemed for merchandise. Named after the Arabic word for money, the plan failed to catch on, and the company folded in 2001.

3. BETAMAX

If you look closely at several episodes of *The Simpsons*, you'll see a video rental store called "VHS Village" with a sign that says, "Formerly 'The Beta Barn.'" Try as it might, Sony was not able to convince the world that the Betamax video system, with its complicated bulk, expensive price tag, and a marketing campaign that was ridiculed by the public, could outmaneuver the VHS format. With a capability of only sixty minutes of recording, as opposed to the six hours that VHS offered, its no surprise that this is one of the biggest techno-failures in history.

4. SWISSAIR

The former national airline of Switzerland, Swissair, was once so financially stable that it was known as the "Flying Bank." Founded in 1931, Swissair epitomized international transportation until the late 1990s, when the airline's board decided to follow an aggressive borrowing and acquisition policy. But when the terrorist attacks of September 11, 2001, put a halt to the company's plans, Swissair found itself hamstrung with debt. Mismanagement and bad ideas—trundling large sums of cash to purchase fuel at foreign airports, for example—left the airline gasping for oxygen. In 2002, Switzerland was embarrassed to lose its national icon for good.

5. PREMIER SMOKELESS CIGARETTE

A smokeless cigarette has long been the holy grail of the tobacco industry. In an effort to reduce the harmful effects of inhaling cigarette smoke, R. J. Reynolds launched the Premier cigarette, a "smokeless nicotine delivery mechanism that looks and feels like a premium cigarette," in 1988. The product ended up a miserable flop. Not only did this expensive cig taste like charcoal, it ended up being employed by drug users as a handy "delivery mechanism" for substances other than tobacco. The cost of the project? A cool billion dollars.

6. BRE-X MINERALS

If someone tells you they've struck gold on the isle of Borneo, grab your money and run the other way. In 1995, Bre-X Minerals was a tiny mining company based in Calgary with stock worth under a dollar when they announced they had found extensive deposits of gold in Busang, Indonesia. As a result, their stock shot to almost $300 a share. A series of strange events, including a man falling from a helicopter and being eaten by tigers, roused enough suspicion to unravel the fraud. By 1999, an outside analysis of the site samples revealed that Bre-X had

faked their findings by "salting" samples with gold dust. Within weeks, the NASDAQ and TSX delisted the company, which at one point held a market cap of $4.4 billion. Investors slapped their foreheads, and Bre-X Minerals disappeared into the mire of failure.

7. TUCKER AUTOMOBILES

The ambitious car company that Preston Tucker started was only in business one year (1947–1948). It produced a mere fifty-one cars, but its story remains enshrined in museums, car clubs, a film, and even a video game in which everyone drives a Tucker. The fatal flaw? Offering customers the option to buy their accessories before their car was built. This program started a witch hunt by the SEC. Amid accusations of fraud and the auto industry's influence over government, Tucker Automobiles went belly-up. Of the original fifty-one cars made, forty-seven still exist today.

8. SHARPER IMAGE

Started in 1977 as a catalog company, the Sharper Image eventually grew into a high-end customer electronics store. As iPods and other branded, high-tech items took over the store's traditional market share, it launched into the infomercial business with the Oreck vacuum and Ionic Breeze. Unfortunately, the Ionic Breeze did not purify the air as it said it did. After losing a lawsuit against *Consumer Reports* for a negative review, the testing company released findings that the Ionic Breeze actually produced trace levels of ozone. In 2008, the store went bankrupt, forcing shoppers to buy their

overpriced, brushed-steel, throwaway executive gifts elsewhere.

9. ENRON

Enron was an energy sector leader that started to dabble in e-commerce and exotic investment areas. In 2001, Enron, once valued at $90 billion and the seventh largest company in the United States, went bankrupt. It took jobs, investor savings, retiree futures, and even some lives with it. In following years, it was revealed that executives had shredded documents, started partnerships with their own shell companies, and engaged in massive insider trading. Today the name Enron is synonymous with galloping greed.

10. POLAROID CORPORATION

The multinational company was founded in 1937 by Edwin H. Land and quickly became famous for the company's flagship product, the Polaroid camera, which made instant images available to the masses. Now moments could be captured—in just moments. But when digital photography took the public by storm in the early 2000s, it pretty much erased the need for the Polaroid camera. The company went bankrupt in 2005.

11. ATKINS NUTRITIONALS

Dr. Robert Atkins released his first book, *Dr. Atkins' Diet Revolution*, in 1972. In 1992, a revised version gained popularity, and the fad really took off at the beginning of the millennium. Questions arose from the medical community about the diet's long-term effects. Countless others, from the FDA to top chefs, also lined up to take shots at it. In 2003, it was reported to a skeptical public that the good doctor slipped on an icy sidewalk and died. The company went bankrupt within two years amid the suspicion that his diet had killed him. A year later, a medical examinations report revealed that Dr. Atkins, 72, had a history of heart attacks and congestive heart failure. He weighed 258 pounds at death. Meanwhile, a fickle public found the next diet fad and moved on, although many still swear by the program.

12. BETHLEHEM STEEL

The company has roots that go back to 1857, when the Saucona Iron Company, which eventually became the Bethlehem Iron Company, was first organized by Augustus Wolle. Eventually known as Bethlehem Steel, the company was the backbone of the first blasting furnace, railroads, skyscrapers, coal mining, nuclear reactors, warships, cargo vessels, large construction projects like arenas, and other major infrastructural accomplishments. However, the company never adjusted to the new service-based economy that gained ground in the 1990s. Cheap imports worsened the situation. Bethlehem Steel, a piece of American history, disappeared forever when it filed for bankruptcy in 2001.

13. PETS.COM

Pet's can't drive, and sock puppets make bad spokespeople, but Pets.com made the dot-com bubble their own in 2000. They over-expanded by opening a nationwide network of warehouses too quickly, and profits never caught up with media buys for commercials. In marketing, nothing is worse than having everyone know who you are and no one interested in what you sell. Widely recognized as the poster child for dot-com failure, its stock went from eleven dollars in early 2000 to just nineteen cents on Election Day that same year, when the company closed its doors.

14. COMMODORE COMPUTERS

Between 1983 and 1986, Apple, IBM, and Atari were quaking in their boots. The Commodore 64 was selling two million units a year and dominated nearly 50 percent of the total market. As the company tried to innovate by releasing the Commodore Plus/4, a faster, smarter version with a color screen, they alienated their original customer base. The new model was incompatible with the cherished C64. By 1994, the company had gone bankrupt.

15. DELOREAN MOTOR COMPANY

John DeLorean was a hero among the very rich for creating the kind of car the future promised. With a stainless steel–skinned body, sleek lines, and doors that opened vertically (gull wings), his DMC-12 hit the streets in 1980. Over the next three years, only 8,900 cars would be made. However, in 1983, a sting operation revealed DeLorean's connection to a suitcase full of drugs valued at $24 million. Later acquitted on entrapment grounds and cleared of defrauding his partners, he would never gain the investors' trust again.

16. PAN AM

Founded in 1927, the airline was a part of American culture for the better part of the twentieth century. It led the industry in international flights and luxury travel. It was also the first airline to make widespread use of jumbo jets, and the first to use an air staff of stewardesses as a PR focal point. Little girls grew up wanting to be Pan Am stewardesses, and boys grew up wanting to pilot one of the fleet. Unfortunately, as an American icon, Pan Am was also a target for terrorism. A few horrific incidents, coupled with the increased global competition that came with deregulation, caused the airline—and its accompanying era—to collapse in 1991.

ABOVE: The DeLorean was the only car model ever produced by the DeLorean Motor Company.

A DOLLAR IS A TERRIBLE THING TO WASTE

9 EXAMPLES OF OVER-THE-TOP GOVERNMENT SPENDING

Government waste doesn't just deprive citizens of the resources to which their taxes entitle them, it also promotes a feeling of despair among people who are already frustrated by their inability to earn a living wage. We've all heard of the $800 hammers, but examples continue to abound: At the time of this writing, $3 billion is missing from a government trust fund for Native Americans; the IRS has paid a $15,000 refund to an individual who owes $350,000 in back taxes; and a NASA probe built to explore Mars has failed because half the team that designed the probe used English measurements in their plans while the others used the metric system.

A war on government waste could easily save over $100 billion annually without harming the legitimate operations and benefits of government programs. As a first step, lawmakers might address the following examples of egregious waste, according to the Heritage Foundation, a public policy research institute:

1 Buried in the Department of the Treasury's 2003 *Financial Report of the United States Government* is a short section titled "Unreconciled Transactions Affecting the Change in Net Position," which explains that unreconciled transactions for 2003 totaled $24.5 billion. The government knows that $25 billion was spent by someone, somewhere, on something, but auditors do not know who spent it, where it was spent, or on what it was spent. The Treasury blamed the fiasco on the failure of federal agencies to report their expenditures adequately.

2 An audit revealed that between 1997 and 2003, the Defense Department purchased and then left unused approximately 270,000 commercial airline tickets at a total cost of $100 million. Even worse, the Pentagon never bothered to get a refund for these fully refundable tickets. Auditors also found 27,000 transactions between 2001 and 2002 in which the Pentagon paid twice for the same ticket. The department would purchase the ticket directly and then inexplicably reimburse the employee for the cost of the ticket. (In one case, an employee who allegedly made seven false claims for airline tickets professed not to have noticed that $9,700 was deposited into his account.) These additional transactions cost taxpayers $8 million.

3 Federal employee credit card programs were designed to save money. Rather than weaving through a lengthy procurement process to acquire basic supplies, federal employees could purchase job-related products with credit cards that would be paid by their agency. What began as a smart way to streamline government has since become a corrupted system at best. An audit revealed that employees of the Department of Agriculture diverted millions of dollars to personal purchases through their government-issued credit cards. Sampling three hundred employees' purchases over six months, investigators estimated that 15 percent abused their government credit cards, at a cost of $5.8 million. Taxpayer-funded

purchases included Ozzy Osbourne concert tickets, tattoos, lingerie, bartender school tuition, car payments, and cash advances.

4 The Defense Department suffers from its own credit card scandal. Over one eighteen-month period, Air Force and Navy personnel used government-funded credit cards to charge at least $102,400 for admission to entertainment events; $48,250 for gambling; $69,300 for cruises; and $73,950 for exotic dance clubs and prostitutes.

5 Medicare wastes more money than any other federal program, yet its strong public support leaves lawmakers hesitant to address program efficiencies, which cost taxpayers and Medicare recipients billions of dollars annually. For example, Medicare pays as much as eight times what other federal agencies pay for the same drugs and medical supplies. The Department of Health and Human Services recently compared the prices paid by Medicare and the Department of Veterans Affairs (VA) healthcare program for sixteen types of medical equipment and supplies. The evidence showed that Medicare paid an average of more than twice what the VA paid for the same items. The largest difference was for saline solution, with Medicare paying $8.26 per liter compared to the $1.02 paid by the VA. Medicare also overpays for drugs: Inflated prices for drugs and basic payment errors cost some $12.3 billion annually.

6 In 2002, the Department of Education received an application to certify the student loan participation of the Y'Hica Institute in London, England. After approving the certification, the department received and approved student loan applications from three Y'Hica students and disbursed $55,000. The Department of Education administrators overlooked one detail: Neither the Y'Hica Institute nor the three students who received the $55,000 existed. The fictitious college students were created (on paper) by congressional investigators to test the Department of Education's verification procedures. All of the documents were faked, right down to naming one of the fictional loan student applicants "Susan M. Collins," after the Senator requesting the investigation. Such carelessness helps to explain why federal student loan programs routinely receive poor management reviews from government auditors. At last count, $21.8 billion worth of student loans are in default, and many cases of fraud are left undetected. Tracking students across federal programs, verifying loan application data with IRS income data, and implementing controls to prevent the disbursement of loans to fraudulent applicants could save taxpayers billions of dollars.

7 The Army Corps of Engineers spends $5 billion annually constructing dams and other water projects. Yet, in a massive conflict of interest, it is also charged with evaluating the science and economics of each proposed water project. The Corps's

"strategic vision" calls on managers to increase their budgets as rapidly as possible, which requires approving as many proposed projects as possible. Consequently, the Corps' has repeatedly been accused of deliberately manipulating its economic studies to justify unworthy projects.

Government and private investigations have found that the Corps's studies routinely contain dozens of basic arithmetic errors, computer errors, and ridiculous economic assumptions that artificially inflate the benefits of water projects by as much as 300 percent.

8 Significant waste, fraud, and abuse pervade Medicaid, which provides health services to 44 million low-income Americans. While states run their own Medicaid programs, the federal government reimburses an average of 57 percent of each state's costs. This system gives states an incentive to over-report their Medicaid expenditures in order to receive larger federal reimbursements, and many such schemes have been uncovered. Some states have also been shown to spend their Medicaid payments on unrelated programs—a practice that costs the federal government well over $2 billion per year.

9 Government's layering of new programs on top of old ones inherently creates duplication. Having several agencies perform similar duties is wasteful and confuses program beneficiaries who must navigate each program's distinct rules and requirements. Some overlap is

inevitable because some agencies are defined by whom they serve (e.g., veterans, Native Americans, urbanites, and rural families), while others are defined by what they provide (e.g., housing, education, healthcare, and economic development). When these agencies' constituencies overlap, each relevant agency will often have its own program. Some consolidation has been accomplished in recent years, but in 2003, our tax dollars were pretty much wasted on redundancies in:

342
economic development programs

130
programs serving the disabled

130
programs serving at-risk youth

90
early childhood development programs

75
programs funding international education, cultural, and training exchange activities

72
federal programs dedicated to assuring safe water

50
homeless assistance programs

45
federal agencies conducting federal criminal investigations

40
separate employment and training programs

28
rural development programs

27
teen pregnancy programs

26
small, extraneous K–12 school grant programs

23
agencies providing aid to the former Soviet republics

19
programs fighting substance abuse

17
rural water and wastewater programs in eight agencies

17
trade agencies monitoring 400 international trade agreements

12
food safety agencies

11
principal statistics agencies

4
overlapping land management agencies

THE IMMEDIATE ECONOMIC EFFECTS OF 9/11

Like all major disasters, natural or manmade, the terrorist attacks of September 11, 2001, resulted in a tragic loss of life and destruction of property, as well as short-term disruption of economic activity. In addition, because of the size and premeditated nature of the attack, there are likely to be more lasting effects in some industries and segments of the U.S. economy. Here are some of the immediate and short-term economic effects resulting from this tragic event:

1 The World Trade Center and the adjacent buildings were insured for $4 billion.

2 The damage to the Pentagon cost a billion dollars to repair.

3 The four planes involved were worth between $50 million and $100 million each.

4 The New York City projected budget deficit for fiscal year 2003 ballooned from $2–$2.5 billion to approximately $4 billion, though most direct expenses related to the rescue and recovery effort would be covered by $40 billion in federal aid.

5 Tourism in New York City plummeted, causing massive losses in a sector that employed 280,000 people and generated $25 billion per year. In the week following the attack, hotel occupancy fell below 40 percent, and three thousand employees were laid off. Tourism and hotel occupancy also fell drastically across the nation.

6 Many of the people and companies housed in the World Trade Center towers were engaged in offering financial services. Insurance estimates on these losses accounted for by goods and services that were not provided total another $10 billion.

7 The war on terrorism, and ancillary increases approved in defense spending because of that war, have added nearly $100 billion annually to the federal budget.

8 Insurance estimates of the cost of the New York attacks total between $25 billion and $30 billion.

9 If you assume that the average person killed earned $75,000 in salary and benefits, was forty years old, and had a life expectancy of seventy-five years, then such a calculation would have each person worth approximately $1.7 million in earning power. With three thousand dead, that comes to a little more than $5 billion.

10 The money needed to tear down the damaged buildings and to start rebuilding of New York World Trade Center site and Washington's Pentagon came from two main sources. The federal government put forward $40 billion for this effort and insurance companies were responsible for another $25 billion.

11 Lower Manhattan lost approximately 30 percent of its office space and a number of businesses ceased to exist. Close to 200,000 jobs were destroyed, or relocated out of New York City, at least temporarily. The destruction of physical assets was estimated in the national accounts to amount to $14 billion for private businesses, $1.5 billion for state and local government enterprises, and

$0.7 billion for federal enterprises. Rescue, cleanup, and related costs have been estimated to amount to at least $11 billion, for a total direct cost of $27.2 billion.

12 The losses from the terrorist attacks for the insurance industry (including reinsurance) are estimated to be between $30 and $58 billion.

13 The United States' airline industry was already in a weak financial position before the attacks, with rising debt ratios and falling returns on investment. Even with cutbacks in service of the order of 20 percent and significant government support, airline passenger traffic has apparently remained below normal. Approximately 100,000 layoffs were announced and employment in October and November of 2001 fell by 81,000 (almost 8 percent).

14 Shipping rates increased by 5 to 10 percent on average in the two weeks following the attack. Airfreight rates were about 10 percent higher in late 2001 than before the attacks.

15 A significant increase in security-related programs was seen in the context of the budget for fiscal year 2003. Additional spending of $48 billion was proposed for national defense (an increase of 14 percent from the previous year). In addition, President Bush asked Congress for an appropriation of $38 billion

for homeland security, compared to $20 billion spent in 2001.

16 The stock market was closed on September 11th and did not reopen until September 17th. When the market reopened, the Dow Jones Industrial Average stock market index fell 684 points, which set a record for a one-day point decline.

9 GOOD THINGS ABOUT BAD ECONOMIES

A recession is not necessarily all about doom and gloom. According to Jennifer Senior's 2009 article in *New York Magazine* entitled "Recession Culture," the year's economic challenges resulted in some positive changes throughout the city. Here are some of the silver linings that lurked inside the clouds of economic downturn.

1 There was an increase in volunteerism, as people became less self-insulated, and more group oriented. New York City's Meals-on-Wheels program, for example, saw a 32 percent rise in volunteerism in 2009 over the previous year.

2 Enrollments at graduate and divinity schools went up dramatically, as many found it easier to continue their education than to find a job.

3 Fewer college graduates entered financial and consulting fields, opting instead for careers that are more meaningful than financially rewarding.

4 Speculative investing became far less attractive.

5 Apartment rentals became more affordable, and landlords were more willing to make more concessions to prospective renters.

6 Practitioners of conspicuous consumption took a second look at their spending habits and realized that more satisfaction can be derived from life experience than from material possessions.

7 Gym prices fell, making good health a little more affordable, and less eating out meant a more nutritious lifestyle for many.

8 Cigarette and alcohol use declined.

9 Attendance at museums, zoos, libraries, aquariums, and other cultural events increased, as people sought out cheaper forms of entertainment.

Q: What's the difference between a banker who's lost everything and a pigeon?
A: The pigeon can still make a deposit on a new Ferrari.

THE 10 BEST MOVIES ABOUT MONEY

Money has been the subject of movies from the very start of filmmaking. The silent film *Greed*, directed by Erich von Stroheim and based on the classic novel *McTeague* by Frank Norris (1899), is considered one of the greatest films ever made. Its plot follows the story of a dentist and his money-obsessed wife. He kills her, but takes on her lust for gold. In the end, he loses everything and winds up handcuffed to his dead pursuer in the fateful conclusion. It's a cautionary tale about the evils of the pursuit of money, and the theme has been drawing us to films for almost a hundred years.

In fact, it's difficult to imagine any plot at all that doesn't have money at its heart. Even films that are not about money per se feature characters motivated in one way or another by the pursuit of the almighty dollar: Vivian Ward in *Pretty Woman*, the Joker in *Batman*, and flim-flam men Johnny Hooker and Henry Gondorff of *The Sting*, for instance. Art imitates life in our inability to escape the subject of money.

In 2006, *Forbes* employed a panel of experts to select nominations for the best films about money. Readers voted. Although the final list could be fodder for barroom brawls everywhere (why didn't Jerry Maguire and his famous refrain "Show me the money!" make this list?), here are the top ten winners chosen by *Forbes* readers:

1. *WALL STREET* (1987)

Enterprising stockbroker Bud Fox (Charlie Sheen) falls under the enticing spell of Gordon Gekko (Michael Douglas), an unabashedly greedy Wall Street broker. But when Gekko embroils his protégé in an insider-trading scheme that may risk the jobs of kith and kin, Fox develops a conscience and decides to turn the tables.

"The point is, ladies and gentlemen, that greed, for lack of a better word, is good. Greed is right. Greed works. Greed clarifies, cuts through, and captures the essence of the evolutionary spirit. Greed, in all of its forms—greed for life, for money, knowledge—has marked the upward surge of mankind."
—Michael Douglas as Gordon Gekko

2. *TRADING PLACES* (1983)

Eddie Murphy, as streetwise hustler Billy Ray Valentine, unwittingly trades places with wealthy investment executive Louis Winthorpe III (Dan Aykroyd). It's all part of a bet cooked up by the rich, greedy Duke brothers (Don Ameche and Ralph Bellamy), who want to see whether circumstances truly do make the man.

"Nothing you have ever experienced will prepare you for the unlimited carnage you are about to witness. Super Bowl, World Series—they don't know what pressure is. In this building, it's either kill or be killed. You make no friends in the pits, and you take no prisoners. One moment you're up half a mil in soybeans and the next, boom, your kids don't go to college and they've repossessed your Bentley."

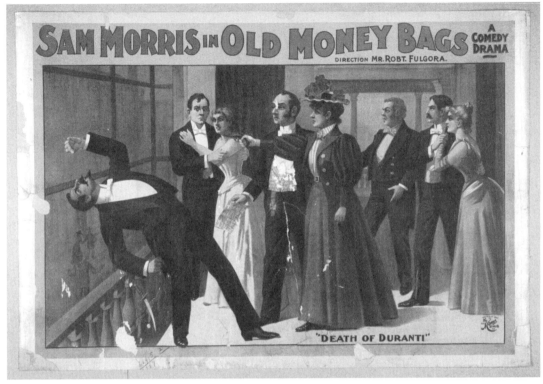

ABOVE: Poster for a dramatic play staged in 1897

—Dan Aykroyd as Louis Winthorpe III, on working at the Chicago Mercantile Exchange

3. *THE STING* (1973)

Rookie grifter Johnny Hooker (Robert Redford) tracks down veteran flim-flam man Henry Gondorff (Paul Newman) in 1930s Chicago, and the duo fleece a homicidal racketeer (Robert Shaw) through a phony racetrack scam.

4. *BOILER ROOM* (2000)

Underground casino operator and college dropout Seth Davis (Giovanni Ribisi) becomes involved in a sham New York brokerage firm and decides to go straight after his stern father disowns him. He risks everything when he turns his back on his greedy, hard-partying colleagues.

"Anybody who tells you money is the root of all evil doesn't have any."
—Ben Affleck as brokerage recruiter Jim Young

5. *OCEAN'S ELEVEN* (1960)

The summit meeting of Frank Sinatra's "Rat Pack" of cronies (Dean Martin, Sammy Davis, Jr., Joey Bishop, and Peter Lawford), *Ocean's Eleven* was filmed on location in Las Vegas. Sinatra and his ex-Army buddies decide to knock over a few casinos on the Strip in one of the merriest heists ever. The original is still the best of 'em.

6. IT'S A MAD, MAD, MAD, MAD WORLD (1963)

Before literally kicking the bucket when his car careens over an embankment, "Smiler" Grogan (Jimmy Durante) tells onlookers he's stashed $350,000 in stolen loot beneath "the big W" in the town of Santa Rosita . . . and thus begins a mad dash to recover the dough. But unbeknownst to the greedy motorists, police captain T. G. Culpepper (Spencer Tracy)—who's been awaiting a break in the Grogan case for twenty years—is stalking their every move.

"I'll wager you anything you like that if American women stopped wearing brassieres, your whole national economy would collapse overnight."
—Terry-Thomas as British treasure hunter J. Algernon Hawthorne

7. CASINO (1995)

With colorful Las Vegas of the 1970s as a backdrop, the story chronicles the rise and fall of three central characters: a play-by-the-rules casino owner with mob connections (Robert De Niro), his childhood friend and Mafia underboss (Joe Pesci), and an ex-prostitute with expensive taste and a driving will to get what she wants (Sharon Stone).

8. GLENGARRY GLEN ROSS (1992)

A group of real estate salesmen (Jack Lemmon, Al Pacino, Ed Harris, and Alan Arkin) in Chicago vies for the best "leads" at a small real estate firm. Competition gets stiff when a hotshot executive (Alec Baldwin) from the head office proposes a vicious sales contest.

9. THE TREASURE OF THE SIERRA MADRE (1948)

A trio of gold prospectors sets out to strike it rich and agrees to split the take, but as the gold is mined the men become increasingly distrustful, and soon turn against one other. Directed by John Huston, this is one of the definitive films on greed.

"Gold's a devilish sort of thing. . . . You start out, you tell yourself you'll be satisfied with twenty-five thousand handsome smackers' worth of it. So help me, Lord, and cross my heart. Fine resolution. After months of sweating yourself dizzy, growing short of provisions and finding nothing, you finally come down to fifteen thousand, then ten. Finally, you say, 'Lord, let me find just five thousand dollars' worth and I'll never ask for anything more the rest of my life.'"
—Walter Huston as gold miner Howard

10. AMERICAN PSYCHO (2000)

With a chiseled chin and an iron physique, Patrick Bateman (Christian Bale)'s looks make him the ideal yuppie—and the ideal serial killer. That's the joke behind American Psycho, which follows a killer at large during the 1980s junk-bond boom.

"I have all the characteristics of a human being—blood, flesh, skin, hair—but not a single, clear, identifiable emotion, except for greed and disgust."
—Christian Bale as homicidal stockbroker Patrick Bateman

8 *SIMPSONS* EPISODES ABOUT MONEY

1. "OLD MONEY"

Season 2, Episode 17

March 28, 1991

Grampa's new girlfriend at the Retirement Castle passes away and leaves him with $106,000. He heads for a casino to spend the money, but he's stopped by Homer and winds up spending the inheritance money on renovating the retirement home instead.

2. "LISA THE GREEK"

Season 3, Episode 14

January 23, 1992

In an effort to connect with Homer, Lisa starts watching football games and soon discovers that she can pick winners. Lisa is thrilled that Homer is now paying more attention to her until she realizes that "Daddy-Daughter Day" was just about winning bets. Homer is finally able to win her love back in the end, and the two go hiking up Mt. Springfield.

3. "BROTHER CAN YOU SPARE TWO DIMES?"

Season 3, Episode 24

August 27, 1992

In an attempt to get Homer to sign a waiver freeing the nuclear plant of all liability for Homer's recently discovered sterility, Mr. Burns concocts a phony prize and "awards" it to Homer. He plans on spending his $2,000 prize on a Spinemelter 2000 vibrating chair but agrees to lend the money to his half-brother Herb Powell, who is a hobo, thanks to Homer. Herb invents a machine that translates baby babbling and gets rich. To show his gratitude, he buys the whole family presents, including a Spinemelter 2000 for Homer.

4. "BART SELLS HIS SOUL"

Season 7, Episode 4

October 8, 1995

After perpetrating a prank on the First Church of Springfield, Bart sells his soul to Milhouse for five dollars, but comes to regret it and goes on a desperate quest to regain it. In the end, he gets it back, with unexpected help from Lisa.

5. "SCENES FROM THE CLASS STRUGGLE IN SPRINGFIELD"

Season 7, Episode 14

February 4, 1996

Marge meets an old friend who invites her and the family to the country club, where Marge becomes obsessed with trying to fit in. Homer takes up golf and catches Mr. Burns cheating at the game. Mr. Burns agrees to help Homer's family become members of the country club if he doesn't tell anyone. Homer and Marge both abandon their high social ambitions in the end.

6. "THE TROUBLE WITH TRILLIONS"

Season 9, Episode 20

April 5, 1998

The IRS makes Homer a deal: If he helps them out, he won't be prosecuted for cheating on his taxes. He has to find a trillion-dollar bill that Mr. Burns stole from the government long ago. He finds it, but before the IRS can move in, Homer foils their attempt and runs away with Burns and Smithers. They wind up in Cuba, where Castro steals the bill, and they have to return in disgrace. Mr. Burns vows to bribe the jury and get them all off scot-free.

7. "THE GREAT MONEY CAPER"

Season 12, Episode 7

December 10, 2000

Homer and Bart realize that they can make a lot of money grifting, and so with help from Grampa, they go into business. But the venture is destroyed when Homer and Bart are arrested. But soon the citizens of Springfield reveal that they have actually staged this trial to teach Homer and Bart a lesson.

8. "NO LOAN AGAIN, NATURALLY"

Season 20, Episode 12
March 8, 2009

When the adjustable rate on Homer and Marge's mortgage is raised to more than they can afford, they put the house up for sale. Good Samaritan Ned Flanders buys it and rents it out to them at an affordable rate. But Homer pushes his luck too far when he takes advantage of Ned's generous landlording duties.

HOMER SIMPSON ON MONEY

1 "I can't take his money. I can't print my own money. I've got to work for money. Why don't I just lie down and die?"

2 "You say I don't make money? I found a dollar when I was waiting for the bus."

3 "Bart! With ten thousand dollars, we'd be rich! We could buy all kinds of useful things like love."

4 "When you gave me that money, you said I wouldn't have to repay it 'til the future. This isn't the future. It's the lousy, stinking now!"

5 "Please don't humiliate me in front of the money."

6 Homer: "Aaaw, twenty dollars! I wanted a peanut!"
Homer's Brain: "Twenty dollars can buy many peanuts!"
Homer: "Explain how!"
Homer's Brain: "Money can be exchanged for goods and services!"
Homer: "Woo-hoo!"

7 "I have three kids and no money, why can't I have no kids and three money?"

8 "All right, let's not panic. I'll make the money by selling one of my livers. I can get by with one."

9 "Oh, used grease is worth money, eh? Then my arteries are filled with liquid gold!"

10 "A hundred bucks for a comic book? Who drew the pictures, Michaelmelangelo?"

FOR A SONG: 101 SONGS ABOUT MONEY

1. "Adan Garcia"
   —Ruben Blades (1992)

2. "Ain't Nothing Going On but the Rent" —Gwen Guthrie (1986)

3. "Ain't With Being Broke"
   —Geto Boys (1992)

4. "Another Day in Paradise"
   —Phil Collins (1989)

5. "Atlantic City"
   —Bruce Springsteen (1982)

6. "Big Money"
   —Rush (1985)

   "Big money got a mighty voice
   Big money make no sound"

7. "Bills, Bills, Bills"
   —Destiny's Child (1999)

8. "Bright Future in Sales"
   —Fountains of Wayne (2003)

9. "You Can't Always Get What You Want" —Rolling Stones (1969)

10. "Can't Buy Me Love"
    —The Beatles (1964)

    "I don't care too much for money, money can't buy me love."

11. "Career Opportunities"
    —The Clash (2000)

12. "Cash Car Star"
    —Smashing Pumpkins (2000)

13. "Cats in the Cradle"
    —Harry Chapin (1974)

14. "Coal Miner's Daughter"
    —Loretta Lynn (1980)

15. "Coat of Many Colors"
    —Dolly Parton (1971)

16. "Common People" —Pulp (1995)

17. "Did You Steal My Money?"
    —The Who (1981)

18. "Don't You Want Me Baby"
    —Human League (1981)

19. "Eat the Rich" —Aerosmith (1988)

20. "For the Love of Money"
    —The O'Jays (1994)

    "Give me a nickel, brother can you spare a dime
    Money can drive some people out of their minds"

21. "Fortunate Son" —Creedence Clearwater Revival (1969)

22. "Free Money" —Patti Smith (1975)

23. "Funky Dollar Bill" —George Clinton and the Funkadelics (1970)

24. "The Gambler"
    —Kenny Rogers (1978)

25. "Get a Job"
    —The Offspring (1998)

26. "Get Rhythm"
    —Johnny Cash (1969)

27. "Gimme Some Money"
    —Spinal Tap (1997)

    "Don't get me wrong, try getting me right
    Your face is ok but your purse is too tight"

ABOVE: The Civil War created an avalanche of financial difficulties for both the North and the South. The sheet music here and on the following page, from 1863–64, attests to the sentiments of the time.

28. "God Bless the Child"
    –Billie Holiday (1941)

29. "Gold Digger"
    –Kanye West (2005)

30. "Gypsy Woman (She's Homeless)"
    –Crystal Waters (1998)

31. "Hard Knock Life" –Broadway
    musical Annie (1982)

32. "Hard Knock Life" –Jay-Z (2001)

33. "Hard Times" –Run DMC (1984)

34. "Head Like a Hole"
    –Nine Inch Nails (1989)

35. "Hey Little Rich Boy"
    –Sham 69 (2001)

36. "Holiday" –Green Day (2005)

37. "How Can a Poor Man Stand Such
    Times and Live?"
    –Blind Alfred Reed (1972)

38. "How to Be a Millionaire"
    –ABC (2005)

    "I've seen the future, I
    can't afford it"

39. "I Wanna Be Rich"
    –Rich Calloway (1994)

40. "I Wish" –Stevie Wonder (2000)

41. "If I Had a Million Dollars"
    –Barenaked Ladies (1992)

42. "If You've Got the Money, I've Got
    the Time" –Willie Nelson (1976)

43. "I'm Busted" –Ray Charles (1963)

44. "In the Ghetto" –Elvis Presley
    (1969)

45. "Independent Women"
    –Destiny's Child (2001)

46. "The Israelites"
    –Desmond Dekker (1969)

47. "King of the Road"
    –Roger Miller (1965)

48. "Life in the Fast Lane"
    –The Eagles (1976)

    "He said, 'Call the doctor.
    I think I'm gonna crash.'
    The doctor say he's
    comin', but you gotta
    pay him cash."

49. "Life's Been Good"
    –Joe Walsh (1978)

50. "Little Ghetto Boy"
    –Donnie Hathaway (1972)

51. "Livin' on a Prayer"
    –Bon Jovi (1986)

52. "The Man Who Sold the World"
    –David Bowie (1970)

53. "Manic Monday" –Bangles (1986)

54. "Masters of War"
    –Bob Dylan (1963)

    "Is your money that
    good, Will it buy you
    forgiveness?"

55. "Material Girl" –Madonna (1985)

56. "Mo' Money Mo' Problems"
    –Notorious B.I.G. (1997)

57. "Money" –Pink Floyd (1973)

58. "Money"
    –The Flying Lizards (1984)

59. "(I'll Give you) Money"
    –Peter Frampton (1996)

60. "Money (That's What I Want)"
    –Barret Strong (1959)

    "The best things in life
    are free
    But you can keep them
    for the birds and bees"

61. "Money, Money"
    –Liza Minnelli (1968)

62. "Money, Money, Money"
   –ABBA (1976)

63. "Money Changes Everything"
   –Cyndi Lauper (1983)

64. "Money Honey"
   –The Drifters (1953)

65. "Money Is Not Our God"
   –Killing Joke (1991)

"So busy trying to make
a living i forgot about
living . . .
So busy trying to make a
living i forget about life"

66. "Money for Nothing"
   –Dire Straits (1985)

67. "Money for the Weekend"
   –Loverboy (1981)

68. "Money-Spending Woman"
   –Brownie McGhee (1941)

69. "Money Talks"
   –AC/DC (1993)

"Come on, come on, love
me for the money"

70. "Money's Too Tight to Mention"
   –Simply Red (1985)

71. "The Money Will Roll Right In"
   –Nirvana (1992)

72. "Mr. President (Have Pity on the
   Working Man)" –Randy Newman
   (1994)

73. "My Hero"–Foo Fighters (1998)

74. "9 to 5"–Dolly Parton (1985)

75. "Notorious"–Duran Duran (1986)

76. "Opportunities (Let's Make
   Lots of Money)"
   –Pet Shop Boys (1985)

"I've got the brains,
you've got the looks—
Let's make lots of money"

77. "Paid in Full"
   –Erik B. and Rakim (1987)

78. "Papa Was a Rolling Stone"
   –The Temptations (1972)

79. "Paper Planes" –M.I.A. (2007)

80. "Patches"
   –Clarence Carter (1970)

81. "A Poor Man's Roses
   (Or a Rich Man's Money)"
   –Patsy Cline (1956)

"For the rose of love
means more to me
More than any rich
man's gold"

82. "The Pretender"
   –Jackson Browne (1976)

83. "Proud Mary" –Creedence
   Clearwater Revival (1969)

84. "Puttin' on the Ritz"
   –Fred Astaire (1946)

85. "Rent" –Pet Shop Boys (1987)

86. "Rich Girl"
   –Hall and Oates (1975)

87. "Satisfied Mind"
   –Jeff Buckley (1997)

"The wealthiest person
is a pauper at times,
Compared to the man
with a satisfied mind"

88. "She Got the Goldmine, I Got the
   Shaft" –Jerry Reed (1985)

89. "She Works Hard for the Money"
   –Donna Summer (1983)

90. "Silver and Gold" –U2 (1988)

91. "Simple Kind of Man"
   –Lynyrd Skynyrd (1973)

"Forget your lust for rich
man's gold
All that you need is in
your soul"

92. "Sixteen Tons"
   –Merle Travis (1947)

93. "Sweetest Girl"
   –Wyclef Jean (2007)

94. "Take the Money and Run"
   –The Steve Miller Band (1976)

95. "Takin' Care Of Business"
   –Bachman Turner Overdrive
   (1973)

96. "Taxman"
   –The Beatles (1966)

"If you drive a car, I'll
tax the street;
If you try to sit, I'll tax
your seat"

97. "Welcome to the Jungle"
   –Guns N' Roses(1987)

"You can have anything
you want
But you better not take
it from me"

98. "We're in the Money
   (The Gold Diggers' Song)"
   –Ginger Rogers

99. "With Plenty of Money and You"
   –Tony Bennett (1958)

100. "Workingman Blues"
   –Merle Haggard (1987)

101. "Young Man Blues"
   –The Who (1974)

"Money doesn't talk,
it swears." —Bob Dylan

The cost of the gift list in the song "The Twelve Days of Christmas" may have sounded like a good idea when it was first performed in 1882. But at today's prices, who can afford more than just a day or two? In 2008, PNC Wealth Management reported that all twelve days, given inflation, would carry an $86,609 price tag, up $8,508 or 10.9 percent from $78,100 the previous year. The definitions and sources of these goods can be found at www.pncchristmaspriceindex.com. Here are the prices they used in their computations:

PARTRIDGE

$20

PEAR TREE

$200

TWO TURTLE DOVES

$55

THREE FRENCH HENS

$30

FOUR CALLING BIRDS (CANARIES)

$600

FIVE GOLDEN RINGS

$350

SIX GEESE A-LAYING

$240

SEVEN SWANS A-SWIMMING

$5,600

EIGHT MAIDS A-MILKING

$52

NINE LADIES DANCING

$4,759

TEN LORDS A-LEAPING

$4,414

ELEVEN PIPERS PIPING

$2,285

TWELVE DRUMMERS DRUMMING

$2,475

DO NOT PASS GO: ALL ABOUT MONOPOLY

In 1934, Charles B. Darrow of Germantown, Pennsylvania, showed what he called the Monopoly game to the executives at Parker Brothers. By the next year, it was the best-selling game in America. Over its long history, an estimated 500 million people have played the game. Today, Monopoly is still the best-selling board game in the world, sold in 103 countries and produced in thirty-seven languages.

More Monopoly money is printed in a year than real money printed throughout the world.

Unlike the U.S. government, Hasbro allows you to print your own money—Monopoly money, that is. Visit Hasbro.com.

More than two hundred million Monopoly games have been sold worldwide.

More than five billion little green houses have been "built" since 1935.

A set valued at $2,000,000 and made of 23-karat gold, with rubies, diamonds, and sapphires atop the chimneys of the houses and hotels is the most expensive Monopoly set ever produced, according to the *Guinness Book of World Records*.

Monopoly has been inducted into *Games Magazine*'s Hall of Fame. The game's famous monocled mascot is named Mr. Monopoly.

The longest Monopoly game in history lasted seventy straight days.

The longest Monopoly game played in a bathtub lasted ninety-nine hours.

65 PLACES THAT HAVE THEIR OWN MONOPOLY EDITIONS

In addition to Monopoly versions that celebrate these countries, there are others that address themselves to specific cities and even streets. England and France, for instance, have more than fifty editions each.

1. Argentina
2. Australia
3. Austria
4. Belgium
5. Brazil
6. Canada
7. Chile
8. China
9. Colombia
10. Costa Rica
11. Czech Republic
12. Denmark
13. Ecuador
14. Egypt
15. England
16. Estonia
17. Europe
18. Finland
19. France
20. Germany
21. Greece
22. Guatemala
23. Hungary
24. Iceland
25. India
26. Indonesia
27. Iran
28. Iraq
29. Ireland
30. Israel
31. Italy
32. Japan
33. Jersey
34. Latvia
35. Luxembourg
36. Malaysia
37. Malta
38. Mexico
39. Netherlands
40. New Zealand
41. Northern Ireland
42. Norway
43. Pakistan
44. Panama
45. Paraguay
46. Peru
47. Philippines
48. Poland
49. Portugal
50. Rhodesia
51. Romania
52. Russia
53. Saudi Arabia
54. Scotland
55. Serbia
56. Singapore
57. South Africa
58. Spain
59. Sweden
60. Switzerland
61. Turkey
62. Uruguay
63. Venezuela
64. Wales
65. Yugoslavia

It seems that folks in Nevada really take their gambling seriously. In 1910, Nevada was the last western state to outlaw gaming, and after the Great Depression, it was the first state to legalize casino-style gambling. Today, more than 43 percent of the state budget is funded by gambling.

Year first casino was licensed:	Number of slot machines in the city:	Percent of visitors who end up gambling during their stay:	Annual state gaming revenue, in billions of dollars:
1931	197,144	87	9

Current number of licensed gambling places in Las Vegas:	Percent of visitors who say they come to Vegas mainly to gamble:	Hours per day average visitor spends gambling:	Average gambling budget per trip, in dollars:
1,701	5	3.9	$559

"Horse sense is good judgment which keeps horses from betting on people."
—W.C. Fields

LEFT: Taking a chance in Reno, Nevada, 1910

THE GOOD LIFE: 19 EXPENSIVE LUXURIES

Merriam-Webster defines *hedonism* as "the doctrine that pleasure or happiness is the sole or chief good in life." While we tend to scoff at its practitioners, the fact is that most of us carry around just a tiny bit of envy for people who can afford $2,600-a-pound chocolates and million-dollar Stratocasters. This list—and those that follow—gives us a sneak peek at the lives of all those "rich bastards" we hear so much about. Perhaps the economic recession curtailed some of these purchases; we doubt it. In fact, we're sure that by the time this book has been published, most of these entries are trumped by even more decadent offerings.

1. AIRLINE TICKET

In September 2007, Australian Julian Hayward dished out US$100,380 for a seat aboard Singapore Airlines's Airbus A380 for a flight from Singapore to Sydney. The seat would normally sell for a measly $3,391, but Hayward outbid all bidders on eBay for the privilege of being the world's first commercial passenger aboard the A380. Extra perks included a trip to France to see the airline take delivery of the A380 aircraft, and the warm fuzzy feeling one gets knowing that his charitable donation will be appreciated by those in need.

2. APARTMENT

One Hyde Park in London contains four penthouses in addition to eighty apartments whose occupants have access to communal spas, squash courts, and a wine-tasting facility. The cost of the building is estimated at $3 billion; it was funded by Qatar's foreign minister. The penthouses each cost about $200 million and include bulletproof glass, panic rooms, and an underground tunnel that leads to a hotel nearby, among other security features. The rest of the apartments are a bargain, at $40 million each.

3. AUTOGRAPH

The world's most expensive autograph is that of William Shakespeare. Only six known authenticated copies of his autograph are known. Should one come up for auction, it would fetch an estimated $5 million.

4. BUGATTI

The Type 41 Royale was the brainchild of Bugatti—and also a hugely expensive misstep in the history of his firm. In the 1920s, Ettore Bugatti was expecting to get a contract from the French military to build 16-cylinder aircraft engines. The contract never materialized, but Bugatti felt he could use half that engine, an eight-cylinder, to form one of the most amazing luxury cars in history. Only six were produced, and two were never sold, remaining with the Bugatti estate. Current value of one of these cars is estimated to be $10 to $12 million.

5. CHESS SET

Renowned French artist and master jeweler Bernard Maquin created the Royal Diamond Chess set in 2005. Thirty craftsmen working under Maquin's direction spent 4,500 hours constructing the set, which incorporates 1,168.75 grams of 14-karat white gold and about 9,900 black and white diamonds with a total weight of 186.09 karats. The set is valued at half a million dollars.

6. CIGAR

The Gurkha premium cigar, His Majesty's Reserve, is known as the "Rolls-Royce" of the cigar industry. Each is handcrafted by the world's leading rollers, contains blends of the finest tobaccos in the world, and is infused with a generous portion of Louis XIII cognac. Only one hundred boxes of HMRs, each containing twenty cigars, are produced annually, and sell for $15,000, or $750 per cigar. Perfect for those who enjoy watching their money go up in smoke.

7. COMIC BOOK

When it comes to comics, condition is everything. *Action Comics* #1, published in 1938, saw the birth of Superman. It is estimated that the highest graded copy could fetch a million bucks.

8. COGNAC

The most expensive cognac is Henri IV Dudognon Heritage. The wine is placed in barrels and aged for more than a hundred years. The bottle in which the cognac is placed also contributes to its expense: It is dipped in twenty-four karat gold and sterling platinum before being decorated with 6,500 brilliant-cut diamonds. Goes for $2 million a pop—no kidding.

9. DIAMOND

Mined in India, the Wittelsbach Blue Diamond, weighing in at 35.56 karats was sold for a staggering $24.3 million at Christie's auction house in December 2008. The historic gem, prized by European royals for centuries, was sold to London-based jeweler Laurence Graff at its record-setting price.

10. FERRARI

The most expensive Ferrari ever sold brought in a whopping $9,252,375 at auction. Not only is the 330 TRI/LM the only four-liter Testa Rossa ever built, it is also the very last Testa Rossa (1962) and last front-engine racing car that Ferrari would ever build. (Ferrari's Testarossa, produced from 1984 to 1991, bears no relation save the similarity in names.) The car was also a huge part of the win at the 24 Heures de Mans when it was driven by Phil Hill and Olivier Gendebien. This would mark the third win for the famous racing pair and it would also be the last win at the competition by a front-engine car.

11. GOLF CART

If you want an electric golf cart that looks like a mini-Hummer; can go 20 mph; has a cooler under its hood, a tinted windshield, a fold-down tailgate, and fog lights; and gives you the option of either a carbon fiber or wood grain dashboard, then the Hummer H2 golf cart is for you. This over-the-top toy will only set you back a mere twenty Gs.

12. HOTEL ROOM

The decadent Mardan Palace resort in Antalya, Turkey, boasts gold-plated mirrors on the floors of the bathrooms, and there is real snow in one of the rooms at the spa. The place also includes 23,000 square meters of Italian marble, remote-controlled toilets, a five-acre pool for a thousand guests, seventeen bars, a three-story night club, and a pool and sunken aquarium that must be crossed by gondola. The beach contains nine thousand tons of fine, white sand flown in from Egypt. The $18,000-a-night price tag keeps out the riffraff.

13. PERFUME

Clive Christian No. 1 perfume is the world's most expensive over-the-counter perfume, available at just

---

"Give us the luxuries of life and we will dispense with necessaries."
—Oliver Wendell Holmes

under $2,000 per ounce. The bottle can be customized to suit one's whim, which is just what Sir Elton John did, paying about $250,000 for a bottle of Clive Christian No. 1 in the shape of a piano.

14. SHOES

Designed by Ronald Winston of the House of Winston, these Ruby Slippers, valued at $3 million, boast 4,600 rubies with a total weight of 201,350 karats as well as 50 karats of diamonds. The shoes were made by Javiar Barerra and took two months to set; they were created to celebrate the fiftieth anniversary of the film *The Wizard of Oz*.

15. GUITAR

Blackie, a Stratocaster owned by Eric Clapton sold at auction for $959,500 in 2004, making it the most expensive guitar in history.

16. VODKA

At $100 per bottle, the world's most expensive vodka is Diaka Vodka, and as of this writing, it is not yet available in the trade market. It is made in Poland with a filtration system that uses around one hundred diamonds, each approximately one karat in size. The diamonds give the vodka a clarity and smoothness unlike that of any other vodka in the world.

17. WATER

When Bling H20 first made the scene, it was made available only to "hand-selected athletes and actors," but mere mortals can now get in on the action. The high cost—$42 per regular bottle at the time of this writing—doesn't have much to do with the water, which comes from Dandridge, Tennessee, but rather the bottle itself, on which Swarovski crystals spell out "bling." And as of December, 2009, you can buy a $2,600 bottle from Bling's "Dubai Collection," called "The Ten Thousand," as it claims to have that number of hand-applied Swarovski crystals. Quenching, to be sure.

18. WHISKEY

Produced in the late 1800s at the Nun's Island Distillery in Galway, Ireland, the world's most expensive bottle of whiskey is valued at $143,020. The bottle, labeled "25 Year Old Pure Pot Still Whiskey," is currently on sale at Thomas' Arkwrights Whiskey and Wine store in Highworth, Wiltshire, England. To date the bottle remains unsold.

19. YACHT

The world's most expensive yacht has gone by three names since its inception—*Platinum 525*, *Golden Star*, and, most recently, *Dubai*. The *Platinum 525* was commissioned by Prince Jefri Bolkiah of Brunei in 1996, but a lack of funds put a stop to the project. In 2001, Sheikh Mohammed bin Rashid Al Maktoum, then Crown Prince and now ruler of Dubai, took over the project and renamed it the *Golden Star*. *Dubai*, as it is now called, is as expansive as it is expensive. The 525-foot yacht is powered by four diesel engines with more than 9,000 horsepower altogether. At $300 million, it is the world's most expensive yacht.

Some features of the *Dubai*:
 » Owner's suite
 » Five VIP guest bedrooms
 » Submarine
 » Helipad
 » Hangar for small aircraft
 » Jet-skis
 » Screening room
 » Squash court
 » Complete gym
 » Swimming pool
 » Spa

OPPOSITE: The Hummer H2 golf cart gets you around the green in style—for just under $20,000.
ABOVE: Elton John's favorite scent: Clive Christian No. 1

A thousand dollars for an ice-cream sundae? Sixteen grand for a cocktail? Believe it or not, there really are foods and drinks that sell for this much—and there really are people who are willing to pay for them. Here are ten of the world's most expensive indulgences. Are they worth the hefty price tag? You be the judge.

1. SAFFRON
Grown worldwide, this spice is derived from the saffron crocus flower. A pound of dry saffron requires 50,000 to 75,000 flowers (enough flowers to fill an entire football field), and because of the massive amount of resources and labor needed, saffron prices range from $500 to $5,000 a pound.

2. ALMAS CAVIAR
The word *almas* is Russian for "diamond," which is a fitting name for the world's most expensive caviar. This beluga variety hails from a fish (not the beluga whale) that is believed to have once lived at the same time as the dinosaurs. Packed in none other than a 24K gold tin, Almas caviar is white in appearance and sells for an unbelievable price of $23,308 per 32 ounces.

3. WHITE TRUFFLE MUSHROOM
These fancy fungi have their origins in the Piedmont region of northern Italy. Typically sold for $1,350 to $2,700 per pound, the record price paid for a single white truffle was set in December 2007, when casino owner Stanley Ho shelled out $330,000 for a truffle weighing just over three pounds.

4. KOBE-STYLE BEEF
This meat from Wagyu cattle is known worldwide for its incredible taste, texture, and marbled appearance. Because of the animal's genetic predisposition and special diet, including beer and sake, Wagyu yields a beef that contains a higher percentage of omega-3 and omega-6 fatty acids than typical beef. Grocery stores in the United States generally sell this sought-after meat anywhere from $40 to $150 a pound.

5. KOPI LUWAK COFFEE
The world's most expensive coffee, Kopi Luwak is made from coffee berries that have been eaten by and passed through the digestive tract of the Asian Palm Civet, a catlike animal. The animal eats the berries, but the beans inside pass through its system undigested. This process

takes place on the islands of Sumatra, Java, and Sulawesi in the Indonesian Archipelago, and in the Philippines. The total annual production is only around 500 pounds of beans, which may explain the outrageous price of a pound—$300 or more.

6. "DIAMONDS-ARE-FOREVER" MARTINI

This ain't your everyday cocktail. The olive has been replaced by a 1.6 karat diamond, partially accounting for the martini's $16,000 price tag. If you're looking for a taste of this divine drink, though, you'll have to travel to the only place it's served: the Ritz-Carlton in Tokyo.

7. KONA NIGARI WATER

This seaweed mineral concentrate, which sells for $16.75 per ounce, must first be mixed with regular drinking water before consuming. The concentrated water is said to be high in minerals and free of contaminants. If you're thinking about purchasing a gallon, though, you'd better have more than $2,000 set aside.

8. CHOCOPOLOGIE TRUFFLE

At $2,600 per pound, these handmade dark-chocolate treasures are available by pre-order only from Knipschildt Chocolatier in Norwalk, Connecticut. Each truffle, made from Valrhona cacao, is blended into a creamy ganache, hand-rolled, and dusted with cocoa powder. How's that for your next Valentine's Day gift?

9. NINO'S BELLISIMA PIZZA

They say there's nothing like New York City pizza, and Upper East Side restaurateur Nino Selimaj proves it. This specialty twelve-inch pie features lobster tail, crème fraîche, and six types of caviar. If you've got $1,000 to spare, the pie is yours. Just make sure you call 24 hours ahead because the ingredients must be specially ordered.

10. SERENDIPITY SUNDAE

Prepared with five scoops of the richest Tahitian vanilla bean ice cream and drizzled with some of the world's most expensive chocolates, this $1,000 dessert created by Serendipity in New York City certainly lives up to its name: Grand Opulence sundae. What's more, the treat is topped with special dessert caviar, adorned with a 23-karat edible gold leaf, and served in a crystal goblet complete with an 18-karat-gold spoon.

THERE'S NO SUCH THING AS A FREE LUNCH

Even though there are no prices on the menu, the food at Denver's Same Café isn't free. Patrons are asked to pay whatever they feel is fair and affordable. Those who can't pay anything at all work in the kitchen to prepare the restaurant's simple, wholesome menu. Brad Birky founded the restaurant when his well-paying position in the IT industry left him uninspired. "You might assume that if people have any chance to freeload, they will," says Brad, who runs the café with his wife, Libby. "But economic theory is just inept at explaining real life behavior." The restaurant's menu "suggests" a payment of $5 to $15 for a full meal and $3 to $6 for, say, soup, but that's all it is, a suggestion.

Can this be a business model for the future? Probably not. The Birkys have applied for nonprofit status for the café, and they both moonlight for extra money.

THE 13 MOST EXPENSIVE MEDICAL PROCEDURES

According to Writers-Free-Reference.com, the following are the costliest medical operations:

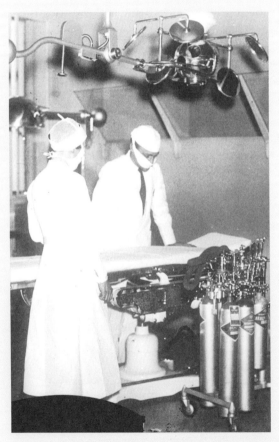

PROCEDURE	COST IN U.S. DOLLARS
Open-heart surgery	$324,000
Heart transplant	$287,000
Liver transplant	$235,000
Tracheotomy	$205,000
Bone marrow transplant	$186,000
Destruction of lesion of retina	$153,000
Pancreas transplant	$135,000
Heart valve procedures	$133,000
Kidney transplant	$130,000
Arterial bypass and shunt	$110,000
Coronary artery bypass graft	$97,000
Gastrectomy (removal of all or part of the stomach)	$93,000
Small-bowel resection	$81,000

"There's [an] advantage to being poor—a doctor will cure you faster."
—Frank "Kin" Hubbard

LEFT: These days, most medical procedures cost an arm and a leg.

THE 11 MOST EXPENSIVE MOVIES OF ALL TIME

As reported by Blog.knowyourmoney.co.uk: When money is tight, we can always stay home and watch a good movie. It's convenient and it's cheap. But making movies isn't. In fact, the multimillion-dollar blockbusters that pop up every summer and Christmas tell us much about how much we value entertainment. Too bad that a film's budget doesn't guarantee any level of quality. The following list is based on estimated costs, adjusted for inflation.

1. *AVATAR* (2009)

Although of too recent a vintage to be reported on Know Your Money's list (compiled in November 2008), this movie would be difficult to ignore. At an estimated $500 million, James Cameron, of *Titanic* and *Terminator* fame, certainly outbudgeted himself—and everyone else in Hollywood—with *Avatar*.

Fourteen years after writing the script (production was delayed until the technology caught up), Cameron began filming his vision. Regrettably, it is pretty much the poster child of technological dazzle over coherent scripting, developed characters, and good dialogue.

2. *PIRATES OF THE CARIBBEAN: AT WORLD'S END* (2007)

The second most expensive movie of all time is arguably the worst of all those on this list. Despite spending the $316.6 million budget filming on the open ocean and in several exotic locations including St. Vincent, Dominica, the Exumas, and Grand Bahama Island, as well as California and Hawaii; constructing giant water tanks; designing hugely complex action scenes; and employing an extensive use of special effects, the movie met lukewarm reviews.

3. *CLEOPATRA* (1963)

This is a scrappy, over-long, and over-ambitious film, riddled with historical inaccuracies and pantomime performances. A commercial and critical flop, the film wound up costing $314.6 million to make, largely because a catalog of production problems resulted in a twenty-two-fold increase of the original $2 million budget. Lead actors left due to other commitments. The first director was sacked after spending $7 million with no footage to show for it. The subsequent director was fired, then rehired, transferring the entire shoot from Rome to London and back to Rome again. And the list goes on.

4. *SUPERMAN RETURNS* (2006)

With a series of abandoned productions, an eternity in that notorious Hollywood netherworld known as "preproduction hell," and just about half of Hollywood attached to the project at some point, it's not surprising that preproduction development costs alone have been estimated at somewhere between $40 and $65 million. Total damages: $294.6 million.

5. *TITANIC* (1997)

Titanic's massive $272.6 million budget can be attributed to producer James Cameron's uncompromising adherence to his creative vision. This translated into an arduous 160-day shoot featuring meticulous re-creations of the doomed ship, including some of the largest and most expensive movie sets ever built: a 17-million-gallon outdoor tank in which to film the exterior ship scenes, and a 5-million-gallon indoor tank in which to film the interior sinking scenes. Still, it was less expensive than the damage caused by the original Titanic—adjusted for inflation, of course.

6. *SPIDER-MAN 3* (2007)

Standard Superhero Sequel Success Strategy (SSSSS) equation: More supervillains + more special effects = more money ($272.2 million in this case).

7. *WATERWORLD* (1995)

An infamously troubled production, *Waterworld*'s eighteen-month shoot took place almost entirely on water (vastly more expensive than filming on dry land), and the shoot was beset by a range of expensive setbacks and difficulties including cast and crew seasickness, violent storms, transportation problems, and the accidental sinking—and subsequent salvaging—of a 180-ton floating set.

8. *TERMINATOR 3: RISE OF THE MACHINES* (2003)

The most expensive independently produced movie in history carried a $237.8 million price tag. The budget included future Governor Schwarzenegger's share, which is reported to be around $30 million.

9. *KING KONG* (2005)

After the huge success of the *Lord of the Rings* trilogy, Peter Jackson decided to focus his talents on a remake of a classic movie that had already been remade into a flop thirty years earlier. The thing wound up costing some $231.9 million. Jackson extended the budget by more than $30 million by running overtime and

by spending endless hours trying to recapture the pioneering special effects of the 1933 original.

10. *SPIDER-MAN 2* (2004)

Most of the $231.6 million budget for this film went into special effects, ensuring that this time around, Spidey wouldn't look like a red blur, as he had in the first movie. Then there was an enormous cast and that pesky $20 million licensing fee to Marvel. How do you top that? With an even more expensive *Spider-Man 3*.

11. *QUANTUM OF SOLACE* (2008)

The usual culprits are to blame for the twenty-second Bond film's budgetary explosion that included huge action set-pieces and a variety of exotic shooting locations. The product placement to which Bond sold out a long time ago helped foot the massive bill, which came to some $230 million.

ALL-TIME HIGHEST GROSSING MOVIES AT THE U.S. MOVIE BOX OFFICE*

1. *AVATAR* (2009)
$747,292,481

2. *TITANIC* (1997)
$600,779,824

3. *THE DARK KNIGHT* (2008)
$533,316,061

4. *STAR WARS* (1977)
$460,935,665

5. *SHREK 2* (2004)
$436,471,036

6. *E.T.: THE EXTRA-TERRESTRIAL* (1982)
$434,949,459

7. *STAR WARS: EPISODE I—THE PHANTOM MENACE* (1999)
$431,065,444

8. *PIRATES OF THE CARIBBEAN: DEAD MAN'S CHEST* (2006)
$423,032,628

9. *SPIDER-MAN* (2002)
$403,706,375

10. *TRANSFORMERS: REVENGE OF THE FALLEN* (2009)
$402,076,689

*Totals as of 2010

9 VERY EXPENSIVE TOYS

Here are a few examples of gift ideas that most mortals could never afford:

1. *STAR WARS* MOVIE PROP

The Darth Vader fighting helmet from *The Empire Strikes Back* is valued at $115,000. It was used extensively throughout the fight sequences in the film and was specially created to provide clearer vision for Bob Anderson, the Olympic fencing champion who took over the role of Darth Vader for the fight sequences.

2. HAND-HELD VIDEO GAME

The world's most expensive Gameboy is made of 18K gold and features a display screen surrounded by diamonds. Created by Aspreys of London, this little toy will set you back a playful $25,000. Aspreys will, however, toss in a case, cables, and a few games for free.

3. PEZ DISPENSER

A 1982 World's Fair Astronaut PEZ dispenser, one of only two ever created, sold at auction on eBay for $32,205.

4. RIDE-ON TOY

The world's most expensive ride-on toy is the Junior Off Roader, offered by Mobileation.com for $40,000. It comes with an all-weather fiberglass body with a protective frame, dual hydraulic disk brakes, rack-and-pinion steering, manual emergency brake, full front and rear suspension, three-speed transmission, radio and CD player with speakers on the side doors, and upholstered leather seats. It does a blistering 30 mph.

5. TOY SOLDIER

The most expensive toy soldier in the world is the 1963 G.I. Joe prototype. Baltimore businessman Stephen A. Geppi bought the toy soldier at Heritage Comics Auctions of Dallas, Texas, for $200,000.

6. TEDDY BEAR

To celebrate the 125th anniversary of the Teddy Bear, a German company created a limited edition of 125 bears. The mouths were made of solid gold, the eyes of sapphires and diamonds. The Teddy is valued at $193,000.

7. TOY GUN

The M134, a Gatling-type air gun made by Craft Apple Works, sells for more than $9,000. With its steel 6mm BBs and 3,000-round magazine, this mini-gun blows away all other air guns.

8. MATCHBOX CAR

The priciest of all of the original Matchbox Cars is a boxy sea-green sedan, the 1966 Opel Diplomat. Only a handful are for sale and at $9,000 they're beyond most budgets. If you had bought one when they first hit the market, the price tag would have been 48 cents.

9. BARBIE

Diamond Barbie comes with a gown that boasts 160 diamonds and white-gold miniature jewelry. This one-of-a-kind Fortieth Anniversary Barbie created in 1999 comes with a full-figured price tag of about $85,000. It is available at De Beers diamond boutique stores.

Fred collected lots of money from trick-or-treating and he went to the candy store to buy some chocolate. "You should give that money to charity," said the salesgirl. Fred thought for a moment and said, "No, I'll buy the chocolate. You give the money to charity."

1. *PORTRAIT OF ADELE BLOCH-BAUER*
by Gustav Klimt
($135,000,000)

This painting was the subject of a restitution battle between the Austrian government and a niece of Mrs. Bloch-Bauer, who claimed that it had been seized from her home along with four other Klimt paintings by the Nazis during World War II. Skillfully painted in 1907 by the art nouveau master, the painting was purchased by Ronald S. Lauder, the cosmetics heir, in 2006.

2. *NU AU PLATEAU DE SCULPTEUR*
by Pablo Picasso
($106,500,000)

The painting shows Picasso's mistress, Marie-Thérèse Walter, both reclining and as a bust. Picasso's profile can be seen in the blue background. Sold at auction on May 4, 2010, this work, measuring 5 by 4 feet, is regarded as a turning point in Picasso's career.

3. *GARÇON À LA PIPE*
by Pablo Picasso
($104,100,000)

Garcon à la Pipe showcases Picasso's exceptional use of a cheerful orange and pink palette. The oil on canvas painting, measuring slightly more than 39 by 32 inches, portrays a Parisian boy holding a pipe in his left hand. The record price, at the time, on May 4, 2004, at Sotheby's, was a surprise to the art world because it was painted in a style that was unusual for the artist.

ABOVE: *Portrait of Adele Bloch-Bauer*, by Gustav Klimt, is the most expensive painting ever sold.
RIGHT: *Garçon à la Pipe*, by Pablo Picasso

4. *DORA MAAR WITH CAT*
by Pablo Picasso
($95,200,000)

Another surprise followed in 2006, when this painting nearly doubled its presale estimate and brought in a new record at auction at Sotheby's on May 3, 2006. Painted in 1941, Picasso's controversial portrait (one of his last) is sometimes described as an unflattering depiction of his mistress, Dora Maar.

"Two hundred thousand dollars." —Picasso, when asked by an American millionaire what one of his paintings represented

"I can't afford them." —Picasso, when asked why none of his paintings adorned the walls of his home

---

5. *PORTRAIT OF DR. GACHET*
by Vincent van Gogh
($82,500,000)

This painting suddenly became world-famous when Japanese businessman Ryoei Saito paid $82.5 million for it at auction in Christie's, New York, on May 17, 1990. Saito was so attached to the painting that he wanted it to be cremated with him when he died. Saito died in 1996–but the painting was saved. Vincent van Gogh actually painted two versions of Dr. Gachet's portrait. The other version, with a slightly different color scheme, is on display at the Musée d'Orsay in Paris.

6. *BAL AU MOULIN DE LA GALETTE*
by Pierre-Auguste Renoir
($78,000,000)

Painted by Renoir in 1876, it was sold on May 17, 1990, at Sotheby's in New York City to Ryoei Saito, who also purchased the *Portrait of Dr. Gachet* (see above).

7. *MASSACRE OF THE INNOCENTS*
by Peter Paul Rubens
($76,700,000)

This painting from 1611 is the only one on this list that was not painted in the nineteenth or twentieth century. It was sold to Kenneth Thomson at a 2002 Sotheby's auction.

8. *PORTRAIT DE L'ARTISTE SANS BARBE*
by Vincent van Gogh
($71,500,000)

One of many self-portraits by Dutch painter Vincent van Gogh, it is unusual in that it lacks the artist's familiar beard. The 16 by 13-inch oil on canvas became one of the most expensive paintings of all time when it sold in 1998 in New York.

9. *RIDEAU, CRUCHON, ET COMPOTIER*
by Paul Cézanne
($60,500,000)

Painted around 1893 to 1894, it was sold at Sotheby's New York on May 10, 1999, to the wealthy Whitney family.

10. *FEMME AUX BRAS CROISÉS*
by Pablo Picasso
($55,000,000)

Painted in 1901, during the artist's Blue Period, the painting depicts a woman with her arms crossed and staring, it seems, at nothing. It was sold on November 8, 2000, at Christie's Rockefeller in New York City.

Unconfirmed rumors buzzing in the art world now place the painting called *No. 5, 1948* by Jackson Pollock at the top of the list of most expensive paintings ever sold. If true, the $140 million price tag would be the highest ever for a painting. It was said to have been privately sold by entertainment magnate David Geffen, who is also thought to have sold *Woman III* by Willem de Kooning for $137.5 million at around the same time.

6 WEDDING EXTRAVAGANCES

Too bad that paying big bucks for a wedding doesn't guarantee its longevity. In some cases, people find themselves making payments long after the divorce decree has been signed. Here are some of the most expensive wedding trappings in history:

1 The wedding of Sheikh Mohammed to Princess Salama, held in 1981, lasted seven days. The ceremony was held in a stadium especially built for the occasion and was attended by twenty thousand guests. Rashid bin Sayid al-Maktoum, the groom's father and sheikh of Dubai, shelled out more than $44.5 million (the equivalent of $100 million in today's dollars) for the festivities. It was the most expensive wedding ever until, in 2004, the "Mittal Affair" grabbed the crown. Lakshmi Mittal, an Indian steel magnate based in London, spared no expense for his daughter Vanisha Mittal's wedding to Amit Bhatia. The wedding ceremony was the culmination of a six-day event held at Vaux le Vicomte, a seventeenth-century French chateau. The engagement ceremony had been held at the Palace of Versailles two days earlier. As part of the wedding celebration, Mittal hosted a "Bollywood night" that featured performances by Indian superstars Rani Mukerji and Shahrukh Khan. The estimated cost was $70 million. Mittal is one of the wealthiest people in the world, with an estimated worth of $32 billion.

2 Paris Hilton was given a choice of two engagement rings by her one-time fiancé Paris Latis. The first was a 24-karat emerald-cut diamond ring worth approximately $4.5 million dollars; the second was a 15-karat white diamond ring valued at $2.1 million. She opted for the 24-karat model. The ring was put up for auction after the five-month engagement ended.

3 Valued at $125,000, a wedding bouquet made of red and white gemstone flowers is the most expensive ever created. Displayed at Ruby Plaza on Vietnam's Le Ngoc Han Street, this over-the-top nosegay includes nine diamonds, a star-shaped ruby, and ninety other gemstones.

"The wages of sin is alimony."
—Carolyn Wells (1862–1942), American writer

"You never realize how short a month is until you pay alimony."
—John Barrymore

The average bride spends anywhere from $500 to $12,000 on a wedding gown, with $800 representing the norm. Here are some gowns that broke the bank:

4 A collaboration between Martin Katz Jewelers and Renee Strauss, a bridal couture designer, resulted in the creation of a wedding gown worth $12 million. The dress, known as the Diamond Wedding Gown, was displayed at the Bridal Show held at the Ritz-Carlton Hotel on Rodeo Drive in Marina Del Rey, California, on February 26, 2006. More than 150 karats of diamonds were used in its creation. It was the most expensive wedding gown in history at that time.

5 On February 18, 2007, another "Diamond Wedding Gown," with an estimated worth of $19 million, went on display at the Spectacular Bridal Show held at the same hotel. The gown was a collaboration between Kazanjian Brothers, who supplied the jewels, and Simin Haute Couture, a custom bridal and high-fashion salon that designed the dress. The gown included priceless diamonds and was created specifically for the show.

6 On Oct. 17, 2006, the world's most expensive wedding cake went on display at the Luxury Brands Bridal Show on Rodeo Drive in Beverly Hills, California. The cake, adorned with priceless diamonds and not meant for human consumption, ironically contained the finest ingredients. The cake was the result of a team effort by Mimi So Jewelers and cake designer Nahid of La Patisserie Artistique. Valued at a whopping $20 million, the cake was guarded by a team of uniformed security guards during the event.

HOW TO GET A FREE WEDDING

Tom Anderson and his bride-to-be Sabrina Root took advertising to a higher level—they sold advertising space to pay for their August 1999 wedding.

A total of twenty-four companies were more than happy to provide the couple with their $34,000 Philadelphia wedding and honeymoon suite in Cancun, Mexico. In exchange, the couple agreed to have the name of each sponsor printed on the invitations, thank-you notes, placement cards, and on scrolls at each dinner table. The groom also agreed to mention each sponsor by name after his first toast.

INTRODUCTION TO COIN COLLECTING

The systematic collecting of coins for their rarity and historical value didn't actually begin until the sixteenth century, when the resurgence of interest in Greek and Roman cultures gave rise to coin collecting as a popular and prestigious hobby among wealthy Europeans.

By the late 1590s, the hobby had become extremely popular among the nobility, and the first coin catalog was created. One of the first known coin auctions was held in Leyden, Holland, in 1598.

Since then, collecting rare coins has attracted such diverse enthusiasts as John Quincy Adams, Cornelius Vanderbilt, Enrico Caruso, Theodore Roosevelt, Buddy Ebsen, Chris Schenkel, and Wayne Gretzky. Today, coin collecting has gained a worldwide following.

It is estimated that there are seven to ten million coin collectors in the United States alone and that there are perhaps four to five times that many collectors around the world. Once known as "the hobby of kings," it is now called "the king of hobbies."

Some of the world's greatest coin collections are now housed in museums. The Smithsonian Institution in Washington, D.C. and the Metropolitan Museum of Art in New York City, as well as the great city museums of London, Paris, Vienna, and Berlin, boast extensive collections of world coinage.

Because coins have been minted for more than 2,500 years, today's coin enthusiast has an almost inexhaustible range of collecting choices available: Ancient coins, rare U.S. coins, modern proof coins, and bullion issues are just a few examples.

The value of a coin is established in a free marketplace by investor and collector activity. The size and intensity of that activity is influenced by three major criteria: rarity, demand, and quality (condition).

The beauty of a coin can attract collectors as well as investors, and therefore increase demand for a particular coin or set. This in turn can result in rising values. Eye appeal is affected by several factors including the beauty of a coin's design, the minting process used, the fullness and sharpness of its strike, the toning, the brilliance of its luster, and the amount of wear and number of blemishes on the coin's surface.

RARITY

The rarity of a particular coin helps to determine its value. Because many collectors and investors prize the scarcer issues and target them for acquisition, they naturally bid up the prices of those coins.

DEMAND

Demand comes from two primary areas: collectors, who build lifelong collections of coins with no intent to sell, and investors, who buy coins in order to earn a profit. Some important factors that can create strong demand for a coin include rarity, historical significance, quality, and a successful investment track record.

CONDITION

The overwhelming majority of minted U.S. coins were circulated. Many coins were lost through attrition and others were damaged by use, thus eliminating any potential for numismatic value.

The few surviving uncirculated coins are in a much more pristine condition. Investment-quality coins are primarily those coins rated in the eleven uncirculated grades, 60 and above, on the American Numismatic Association's 70-point grading scale. A coin's *grade* is a measure of its condition or state of preservation. The higher the grade, the better the condition.

Uncirculated coins fall into two broad categories: Proof (PF or PR) and Mint State (MS). Mint State coins were originally meant for circulation but never were circulated, so they remain in the same condition today as when they were minted. Proof coins were never meant for circulation, thus they received very careful handling and were specially struck at least twice on highly polished planchets.

WHERE TO FIND MONEY

The best way to find coins is through dealers, and the best way to find dealers is at the coin shows and conventions they routinely attend. The most prestigious of these shows is the annual New York International Numismatic Convention. The show features hundreds of dealers from all over the world, educational programs, special events for young numismatists, extensive exhibits, and approximately a dozen different auctions. Visit www.nyinc.info for more information.

One of the most prestigious of the numismatics organizations is the American Numismatic Society, founded in 1858 in New York. Its main objectives are the collection and preservation of coins and medals and the popularization of numismatics. The society maintains an extensive library, with educational facilities that are available to international scholars, students, and the general public. The numismatics collection, estimated at approximately 800,000 coins and related objects, is of international caliber, rivaled only by the largest state collections of Europe and includes many great rarities. The collection is particularly strong in the areas of coinage from ancient Greece, the Far East, Latin America, and the United States. The library houses more than 100,000 items, comprising bound volumes, pamphlets, manuscripts, auction catalogs, and microforms. Access to the fully catalogued collections is facilitated by a specially designed subject guide and authority file. Located in New York City, the ANS facilities are open to the public four days each week. Visit Numismatics.org.

When we think of a coin, we tend to picture something in the shape of a disk. But several countries have issued a variety of odd-shaped coins, and these are avidly pursued by collectors.

While round coins continue to be the norm in modern coinage, some fifty nations have issued coins of other shapes for both circulation and commemorative purposes.

OVAL COINS

To commemorate the "unsinkable" *RMS Titanic*, which sank on April 14, 1912, and its 1985 recovery effort, Liberia issued an oval silver Proof 10-Dollar coin. The coin depicts the doomed ship, with a small piece of coal from the *Titanic* incorporated into the coin at the coal bunker section of the ship. The reverse of the coin shows the arms of Liberia. The coin is dated 2005 and has a mintage of only five thousand pieces.

A crouching Mongolian Snow Leopard appears on an oval coin from Mongolia with a face value of 500 tugrik. The coin is made of niobium and silver and has a mintage of only five thousand pieces.

SCALLOPED-EDGE COINS

Flower-shaped coins are also common. A 10-poisha coin from Bangladesh that featured a scalloped shape was minted from 1973 to 1984. In 2003, the Cook

Islands issued a very unusual set containing (among other odd shapes) the scalloped-edge 1-dollar coin featuring the recent, frumpy Ian Rank-Broadley portrait of Queen Elizabeth on the obverse side and the very well-endowed fertility god Tangaroa on the reverse. In Europe, Spain's 50-peseta coins first featured a scalloped shape in 1990 and each year between 1990 and 1998 carried a new circulating commemorative design. The Republic of Tanzania issued a scalloped-edge nickel-brass 10-senti coin from 1977 to 1984 featuring a zebra. Israel's copper-nickel agorah coins from 1960 to 1980 feature a scalloped edge and a wheat design on their obverses. Other scalloped-edge coins have been issued in Swaziland, the Maldives, and the kingdom of Bhutan.

TRIANGULAR COINS

Bermuda trades upon the so-called Bermuda Triangle with its triangular dollar coins. Queen Elizabeth II's portrait appears on their obverses and shipping scenes on their reverses. Bermuda's Proof 1998 sterling silver $3 coin was also struck on a rectangular planchet. In 2003, the Cook Islands issued a triangular 2-dollar coin featuring the aforementioned frumpy portrait of Queen Elizabeth on the obverse side and a ceremonial table and a bottle on the reverse.

SQUARE, RECTANGULAR, PENTAGONAL, AND HEXAGONAL COINS

Special-edition klippe coins to commemorate the tenth anniversary of the National Bank of Poland's new coinage system were struck by the Polish State Mint in 2004. Klippe coins are usually square or rectangular in shape and are reminiscent of the centuries-old

European silver coins, like the 1627 Transylvania 2-taler klippe.

Leonardo da Vinci's famed Equestrian statue is featured on a square silver 500-tugrik coin from Mongolia minted in 2005. The statue, now in Budapest, Hungary, is the only known original surviving sculpture by da Vinci. There are two versions of the coin: one with an antique finish and depicting the sculpture in bronze; the other version has a Proof finish and depicts the sculpture in gold. Only 2,500 were minted.

Tonga issued a few rectangular pa'anga coins in the late 1970s and early 1980s. The coins were struck in copper-nickel and in .999 fine silver versions.

Aruba issued two square-shaped denominations, 50 cents and 5 florins. The Netherlands, Swaziland, and Yemen have also issued square coins.

POLYGONAL COINS

A number of the United Kingdom's 50-pence coins are seven-sided. The United Kingdom has used this shape in its 20-pence coins since 1985 and since 1969 for its 50-pence coins. The 20-pence design features the Tudor rose on its reverse, topped by a crown. In 2003 the Cook Islands issued a twelve-sided 5-dollar coin featuring their favorite portrait of Queen Elizabeth on the obverse side and a conch shell on the reverse.

Many countries that currently have or used to have ties to the United Kingdom have also issued seven-sided coins: the Isle of Man, Jersey, Ireland, Papua New Guinea, Uganda, Barbados, and Gibraltar. Still other countries have struck six-, eight- or ten-sided coins. Chile's circulation peso and 5-peso coins have eight sides.

Hong Kong's 1976 to 1979 $5 copper-nickel coin is ten-sided, and Argentina has also issued several octagonal and twelve-sided coins. Canada has issued the eleven-sided Loon dollar since its introduction in 1987 and also boasts a number of 1-cent and 5-cent issues that are twelve-sided; the Republic of Tanzania issued a twelve-sided 5-senti coin from 1966 through 1984 featuring a sailfish design; and Swaziland issued a twelve-sided bronze cent in 1975 as a commemorative for the World Food and Agriculture Organization.

OTHER SHAPES

A fan-shaped Proof sterling silver 10-złoty commemorative coin marking the occasion of the World Exhibition Expo 2005 held in Aichi, Japan, was issued in March by the National Bank of Poland.

The most oddly shaped coin has to be the silver 2002 $10 issue from the Republic of Nauru, an island republic located in the western Pacific Ocean. The Proof coin celebrates the introduction of the euro with a coin shaped in the outline of the nations that comprise the European Economic Union.

The silver Proof 5000-kwacha coin issued by Zambia to commemorate the 2000 Sydney Olympics is another of the strangest shaped coins ever issued. The unusual coin was made in the shape of the conjoined maps of Australia and Zambia. Though Australia is approximately ten times the size of Zambia, the two are shown to be roughly the same area on the coin. The large coin is approximately 49 by 42 mm and contains approximately one troy ounce of silver.

Somali Republic's 2004 commemorative dollar coin is shaped like a guitar to mark the fiftieth anniversary of rock 'n' roll music and the Stratocaster guitar. The non-denominated side is enameled. The multicolored guitar coins have proved to be unbelievably popular. They are designed after famous electric guitars, including the classic red and white Fender Stratocaster, an American Flag Stars and Stripes Gibson Flying V, a black Gibson Flying V, a pink star-bodied guitar used by various rock bands including ABBA, a blue Gibson X-Plorer, and a yellow Klein. The coins are 1-dollar legal tender coins and are approximately 44.5 mm long.

The Bahamas's 15-cent coins are diamond shaped. First issued in 1966, the coins feature Queen Elizabeth II's portrait on the obverse and a hibiscus on the reverse. Bhutan, India, Myanmar, the Netherlands, Oman, and Pakistan are among other countries that have released circulating diamond-shaped coins.

HOW COINS ARE MADE

Making coins is a long and arduous process that was even more laborious in centuries past, before automated equipment and modern technology made it possible for the U.S. Mint to churn out some ten to twenty billion coins annually. Understanding how they are made today gives us a greater appreciation for the art of money. To see a video of the process, visit USMint.gov.

Coins are made of different metals (silver, copper, gold, nickel, etc.). The metal is delivered in the form of coils that are wound up in a roll, each approximately a foot wide and fifteen hundred feet long and weighing up to six hundred pounds. This roll of metal is fed into a machine that cuts out disks the size of whatever coin is being produced at the time.

These metal disks are called blanks. After the blanks are cut out, they are washed and polished. If the disks are meant for making proof coins, they are given some extra care and polishing. Once they are washed and polished, the disks are called planchets. They are now ready to be made into coins.

In the meantime, artists have been hand-carving and molding the design to be used on the coins. These designs are many times larger than the actual size of the coin, so a duplicating machine is used to reduce the design and carves it into a very hard metal hub. These hubs are used to create the "dies" that will transfer the design to the coin.

When the dies are ready—one for the front of the coin and one for the back—the planchets are then "squeezed" between them under great pressure. If the coin is a proof coin, it will be struck (squeezed) more than once. Once the coins have been struck, they are carefully inspected before being stored.

ABOVE: Punching out blanks at the U.S. Mint in New Orleans, c1897

THE TOP 10 RARE COINS

The following list, compiled by Van Simmons, president of David Hall Numismatics, represents the rare coin market's ten best bets for short-term, medium-term, and long-term potential. The list includes at least one coin from each of the five major areas of the market: "type" coins (design/denomination, e.g., Kennedy half-dollars), rare gold, silver dollars, twentieth-century singles, and silver commemoratives.

$20 SAINT-GAUDENS DOUBLE EAGLE

1919 MERCURY DIME

1885 LIBERTY SEATED DOLLAR

WALKING LIBERTY HALF-DOLLAR

1917 TYPE ONE STANDING LIBERTY QUARTER

PROOF GOLD

1. $20 SAINT-GAUDENS DOUBLE EAGLE

Minted in 1849, this is probably the world's best-known coin and one of the most beautiful coin designs in numismatic history. The coin has it all—beauty, popularity, rarity, top condition, and good past investment performance. In fact, the Saint-Gaudens seems to retain its value independent of the price of gold. This coin in Uncirculated condition can fetch as much as $1,800.

2. TEXAS COMMEMORATIVE HALF-DOLLAR

This coin was first minted in 1934 to commemorate the hundredth anniversary of Texas Independence. Between 1934 and 1938, approximately 150,000 were minted, and it's likely that 60 to 80 percent survive today, so this is not a truly rare coin, just a scarce one. The thing that sets the Texas apart is the beauty of its design and the coin's extreme popularity. Today, this coin in Uncirculated condition is valued at about $350.

3. WALKING LIBERTY HALF-DOLLAR

Like the $20 Saint-Gaudens, this is one of the world's most beautiful coins and is extremely popular. For the collector, this 1916 coin fits the "most affordable" category, though these coins are certainly not easy to find in top condition. A mint-condition Walking Liberty Half-Dollar is valued at about $100.

4. MERCURY DIME

Mercury dimes and Walking Liberty halves represent the ultimate in twentieth-century numismatic beauty and importance. Though the Mercury dime series stretched between 1916 and 1945, proofs were made only between 1936 and 1942.

Circulation-strike Mercury dimes circa 1940 to 1945 are very reasonably priced, starting at less than $50. A 1945 proof is valued at about $350.

5. 1917 TYPE ONE STANDING LIBERTY QUARTER

Though this is one of the truly beautiful U.S. coin types, it was made for only two years. The exposed breast of Ms. Liberty caused such an uproar that the design was radically changed halfway through 1917. It makes the rare coin price list thanks to its beauty, popularity, and historical importance. A high-grade coin is valued at around $12,000.

6. BARBER HALF-DOLLAR

Barber halves were minted between 1892 and 1915 and are one of the coin market's most important issues. They are collected both by date and by "type" collectors and are the rarest of the twentieth-century silver type issues. An 1892 Barber half-dollar in excellent condition is worth around $1,100.

7. 20-CENT PIECE

This odd coin was only made from 1875 through 1878. It looked too much like a quarter to catch on with the public and there really wasn't a commercial need for the denomination. Today, twenty-cent pieces are highly prized collector's items; if you are lucky enough to stumble upon one in top condition, expect to pay about $1,200.

8. LIBERTY SEATED DOLLAR

This is one of the most beautiful coins ever made and one of the rarest of the major nineteenth-century U.S. types, issued from 1840 to 1873. Both circulation strikes and proofs are very rare. An 1872 Liberty seated dollar in gem condition is worth $800 to $900.

9. EARLY U.S. GOLD COINS

From 1795 to 1834, the U.S. minted $2.50, $5, and $10 gold coins. In 1834, the gold content of our coins was lowered slightly and most pre-1835 gold coins hit the melting pot. Today, these early treasures of American financial history are rare in all grades. A 1795 $5 Small Eagle, for instance, in top condition is worth about $25,000, and an 1800 $10 gold coin in Extra Fine condition is worth about $13,000.

10. PROOF GOLD

Today the Mint strikes millions of proof coins a year and sells them to collectors all over the world. But in the nineteenth century, the Mint struck a few thousand proof coins each year and only a handful of proof gold coins. Proof gold coins are the caviar of the numismatic marketplace—the beachfront property of rare coins. They are expensive, but they are super rare and demand is always sky high in both good and bad markets. An 1880 set of pristine proof coins sold for $1.4 million in 2000.

THE POCKET CHANGE LOTTERY

6 VALUABLE COINS YOU CAN FIND IN POCKET CHANGE

Scott Travers, a New York City coin dealer and author of *The Coin Collector's Survival Manual* and *One-Minute Coin Expert*, writes: "There are still golden opportunities to find worthwhile coins in pocket change today. If you pay very close attention to the coins that pass through your hands you may be pleasantly surprised, and while you may not always enjoy the thrill of discovery, you're bound to derive pleasure and satisfaction from the hunt." Here is Travers's list of six valuable coins that may be in your pocket right now:

1. 1943 BRONZE OR COPPER LINCOLN CENT

Although popularly termed "copper," this coin is actually made from bronze—an alloy of copper, tin, and zinc. By 1943, copper was urgently needed for battlefield uses. To help conserve the supply of this critical metal, the U.S. Mint suspended production of "copper" cents and made more than a billion cents instead from steel with a coating of zinc. These "white" cents rusted rapidly and today are of little value.

But at the end of production of the "copper" cents, a small number of bronze coin blanks—possibly fewer than forty—somehow got stamped along with the new steel cents in 1943. The rarest examples carry the "D" (Denver) or "S" (San Francisco) Mint marks underneath the date.

Value: as much as $200,000

2. 1965 SILVER ROOSEVELT DIME

The U.S. Mint officially stopped the manufacture of silver Roosevelt dimes in 1964, so virtually every Roosevelt dime you find dated "1965" will not be silver; it will be composed of copper and nickel "clad." This rare 1965 dime mistake is made of 90 percent silver and, as such, is one of only a few accounted for. You can tell silver from clad by examining the coin's edge: The rare silver coin has a silver edge; the common clad coin has a strip of brown around the edge. Experts believe that a small number of 1965 silver dimes were manufactured by mistake at the Mint, and many of those are still waiting to be discovered.

Value: as much as $20,000

ABOVE: 1955 Doubled Die Lincoln Cent

3. 1972 DOUBLE DIE LINCOLN CENT

Doubling is visible on the front or "obverse" of the coin. The "die" (engraved master impression that strikes the coin) was engraved twice. Noticeable doubling is visible on the words "Liberty" and "In God We Trust," as well as on the date. Although nobody knows with certainty how many 1972 Double Die cents the Mint manufactured, several thousand are estimated to exist. The demand by thousands of Lincoln cent collectors has outstripped the supply.

Value: from $50 to $600, depending on condition

4. 1913 LIBERTY HEAD NICKEL

Until recently, experts could account for only four of the five specimens of this coin. A million-dollar offer led to the discovery of a "missing" fifth specimen. It had been stashed in a closet in North Carolina for many years after one of the nation's oldest and largest coin firms looked at it in 1962 and incorrectly concluded that the date had been altered. Re-examination by a blue-ribbon panel revealed it was genuine and unaltered after all.
Value: approximately $3 million

5. 2001-P DOUBLE STRUCK WASHINGTON QUARTER

("Fifty States" quarter/New York)

Instead of being ejected after it was struck, this coin stayed in the coining chamber and was struck again. This type of quarter is very much in demand and quite dramatic with its doubled Statue of Liberty.
Value: $3,000

6. 1995-P ROOSEVELT DIME

(accidentally manufactured with a staple in the body of the coin)

A staple somehow found its way into the minting process of this coin, resulting in a rare type of error.
Value: $1,000

LOOSE CHANGE

In 2006, Scott Travers, former vice president of the American Numismatic Association, came up with a unique way of introducing the general public to the excitement of coin collecting. He deliberately spent three valuable pennies while shopping in Manhattan, stating, "I'm planting a seed, and I hope that a new generation of people will come to appreciate the history that coins represent." The pennies Travers spent were a 1908-S Indian Head cent, a 1909-S VDB cent, and a 1914-D cent, worth approximately $200; $1,000; and $4,300 respectively. None of the coins was ever reported to have been discovered.

Daniel J. Goevert, of www.US-coin-values-advisor.com, specializing in coin value trends, considers these the most desirable pennies:

The 1793 Chain Cent was the first regular issue coin produced by the United States Mint

1. 1793 CHAIN CENT

The 1793 Chain Cent was the first regular issue coin produced by the United States Mint. The reverse featured a fifteen-link chain, to symbolize a strong bond between the fifteen states in the Union at that time. Many people objected to the chain, for it seemed a bad omen to liberty. Within a few weeks, the chain was replaced by a wreath. A 1793 Chain Cent in Good condition (a numismatic term describing a coin with heavy wear) is worth about $10,000 in today's market. There are approximately 1,500 in existence.

2. 1793 STRAWBERRY LEAF CENT

The Strawberry Leaf Cent gets its name because of the leaves located just below Miss Liberty, although no botanist would ever say the foliage is that of the popular fruit-bearing plant. Only four Strawberry Leaf Cents are known to exist today. In January 2009, the best of the four sold for $862,500.

3. 1794 STARRED REVERSE CENT

This coin is noted for having 94 tiny five-pointed stars located between the dentils (toothlike devices encircling the rim of some coins) on the reverse. The existence of the stars did not gain publicity until the 1870s. Despite extensive research, numismatists have never understood their symbolism or purpose for being there. In 2008, an example with only traces of wear was auctioned off for $632,500.

4. 1795 REEDED EDGE CENT

Only six 1795 cents are known to have a reeded edge. Copper coins generally do not have reeded edges, leading scholars to believe this was most likely an experimental piece of some kind. The finest of these six specimens, graded VG, was sold in September 2009 for $1.265 million, the only U.S. cent ever to break the million-dollar barrier.

5. 1856 FLYING EAGLE CENT

By the 1850s, the Large Cent, a staple in U.S. coinage since 1793, had become too costly to mint because of its clunky size. The 1856 Flying Eagle Cent was the first penny with a reduced diameter. It is estimated that only one thousand of the 1856 Flying Eagle Cents were minted. The coin is valued anywhere from $5,000 to more than $100,000, depending on condition.

6. 1877 INDIAN HEAD CENT

The Indian Head Cent, which debuted in 1859, averaged a mintage of 18 million annually until 1877, when production suddenly declined to only 852,000. Relatively few cents were issued in 1877 because the Mint had a sufficient supply of older cents in storage to meet reduced demand for coinage that year, due to softening economic conditions. The starting price of an Uncirculated 1877 is about $5,000, and could go as high as $75,000.

7. 1909-S VDB LINCOLN CENT

This Lincoln Cent was first minted in 1909. Designed by Victor D. Brenner, the Lincoln Cent was the first United States circulating coin to bear the image of a real person. The public loved the coin, but was less enthused about the designer's initials, V.D.B., appearing conspicuously at the bottom of the reverse. Mint officials quickly removed the V.D.B., but not before a very small mintage of 484,000 was released. The initials were restored in 1918 on the front of Lincoln's shoulder, in much smaller letters, where they remain today. Owning a 1909-S VDB is a dream come true for every Lincoln Cent collector, many of whom are prepared to pay a minimum of $900 to acquire this favored rarity. A price tag of $100,000 for the highest quality example is not out of line.

8. 1943 COPPER LINCOLN CENT

In 1943, the Mint produced steel pennies, to preserve the copper supply for use in World War II. Somehow, a tiny number of 1943 cents were made of copper and escaped into circulation. Whether this was accidental or not is something we'll probably never know. Today, the 1943 copper cent ranks among the most famous and valuable of all United States coins. The average collector can forget about owning one, since only a dozen or so examples are known to exist. A genuine 1943 copper cent is worth in the range of $50,000 to $200,000.

9. 1955 DOUBLE DIE LINCOLN CENT

Coin dies are made by hitting steel tooling several times with a master die, or hub, to form an inverse image of the coin. The dies are then used to strike round blanks to make coins. While preparing a Lincoln Cent die at the Philadelphia Mint in 1955, somehow a slight misalignment occurred in between hub hits, causing the lettering and date to appear doubled. The die was placed into service and the goof discovered soon thereafter, but not until 24,000 doubled cents were dumped in with normal production runs, meaning the Mint had little choice but to release them. The incident created quite a stir within the numismatic community, one that has not subsided with time. A 1955 Double Die Lincoln Cent has a value of more than $1,000 in Good condition, and if Uncirculated, is worth somewhere from $2,500 to $40,000.

10. 1969-S DOUBLE DIE LINCOLN CENT

In 1969, another double die sensation captured headlines, this time courtesy of the San Francisco Mint. The date, the word "liberty," and the motto "In God We Trust" all displayed the doubling effect. Only a few dozen of them are known to exist, but there are probably more. If you think valuable coins cannot be found in pocket change, think again. In 2007, a keen-eyed collector stumbled across an Uncirculated 1969-S Double Die Lincoln Cent, and sold it for an astounding $126,500!

THE MOST VALUABLE NOTES, BY DENOMINATION

Here are the most sought-after currency notes according to *100 Greatest American Currency Notes* by Q. David Bowers and David M. Sundman:

ONE-DOLLAR BILL: The most valuable example is the Legal Tender "Rainbow Note," which was first produced in 1869. This bill, featuring a portrait of George Washington and a scene of Christopher Columbus discovering America, was printed using multiple colors, such as green, blue, red, and black, hence the nickname, "Rainbow." It is valued at $4,500 in Uncirculated condition.

TWO-DOLLAR BILL: The finest example of the "Lazy Deuce" or "Lazy Two" National Bank Note printed in 1849 is the Rhode Island version, featuring portraits of George Washington, John Adams, and Zachary Taylor. The name, "Lazy Deuce," refers to the large horizontally oriented number two on the face of the note. It is valued at $12,000 in Uncirculated condition.

FIVE-DOLLAR BILL: The $5 Demand Note of 1861 features the image of the statue Freedom, as well as a portrait of Alexander Hamilton. The back of the note is printed entirely in green, and is therefore often referred to as the "Greenback Issue." A crisp Uncirculated bill is valued at approximately $40,000.

TEN-DOLLAR BILL: The $10 Compound Interest Treasury Note was first issued in 1864. This bill features a portrait of Salmon P. Chase, and it also features an overprinting with a bronze color. This note, in pristine condition, is valued at $95,000.

TWENTY-DOLLAR BILL: The $20 National Gold Bank Note Original and Series of 1875 features a vignette of the Battle of Lexington on the face and a montage of gold coins on the back. All these images were printed on gold-tinted paper. An Uncirculated note, in mint condition, is valued at $50,000.

FIFTY-DOLLAR BILL: The $50 Interest Bearing Note was first issued in 1861. This note is one of the rarest of all bills, and only two are known to exist—one is owned by a private collector, who paid nearly $400,000 for it at auction; the other is owned by the U.S. government. The goddess Justice appears at the center of the bill, and portraits of Andrew Jackson and Salmon P. Chase appear on either side.

ONE-HUNDRED-DOLLAR BILL: The $100 "Watermelon Note" series was first issued in 1890. This note was given its nickname, "Grand Watermelon," because the design on the back featured enormous zeroes. The portrait of Admiral David G. Farragut, who is credited with the famous quote, "Damn the torpedoes, full speed ahead!", is featured on the face of this bill. In pristine condition, this bill is valued at $356,500.

ONE-THOUSAND-DOLLAR BILL: The most valuable $1,000 dollar bill is another "Watermelon Note," series of 1890, with a vignette of General George Meade, the Union general credited with winning the Battle of Gettysburg. The current value of this bill is estimated at more than $2.25 million, in Uncirculated condition. There are only seven in existence.

TEN-THOUSAND-DOLLAR BILL: The $10,000 Federal Reserve note, issued in 1918, is perhaps the most valuable of all American currency notes. The face of the bill features a portrait of Salmon P. Chase, while the back has an illustration entitled "Embarkation of the Pilgrims." All five examples of this bill are owned by the U.S. government. It has an estimated value of $2,000,000.

From TheFunTimesGuide.com:

More than two-thirds of all coins produced by the U.S. Mint are pennies. In fact, the penny is the most widely used denomination currently in circulation.

Each year, the U.S. Mint produces from 1 to 2 billion to as many as 14 billion pennies.

The average American household has $93.75 worth of pennies stashed in jars, empty five-gallon water bottles, and old purses, or lost behind sofa cushions.

Pennies were the very first coins minted in the United States. In March 1793, the mint distributed 11,178 copper cents, a whopping $111.78 worth. Each penny bore the motto "Mind your business."

There are about 200 billion U.S. pennies in circulation today.

The penny was the only coin to feature an image of the same president on both sides of the coin—until the New Jersey State Quarter came along in 1999 bearing an image of Washington (among others) on the reverse.

A penny weighs more than a hummingbird.

The Lincoln penny was first minted and circulated in 1909, the hundredth anniversary of his birth.

If you doubled one penny every day for thirty days, you would have $5,368,709.12.

If you toss a penny 10,000 times, it will not be heads 5,000 times, but more like 4,950. The heads picture weighs more, so it ends up on the bottom.

The two-cent penny was the first U.S. coin to bear the motto "In God We Trust."

The average penny lasts twenty-five years.

PENNY LEXICON

A PENNY FOR YOUR THOUGHTS: Tell me what you're thinking

NOT ONE RED CENT: Not giving up a single penny

PENNY WISE AND POUND FOOLISH: Being thrifty in small things but wasteful in important things

PUT YOUR TWO CENTS IN: Give your opinion

PENNIES FROM HEAVEN: Small blessings

PENNY-PINCHING: Stinginess

PENNY ANTE: Small-time

PENNY ARCADE: Part of an amusement park with coin-operated machines

"A penny saved is 2.5 grams of zinc alloy." —Anonymous

NOT ALL PENNIES ARE CREATED EQUAL

The Lincoln Memorial Reserve penny made from 1959 to mid-1982 weighs 3.11 grams, while the ones made after that weigh in at 2.5 grams. The following calculations use the exact dimensions of the coin rounded off to the nearest ounce and inch.

NUMBER OF PENNIES	WEIGHT	HEIGHT WHEN STACKED
1	0.1 ounces	0.05 inches
16	1.6 ounces	1 inch
1,000	6.25 pounds	62.4 inches
50,000	307.2 pounds	256 feet
100,000	614.4 pounds	512 feet
1 million	3.14 tons	0.99 miles
10 million	31.3 tons	9.88 miles

NUMBER OF PENNIES	WEIGHT	HEIGHT WHEN STACKED
100 million	312.5 tons	99 miles
1 billion	3,125 tons	987 miles
10 billion	31,250 tons	9,864 miles
100 billion	312,555.2 tons	98,660 miles
1 trillion	3,125,000 tons	986,426 miles
1 quadrillion	3,125,000,000 tons	986,426,768 miles
1 quintillion	3,125,000,000,000 tons	986,426,767,677 miles

1,818,624,000,000
pennies would fill the Empire State Building.

2,623,684,608,000
pennies would fill the Sears Tower.

For many, the penny seems like little more than an inconvenience, and a debate has raged for decades among numismatists and economists alike as to whether it deserves to be kept around. Here are both sides of the argument:

PROS

Gallup polls show that two-thirds of Americans want to keep the cent around. A pro-penny lobby even exists called Americans for Common Cents (in 2006, Kevin Federline, the husband of Britney Spears at the time, was hired by Virgin Mobile and ACC to spearhead their Save the Penny campaign). Polls found that 58 percent of Americans stash pennies in piggy banks, jars, or drawers instead of spending them like other coins. Some people eventually redeem them at banks or coin-counting machines, but 2 percent admit to throwing pennies out. Still, the majority recognizes the penny as part of American history and tradition.

It's a hedge against inflation, by virtue of the accurate pricing it can offer consumers.

Charities love pennies, as they are a common form of donation. In fact, it is the most frequently donated coin; charitable organizations receive tens of millions of dollars a year in pennies alone.

It is believed that doing away with the penny would hurt the economy by causing nearly $650 dollars per year in a sort of "penny tax" that would only benefit businesses. Prices would be changed so that store owners would keep the change from the rounding required without pennies.

During economic recessions, penny circulation increases dramatically as people roll and spend them.

If we eliminate the penny, we will need more nickels in circulation, and nickels cost even more to make than pennies. In fact, they cost 7.7 cents to make (2.7 cents over face value, as opposed to 0.26 cents over face value to make a penny).

Pennies are sentimental. The fact is that Americans love their pennies and hate to change things. We've always had pennies and therefore always *should* have pennies, claim some. (This is the same thinking that rejects the metric system despite the fact that virtually the entire rest of the world uses it.) Americans are traditionalists, and the Lincoln Cent is the epitome of modern day circulating coin tradition.

CONS

The penny is called the "nuisance coin" because it's bulky to carry around in quantity, and there's nary a vending machine that will accept one. Most pennies are never used, but rather stored or hoarded.

It costs more to produce than its face value due to today's higher metal prices. (Some shrewd folks have suggested that pennies can be melted down and sold for their base metal at a profit.)

Pennies are basically worthless, and you really can't buy anything with them. According to the *New Yorker* magazine, unless you can stoop down and pick a penny off the floor in less than 6.15 seconds, picking them up doesn't even pay minimum wage.

Pennies waste time. The average American wastes 2.4 hours a year handling pennies or waiting for people who handle them, claimed RetireThe Penny.org, after compiling data relating to a number of penny-handling-related events, including the ubiquitous thirty-second period we sometimes spend waiting for someone who just *has* to dig through their pockets or purse to find that last cent so they can pay for something with exact change—so they don't get stuck with any more pennies.

Making pennies wastes time. The U.S. Mint makes an average of 20.27 *million* pennies per day to produce as many as 14 billion pennies a year depending on demand, and that's not even counting the time, fuel, expense, and hassle of carting all of those pennies around to the banks, merchants, etc.

Rounding-up prices wouldn't matter. The anti-penny folks point out that we wouldn't pay more for each item we buy, only for the *total* price of what we buy. Even if you shop two or three times a day (which most people don't) and even if the rounding goes against you two times out of three (which it shouldn't), we're still only talking about three or four cents per day at the most. Most people throw more than four cents' worth of pennies into the jar (or trash) each day anyway.

Q: Who invented copper wire?
A: Two tax attorneys fighting over a penny.

The word "nickel" is derived from the German word *Kupfernickel*, referring to the deceptive copper color of the ore.

Before we had nickels, we had small silver coins called "half dimes."

The first 5-cent piece minted in the United States appeared in 1866.

First minted in 1883, the Liberty Head Nickel did not have the word "cents" imprinted on it, making it possible for some enterprising individuals to gold-plate these coins and pass them off as $5 gold pieces. The word "cents" was soon added.

President Thomas Jefferson took his place on the obverse of the nickel in 1938 with Monticello, his Virginia home, on the reverse. These designs were produced until 2003. In 2004, the United States Mint began to commemorate the bicentennials of the Louisiana Purchase and the Lewis and Clark Expedition with the Westward Journey Nickel Series. The nickel's current design is the last of that series.

The U.S. Mint loses $14 million each year producing the nickel; they each cost 7.7 cents to manufacture.

The Big Nickel, located in Sudbury, Ontario, Canada, is the largest coin replica in the world, according to the *Guinness Book of World Records*. It stands 27.5 feet high and 2 feet thick. It is not made of nickel.

Five-cent coins minted from 1942 to 1945 don't have any nickel in them. During that time, the United States Mint used a special wartime alloy instead—copper (56 percent), silver (35 percent), and manganese (9 percent)—so that the available nickel could be used in the war effort.

There's still nickel in the nickel. The 2006 five-cent coin is the same weight and metal alloy as when it was first made in 1866 (except when its nickel was replaced during World War II). Although its design has changed, the nickel is the circulating coin whose weight and composition have stayed the same for the longest time.

NICKEL LEXICON

NOT WORTH A PLUGGED NICKEL: Worthless; a plugged nickel has a hole shot through it by a marksman

DON'T TAKE ANY WOODEN NICKELS: Be careful

NICKEL-AND-DIME: Small-time

FIVE-AND-TEN-CENT STORE OR FIVE-AND-DIME: Store that sold goods for five or ten cents

NICKELODEON: An early movie theater, which usually cost five cents to enter

THE DIME

Even though it was pronounced in the same way, the original spelling was "disme" because the word is based on the Latin word *decimus*, meaning "one-tenth." The French used the word *disme* when they came up with the idea of money divided into ten parts in the 1500s.

The current design on the obverse of the dime first appeared in 1946, soon after the death of President Franklin Delano Roosevelt. It was released on the late president's birthday after citizens petitioned the Treasury Department to depict the beloved president on some form of currency. The dime was a good choice because Roosevelt supported the March of Dimes, a program that raised funds for research to find a cure for polio. Roosevelt had contracted the polio virus when he was thirty-nine years old.

The reverse of the coin shows a torch signifying Liberty, with an olive branch on the left signifying Peace and an oak branch on the right signifying Strength and Independence.

The dime is the smallest, thinnest coin we Americans use today.

Lady Liberty reigned on the dime in different forms for many years. Usually just her head was shown, but her full body, seated on a rock, was used during the 1800s. She was shown with wings on her head from 1916 to 1945 (the coin was often called the Mercury dime) to symbolize freedom of thought.

DIME LEXICON

DIME NOVEL: Cheap novel of the late 1800s

A DIME A DOZEN: Easy to get

DIME STORE: Five- and ten-cent store

STOP ON A DIME: Stop very quickly

GET OFF THE DIME: Get moving as you should

SPARE A DIME: Lend money

FIVE THINGS YOU COULD BUY FOR A DIME IN 1897

1. A cast-iron toy bank
2. An embroidered handkerchief
3. One pound of boneless ham
4. Three bars of Pears soap
5. A box of 24 doses of "Stop Drinking German Liquor Cure"

The 50 State Quarters Program Act began in 1999 and ran through 2008, with five new quarters released every year. The quarters were released in the order that the states joined the union. Each quarter features a different state design on the back.

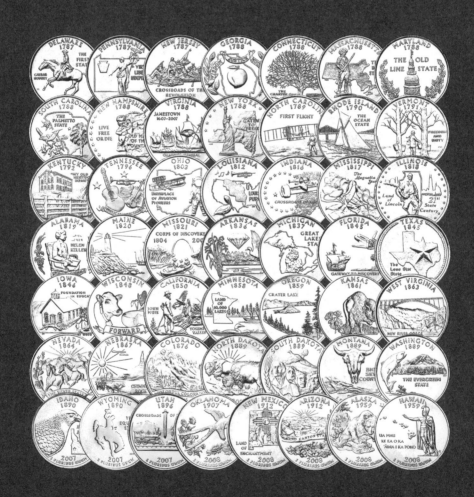

STATE	DATE OF STATEHOOD	ISSUED	DESIGN	INSCRIPTIONS
Delaware	Dec. 7, 1787	1999	Caesar Rodney's horseback ride	"The First State"
Pennsylvania	Dec. 12, 1787	1999	Commonwealth statue, keystone, and outline of state	"Virtue, Liberty, Independence"
New Jersey	Dec. 18, 1787	1999	Washington crossing the Delaware River	"Crossroads of the Revolution"
Georgia	Jan. 2, 1788	1999	Peach, live oak, and outline of state	"Wisdom, Justice, Moderation"
Connecticut	Jan. 9, 1788	1999	The charter oak	"The Charter Oak"
Massachusetts	Feb. 6, 1788	2000	Minuteman statue and outline of state	"The Bay State"
Maryland	April 28, 1788	2000	Maryland statehouse and white oak	"The Old Line State"
South Carolina	May 23, 1788	2000	Palmetto tree, Carolina wren, and jessamine	"The Palmetto State"
New Hampshire	June 21, 1788	2000	Old Man of the Mountain rock formation	"Old Man of the Mountain"; "Live Free or Die"
Virginia	June 25, 1788	2000	First three ships to Jamestown	"Jamestown 1607–2007," "Quadricentennial"
New York	July 26, 1788	2001	Statue of Liberty, state outline, 11 stars	"Gateway to Freedom"
North Carolina	Nov. 21, 1789	2001	First flight at Kitty Hawk	"First Flight"
Rhode Island	May 29, 1790	2001	A sailboat on the open sea	"The Ocean State"
Vermont	March 4, 1791	2001	Camel's Hump Mountain, maple trees with sap buckets	"Freedom and Unity"
Kentucky	June 1, 1792	2001	Federal Hill, race horse behind a fence	"My Old Kentucky Home"
Tennessee	June 1, 1796	2002	Fiddle, trumpet, guitar, and musical score	"Musical Heritage"
Ohio	March 1, 1803	2002	Early airplane, astronaut, and state outline	"Birthplace of Aviation Pioneers"
Louisiana	April 30, 1812	2002	Pelican, horn with musical notes, and outline of Louisiana Purchase	"Louisiana Purchase"
Indiana	Dec. 11, 1816	2002	Race car and state outline	"Crossroads of America"
Mississippi	Dec. 10, 1817	2002	Blossoms and leaves of two magnolias	"The Magnolia State"
Illinois	Dec. 3, 1818	2003	Abraham Lincoln, state outline, and Chicago skyline	"Land of Lincoln;" "21st State"; "Century"
Alabama	Dec. 14, 1819	2003	Helen Keller, with her name in English and Braille	"Spirit of Courage"
Maine	March 15, 1820	2003	The Pemaquid Point Light House and a schooner	

OPPOSITE: The fifty state quarters

STATE	DATE OF STATEHOOD	ISSUED	DESIGN	INSCRIPTIONS
Missouri	Aug. 10, 1821	2003	Lewis and Clark travelling down the Missouri River	"Corps of Discovery 1804–2004"
Arkansas	June 15, 1836	2003	Rice stalks, a diamond, and a mallard	
Michigan	Jan. 26, 1837	2004	Outline of state	"Great Lakes State"
Florida	March 3, 1845	2004	Galleon, space shuttle, strip of land with palm trees	"Gateway to Discovery"
Texas	Dec. 29, 1845	2004	State outline and star encircled by lariat	"The Lone Star State"
Iowa	Dec. 28, 1846	2004	One-room schoolhouse, based on a Grant Wood painting	"Foundation in Education"; "Grant Wood"
Wisconsin	May 29, 1848	2004	Cow's head, cheese, corn	"Forward"
California	Sept. 9, 1850	2005	John Muir, Yosemite Valley, and California condor	"John Muir"; "Yosemite Valley"
Minnesota	May 11, 1858	2005	People fishing, a loon, and state outline	"Land of 10,000 Lakes"
Oregon	Feb. 14, 1859	2005	Crater Lake	"Crater Lake"
Kansas	Jan. 29, 1861	2005	Buffalo and sunflowers	
West Virginia	June 20, 1863	2005	New River Gorge Bridge	"New River Gorge"
Nevada	Oct. 31, 1864	2006	Mustangs, sun rising over mountains, and sagebrush	"The Silver State"
Nebraska	March 1, 1867	2006	Covered wagon, Chimney Rock	"Chimney Rock"
Colorado	Aug. 1, 1876	2006	Rocky Mountains, evergreens	"Colorful Colorado"
North Dakota	Nov. 2, 1889	2006	Bison grazing in the Badlands	
South Dakota	Nov. 2, 1889	2006	Pheasant in flight over Mount Rushmore	
Montana	Nov. 8, 1889	2007	Bison skull	"Big Sky Country"
Washington	Nov. 11, 1889	2007	King salmon, Mount Rainier	"The Evergreen State"
Idaho	July 3, 1890	2007	Peregrine falcon, state outline	"Esto Perpetua"
Wyoming	July 10, 1890	2007	Bucking horse and rider	"The Equality State"
Utah	Jan. 4, 1896	2007	Locomotives moving toward golden spike	"Crossroads of the West"
Oklahoma	Nov. 16, 1907	2008	State bird soaring over the State wildflower	"Oklahoma 1907"
New Mexico	Jan. 6, 1912	2008	Zia sun symbol over outline of the State	"Land of Enchantment"
Arizona	Feb. 14, 1912	2008	Image of the Grand Canyon with a saguaro cactus	"Grand Canyon State"
Alaska	Jan. 3, 1959	2008	The North Star, a grizzly bear	"The Great Land"
Hawaii	Aug. 21, 1959	2008	The Hawaiian monarch King Kamehameha I and eight islands	"UA MAU KE EA O KA ʻĀINA I KA PONO"

QUARTER NOTES

ALABAMA: The Alabama state quarter is the first coin circulated in the U.S. that features Braille writing. It also is the first coin circulated in the United States featuring a member of the Socialist Party.

ARIZONA: The banner reading "Grand Canyon State" in the design is intended to split the quarter into two sections and indicate the Grand Canyon and the saguaro cactus are in two different Arizona scenes, as the saguaro cactus is not found near the Grand Canyon.

CONNECTICUT: The charter oak on the back of the Connecticut quarter fell during a storm on August 21, 1856. It also appears on a 1936 half-dollar commemorating the three-hundredth anniversary of the state's settlement by Europeans.

GEORGIA: An apparent mistake in the outline of the state of Georgia on the quarter appears to have accidentally left out Dade County, which is in the extreme northwestern part of the state.

ILLINOIS: The Illinois quarter is the only quarter to directly reference and portray an urban area, with a picture of the Chicago skyline. It is also the first coin to feature George Washington and Abraham Lincoln on the same coin.

INDIANA: The Indiana quarter—having a problem similar to Georgia's quarter—is missing part of its northwestern corner. Lake County is either partially or completely missing (where it borders Lake Michigan). The error did not garner considerable notice.

The edge of the quarter has 119 ridges.

MINNESOTA: Many safety groups have pointed out that the men fishing from the boat are not wearing life jackets.

NEBRASKA: One of the final concepts for the Nebraska quarter was based on the Ponca leader Standing Bear, who, in a suit brought against the federal government, successfully argued that Native Americans were citizens entitled to rights under the U.S. Constitution.

NEW HAMPSHIRE: The Old Man of the Mountain, the rock formation featured on the back of the New Hampshire quarter, collapsed in 2003.

TENNESSEE: Some claim that the details on the musical instruments depicted on the quarter are inaccurate, such as the number of strings on the guitar and the location of the tubing on the trumpet.

WISCONSIN: A number of the Wisconsin quarters featured a small mint error: The ear of corn features an extra leaf. Some of the affected coins feature a "low leaf," others feature a "high leaf." All of these "error coins" were minted at the Denver mint. It is unclear whether the error was deliberate or accidental, but the error sparked a collector frenzy. Sets of the flawed coins have been sold on eBay for up to $2,800.

WYOMING: Some Wyoming quarters were released in 2007 with indications of inadequate quality control. Many persons, upon first seeing the same cowboy outline design used on the state's automobile license plates, have mistakenly believed that the lack of detail is itself a flaw, the result of an incomplete striking. However, evidence of cracks in the die and subsequent hasty repairs have been observed in a few circulation specimens.

In 1965, copper-nickel quarters were minted to replace the Washington silver quarter, which had been produced between 1932 and 1964. As a result, the production of the quarter costs only a few cents, and yet its face value remains 25 cents, making it the most cost-effective of all coins to mint. This profit helps to run the U.S. Mint and puts extra funds into the country's Treasury—funds then spent on education, healthcare, defense, and other services for the nation.

THE HALF-DOLLAR COIN

1 From 1794 to 1947, half-dollars, like many coins of the time, were made of silver and decorated with an image that symbolized liberty. In 1948, Benjamin Franklin's likeness was placed on the obverse of the coin and he's been there ever since.

2 The Liberty Bell, which had been on the reverse of Franklin's half-dollar, was replaced by the eagle from the presidential seal, except during 1975 and 1976, the nation's bicentennial. These coins showed an image of Independence Hall in Philadelphia, the site of many important national events.

3 Lady Liberty, in her many forms, adorned the half-dollar coin from 1794 until 1947.

4 Flowing Hair half-dollars were minted between 1794 and 1795.

5 Draped Bust half-dollars were minted between 1796 and 1807.

6 Capped Bust half-dollars were minted between 1807 and 1839.

7 Seated Liberty half-dollars were minted between 1839 and 1891.

8 Walking Liberty half-dollars were minted between 1916 and 1947.

9 Franklin half-dollars were minted between 1948 and 1963.

10 Kennedy half-dollars were minted from 1964 to the present.

ABOVE: A Kennedy half-dollar

THE DOLLAR COIN

The word "dollar" comes from the German word *Thaler*, which was a large silver German coin. Because these silver *Thalers* were popular everywhere, other countries began making their own versions. Dollar coins have been minted intermittently since 1794; currently there are three dollar coin series in production: the Presidential $1 Coin Series (begun in 2007), the Sacagawea Golden Dollar (first issued in 2000), and the Native American Dollar Coin (first issued in 2009).

Our first dollars were coins made of silver.

All three dollar coins are golden in color, created by a mixture of metals (none of them gold). These dollar coins have the same "electromagnetic signature" as their predecessor, the Susan B. Anthony dollar, which was silver in color. Keeping this signature allows older vending machines to accept the new coins without being retrofitted.

Since it was first minted in 1794, the dollar coin has been minted periodically with different versions of Liberty and other individuals on the obverse, including those of President Dwight D. Eisenhower (made 1971–1978) and suffragist Susan B. Anthony (1979–1981, 1999).

DOLLAR LEXICON

ANOTHER DAY, ANOTHER DOLLAR: Another workday has ended

I BET DOLLARS TO DONUTS: I'm sure enough to bet at good odds

BET YOUR BOTTOM DOLLAR: Bet your last coin

MAKE A BUCK: Earn money

MORE BANG FOR THE BUCK: More value or power for the same amount of money

DOLLAR DAYS: Days when a store offers major sales

5 THINGS YOU COULD BUY FOR A DOLLAR IN 1897

1. A folding ironing board
2. A stepladder
3. A pair of shoes
4. A pocket compass
5. A child's high chair

5 HOUSEHOLD USES FOR COINS

We use them to scratch our lottery tickets, we flip them to make heads-or-tails bets, and we wear them as jewelry. Here are some other uses for coins:

TEST TIRE TREAD
Insert an American penny into the tread. If you can't cover the top of Honest Abe's head inside the tread, it's time to, er, head for the tire store.

GIVE THE CARPET A LIFT
When you've moved a piece of furniture that leaves telltale indentations in your carpet, hold a coin on its edge and scrape it against the flattened pile.

KEEP CUT FLOWERS FRESH
They'll stay fresh longer if you add a copper penny and a cube of sugar to the vase water.

INSTANT MEASURE
If you need to measure something but you don't have a ruler, use a quarter. It measures exactly 1 inch (2.54 centimeters) in diameter.

HANDY TOOL
Coins come in handy as impromptu screwdrivers.

HOW TO COLLECT PAPER MONEY

Notaphily, as it's called, is popular throughout the world, and collectors have long admired the stories that these artifacts tell. Collecting paper money enables hobbyists to pursue specific areas of interest and often sheds light on the culture from which the money originates. Here's a starter kit for prospective notaphiles:

Generally, collectors focus on one or more of these ten categories:

1. Large-size U.S.–type notes (see p. 196)
2. U.S. national bank notes (issued by local banks chartered by the federal government)
3. U.S. fractional currency (notes of less than one dollar face value from the 1800s)
4. Colonial currency
5. Confederate States of America notes
6. Small-size U.S.–type notes (the size we're familiar with now)
7. Recent and general world paper money
8. Older and rare world paper money
9. Error notes, including printing, paper, and cutting errors
10. Souvenir cards

In recent times, collectors have begun to include traveler's checks, stocks, and bonds, but purists do not consider these to be money.

During and after the Civil War, the United States began to run short on change, so it printed paper money with denominations of less than one dollar. These are generally smaller than other paper notes and are more affordable than the larger notes of that era. Denominations are 3, 5, 10, 15, 25, and 50 cents.

Collections can be defined by historical interests, such as portraits of Queen Elizabeth, political events, or advances in transportation. Some seek out notes with specific serial numbers (all the same digit or very low serial numbers), while others collect notes primarily for their artistic merit. Many collections include notes from every country on the globe, and these can get quite expensive.

The Internet has revolutionized the world of collecting by putting collectors across the globe in close touch, and postings on various sites regularly announce auctions and shows, which are a great place to learn about money. Newsletters and other periodicals keep enthusiasts informed. Although mail auctions are another common way to acquire notes, reputable dealers are the very best way to develop paper money collections. Their expertise is invaluable, and they often have large stocks of notes to keep everyone happy.

Note that most paper money dealers don't have stores in the same sense as coin dealers. Transactions take place through the mail and over the phone. Lenient return policies make this easy and practical.

During World War II, German concentration camps produced high-quality counterfeits of the British pound as well as currency that was used exclusively within the camps. The notes made by Jewish prisoners are highly collectible today.

The condition of a note is critical to its value, and so much attention is paid to its precise condition. Although there is no formally accepted scale, the following guidelines are universally accepted:

CRISP UNCIRCULATED, UNC OR CU: This means absolutely not the slightest sign of any handling or wear or folding or *anything*.

Some people use additional grades to distinguish qualities such as perfect centering or other printing characteristics.

ALMOST UNCIRCULATED (OR ABOUT UNCIRCULATED), AU: This means there is a slightly detectable imperfection such as a counting fold on one corner or slightest fold in the center (but nothing which breaks the surface of the paper) or a pinhole. At first glance, it looks like a UNC note.

EXTREMELY FINE, EF OR XF: Generally three light folds or one strong fold that breaks the surface. There may be slight rounding at the corners.

VERY FINE, VF: May have several folds although the note is still crisp and has a minimum amount of dirt. There may be minor tears or very small holes but nothing that distracts from the overall appearance of the note. Take an uncirculated note and crumple it once in your hand, then flatten it out: this is a Very Fine note. Repeat the crumpling and it's still pretty much a VF note.

FINE, F: A circulated note on which individual folds and creases may no longer be visible. To distinguish this from a VF note, a Fine note clearly does not look like a note that has merely been crumpled a few times; it doesn't have the crispness and brightness of a VF note. No tears may extend into the printing. This is your average in-the-wallet note.

VERY GOOD, VG: Tears and small holes can be present. The note is not crisp at all. This is your lower quality in-the-wallet note. Lots of people don't realize that a note in "very good" condition is really pretty lousy.

GOOD, G: Small pieces missing, graffiti. A worn-out note.

FAIR: Major tears, etc. A badly worn-out note.

POOR: Even worse.

To grade a note precisely, it should be examined under a magnifying lens and with a strong light source.

One of the best ways to get started collecting is to read the monthly newsletter *Bank Note Reporter*, which contains all the latest news about new issues, currency changes, etc., and carries advertising from a very large number of dealers around the world. Visit BanknoteReporter.com.

The Bureau of Engraving and Printing (BEP) sells various sheets of uncut one- and two-dollar notes (4, 16, and 32 per sheet) through the mail. They cycle through the various Federal Reserve Banks over time. The cost varies from $10.25 (four 1-dollar notes) to $79.00 (thirty-two 2-dollar notes in a cardboard frame). You can order these online at www.money factorystore.gov or from:

Order Processing Center
Bureau of Engraving and Printing
P.O. Box 371594
Pittsburgh, PA 15250-7594
(202) 874-3315

Sheets may be ordered flat or rolled.

On July 10, 1929, the United States replaced its large size currency, which measured approximately 7.42 by 3.125 inches, with small-size notes, measuring 6.14 by 2.61 inches–like the ones in use today.

The purpose of this change was simply to save some money on paper, but the timing inadvertently signified a new era in United States money. When the change was made, there were six kinds of United States paper currency in circulation, but only three months later, the stock market crash ushered in the era of the Great Depression, during which three of those kinds of currency would disappear. Thirty years later, two of the remaining types would also disappear, leaving only one.

The six kinds of paper currency in 1929 were:

United States Notes: These were the first permanent kind of federal paper money, the original "greenbacks." Previously, what the Treasury had issued in wartime were bonds and interest-bearing notes. These were also issued during the Civil War, but then the public was introduced to Legal Tender Notes, which paid no interest but were intended for "all debts public and private, except duties on imports and interest on the public debt"–the purest kind of fiat paper money.

Gold Certificates: First issued in 1863, perhaps to reassure people that the United States Government did not intend to replace all U.S. money with greenbacks. "Certificate" signified that the notes were backed by 100 percent reserves of gold coins, for which they could be redeemed on demand. This was the hardest of hard money short of gold coin itself, since the Treasury would never maintain more than a fractional gold reserve for other currencies.

National Bank Notes: Also called "National Currency," these were established by the National Banking Act of 1863. At this time, states and even private concerns were allowed to print their own money. The federal government, finding itself in need, levied a tax on state banknotes that made them far less desirable than this new currency. The other rationale for the National Banking Act was to "protect" the public from fraudulent and poorly managed banks, whose banknotes might become worthless. The device of "National Currency" made the notes obligations of the Treasury, which meant they were good even if the banks failed.

Silver Certificates: These were created by an Act in 1878. Except for the rare 1928 $1 United States Note, all small $1 bills until 1963 were Silver Certificates. Starting in 1934, these simply said they were redeemable "in silver" instead of "in silver dollars" and, strangely enough, they *could* be redeemed in silver (small bars) at the United States Treasury up until 1968.

Federal Reserve Bank Notes: Identical to National Banks Notes in form and function but issued by Federal Reserve Banks, these notes were retired in 1945.

Federal Reserve Notes: The Federal Reserve Note is the only type of U.S. banknote that is still produced to this day.

The three kinds of currency that remained after the Depression were:
• United States Notes
• Silver Certificates
• Federal Reserve Notes

And all that remained by 1970 were:
• Federal Reserve Notes

All this was part of a plan to unify the design of all currency. The variety of large-note designs gave way to shared elements and a common look for the small notes. This changed little over the years, until a radically redesigned $100 bill was introduced in the 1990s, inaugurating a gradual change in all the currency for security reasons. United States currency had never before featured anti-counterfeiting devices like watermarked paper and security threads, which had appeared in foreign money decades earlier.

One peculiarity of the small note series is that until 1976 the only $2 bill issued was a United States Note. These turned up occasionally in the 1950s. Why so little use was made of the $2 denomination is a little mysterious. Part of the problem may have been the peculiar reputation that $2 bills had gotten; they were thought of either as bad luck or as the proper tender for "gentlemen's clubs," neither of which made them appealing for most people.

Issuing any notes larger than $100 was discontinued during World War II because of fears of German counterfeiting. With the development of other financial instruments and wire transfers, there was felt to be no need for larger notes. Another consideration was the War on Drugs. Drug dealers relied on those big bills for easier transport of funds; eliminating them could thwart at least some commerce, it was believed.

PORTRAITS ON CURRENT BANKNOTES

$1	George Washington
$2	Thomas Jefferson
$5	Abraham Lincoln
$10	Alexander Hamilton
$20	Andrew Jackson
$50	Ulysses S. Grant
$100	Benjamin Franklin
$500	William McKinley
$1,000	Grover Cleveland
$5,000	James Madison
$10,000	Salmon P. Chase
$100,000	Woodrow Wilson

BELOW: Four examples of Confederate paper currency

19 FUN FACTS ABOUT PAPER MONEY

1 The beginning of an establishment for the engraving and printing of U.S. currency can be traced as far back as August 29, 1862, to a single room in the basement of the Main Treasury Building, where two men and four women separated and sealed by hand $1 and $2 U.S. notes that had been printed by private banknote companies. Today there are approximately 2,800 employees who work out of two buildings in Washington, D.C., and a facility in Fort Worth, Texas.

2 During fiscal year 2008, the Bureau of Engraving and Printing produced approximately 38 million notes a day with a face value of approximately $629 million.

3 About 95 percent of the notes printed each year are used to replace notes already in, or taken out of, circulation.

4 The first paper currency issued by the U.S. Department of the Treasury was the Demand Notes Series of 1861.

5 During the Civil War period, the Bureau of Engraving and Printing was called upon to print paper notes in denominations of 3, 5, 10, 15, 25, and 50 cents. The reason for this is that people hoarded coins because of their intrinsic value, thus creating a drastic shortage of circulating coins.

6 In 1929, the size of currency was reduced to about two-thirds of its former size when production was converted to twelve-subject plates. The familiar portraits and back designs of our currency were also established at that time.

7 The approximate weight of a currency note, regardless of denomination, is one gram. There are 454 grams in one U.S. pound, or 450 notes to the pound.

8 If you had ten billion $1 notes and spent one every second of every day, it would require 317 years for you to go broke.

9 A stack of currency one mile high would contain more than 14 million notes.

10 Currency paper is composed of 25 percent linen and 75 percent cotton. Red and blue synthetic fibers of various lengths are distributed evenly throughout the paper. Prior to World War I, the fibers were made of silk.

11 There are traces of cocaine in 95 percent of all notes.

12 Between the Fort Worth, Texas, and the Washington, D.C., facilities approximately eighteen tons of ink per day are used.

13 About four thousand double folds—first forward and then backward—are required before a note will tear.

14 The average lifespan of a Federal Reserve Note by denomination:
$1: 21 months
$5: 16 months
$10: 18 months
$20: 24 months
$50: 55 months
$100: 89 months

15 The hundred-dollar note has been the largest denomination of currency in circulation since 1969.

16 The legend "In God We Trust" became a part of the design of United States currency in 1957 and has appeared on all currency since 1963.

17 The largest note ever printed by the Bureau of Engraving and Printing was the $100,000 Gold Certificate, Series 1934. These notes were printed from December 18, 1934, through January 9, 1935, and were issued by the Treasurer of the United States to Federal Reserve Banks only against an equal amount of gold bullion held by the Treasury. These notes were used for transactions between Federal Reserve Banks and were not circulated among the general public.

18 During fiscal year 2008, the BEP delivered 7.7 billion notes at an average cost of 6.4 cents per note.

19 One-, five-, and ten-thousand dollar bills were last printed in 1945, and officially discontinued on July 14, 1969, by the Federal Reserve System.

"If you can actually count your money, then you are not really rich."
—John Paul Getty

COUNTING CASH

Just how much money is there? Here are the figures for each paper denomination in 2009, according to CNBC.com:

1. $1 bill: 9,159,020,972 in circulation
2. $20 bill: 6,088,154,763 in circulation
3. $100 bill: 5,692,248,601 in circulation
4. $5 bill: 2,126,211,930 in circulation
5. $10 bill: 1,613,477,396 in circulation
6. $2 bill: 774,526,357 in circulation
7. $50 bill: 259,350,007 in circulation
8. $500 bill: 284,288 in circulation
9. $1,000 bill: 165,444 in circulation
10. $5,000 bill: 342 in circulation

A TON OF MONEY

Just how much is a ton of money? Well, that depends on the denomination you have at hand.

A ton of pennies	$3,478
A ton of nickels	$9,091
A ton of dimes	$40,000
A ton of quarters	$40,000
A ton of one-dollar bills	$888,890
A ton of five-dollar bills	$4,444,445
A ton of ten-dollar bills	$8,888,890
A ton of fifty-dollar bills	$44,444,450
A ton of hundred-dollar bills	$88,888,900

RIGHT: The packages seen here, from the vault at the U.S. Treasury in 1914, contain over $80 million.

Even though United States currency is strong and durable, it does wear out with constant handling.

About 13 percent of coins and 42 percent of bills test positive for unpleasant bacteria, such as fecal bacteria.

All currency in circulation is routinely deposited to Federal Reserve Banks by commercial banks. Worn notes are systematically destroyed by Federal Reserve Banks during ordinary currency processing. The destroyed notes are replaced by new currency provided by the Bureau of Engraving and Printing. The note most frequently replaced is the $1 denomination. Since larger denominations are handled less, they last longer.

When a note is partially destroyed, the Treasury Department will replace it if clearly more than half of the original remains. Fragments of mutilated currency that are not clearly more than one half of the original whole note may be exchanged only if the Director of the Bureau of Engraving and Printing is satisfied by the evidence presented that the missing portions have been totally destroyed.

Damaged or mutilated notes should be taken to a bank for redemption. When partially destroyed currency is of questionable value, the fragments should be sent by registered mail to the Department of the Treasury, Bureau of Engraving and Printing, OCS/BEPA, P.O. Box 37048, Washington, D.C. 20013. The Bureau of Engraving and Printing can be accessed at www.moneyfactory.gov.

HOW TO DETECT COUNTERFEIT MONEY

Look at the money you receive. Compare a suspect note with a genuine note of the same denomination and series, paying attention to the quality of printing and paper characteristics. Look for differences, not similarities. Here are some things to look for:

PORTRAIT

The genuine portrait appears lifelike and stands out distinctly from the background. The counterfeit portrait is usually lifeless and flat. Details merge into the background, which is often too dark or mottled.

FEDERAL RESERVE AND TREASURY SEALS

On a genuine bill, the sawtooth points of the Federal Reserve and Treasury seals are clear, distinct, and sharp. The counterfeit seals may have uneven, blunt, or broken sawtooth points.

BORDER

The fine lines in the border of a genuine bill are clear and unbroken. On a counterfeit, the lines in the outer margin and scrollwork may be blurred and indistinct.

SERIAL NUMBERS

Genuine serial numbers have a distinctive style and are evenly spaced. The serial numbers are printed in the same ink color as the Treasury Seal. On a counterfeit, the serial numbers may differ in color or shade of ink from the Treasury seal. The numbers may not be uniformly spaced or aligned.

> Three in every ten thousand U.S. bills is counterfeit.

PAPER

Genuine currency paper has tiny red and blue fibers embedded throughout. Often counterfeiters try to simulate these fibers by printing tiny red and blue lines on their paper. Close inspection reveals, however, that on the counterfeit note the lines are printed on the surface, not embedded in the paper. It is illegal to reproduce the distinctive paper used in the manufacturing of United States currency.

> Around 75 percent of counterfeit currency is found and destroyed before it ever reaches the public.

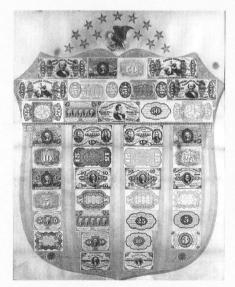

LEFT: Fractional currency shields were first produced by the Treasury Department in 1866 and were sold to banks as a useful comparison in detecting counterfeit notes.

8 INTERESTING FACTS ABOUT THE ONE-DOLLAR BILL

1 The one-dollar bill you have in your possession first came off the presses in 1957 in its present design. This so-called paper money is in fact a cotton and linen blend, with minute red and blue silk fibers running through it to deter counterfeiters, as does the secret blend of ink that is used to print this and other paper notes. The bills are actually starched to make them water resistant, and they are pressed to give them that nice crisp look.

2 The first $1 notes were issued by the Federal Government in 1862 and featured a portrait of Secretary of the Treasury Salmon P. Chase, who served from 1861 to 1864.

3 The first use of George Washington's portrait on $1 notes was on Series 1869 United States Notes.

4 The average life of a dollar bill is 21 months.

5 Almost half of the notes printed by the Bureau of Engraving and Printing are $1 notes.

6 Martha Washington is the only woman whose portrait has appeared on a U.S. currency note. It appeared on the face of the $1 Silver Certificate of 1886 and 1891, along with the back of the $1 Silver Certificate issued in 1896.

7 The $1 bill's famous nickname, "greenback," derives from the Demand Note dollars created by Abraham Lincoln in the mid 1800s to finance the Civil War. These notes were printed in black on one side and green on the other.

8 The motto "In God We Trust" first appeared on U.S. coins in 1864. However, it was not until 1955 that a law was passed that stated that thereafter all new designs for both coins and currency would bear that inscription.

HOW TO READ A ONE-DOLLAR BILL

Front: The black seal to the left of the portrait is the Federal Reserve Seal and Letter. The green seal to the right is the U.S. Treasury Seal. The four black numbers near the corners are Federal Reserve Numbers.

Back: The pyramid on the dollar bill is a Freemason emblem.

The eye in the triangle is a symbol of God.

The motto "Annuit Coeptis" is usually translated as "He hath smiled on our undertakings."

"Novus Ordo Seclorum" means "a new order of the centuries."

The unfinished pyramid stands for permanence and strength and is unfinished to symbolize the future growth of the United States.

The year "1776" in Roman numerals appears at the base of the pyramid.

The various little numbers and letters on the front and back are check letters, face plate letters, quadrant numbers, and back plate numbers. They are used to identify the printing plates and the position of the note on the printing plate.

The right-hand side roundel shows the coat of arms of the United States.

Some people say they see an owl in the upper left-hand corner of the "1" encased in the "shield," and a spider hidden in the front upper right-hand corner.

The U.S. Treasury Seal that appears on the front of the bill and to the right of George Washington depicts a key, representing security.

The number 13 (corresponding to the thirteen colonies) figures prominently on the $1 bill:

» The number of letters and digits in 1776 and its Roman numeral equivalent MDCCLXXVI adds up to 13.

» The dollar has 13 stars above the eagle.
» There are 13 steps on the pyramid.
» There are 13 letters in "Annuit Coeptis."
» There are 13 vertical bars on the shield.
» The top of the shield has 13 horizontal stripes.
» You can count 13 leaves on the olive branch.
» There are 13 berries on the olive branch.
» The dollar bill also features 13 arrows.

8 INTERESTING FACTS ABOUT THE TWO-DOLLAR BILL

1 The common phrase "as phony as a two-dollar bill" is a misnomer, as one Best Buy employee learned the hard way in 2005 after calling the police when a customer attempted to pay for his purchase with a stack of them. The customer remained in custody for three hours until a Secret Service agent was called in to declare the money legal tender.

2 The first $2 notes were issued by the Federal Government in 1862 and featured a portrait of the first Secretary of the Treasury, Alexander Hamilton.

3 Monticello, Thomas Jefferson's estate in Virginia, was first featured as the vignette on the back of the Series 1928 $2 note.

4 In celebration of the United States bicentennial, a $2 Federal Reserve Note, series 1976, was introduced. The new design maintained the portrait of Jefferson on the face, but the back was changed from Monticello to an engraving of John Trumbull's painting *The Signing of the Declaration of Independence*. The original Trumbull painting portrayed forty-seven people, but limited space only allowed for depiction of forty-two of them.

5 It is a common misconception that the $2 bill is no longer in circulation, but according to the U.S. Treasury Department, there are $1,549,052,714 worth of $2 bills out there today. Sixty-one million of them were printed in 2005.

6 Most modern cash registers don't have space for them.

7 Most banks will only give out the $2 bill on special request.

8 Strip clubs will often hand out $2 bills as change instead of singles to encourage larger tips for the dancers.

The $5 bill is sometimes called a "fin," derived from the Yiddish word *finf*, which came from the German *fünf*, meaning "five."

On March 13, 2008, the Federal Reserve issued a new $5 bill. It was debuted during a commemorative transaction at President Lincoln's Cottage at the Soldiers' Home in Washington, D.C. The bill was first ushered into circulation at the Lincoln Cottage gift shop.

The redesigned $5 bills incorporate state-of-the-art security features that are easily recognizable by merchants and consumers. If you hold up the bill, you will see a large number "5" watermark located in a blank space to the right of the watermark portrait of President Lincoln. There is also an imbedded security thread that runs vertically and is located to the right of Lincoln's portrait. This thread glows blue when held under ultraviolet light.

You don't have to trade in your old bills for new ones. Both the new $5 bills and the older-design $5 bills happily co-exist.

The new $5 bill design includes a large, easy-to-read number "5" in the lower right corner on the back of the bill, which helps those with visual impairments distinguish the denomination, and the number is printed in high-contrast purple ink.

The new bill also features a splash of light purple next to Lincoln's portrait that fades to gray as it spreads toward the bill's edges.

The $5 bill now contains microprinted words that are difficult to duplicate. For example, on the face of the bill, the words "Five Dollars" can be found repeated inside the left and right borders.

On the new $5 bill, the left serial number has shifted slightly to the right, compared with previous designs.

The average lifespan of a $5 bill in circulation is 16 months. Approximately 9 percent of all paper currency produced by the U.S. Treasury's Bureau of Engraving and Printing today is $5 bills.

The new ten-dollar bill was first introduced in 2000.

The most noticeable difference in the redesigned $10 bill is the addition of subtle background colors of orange, yellow, and red. The words "We the People," from the United States Constitution, have been printed in red in the background to the right of the portrait. Small yellow "10"s have been printed in the background to the left of the portrait on the face of the bill and to the right of the vignette on the back of the bill. The major design changes to the bill include a revised portrait of Alexander Hamilton and a revised vignette of the U.S. Treasury building.

The redesigned $10 bill retains three of the most important security features that were first introduced in the 1990s, but with improvements. If you tilt the bill and look at the "10" on the lower right-hand corner, the face of the bill changes color from copper to green. This color shift is even more dramatic on the new bills. If you hold the bill up to the light, a faint image of Hamilton appears to the right of his large portrait. It can be seen from both sides. There is also a new security thread that glows orange when held under ultraviolet light.

New symbols of freedom representing icons of Americana are part of the new design series. Two images of the torch carried by the Statue of Liberty are printed in red on the face: a large one in the background to the left of the portrait of Secretary Hamilton, while a second, smaller metallic red one can be found on the lower right side of the portrait.

The oval borders and fine lines surrounding the portrait on the face and the vignette on the back have been removed. The portrait has been moved up and the shoulders have been extended into the border. Additional engraving details have been added to the vignette background.

The redesigned $10 bill also features microprinting on the face of the bill in two areas: The word "USA," and the numeral "10" can be found repeated beneath the large printed torch and the phrases "The United States of America" and "Ten Dollars" can be found below the portrait, as well as vertically inside the left and right borders of the bill.

The large number "10" in the lower right corner on the back of the bill is easy to read and serves as an aid to the visually impaired.

THE TWENTY-DOLLAR BILL

Because President Andrew Jackson is featured on the front of the bill, it is often referred to as a "Jackson." It was also known as a "double-sawbuck" because it is twice the value of a $10 bill. (The Roman numeral ten, an "X," which once appeared on the $10, resembled the legs of a sawbuck, a framework for holding wood that is being sawed.)

Twenty-dollar bills account for about 22 percent of all notes printed today.

The $20 bill got a facelift in October 2003, complete with new colors, a new number arrangement, and a new background. The bill still features Andrew Jackson, but without the old circle. A subtle green background with peach and light blue shades was also added to the new bill.

Many people, especially Native Americans, feel that the image of Andrew Jackson is unsuitable for any denomination of currency, as he is considered the leading exterminator of Native Americans in the United States. Furthermore, Jackson spent a great deal of his presidency opposing central banking, making his appearance on a Federal Reserve Note questionable.

THE FIFTY-DOLLAR BILL

President Ulysses S. Grant is currently featured on the face of the bill, while the U.S. Capitol is featured on the reverse. These bills are often referred to as "Grants."

The average life span of a $50 bill in circulation is 55 months.

Approximately 5 percent of all notes printed today are $50 bills.

In 1969, the $50 bill began bearing the new Treasury Seal with wording in English rather than Latin.

On September 28, 2004, a revised design was introduced, featuring a subtle blue and red background around the borderless image of Grant. In addition, a small silver-blue star was added to the lower right of Grant's portrait.

Some southerners consider it unlucky to carry a $50 bill because it bears the image of the general who won the Civil War for the North.

THE HUNDRED-DOLLAR BILL

The first $100 notes were issued by the Federal Government in 1862 and featured a vignette of an American eagle.

The first use of Benjamin Franklin's portrait on $100 notes was on the first series of Federal Reserve Notes, Series 1914.

The $100 note is the largest denomination currently issued in the United States.

The life span of a $100 Federal Reserve Note is 89 months.

Beginning with Series 1996, $100 Federal Reserve Notes feature a larger portrait, watermarks in the paper, and color-shifting ink. The notes also include microprinting—small lettering that is hard to replicate—on the face.

The vignette on the back of the $100 note since Series 1928 features an engraving of Independence Hall in Philadelphia.

The hands of the clock on Independence Hall are set at approximately 4:10. There are no records explaining why that particular time was chosen.

In 2010, the U.S. Department of the Treasury unveiled a new design for the $100 note. The new design retains the images of its precursor, but it has an array of security features (the $100 bill is the most frequently counterfeited). These include an image of the Liberty Bell that changes color from copper to green when the note is tilted and a "3-D security ribbon" that employs the same technology used for 3-D movies. Just tip the note and the strip of bells and digits on the bill comes into 3-D relief. And you don't even need special glasses to see it.

THE THOUSAND-DOLLAR BILL

The U.S. government first issued $1,000 bills in 1861; they bore the portrait of Grover Cleveland. Other high-denomination bills were issued around this time as well. The last such note was issued in 1934.

The $1,000 bill, along with those of other high denominations, was last printed in 1945.

The most valuable $1,000 bill is the "Grand Watermelon Note," series of 1890, with a vignette of General George Meade, the Union general credited with winning the Battle of Gettysburg. This note was given the nickname "Grand Watermelon" because the design on the back featured enormous zeroes. The current value of one of these bills is estimated at more than $2.25 million; there are only seven in existence.

"A billion dollars doesn't go as far as it used to."
—John Paul Getty

THE TEN-THOUSAND-
DOLLAR BILL

Although it is still legal tender, the $10,000 bill was last printed in 1945 and was officially discontinued in 1969 by the Federal Reserve System, when President Richard Nixon ordered the destruction of the remaining notes. The bills were never publicly issued, and were used for bank transactions only.

They were printed in orange on the reverse.

It is illegal to own a $10,000 bill. All known pieces are in government museums.

One such bill made front-page headlines in 1910 when a messenger boy lost one on Wall Street in the course of completing a bank transaction.

THE HUNDRED-THOUSAND-
DOLLAR BILL

The largest currency ever printed by the United States was the $100,000 Gold Certificate. These notes were printed from December 18, 1934, through January 9, 1935, and were issued by the Treasurer of the United States to Federal Reserve Banks only against an equal amount of gold bullion held by the Treasury. These notes were used for transactions between Federal Reserve Banks and were not circulated among the general public.

The $100,000 bills were last printed in 1945 and officially discontinued on July 14, 1969, by the Federal Reserve System.

Although the bills exist, they were not publicly issued and were used only for intra-government transactions. They are printed in orange on the reverse, and are illegal to own. All known pieces are in government museums.

1 The world's highest denomination note is the Hungarian 100 Million B-Pengő, issued in 1946. That's one hundred quintillion (100,000,000,000,000,000,000) pengő, using the European "long scale" system for naming numbers. It was worth about twenty U.S. cents. Hungary also printed a 1 Milliard B-Pengő (one sextillion, or 1,000,000,000,000,000,000,000 pengő) note that year. Overtaken by hyperinflation, it was never issued. In August 1946, the Hungarian economy was stabilized by the introduction of a new currency, the forint, worth about 8½ U.S. cents, at a rate of 4×10^{29} pengő to the forint.

In the years 1993 through 1998, when there was lack of financing from the federal government, Tatarstan invoked its status as a national autonomy in the Russian Federation and issued a series of currency notes without any denomination printed. They were single sided and had no known exchange rate but were nevertheless used as a local substitute for the Russian ruble.

2 To commemorate the Centennial of Independence from more than three hundred years of Spanish colonial rule in 1998, the government of the Philippines wanted to do something very special. It issued the world's largest banknote (in terms of size), beating the previous record, the 1 kuan issued during China's Ming Dynasty (1368–1398), which measured 222 by 340 mm (8.7 by 13.4 inches). The Philippine 100,000 piso note, measuring 356 by 216 mm (about the size of a sheet of legal paper, 8.5 by 14 inches), is credited by the *Guinness Book of World Records* as the world's largest legal tender note. Only a thousand of these notes were issued.

3 The note with the most zeros in circulation today is Zimbabwe's 50 trillion (50,000,000,000,000) dollar note, worth about 150 U.S. dollars.

4 Four cars appear on the back of $10 bills. Because legal regulations by the Treasury would not permit a government agency to endorse a particular commercial firm or product, Louis S. Schofieldare, the engraver at the time, designed a car that was a composite of four different then-popular models. The car first appeared on the note in 1927.

5 Coins are usually in short supply during times of war, as gold and silver are often hoarded for their intrinsic value. Ivory Coast, Macao, Monaco, Morocco, New Caledonia, Romania, Russia, Spain, and the United States have all resorted to printing small denomination banknotes as temporary substitutes for coins. Morocco's 50 Centimes 1944 emergency issue, measuring only 41 by 32 mm (about 1⅝ by 1¼ inches), is the world's smallest banknote.

6 During World War II, perfect forgeries of Bank of England pound notes were produced by Germany. The bills were manufactured by prisoners in various German concentration camps.

THE FUTURE OF MONEY

Is money going the way of the dinosaurs? It seems so. Money has changed more in the past twenty years than it has in the past two hundred, thanks to the technology explosion of the 1980s and the global consciousness that emerged. Economists and sci-fi writers alike agree that the future of money lies in an electronic approach to it, and already countries and communities around the world are experimenting with new forms of currency. To be sure, the advent of e-cash presents all sorts of problems and questions. Who will be allowed to issue it? How will taxes be paid in cyberspace? How secure will the transactions be?

Microsoft CEO Bill Gates suggested an answer when he attempted to acquire personal-finance software maker Intuit Inc., whose programs, he predicted, would draw millions of consumers to his online network where they could pay bills, get financial advice, and shop, paying him for access. The idea was eventually squelched by the Justice Department.

Here are some recent developments that point to new ways of going about our business:

» The smart card will become an electronic purse. It will work like a phone card: You'll buy a $50 card at 7-Eleven and use it in vending machines, all of which will accept this card. When you're down to a zero balance, you throw it away. These may go so far as to include a chip that contains your DNA signature or some other identifying information. Smart cards have been in use in Europe since 1995 and are predicted to change the face of money throughout the world. Today, in the United States, only 7-Eleven issues smart cards.

» Mobile phones will become a way to pay. Swanky nightclubs in London have already invented a version of money by issuing admission tickets in the form of a barcode that is sent to mobile phones once an (electronic) payment has been made. At one event, clubbers were offered a discount if they purchased electronic tickets.

» Local currencies are already regaining popularity, as they did before central banks were developed. These are currencies that are not backed by a national government and wouldn't be considered legal tender outside of the areas for which they were developed. They can be issued by local governments, businesses, and even individuals. Such currencies were rampant in the early colonies, and today they are flourishing once more: More than two thousand different local community currency systems are in use today throughout the world, and the movement is encouraged by those who argue that local currencies are the only way to enable a poor community to address its problems. Local currencies are especially useful during times of economic turmoil, when the national currency is vulnerable.

» Closely related to local currency is the concept of a new corporate currency in which frequent flyer miles become a sort of corporate scrip. Essentially, this is a private currency that is "earned" by frequenting a certain business, and it can only be used for certain purchases. "Netmarket cash" is already being issued for Internet commerce, and Alan Greenspan, former chairman of the Federal Reserve, foresees "new private currency markets in the twenty-first century."

» In 1997, "Bowie bucks" became available when David Bowie issued bonds using future royalties as security. The idea caught on and has since been employed by Hollywood film studios as well as sports teams.

» The barter system is back—big time. Craigslist and thousands of other services have been set up to enable people to barter. Some of these handle direct exchanges of goods, while others issue scrip that is used for future "purchases." But barter isn't just limited to handbags and woodworking tools. Today barter is used to exchange goods on the national level as well as on the corporate. In fact, futurist Douglas Rushkoff argues for the creation of "craigbucks," saying it is the obvious next step in the evolution of money. "People could buy and sell things exclusively on Craigslist using craigbucks," Rushkoff enthuses. "Sure, they'll want to keep their Visas and their MasterCards, but they'll want a specialized, alternative form of cash too."

» Kenyans use a service called M-PESA that enables people to use mobile-phone minutes as currency—you pay for something at a store by transferring mobile minutes to the store's phone. Today the M-PESA is used for $10 million worth of trades a day.

» In 2006, a Chinese online social network called QQ produced "QQ coins" that were used for almost a billion dollars a year in transactions. The currency was designed just to buy things on the QQ network, but they became so popular that other Web sites started accepting QQ coins for payment of even non-virtual goods, and a black market sprang up to convert QQ coins directly to yuan. The Chinese government cracked down, fearing that QQ coins could trigger inflation of the yuan by increasing the total money supply in China.

» Time is money! In Japan, people trade "elder-care units," which are earned by spending time caring for elders in the community. In the United States, various "time banks" enable people to trade goods and services. For example, you offer to tutor a child, while someone in that family mows your lawn. These exist on both local and national levels.

» Will gold re-emerge as collateral for the money we issue? By the end of the twentieth century, the multi-trillion-dollar global money supply had long since shed its ties to gold or any other tangible asset. Money had gone virtual, and reattaching it to gold made as much historical sense, it seemed, as instant-messaging by pigeon post. But when a slick new digital-gold app for the iPhone shipped in 2009, it allowed holders of GoldMoney—a gold-backed currency, with more than $631 million worth of bullion in its London and Zurich vaults—to touch their iPhone screens and instantly transfer as little as a centigram of gold

(about thirty cents worth) to other GoldMoney users, leading many to rethink the gold standard.

» Bruce Sterling, futurist and science-fiction writer, predicts that price tags will be replaced by radio frequency tags that will calculate a price when they are touched. In his view, prices will rise and fall from minute to minute according to supply and demand. Sterling also predicts that offshore banking will be replaced by "data havens" tucked into satellites, and money will be encrypted so that only its rightful owner is able to spend it.

hen it comes to other people's money, we as a society take a clearly voyeuristic approach. It may be impolite to raise the subject of money in social conversation, but that doesn't stop us from leaping across checkout counters to grab up the latest tabloids for financial gossip about how much money Jennifer Aniston is getting per picture or the latest dirt on the wealthiest women in entertainment. Who are the richest people in America and how much money do they really have? How exactly did they get it? Are they really so different from the rest of us?

Most important, we wonder what they do with all that money. The answers are surprising, and they range from outrageous extravagances like yachts fitted with swimming pools and elevators to meaningful contributions to society from our greatest philanthropists. Some spend little, as our list of self-proclaimed frugal celebrities attests.

This chapter takes a look at the spending habits of the rich and famous but also contains some darker accounts: stories of lottery winners who went bust, some of the more unsavory methods by which folks come upon their fortunes, and mistakes that were made along the way. The stories of those who struck it rich overnight—only to be struck down just as quickly—are intended as cautionary tales for us all in the hopes that we learn, in looking at other people's money, how better to care for our own.

HIGHEST PAID PRESIDENTS AND PRIME MINISTERS

AROUND THE WORLD

Even heads of state have been hit by the recession. If they haven't already done so, most have plans to cut their own salaries. Here are the salaries for eight head honchos for the year 2008 in U.S. dollars:

LEE HSIEN LOONG
Prime Minister of Singapore
Annual salary: $2.46 million

BARACK OBAMA
President of the United States
Annual salary: $400,000

KEVIN RUDD
Prime Minister of Australia
Annual salary: $330,300

ANGELA MERKEL
Chancellor of Germany
Annual salary: $307,340

NICOLAS SARKOZY
President of France
Annual salary: $304,800

STEPHEN HARPER
Prime Minister of Canada
Annual salary: $280,000

GORDON BROWN
Prime Minister of the United Kingdom
Annual salary: $238,266

VLADIMIR PUTIN
Prime Minister of Russia
Annual salary: $81,190

U.S. PRESIDENTIAL AND VICE PRESIDENTIAL SALARIES

(exclusive of perquisites)

YEAR ESTABLISHED	PRESIDENT	VICE PRESIDENT
1789	$25,000	$5,000
1873	$50,000	$10,000
1906	$50,000	$12,000
1909	$75,000	$12,000
1946	$75,000	$20,000
1949	$100,000 $50,000*	$30,000 $10,000*
1951	$100,000 $50,000*	$35,000 $10,000*
1953	$100,000 $50,000**	$35,000 $10,000**
1964	$100,000 $50,000**	$43,000 $10,000**
1969	$200,000 $50,000**	$62,500 $10,000**
1979	$200,000 $50,000*	$62,500 $10,000**
1994	$200,000 $50,000*	$171,000 $10,000**
2001	$400,000	$175,400
2003	$400,000	$198,600

* non-taxable expense account
** taxable expense account

FAMOUS AMERICAN BANK ROBBERS

When Isaac Davis pulled off the first American bank robbery in 1798, he had no way of knowing that he was starting a tradition. One would think that modern technology has all but eliminated bank robberies, but they would be mistaken. Today bank robberies are still a problem, especially in urban areas where bank branches are concentrated. In 2007, for instance, nearly 1,500 bank robberies took place. Yes, they still use notes, and yes, they still take hostages. But they no longer ride off on horses, and we no longer glorify them as we once did by making heroes of these criminals.

BELOW: "Jackrabbit" Dillinger was able to leap over tall bank barriers.

MA BARKER (1873–1935)
Kate Barker employed her own kids, who formed the Barker-Karpis Gang, to execute a number of robberies and kidnappings between 1931 and 1935. She has been portrayed in numerous films, books, and comics as a "tough broad" criminal mastermind.

WILLIAM DADDANO SR.
(1912–1975)
A.k.a. "William Russo" and "Willie Potatoes," Daddano worked for the Chicago mob and was a leader of a gang whose members included the notorious Salvatore Giancana ("Sam," "Momo," or "Mooney") and Sam "Teets" Batagla. At the age of twenty-four, he had already accumulated nine counts of bank robbery, larceny, and auto theft. He was heavily involved in gambling concerns.

EMMETT DALTON (1871–1937)
Dalton and his brother Bob were best known as leaders of the Dalton Gang, whose criminal activities ravaged Oklahoma. The band enjoyed success until one day in 1892 when they attempted to rob two banks in Coffeyville at the same time. The armed citizens of the town ambushed them as they attempted to leave the banks, and four members of the gang, including Bob and another brother, Grattan, were killed. Emmett was sentenced to life in prison but was released after fourteen years. In 1937, he published a book entitled *When the Daltons Rode*.

BENNIE (?–1939)
AND STELLA
MAE DICKSON
(1922–1995)
During an eight-month period in 1938, this husband and wife team stole more than $50,000 from American banks. Bennie and "Sure Shot" Stella embarked on a life of crime on Stella's sixteenth birthday, robbing a South Dakota bank. Bennie was killed by an FBI agent, and Stella was eventually arrested.

JOHN DILLINGER (1903–1934)
Nicknamed "Jackrabbit" for his ability to leap over tall bank barriers, Dillinger has the distinction of being

the first criminal to win the FBI's "Public Enemy #1" designation. During his colorful career, he robbed two dozen banks and four police stations. He escaped captivity twice, and his exploits were followed by the population with zeal. Dillinger was eventually killed as he was leaving a movie theater.

JOHN DILLINGER:

"All my life I wanted to be a bank robber. Carry a gun and wear a mask. Now that it's happened, I guess I'm just about the best bank robber they ever had. And I sure am happy."

"I rob banks for a living, what do you do?"

"My buddies wanted to be firemen, farmers, or policemen, something like that. Not me, I just wanted to steal people's money!"

"Now nobody get nervous, you ain't got nothing to fear. You're being robbed by the John Dillinger Gang, that's the best there is!"

"These few dollars you lose here today are going to buy you stories to tell your children and great-grandchildren. This could be one of the big moments in your life; don't make it your last!"

CHARLES ARTHUR "PRETTY BOY" FLOYD (1904–1934)

Floyd was just eighteen when he robbed his first bank. He managed to get away with it but wasn't so lucky when he tried to rob a grocery. It was after spending five years in prison that Floyd was able to dedicate himself to his career, robbing thirty banks and killing ten men. He was eventually killed by authorities, but not before he had become something of a folk hero, known to be always well groomed and polite to his victims. Woody Guthrie's song "Pretty Boy Floyd" recounts the tale.

FRANK (1843–1915) AND JESSE JAMES (1847–1882)

The most famous robbers of all time, immortalized in both film and song, executed the country's first daytime bank heist, and they perfected the art of train robbery. Despite their exploits, a statue stands in their honor in Kentucky, the only such memorial for an outlaw. It is said that their career was inspired by the killing they witnessed during the Civil War. Their escapades included stints with the James-Younger Gang. Their career lasted for fifteen years until Jesse's death.

HARRY LONGABAUGH (1867–1908? 1937?) AND ROBERT LEROY PARKER (1866–1908)

Harry was just fifteen when he got caught stealing a horse in Sundance, Wyoming. He lost his freedom over it, but he gained his famous nickname, the Sundance Kid. After a short stint in jail, he became associated with Parker, a.k.a. Butch Cassidy, and the two rode with the Wild Bunch gang, robbing banks and trains, always with Pinkertons following close behind. Sundance and Cassidy were eventually tracked to Bolivia. Legend has it that they were both killed there in 1908, but reports abound that Longabaugh escaped back to the United States and died of cancer in 1937. Robert Redford and Paul Newman immortalized the duo in the 1969 film *Butch Cassidy and the Sundance Kid*.

GEORGE "BUGS" MORAN (1896–1957)

In addition to robbing banks, Moran was also famous for cashing counterfeit checks and for bootlegging. He was well known as Al Capone's archenemy, and the famous Saint Valentine's Day Massacre that took place in 1929 comprised their faceoff. Seven members of Moran's gang were left dead, but Moran survived. He died of lung cancer in Leavenworth Prison.

GEORGE "BABY FACE" NELSON (1908–1934)

He was the FBI's "Public Enemy #1" in the 1930s, and he'd already dabbled in his craft by the time he was twelve. His arrest record began the very next year, and after a lucrative solo career in crime, he landed a membership with the Dalton Gang. He suffered a violent death in 1934 after a police chase. Mickey Rooney played the title role in the 1935 film *Baby Face Nelson*; C. Thomas Howell starred in the 1995 remake.

BONNIE PARKER (1910–1934) AND CLYDE BARROW (1909–1934)

The legendary partners in crime met in 1930. Clyde had been arrested for burglary, but he escaped using a gun that Bonnie had slipped him. He was caught but paroled in 1932, and it was then that the couple embarked on a career of robbery and violence. They were killed by a hail of FBI gunfire in 1934 and were promptly elevated to folklore status. The real Bonnie and Clyde looked nothing like Faye Dunaway and Warren Beatty, who played them in the 1967 movie.

J. L. HUNTER "RED" ROUNTREE (1912–2004)

Believed to be the oldest active bank robber in history, Rountree was ninety-one when he was finally arrested in 2003 after a string of bank robberies that stretched from Florida to Missouri. Rountree had plenty to catch up on: He began his criminal career in 1996 at the age of eighty-four. He received a twelve-year prison sentence but eluded authorities again by dying the following year.

HENRY STARR (1874–1921)

Horse thief, train and bank robber, and killer Starr escaped the noose twice during his lifetime by slipping through legal technicalities. He is especially noted for being the first robber to use a getaway car, and he played himself in a 1919 silent movie called *A Debtor to the Law*. He was killed while robbing a bank in Arkansas.

WILLIE SUTTON (1901–1980)

He was known as "The Actor" for his talent with disguises, and executed bank robberies dressed in costume. He posed as a guard, a policeman, a diplomat, and a window cleaner in the course of robbing banks and jewelry stores. He landed in prison numerous times, but reverted back to his first love—stealing money—every time. In his 1953 autobiography *I, Willie Sutton*, he estimated that he had stolen more than $2,000,000 from banks. When asked why he robbed banks, he replied simply, "Because that's where the money is."

THE CRIME OF THE CENTURY

When it happened, it was the largest robbery in history. An eleven-member gang robbed the Brinks Building in Boston of $1.2 million in cash and more than $1.5 million in checks, and left barely a clue behind at the scene. They had attempted the robbery six times before but each time felt that circumstances just weren't right. On January 17, 1950, the stars were aligned, and the gang, dressed in peacoats and Halloween masks, finally pulled it off. The gang then separated, but various members continued their lives of crime, and paid for it with incarceration. One of them, Joseph "Specs" O'Keefe, finally decided to confess after being seriously wounded in a police shoot-out. In 1956, authorities finally apprehended members of the gang, but only $58,000 of the $2.7 million was ever recovered. It is believed that the rest of the money remains buried somewhere in Minnesota.

ALL ABOUT PONZI SCHEMES

Ponzi schemes are a type of illegal pyramid money scam named for Charles Ponzi, a Boston businessman who duped thousands of New England residents into investing in a postage stamp speculation scheme back in the 1920s. Ponzi thought he could take advantage of differences between U.S. and foreign currencies used to buy and sell international mail coupons. He told investors that he could provide a 40 percent return in just ninety days, compared with 5 percent for bank savings accounts. What he was doing, however, was using money from new investors to pay dividends to previous investors, an illegal scheme known as "robbing Peter to pay Paul." Ponzi was deluged with funds from investors, taking in $1 million during one three-hour period. Though a few early investors were paid off to make the scheme look legitimate, an investigation revealed that Ponzi had only purchased about $30 worth of the international mail coupons.

After his operation went bust, Ponzi was sent to prison for five years. The State of Massachusetts sentenced him to an additional nine years after his release, but he fled the country. Ponzi spent the remainder of his life in Brazil, in poverty and ill health.

Decades later, the Ponzi scheme continues to work on the unsuspecting. Here are some of the most notorious practitioners.

WILLIAM MILLER

In 1899, New York con artist William Miller bilked investors out of $1 million, approximately $25 million in today's dollars. Miller claimed he had an inside track on the stock market and promised investors a return of 500 percent on their money in the first year alone. He paid off the initial investors but his scheme was soon exposed when a newspaper suspected him of wrongdoing. Miller spent the next ten years in prison.

DONA BRANCA

Maria Branca dos Santos, a.k.a. "Dona Branca," was a poor Portuguese woman who in 1970 decided to open her own "bank." To make her bank appealing to customers, she guaranteed an interest rate of 10 percent per month, and thousands of clients, many of whom were poor, entrusted their savings to her.

Her scheme lasted more than fourteen years, and as a result, she became known as "The People's Banker." Dona Branca was convicted of fraud and sentenced to ten years in prison. She died alone, blind, and in poverty.

In 1993, her crime inspired a Portuguese soap opera titled *A Banqueira do Povo*, or *The People's Banker*.

DAVID DOMINELLI

In 1985, a San Diego currency trader named David Dominelli bilked more than a thousand investors out of $80 million. Dominelli's girlfriend, Nancy Hoover, was popular in high society, and she gave him an inside track on some of the wealthiest marks. He pleaded guilty after his arrest and was sentenced to twenty years in prison.

SERGEY MAVRODI

Sergey Mavrodi, a Russian scammer, along with his brother Vyacheslav Mavrodi and his future wife, founded the MMM company in the early 1990s. MMM promised dividends of 1,000 percent. The Mavrodis promoted themselves in television ads and initially delivered on their promise. At the height of its success, MMM was taking in more than $11 million a day. Word of mouth as well as their extremely aggressive ad campaign kept the scheme going for nine years, during which time they took in $1.5 billion from at least two million investors. The Mavrodis were eventually arrested for tax evasion but claimed that the government was to blame for investor losses. Sergey Mavrodi then ran for and was elected to office in the Duma, the Russian house of parliament, thereby obtaining parliamentary immunity. This was later revoked, and Mavrodi was sentenced to four and a half years in a penal colony.

REED SLATKIN

Scientology minister Reed Slatkin, a cofounder of Earthlink, posed as an experienced investment advisor and convinced a number of A-list Hollywood types and corporate executives to let him invest their money. Working out of his garage, Slatkin cheated his clients out of roughly $593 million. He created phony statements and fake brokerage firms to cover up his dealings. In 2002,

he was finally busted by the SEC.

SYED SIBTUL HASSAN SHAH

In 2005, Syed Sibtul Hassan Shah, a Pakistani high school teacher, convinced his friends and neighbors to give him their savings, which he would double in just fifteen days based on a new stock program he had learned in Dubai. When he began repaying some of his investors with the money promised, word spread, and more than three thousand people were drawn into the "Double Shah" scheme to the tune of nearly $1 billion. When he was finally charged with fraud in 2007, thousands of trusting citizens took to the streets to protest his arrest.

LOU PEARLMAN

In 2006, it was revealed that former boy-band impresario Lou Pearlman (of N'Sync and Back Street Boys fame) stole $300 million in investor capital over a period of twenty years. In addition, he sold shares to two companies, Trans Continental Airlines Travel Services and Trans Continental Airlines Inc., as well as several other companies, all of which existed on paper only. To perfect his scheme and cover his tracks, Pearlman even went so far as to create a fake accounting firm and German bank. Pearlman was arrested in Indonesia on June 14, 2007. On May 21, 2008, Pearlman was convicted and is currently serving (up to) twenty-five years in a federal prison.

ABOVE: The Madoff urinal gave some victims a way to fight back, although their investments had already gone down the toilet.

NORMAN HSU

On November 27, 2007, Democratic fundraiser Norman Hsu was indicted for operating a $60 million Ponzi fraud. Hsu used his charm, educational credentials, and a list of companies he supposedly owned to attract his victims. He guaranteed his investors a high rate of return for a short-term investment. In order to boost his profile and credentials he asked his investors to help him finance various election campaigns, implying that their other investments with him might suffer if they didn't help.

BERNIE MADOFF

The $50 billion fraud perpetrated by Madoff was the most outrageous Ponzi scheme in history. Madoff supposedly conducted trades and other stock market activities for broker-dealers, banks, financial institutions, and numerous charitable organizations. However, on December 11, 2008, it was revealed that Madoff never conducted a single trade and that, like Charles Ponzi, he was "robbing Peter to pay Paul." His reputation as a businessman and former non-executive chairman of the NASDAQ stock exchange gave him the reputation he needed to perpetuate his scheme, and helped him attract an extremely wealthy clientele that included numerous celebrities. On March 12, 2009, Madoff pled guilty to an eleven-count criminal complaint, admitting to defrauding thousands of investors. Madoff's high-profile investors included many celebrities as well as institutions such as Elie Wiesel's Foundation For Humanity, Yeshiva University, and Tufts University.

TOM PETTERS

In 2009, Minnesota businessman Tom Petters was indicted by a federal grand jury on twenty counts of fraud, conspiracy, and money laundering stemming from his alleged role in a thirteen-year, $3.5 billion Ponzi ring. He had promised fat returns to investors who lent him money to purchase surplus merchandise, which he would then resell to famous retailers. But a federal indictment stated that "There were no such purchases or resale. . . . Mr. Petters used the money to maintain an extravagant lifestyle."

19 OF BERNARD MADOFF'S HIGH-PROFILE VICTIMS

Madoff's scheme left thousands of investors shocked and broke, and some have reported serious psychological problems and sleeplessness since the scam was uncovered. Here are just a few of the many celebs and others who were taken in by Madoff:

1. Barbara Bach, actress and the wife of former Beatles drummer Ringo Starr
2. Kevin Bacon and wife Kyra Sedgwick, actors
3. Norman Braman, former Philadelphia Eagles owner
4. Leonard Feinstein, cofounder of retailer Bed Bath & Beyond
5. Jerome Fisher, founder of the Nine West shoe company
6. Zsa Zsa Gabor, actress
7. Phyllis George, former Miss America
8. Avram and Carol Goldberg, former owners of the Stop & Shop supermarket chain
9. Saul Katz, co-owner of the New York Mets
10. Jeff Katzenberg, film company DreamWorks CEO
11. Larry King, talk-show host
12. Henry Kissinger, former Secretary of State
13. Sandy Koufax, former Los Angeles Dodger pitcher
14. Sen. Frank Lautenberg
15. John Malkovich, actor
16. Larry Silverstein, New York developer who is working with partners to rebuild the World Trade Center
17. Steven Spielberg, film producer and director
18. Tim Teufel, former baseball player
19. Mort Zuckerman, chairman of real-estate firm Boston Properties and owner of the New York Daily News and U.S. News & World Report

8 RAGS-TO-RICHES STORIES

We love rags-to-riches stories. They give us hope and seemingly enforce the American dream and the idea that in this country, at least, one can rise above one's class. Forrest Gump, Eddie Murphy in *Trading Places*, and George Bailey in *It's a Wonderful Life* endear us to themselves simply because they struggle—just as we all do. Here are some real-life stories that inspire us, entertain us, and sometimes make us green with envy.

1. OPRAH WINFREY (1954–)

Oprah was born to unwed teenage parents in Mississippi and was raised by her grandmother, who was poor and unable to provide for her sufficiently, but she did teach Oprah how to read before age three. When Oprah turned six, she relocated to the city of Milwaukee to live with her mother. She did well academically but was rebellious and ran away from home. She was then sent to live with her father in Tennessee, where she proved to be a fine student, impressing all who knew her. She became a radio host, a news anchor, an actress, and finally a television host. Today she is a media icon and one of the richest people in the world.

2. ANDREW CARNEGIE (1835–1919)

Though Andrew Carnegie proved to be one of the titans of the industrial age, he was once a poor boy from Scotland. His father was a hand-loom weaver, but once the industrialization of society reached Scotland, his father's work was no longer needed. At thirteen, Andrew and his family moved to America and he got a job at a cotton mill. He worked twelve-hour days, six days a week. Eventually Andrew got a job as a telegraph messenger. Because of his great work ethic, someone from the Pennsylvania Railroad Company offered him a job, which allowed him to earn more money and make his way up the corporate ladder. He soon started investing in railroad companies, and then hit the jackpot by investing in the steel industry. His investments afforded him his own steel company and a $500 million ($120 billion in today's money) fortune.

3. JIM CARREY (1962–)

Jim Carrey was born in Ontario, Canada, to a financially secure family, but as Jim got older, his family's situation deteriorated. Jim had to work eight hours a day while attending school. Still, it was very hard to keep the family stable, and they found themselves living in a camper van. Eventually, Jim gathered the courage to pursue his dream of becoming a comedian. He did stand-up routines and loved it so much that he dropped out of high school. One gig led to another, and today he is among Hollywood's top paid actors.

4. H. WAYNE HUIZENGA (1937–)

Wayne was born in Chicago, Illinois, and soon learned that his father was not the male figure he should look up to. He abused his wife, and the family was troubled. Wayne dropped out of high school, trained with the Army reserves, and finally got a job collecting garbage. He eventually bought his own garbage truck and started his own company. Soon enough, Wayne's company was known all over the United States. He purchased Blockbuster stores, which became a huge success, and eventually merged it with Viacom. Throughout his lifetime, Wayne has founded three Fortune 500 Companies.

5. RICHARD BRANSON
(1960–)

Branson was born in Blackheath, London. His grandfather was a judge and he received a good education, but he didn't do well in school. Instead, he worked at growing Christmas trees and raising budgerigars (parakeets). Neither venture worked. But at sixteen, he set up a record mail-order business, and in 1972, he was able to open several record stores, which he called Virgin Records. In the 1980s, his stores flourished. Branson then created Virgin Atlantic Airwaves while expanding Virgin Records, which became a music label. Branson is now one of the richest people in the world, and his continued adventures are closely followed by the media.

6. J. K. ROWLING (1965–)

Rowling was born in Yate, Gloucestershire, England. She attended school and found her love for writing fantasy stories. Rowling moved from village to village many times and often traveled. In December of 1990, Rowling's mother died, and she moved to Porto, Portugal, in order to teach English as a foreign language. Before her mother's death, Rowling had already begun writing her first Harry Potter novel. In Portugal, Rowling married and had a daughter, but the couple separated in 1993. She then moved to Scotland, but her situation became progressively bleaker. She was diagnosed with clinical depression and often contemplated suicide. She was unemployed and living on welfare. Eventually, she was able to write and complete her first novel. Today, J. K. Rowling is worth about $1.1 billion and has sold more than 400 million books.

7. OZZY OSBOURNE (1948–)

Osbourne was born in Aston, Birmingham, U.K. His father was a toolmaker and his mother worked in a factory. He had five siblings. Osbourne didn't do well at school and was said to be dyslexic. At fifteen, he dropped out of school and became a construction site laborer. He worked as a plumber, as a toolmaker, and in a slaughterhouse and a car factory. He was accused of the burglary of a clothing store, and, unable to pay the fine, spent time in prison. Eventually, Osbourne would go on to become the singer of a local band, and many would recognize his talent. Soon enough with the help of friends, Ozzy was able to create his own band, Black Sabbath, one of the most influential heavy metal bands of all time.

8. JOHN D. ROCKEFELLER
(1839–1937)

Rockefeller was born in Richford, New York, one of six children. His father was a traveling salesman who challenged conventional morality. Throughout much of his life, Rockefeller's father tried to find tricks and schemes he could use in order to avoid hard work, or any work at all. His mother struggled to keep the home stable, especially when her husband was gone for weeks at a time. After John finished school, he got a job as a bookkeeper, where he made about $50 in three months. In 1859, he decided to start a business with a friend named Maurice B. Clark. The two established a firm and built an oil refinery. The refinery was run by two other men, but soon after, Rockefeller bought out the Clark brothers' firm and renamed it Rockefeller & Andrews. Soon his brother also bought into the oil business. By the end of it all, Rockefeller had founded the Standard Oil Company and became the world's first billionaire.

This was the *Forbes* lineup in 2009.

1. BILL GATES (1955–)

Chairman of Microsoft, which he cofounded with Paul Allen in 1975. He is consistently rated one of the world's wealthiest people and the wealthiest overall as of 2009.
Net worth: $40 billion

2. WARREN BUFFETT (1930–)

One of the world's most successful inventors and chairman and CEO of Berkshire Hathaway, a conglomerate holding company.
Net worth: $37 billion

3. CARLOS SLIM HELU (1940–)

Businessman Helu made his fortune in the telecommunications industry in Mexico and in a large portion of Latin America.
Net worth: $35 billion

4. LAWRENCE (LARRY) ELLISON (1944–)

American computer innovator and cofounder of the Oracle Corporation, known for his extravagant lifestyle.
Net worth: $22.5 billion

5. INGVAR KAMPRAD (1926–)

Swedish businessman and founder of the IKEA furniture company. He is known as the richest person in Europe.
Net worth: $22 billion

6. KARL ALBRECHT (1926–)

German businessman and founder, with his brother Theo, of the supermarket chain ALDI.
Net worth: $21.5 billion

7. MUKESH AMBANI (1957–)

Indian engineer and businessman. He is the chairman of Reliance Industries, the largest privately held industry in India. He also founded Reliance Communications, one of India's largest telecommunication companies.
Net worth: $19.5 billion

8. LAKSHMI MITTAL (1950–)

Indian industrialist and founder of Mittal Steel, but manages his business affairs from his home in England.
Net worth: $19.3 billion

9. THEO ALBRECHT (1922–)

Cofounder of the supermarket chain ALDI. He also owns Trader Joe's grocery stores in the United States.
Net worth: $18.8 billion

10. AMANCIO ORTEGA (1936–)

Spanish industrialist and founder of Inditex Group, one of the world's most successful fashion concerns. He is Spain's richest person.
Net worth: $18.3 billion

11. JIM WALTON (1948–)
Chairman of Arvest bank and the youngest son of Sam Walton, founder of Wal-Mart.
Net worth: $17.8 billion

12. ALICE WALTON (1949–)
Daughter of Sam Walton. In 1988, she founded the Llama Company, an investment bank, and later became the vice chairman of Jim Walton's Arvest bank.
Net worth: $17.6 billion

13. CHRISTY WALTON (1949–)
Wife of John T. Walton, who gained her wealth by inheritance after the passing of her husband.
Net worth: $17.6 billion

14. S. ROBSON WALTON (1945–)
Eldest son of Sam Walton. In 1969, he earned a law degree at Columbia University in New York City; he became the chairman of the board of Wal-Mart in 1992 after his father's passing.
Net worth: $17.6 billion

15. BERNARD ARNAULT (1949–)
French businessman and the richest person in France. He has served as chairman of Moët Hennessy, Louis Vuitton, Christian Dior, and Groupe Arnault SAS. He has also been involved in numerous other ventures, in both France and the United States.
Net worth: $16.5 billion

16. LI KA-SHING (1928–)
Businessman based in Hong Kong. He earned his fortune in telecommunications, shipping ports, and real estate development.
Net worth: $16.2 billion

17. MICHAEL BLOOMBERG (1942–)
American businessman and founder of Bloomberg L.P., a financial software services company, and is currently the mayor of New York City in his third term in office.
Net worth: $16 billion

18. STEFAN PERSSON (1947–)
Businessman who inherited his father's fashion apparel company, Hennes & Mauritz (H&M), and serves as its CEO.
Net worth: $14.5 billion

19. CHARLES KOCH (1935–)
American engineer and CEO of Koch Industries. As CEO, Koch has holdings in numerous American industries, making his Koch Industries the second largest privately held company in the United States. He and his brother, David, each own 42 percent of the company.
Net worth: $14 billion

20. DAVID KOCH (1940–)
Co-owner of Koch Industries. He now serves on the board of directors of the Cato Institute, a libertarian think tank.
Net worth: $14 billion

21. MICHAEL DELL (1965–)
Founder and CEO of Dell, Inc., which was the largest seller of personal computers during the 1980s and 1990s.
Net worth: $13.5 billion

22. LILIANE BETTENCOURT (1922–)
Inherited the L'Oréal cosmetic company and as its major shareholder became the wealthiest woman in Europe.
Net worth: $13.4 billion

23. PRINCE ALWALEED BIN TALAL ALSAUD (1955–)
Saudi Arabian prince and successful entrepreneur and investor, having earned most of his fortune in real estate and the stock market.
Net worth: $13.3 billion

24. MICHAEL OTTO (1943–)
Owner of the world's largest mail-order company, the Otto Group of Germany. His company benefited greatly by the advent of the Internet and is second only to Amazon.com in retail sales. He is also owner of the Crate & Barrel home-furnishings chain in the United States.
Net worth: $13.2 billion

25. DAVID THOMSON (1960–)
Canadian chairman of Thomson Reuters, a media giant that functions in more than ninety countries around the world. He also serves as the chairman of Woodridge Investment Corporation.
Net worth: $13 billion

26. DONALD BREN (1965–)

Businessman who made his fortune in real estate and served as the chairman of the Irvine Co. He is known as the wealthiest real estate developer in the United States.
Net worth: $12 billion

27. SERGEY BRIN (1973–)

American computer scientist born in Moscow. In 1998, he cofounded Google, Inc., the world's largest Internet company, along with Larry Page.
Net worth: $12 billion

28. LARRY PAGE (1973–)

Cofounder of Google, Inc. He attended a Ph.D. program at Stanford University, where he worked on the mathematical principles of the World Wide Web. It was during this time that he developed the initial stages of Google. He met Sergey Brin in 1995.
Net worth: $12 billion

29. STEVEN BALLMER (1973–)

Executive who joined the Microsoft Company in 1980, and became its CEO in 2000.
Net worth: $11 billion

30. GERALD CAVENDISH GROSVENOR, SIXTH DUKE OF WESTMINSTER (1951–)

Member of British royal family who gained his fortune by inheritance, but has also served as the chancellor of the University of Chester. He is known as the wealthiest real estate developer in the United Kingdom.
Net worth: $11 billion

31. GEORGE SOROS (1951–)

American businessman, investor, philanthropist, and political activist.
Net worth: $11 billion

32. PAUL ALLEN (1953–)

Cofounded Microsoft Inc. with Bill Gates in 1975. Since that time he has been involved in more than forty technology and media-oriented businesses.
Net worth: $10.5 billion

33. KWOK FAMILY

Owners of the largest real estate concern in Hong Kong, Sun Hung Kai Properties. Turmoil and disputes within the family, as well as falling real estate prices, have taken their toll on the family fortune in recent years.
Net worth: $10.5 billion

34. ANIL AMBANI (1959–)

Indian businessman with major interests in the Anil Dhiruhai Ambani Group and Reliance Industries, the largest private-sector conglomerate in India and the second largest in the world.
Net worth: $10.1 billion

35. ABIGAIL JOHNSON (1961–)

Johnson is an American businesswoman who worked her way up the corporate ladder and became president of Fidelity Investments. She went from answering phones at Fidelity in 1980 to becoming a research associate, stock analyst, portfolio manager, associate director, senior vice president, and by 2001 president.
Net worth: $10 billion

36. SUSANNE KLATTEN (1962–)

Germany's richest woman after her father passed away in 1982. She inherited 50.1 percent of her father's pharmaceutical company, Altana, and was able to purchase the remaining shares of the company by 2009.
Net worth: $10 billion

37. RONALD PERELMAN (1943–)

Businessman who made his fortune buying corporations on the brink of collapse and later reselling them for huge profits. He made his first acquisition during his freshman year at the Wharton School. Over the following years, he invested in banking, Marvel Comics, communications, and several other ventures.
Net worth: $10 billion

38. HANS RAUSING (1926–)

Swedish-born businessman who inherited Tetra Pak, a liquid food packaging company that his father founded. He later went on to become an investor in Russian and Ukrainian companies.
Net worth: $10 billion

39. BIRGIT RAUSING (1924–)

She, along with Hans Rausing, inherited half of her father-in-law's company.
Net worth: $9.9 billion

40. MICHELE FERRERO (1925–)

Italian chocolatier and owner of Ferrero SpA, one of the leading candy companies in Europe. He is Italy's wealthiest person.
Net worth: $9.5 billion

25 HIGHEST PAID SPORTS STARS

Earnings are based on salary, winnings, endorsements, bonuses, and appearances in 2008, as reported by SportsIllustrated.CNN.com.

1 Tiger Woods (golfer)
$127.9 million

2 Phil Mickelson (golfer)
$62.3 million

3 Lebron James (basketball player, Cleveland Cavaliers)
$40.4 million

4 Floyd Mayweather, Jr. (boxer)
$40.3 million

5 Kobe Bryant (basketball player, Los Angeles Lakers)
$35.5 million

6 Shaquille O'Neal (basketball player, Cleveland Cavaliers)
$35 million

7 Alex Rodriguez (baseball player, New York Yankees)
$35 million

8 Kevin Garnett (basketball player, Boston Celtics)
$31 million

9 Peyton Manning (football player, Indianapolis Colts)
$30.5 million

10 Derek Jeter (baseball player, New York Yankees)
$30 million

11 Allen Iverson (basketball player, Detroit Pistons)
$27.1 million

12 Kevin Durant (basketball player, Oklahoma City Thunder)
$26 million

13 Jeff Gordon (race car driver)
$26 million

14 Ben Roethlisberger (football player, Pittsburgh Steelers)
$25.2 million

15 Tracy McGrady (basketball player, Houston Rockets)
$25 million

16 Dwyane Wade (basketball player, Miami Heat)
$25 million

17 Carmelo Anthony (basketball player, Denver Nuggets)
$22.5 million

18 Tim Duncan (basketball player, San Antonio Spurs)
$22.5 million

19 Manny Ramirez (baseball player, Los Angeles Dodgers)
$22.5 million

20 Michael Finley (basketball player, San Antonio Spurs)
$22.2 million

21 Dwight Howard (basketball player, Orlando Magic)
$21.6 million

22 Jason Giambi (baseball player, Colorado Rockies)
$21.5 million

23 Jason Kidd (basketball player, Dallas Mavericks)
$21.2 million

24 Stephon Marbury (basketball player, currently a free agent)
$21 million

25 JaMarcus Russell (football player, Oakland Raiders)
$20.9 million

SPENDING HABITS OF COLLEGE STUDENTS

While some students struggle to make ends meet, the stereotypical college experience of eating ramen noodles, wearing clothes from Goodwill, and drinking cheap beer is quickly disappearing. Much of this can be explained by the changing demographics of today's students. Less than half (43 percent) of college students are eighteen to twenty-one. The typical college student today is in his or her mid-twenties, lives either at home or on campus, and has a job. Students no longer expect to complete college in four consecutive years, and many fluctuate between full-time and part-time study over a period of five to seven years. The older the student, the more money he or she generally has. Here, according to Stateuniversity.com, is a field guide to college spending habits:

1 By the time they reach college, full-time students represent more than $60 billion in buying power. This amount usually increases once the student graduates and becomes employed. Marketers who can successfully reach these young adults with a quality product, positive message, and clear value may enjoy decades of loyal purchasing and millions of dollars worth of free, word-of-mouth marketing.

2 The typical college student gets an average of $757 a month from jobs, parents, or other sources. Most money comes from work. Approximately 75 percent of students maintain jobs while attending school, earning $645 per month on average; 20 percent have secured an on-campus job; and 42 percent are spending school breaks working. Parents contribute, too, adding an average of $154 to a student's monthly income. A student spends more than $13,000 per year on average, 19 percent of which is discretionary. That adds up to a substantial $211 per month of discretionary spending.

3 Most students—70 percent of males and 75 percent of females—have one, two, or three credit cards.

4 Overall, data reveals college students to be savvy, capable, and influential consumers, balancing the rising cost of tuition with a hardy work ethic, spending a fair portion of their considerable discretionary income on high-end technology, and holding considerable sway over the purchasing decisions of their peers. College students spend most of their discretionary income on food. Students spend more than $11 billion a year on snacks and beverages.

5 Students rely on technology to access information, communicate with friends, and keep themselves entertained. These expenses are seen as necessities. The majority of college students (90 percent) own a computer, and two-thirds (65 percent) of those students have a broadband connection; 62 percent of college students own a stereo, a cell phone (77 percent), a printer (77 percent), and a television (84 percent). A large portion of income goes to cell phone service. The majority of students with cell phone service pay for extras such as text messaging (62 percent) and Internet access through their mobile phone (41 percent).

6 College students spend nearly $3 billion annually on entertainment: movies, DVDs, music, and video games. They spend $474 million on music sales, $658 million on theater tickets, and $341 million on games each year. At home and in the dorms, they're watching movies, spending $600 million to buy and $326 million to rent DVDs. In addition, it is estimated that the average student spends at least $50 per month on beer alone. And that all told, American college students spend $5.5 billion on alcohol.

7 Personal care is another big expense for college students, at $4 billion a year. In addition, they also spend a lot of their money on clothing and shoes—$5 billion a year.

TOP 10 U.S. BUSINESS SCHOOLS

Here, according to BusinessWeek.com, are the top business schools in the U.S. in 2010, along with the salaries their graduates were likely to expect.

1 Mendoza College of Business at Notre Dame University
Length of program: 3 years
Tuition per year: $38,477
Number of students: 1,750
Median starting salary for graduates: $55,000

2 McIntire School of Commerce at the University of Virginia
Length of program: 2 years
Tuition per year: $9,872
Number of students: 662
Median starting salary: $55,000

3 Sloan School of Management at the Massachusetts Institute of Technology
Length of program: 4 years
Tuition per year: $37,782
Number of students: 190
Median starting salary: $62,000

4 The Wharton School at the University of Pennsylvania
Length of program: 4 years
Tuition per year: $38,970
Number of students: 2,560
Median starting salary: $60,000

5 The Johnson School at Cornell University
Length of program: 4 years
Tuition per year: $21,814
Number of students: 692
Median starting salary: $55,000

6 Haas School of Business at the University of California Berkeley
Length of program: 2 years
Tuition per year: $10,333
Number of students: 653
Median starting salary: $55,000

7 Goizueta Business School at Emory University
Length of program: 2 years
Tuition per year: $38,036
Number of students: 652
Median starting salary: $53,000

8 Stephen M. Ross School of Business at the University of Michigan
Length of program: 2 years
Tuition per year: $11,645
Number of students: 1,074
Median starting salary: $59,000

9 Carroll School of Management at Boston College
Length of program: 4 years
Tuition per year: $39,130
Number of students: 1,970
Median starting salary: $55,000

10 McCombs School of Business at Texas University
Length of program: 4 years
Tuition per year: $9,808
Number of students: 3,914
Median starting salary: $54,000

HOW 16 WEALTHY YOUNG ENTREPRENEURS

MADE THEIR FORTUNES

1. SEAN BELNICK (1988–)

At the age of fourteen, Belnick started selling office chairs online. He started the business from his bedroom with $500. Six years later, BizChair.com had seventy-five employees and was taking in $24 million in annual revenues.
Net worth: $42 million

2. RYAN BLOCK (1982–)

Block is best known as the editor-in chief of Engadget.com, a blog that is known for the most thorough coverage of consumer electronics and technology. He is also a tech critic and commentator who is often quoted by the media. His comments have appeared in *Business Week*, the *Chicago Tribune*, the *New York Times*, the *Guardian*, the *London Times*, and the *Wall Street Journal*.
Net worth: $20 million

3. CATHERINE COOK (1987–) AND DAVID COOK (1988–)

The siblings were just seventeen and nineteen respectively when they started MyYearbook.com, a social networking Web site that was an immediate success. Within three years of its inception, it was third in ranking, behind Facebook and MySpace.
Combined net worth: $10 million

4. AODHAN CULLEN (1983–)

When he was sixteen, Cullen invented StatCounter, a type of software that kept track of the number of hits received by a Web site. By 2008, the company had more than 2 million customers, and today StatCounter monitors some three million Web sites.
Net worth: $18 million

5. DAVID HAUSER (1982–) AND SIAMAK TAGHADDOS (1983–)

These two met as undergrads at Babson College, famous for turning out successful entrepreneurs. They had both started their own companies while still in high school. Together they founded GotVMail, which provides small businesses with fancy-schmancy voicemail so that even the smallest business can sound like a large operation. The company was an immediate success.
Combined net worth: $8 million

6. RISHI KACKER (1983–) AND MATT PAUKER (1983–)

For more than a year, Kacker and Pauker worked on their entry for a business-plan competition. Winning the competition gave them access to a host of mentors, and they eventually created Voltage, a successful security software business.
Combined net worth: $12 million

7. DAVID LEVICH (1982–)

David Levich and his buddy Dan Gershon were both fans of hip-hop style when they were in high school. While still there, they started selling hip-hop watches and jewelry on eBay, and they eventually created their own Web site, Icedoutgear.com, expanding the business to include apparel and other furnishings. Today the company is among the most successful online retailers.
Net worth: $10 million

8. ALEXANDER LEVIN (1984–)

While still in his teens, Levin launched ImageShack, an image-hosting Web site that quickly became one of the most popular of its kind. According to Neilsen Net Ratings, it was the fastest-growing Web brand in 2006.
Net worth: $56 million

9. ANDREW MICHAEL (1980–)

He was only seventeen when he started up the Web technology firm Fasthosts.co.uk as a school project. Today he owns 75 percent of the popular U.K. firm.
Net worth: $110 million

10. MATT MICKIEWICZ
(1983–)

Mickiewicz first started dabbling in business at the age of fifteen. He is the creator of 99designs.com, the largest online marketplace for graphic design services and a book publisher.
Net worth: $18 million

11. MATT MULLENWEG
(1984–)

Mullenweg is widely known as a wunderkind of the Internet. When he started blogging at the age of seventeen, he used open source software to develop his own Web tools, which became what we know today as WordPress.org, the most successful blogging service in the world. Today it hosts 103 million global visitors, more than five times that of its main rival, Typepad.com.
Net worth: $40 million

12. BLAKE ROSS (1985–) AND DAVID HYATT (1977–)

These two software developers created the Mozilla Web browser, among other Internet innovations. Ross created his first Web site at the age of ten and was already working for Netscape by the time he was fifteen. David was on the team that developed the Safari Web browser and WebKit.
Combined net worth: $120 million

13. ROBERT SMALL (1983–)

Small and a friend, Tihan Presbie, founded Miniclip, a U.K. gaming company, from Small's bedroom in 2001. Today his company has 34 million users and is one of the biggest gaming networks in the world.
Net worth: $23 million

14. ANGELO SOTIRA (1981–)

With pals Scott Jarkoff, Matthew Stephens, and others, Sotira founded deviantART.com, an online community that showcases various forms of art. Launched in 2000, it had more than 10 million members by 2009 and today receives around 105,000 submissions per day.
Net worth: $75 million

15. JEREMY STOPPELMAN (1979–) AND RUSSEL SIMMONS (1980–)

Simmons graduated from the Illinois Mathematics and Science Academy at sixteen and was the first engineer to be hired by PayPal. Stoppelman dropped out of Harvard Business School. Together they created Yelp.com, a site that invites people to review everything from restaurants to medical services.
Combined net worth: $10 million

16. MARK ZUCKERBERG
(1984–)

The Harvard computer science major created one of the Internet's most popular Web sites, Facebook.com, along with his roommates, Dustin Moskovitz and Chris Hughes. In 2008, *Time* magazine named him as one of the world's most influential people.
Net worth: $700 million

AVERAGE ALLOWANCES FOR KIDS IN THE U.S.

The most common weekly allowance amount for kids between five and thirteen is $5 a week. Here are average allowances for kids aged three to eighteen, according to kidsmoney.org.

AGE	AVERAGE ALLOWANCE
3	$3.20
4	$2.85
5	$3.15
6	$3.85
7	$4.10
8	$4.32
9	$5.52
10	$7.18
11	$7.92
12	$9.58
13	$9.52
14	$13.47
15	$15.57
16	$17.84
17	$30.66
18	$40.10

13 OF THE WORLD'S WEALTHIEST COLLEGE DROPOUTS

According to CNBC.com in 2007:

1. ROMAN ABRAMOVICH
Moscow State Auto Transport Institute, Moscow, Russia
Abramovich made his fortune as the main owner of the private investment company Millhouse, in Russia. He is also the owner of the Chelsea Football Club, an English Premier League soccer team, and is currently the governor of Chukotka.
Net worth: $18.7 billion

2. SHELDON ADELSON
City College of New York, New York
Adelson owns and operates upscale gambling casinos. He purchased the Sands Casino, tore it down in 1996, and replaced it with the Venetian Casino resort in 1999.
Net worth: $26 billion

3. PAUL ALLEN
Washington State University, Pullman, Washington
Allen, along with Bill Gates, founded Microsoft, the world's largest software developer in 1975. He and Gates eventually became co-owners of the Seattle Seahawks football team and the Portland Trailblazers basketball team.
Net worth: $18 billion

4. MICHAEL DELL
University of Texas, Austin, Texas
Dell founded the second largest computer company in the world, named after himself. He started his first company, PCs Limited, with only $1,000 in his pocket.
Net worth: $13.5 billion

5. LARRY ELLISON
University of Illinois, Chicago, Illinois
Ellison was the cofounder of Oracle Systems and served as its CEO for more than thirty years.
Net worth: $22.5 billion

6. BILL GATES
Harvard University, Cambridge, Massachusetts
Cofounder of the Microsoft Corporation, Gates is ranked as the world's wealthiest man. He did eventually get an honorary degree from Harvard in 2007. In the first line of his address, Gates addressed his father: "Dad, I always told you I'd come back and get my degree."
Net worth: $56 billion

7. DAVID GEFFEN
University of Texas, Austin, Texas
Often referred to as Hollywood's richest man, Geffen made it big at Asylum Records in 1970 and at Geffen Records in 1980. In 1995, along with Steven Spielberg and Jeffrey Katzenberg, Geffen cofounded the DreamWorks film studio.
Net worth: $4.7 billion

8. STANLEY HO
University of Hong Kong, Hong Kong, People's Republic of China
Sometimes referred to as "The King of Gambling," Ho made his fortune by building and running gambling casinos in Macau and Hong Kong after receiving a government-granted monopoly for gaming. His casinos account for one-third of Macau's gross domestic product.
Net worth: $7 billion

9. CARL ICAHN
actually has a B. S. degree from Princeton University but dropped out of New York University Medical School
Icahn earned his fortune as one of the world's most successful investors.
Net worth: $13 billion

10. STEVE JOBS
Reed College, Portland, Oregon
Steve Jobs, the CEO of Apple Computers, and the man who introduced the iPhone, iPod, and iMac, dropped out after one semester.
Net worth: $5.7 billion

11. DONALD NEWHOUSE
Syracuse University, Syracuse, New York

Along with brother Samuel, Donald Newhouse owns the *New Yorker* magazine, *Vanity Fair*, and portions of television's Learning and Discovery Channels.
Net worth: $7.3 billion

12. JACK TAYLOR
Washington University, St. Louis, Missouri

Taylor dropped out of college in the early 1940s to join the Navy as a fighter pilot. In 1957, he became the founder and CEO of Enterprise Rent-A-Car.
Net worth: $13.9 billion

13. YC WANG
High School Dropout

In 1978, equipped with only an elementary school education, Wang founded Formosa Plastics, now one of Asia's largest Petrochemical companies.
Net worth: $5.1 billion

THE ART OF THE DEAL

J. S. G. Boggs will never run out of money. Born Steve Litzner, he's an artist known for his drawings of banknotes, which he uses to purchase goods. For instance, he will use a drawing of a $10 bill to purchase ten dollars' worth of goods. If change is due, he takes it in currency and coins. The system works because "Bogg Notes," as they are known, are worth far more than their face value. The notes have become collectible, although Boggs won't sell directly to collectors. Although he denies that his bills are counterfeit (for one thing, they are blank on one side), Boggs has been arrested for producing his funny money in England and Australia, and the U.S. Secret Service has confiscated much of his work. Boggs himself thinks of his work as performance art that examines the real value of money. "It's all an act of faith," he has said. "Nobody knows what a dollar is, what the word means, what holds the thing up, what it stands for.... That's ... what my work is about."

Boggs's complete adventures are recounted in *Boggs: A Comedy of Values* (University of Chicago Press, 2000) by Lawrence Weschler.

21 REALLY GROSS THINGS PEOPLE HAVE DONE

FOR MONEY

What would you do for a million dollars? How about half a mil? What about $50,000? "Chicken feed," you say? Contestants on the NBC TV show *Fear Factor*, which appeared in the United States in 2001 (it was based on a Dutch show), wouldn't agree. This game show from hell gave people opportunities to sink to unimaginable levels, all for a buck, fifty thousand of them, actually. Call it extreme greed, call it depravity. Hollywood calls it entertainment. Here are some of the stunts that contestants performed:

1 Ate a pizza with a crust made from cow bile, coagulated blood paste for sauce, rancid cheese, and topping choices like live red worms and fish eyes.

2 Lay down in a Plexiglas tank and were covered by four hundred rats. They then had to retrieve ten chicken feet from the tank, using only their mouths.

3 Ate bull's testicles.

4 Were stuck inside a morgue drawer, in a body bag filled with giant hissing cockroaches, flesh-eating worms, crickets, and stink beetles.

5 Ate cave-dwelling spiders.

6 Stuck their faces in a jar full of cow eyeballs, picked them up without using their hands and punctured them with their teeth, letting all of the juices fall into a cup. Then drank it all.

7 Ate horse rectum.

8 Ate "spaghetti" made up of live night crawlers and coagulated blood balls.

9 Were covered in hundreds of pounds of cow intestines, which they then had to puncture with their mouth, suck out the liquid, fill a glass with it, and then drink the contents.

10 Ate ten slugs, followed by a shot of cow bile.

11 Ate live beetles.

12 Ate five earthworms and one super-worm in a martini glass.

13 Ate live crickets.

14 Ate a pig's liver, kidney, heart, ear, tongue, or snout.

15 Bobbed for plums in a tank containing fifty water snakes and a boa constrictor.

16 Ate a raw cow brain.

17 Put their faces into a box containing 25,000 live wax worms in order to retrieve twenty chicken feet using only their mouths.

18 Drank a shake made of pig brains, pig intestine, animal fat, rooster testes, cow eyes, veal brain, spleen, cod liver oil, bile, and fish sauce.

19 Stuck their heads in a Plexiglas box containing twenty-four rats and reached into the cage with their hands to pick up black and white rats and put them in separate cages.

20 Ate raw pig uteruses.

21 Drank cocktails made with red snapper fish eggs.

TOP 10 GAME SHOW WINNERS OF ALL TIME

Game shows have been transfixing audiences since 1924, when *Time* magazine sponsored a radio show called *Pop Question*. When television came along in the 1940s, game shows followed. *Spin to Win*, *Hit the Jackpot*, and *Break the Bank* were among the most popular of the many shows on the air. These shows, like those that followed—*The Big Payoff*, *Strike It Rich*, *G.E. College Bowl*, *Play Your Hunch*, *The Price Is Right*, and *The $64,000 Question*, which distinguished itself through scandal—all dealt in "fabulous prizes," everything from vacations, cars, and even homes, to modest amounts of cash. *The $20,000 Pyramid* raised the ante in 1976, and *Who Wants to Be a Millionaire?* did it again in 1999. Ironically, a million-dollar winner appears at the *bottom* of this list of top ten game-show winners.

1. KEN JENNINGS
(*Jeopardy!*, 2004)
$2.52 million

2. KEVIN OLMSTEAD
(*Who Wants to Be a Millionaire?*, 2001)
$2.2 million

3. ED TOUTANT
(*Who Wants to Be a Millionaire?*, 2001)
$1.86 million

4. DAVID LEGLER
(*Twenty-One*, 2000)
$1.77 million

5. CURTIS WARREN
(*Greed*, 2000)
$1.42 million

6. BRAD RUTTER
(*Jeopardy!*, 2001, 2002)
$1.16 million

7. JOHN CARPENTER
(*Who Wants to Be a Millionaire?*, 1999, 2000)
$1.25 million

8. RAHIM OBERHOLTZER
(*Twenty-One*, 2000)
$1.12 million

9. TIM HSIEH
(*It's Your Choice of a Lifetime*, 2000)
$1.04 million

10. DAN BLONSKY
(*Who Wants to Be a Millionaire?*, 2000)
$1 million

FOUND MONEY

What would you do if you found a million dollars? Here are the stories of ten people who did the right thing:

In October of 2007, DEBBIE COLE, 53, an employee at a waste operations plant in Pinellas County, Florida, found $65,000 that was about to be treated as garbage. The bag had fallen off the back of an armored truck.

MARK MORANT found $640,000 that had fallen from the back of an armored truck in 2001, and he thought hard and long—two days—before finally returning the money to the bank to which it belonged. News that the FBI had discovered his identity may have helped him to make his decision.

JOI LYN HONER was about to make a withdrawal from an ATM machine in Brigantine, New Jersey, in 2007 when she realized she didn't have to: Right there next to the machine sat $20,000 in crisp bills. Honer received a $500 reward for returning the money.

TODD LITTLE AND EDWIN WORK-MAN were collecting garbage on New Year's Eve 2004 in Hickory, North Carolina, when they noticed a bulging pocket on a shirt that had been thrown out. In it they discovered fifty-one $100 bills, no doubt someone's year-end bonus. The woman of the house, who had tossed out some of her husband's clothing without checking the pockets, will probably never make that mistake again.

KATSUMASA HIBINO of Nagoya, Japan, was in the process of installing his family in his new home when he discovered $10,000 wrapped in aluminum foil under a heating vent cover. He knew immediately that the money would have to be returned to the previous homeowner, who turned out to be an eighty-one-year-old widow. Appropriately, in Japanese, "Katsumasa" means "kind winner."

In 2007, JERRY MIKA awaited a $15 tax refund. What he received instead was a check for $2,245,342. Sure, the IRS would have discovered the error, but Mika could have cashed the check and laughed all the way to his Swiss bank. He considered it. But in the end, Mika returned the check. In return for his honesty, he received a polite thank-you.

In 2007, JATENDRA CHIRAG, 24, was on his way to work in Malvern, Arkansas, when he saw an envelope by the side of a road. Neatly bundled inside was $10,000. Chirag spent a day considering his options before finally taking the money to the police. The money belonged to an elderly man who had reported the loss, which he had just withdrawn from a bank. Chirag refused the reward that was offered to him.

A landscaper named ELI ESTRADA found a bag filled with $140,000 on a street in Cerritos, California, in 2008. Despite his own credit card debt and serious problems making ends meet, Estrada reported the money, which was traced to a Brinks truck. He received a $2,000 reward.

Legal secretary DHAIMA BROOKES found 1 million Jamaican dollars (about $12,000 U.S.) at an ATM machine in a shopping mall in Jamaica. Others witnessed the discovery and some suggested dividing the money among the crowd, but it was taken to the police and finally returned to the company that serviced the ATM.

Ten-year-old TYLER BUNCH could have purchased the video game system he was saving for—and plenty more—with the $1,714.11 he found on the side of a road in 2006. He took the money home to his family, who turned the money into the sheriff's office. The rightful owner was located, and Tyler bought that video game system with the $300 reward money.

14 LOTTERY WINNERS WHO WENT BUST

Getting your hands on money is only half the battle. These people learned that lesson the hard way:

1 Evelyn Adams struck it rich not only once but twice–in 1985 and 1986–to the tune of $5.4 million. She gambled some of it away and says she fell victim to relatives who swarmed for handouts. She wound up broke, living in a trailer.

2 Michael Carroll, a laborer, won £9.7 million at the age of just nineteen in 2002. He spent it on four homes, a villa in Spain, two BMWs, two Mercedes, and a stake in the Glasgow Rangers Football Club. A string of petty crimes ended in a nine-month prison sentence. By 2007, he was penniless.

3 Jeffrey Dampier won a $20 million jackpot and was then kidnapped and murdered by his own sister, who hoped to inherit the winnings.

4 David Lee Edwards was an unemployed laborer in 2001 when he won $42 million from a $295 million Powerball drawing in Kentucky. Life seemed rosy. He bought a house that had its own golf course, and he purchased numerous sports cars. Then Edwards's wife filed for divorce and both were arrested on drug charges. Edwards's $1.2 million home was eventually auctioned off for $400,000.

5 Big-hearted Missourian lottery winner Janite Lee collected $18 million in 1993 and promptly shared her bounty with all of her favorite causes. By 2001, Lee was down to her last $700 and had filed for bankruptcy.

6 William "Bud" Post wishes he'd never heard of the lottery, despite the fact that he won $16.2 million in the Pennsylvania lottery in 1988. Shortly after pocketing his winnings, his girlfriend sued him for a share of the winnings, his brother put out a hit on him, and other relatives forced him into two losing ventures. When he fired a gun in frustration with a bill collector, he was arrested. Within a year of his win, the money was gone and he was $1 million in debt. Today he lives on $450 a month and food stamps.

7 The first thing Virginia Metcalf Merida and Mack Metcalf did when they heard they'd won $65.4 million in the lottery was to quit their jobs. Married but not living together, they chose a one-time payment of $34 million, divided the money equally, and parted ways. A month later, Mack was ordered to pay $31,000 in child support and another $800,000 toward a trust fund for his child from a previous marriage. He served four days in jail on a DUI charge. Two years later, he was dead from complications having to do with a drinking problem. Virginia fared no better. Her body was found in her home, dead for a few days, within five years of her win. No foul play was suspected.

8 After Vivian Nicholson won £152,300 playing the U.K.'s Castleford football pools in 1961, she was widowed, married five times, suffered a stroke, was treated for alcoholism, got deported from Malta, became a Jehovah's Witness, tried to commit suicide, and spent time in a mental institution. She spent her winnings on clothing, cars, and travel, and her story was the subject of a West End production entitled *Spend, Spend, Spend.* She is now living on an £87 a week pension.

9 Ken Proxmire won $1 million in the Michigan lottery, went into business with his brothers, and filed for bankruptcy five years later.

10 Shefik Tallmadge, of Arizona, used his last $5 to buy a lottery ticket and won a cool $6.7 million. After eighteen years of traveling throughout Asia and Africa, buying expensive cars and real estate, and indulging friends with investments that inevitably failed, he filed for bankruptcy in 2006.

11 Vince Taylor won two lottery fortunes, only to lose them both and end up broke. His initial £1.3 million winnings enabled him to move from a two-room flat to a mansion that boasted stables and a swimming pool, and he filled the garages with flashy cars worth hundreds of thousands of dollars. By 2001 he was broke, but miraculously hit the lottery again, this time picking up £120,000. But his winnings were soon swallowed up by bad investments. Today Taylor is broke. He blames his fall on greedy friends and relatives, and he blames himself for ignoring sound advice. He eventually took a job as a bricklayer to get out of debt.

12 Rhoda Toth won $13 million in the Florida lottery in 1990, and she and her husband quickly spent the winnings. In 2006, they were charged with tax evasion and soon found themselves living in poverty, with electricity provided by a cord rigged to a car engine. While awaiting trial, Toth's husband died, and she was accused of insurance fraud. She was sentenced to two years in prison and ordered to pay $1.1 million to the IRS.

13 In 2002, Jack Whittaker won the biggest lottery pot to date: $314.9 million. He collected $114 million in a one-time payment, and then his life fell apart: Hundreds of thousands of dollars were stolen from his home, office, and vehicle. He had numerous brushes with the law, including a lawsuit from a gambling casino. His granddaughter, Brandi, died of a drug overdose (he had been providing her with a $2,100-per-week allowance), and in her suit for divorce, his wife filed notice against the numerous companies and corporations owned by Whittaker, thereby freezing his assets. In 2008, he settled a wrongful death civil suit and was fined for driving with a suspended license.

14 Callie Rogers was just sixteen years old when she won a $3 million jackpot in England. She blew it all on wild shopping sprees, breast implants, and cocaine. Eight years later, she had $32,000 left to show for her big win.

You could say that Frank Selak, a Croatian music teacher, is both the luckiest and unluckiest man in the world: In 1962, he survived a train derailment where he was thrown into an icy river in which seventeen were killed; in 1963, a door blew off the airplane in which he was riding, upon which he was sucked out of the plane but miraculously fell onto a haystack, unharmed; in 1966, his bus went off the road into a river leaving five dead and Frank with minor injuries; in 1973, his car caught fire, and though he lost more of his hair, he survived. There's more: in 1995, he was hit by a city bus but suffered only minor injuries; and in 1996, his car was forced off a cliff to escape an oncoming truck. He landed safely in a tree, but watched his car explode 300 feet below.

In 2003, Frank's luck changed. He won $1 million in the Croatian lottery. When he was asked to fly to Australia with other winners to take part in a Doritos commercial, he refused, saying he didn't want to press his luck.

When Elvis Presley died, Colonel Tom Parker was asked what he would do now. Smugly, he replied, "I'll keep right on managing him." And so he did. To date, Elvis has generated far more income than he ever realized while he was alive. Here are some more celebs who seem to be worth more dead than alive:

The following figures represent the amount of money the estate of each deceased celebrity earned in 2008, according to Forbes.com:

1. ELVIS PRESLEY
(1935–1977)
the king of rock 'n' roll
Net earnings: $52 million

2. CHARLES M. SCHULZ
(1922–2000)
Peanuts cartoonist
Net earnings: $33 million

3. HEATH LEDGER
(1979–2008)
actor who last appeared in
The Dark Knight
Net earnings: $20 million

4. AARON SPELLING
(1923–2006)
TV producer of *Beverly Hills 90210*,
among others
Net earnings: $15 million

5. DR. SEUSS A.K.A. THEODOR GEISEL
(1904–1991)
children's author and illustrator
Net earnings: $12 million

6. JOHN LENNON
(1940–1980)
founding member of the Beatles
Net earnings: $9 million

7. ANDY WARHOL (1928–1987)
artist
Net earnings: $9 million

8. MARILYN MONROE
(1926–1962)
the one and only
Net earnings: $6.5 million

9. STEVE MCQUEEN
(1930–1980)
film star
Net earnings: $6 million

10. JAMES DEAN
(1931–1955)
actor, poster child for ennui
Net earnings: $5 million

11. MARVIN GAYE (1939–1984)
rhythm 'n' blues singer
Net earnings: $3.5 million

The banker fell overboard from a friend's sailboat.

The friend grabbed a life preserver, held it up, not knowing if the banker could swim, and shouted, "Can you float alone?"

"Obviously," the banker replied, "but this is a heck of a time to talk business."

8 VERY WEALTHY CATS

We love cats. From time to time, newspapers print stories about some elderly widow who died and left her entire estate to her cat. Cats read these stories, too, and are always plotting to get named as beneficiaries in their owners's wills.

Did you ever wonder where your cat goes when it wanders off for several hours? It meets with other cats in estate-planning seminars. We just thought you should know.

1 David Harper, a somewhat reclusive cat owner, died in March 2005 at the age of seventy-nine, leaving an estate worth $1.1 million to his beloved tabby, Red. The United Church of Canada was appointed administrator of the funds, in accordance with Harper's will, and is responsible for the three-year-old cat's care, feeding, and veterinarian bills for the rest of its life.

2 In 1969, Joseph, a striped tomcat, inherited over a million dollars when his owner, Ms. Agatha Higgins, passed away. Joseph remained at the Higgins mansion until his death. After Joseph passed on, the rest of the fortune was divided among Higgins's family members.

3 Margaret Layne, who lived in a small suburb of London, left her entire fortune to her cat, Tinker. Tinker inherited an estimated $900,000, and Layne left detailed instructions regarding specific treats to which Tinker had grown accustomed. The house was not to be sold until Tinker's death.

4 In the 1960s, Dr. William Grier left his cats Brownie and Hellcat $415,000 in his will. The cats died two years later, and the remaining funds went to George Washington University in Washington, D.C.

5 Ben Rea, a British recluse who died in 1988, left $15 million to his cat, Blackie, and various cat charities—but not one farthing to his relatives.

6 In 1996, a businessman from Thailand spent £18,000 for the marriage of his male diamond-eyed pet cat Phet to a female diamond-eyed cat named Ploy. Five hundred guests attended the wedding, after which the cats were given a dowry of more than £23,000.

7 In 1999, two cats became landlords in Queens, New York, when their owners, two elderly sisters who died within months of each other, bequeathed to them their two-story, 1,400-square-foot home. A woman who lived in the apartment building was appointed executor, and all was well until the executor decided to move all of her cats—including the many strays she had been bringing into her apartment—to the country. She was willing to leave the two landlord cats behind, according to the terms of the will, which required that they remain at the Queens residence, but the place was overrun with cats, and no one was quite sure which two were the cats in question. In the end, the woman was allowed to move all her cats, selling the property for just under $1 million.

8 Woodbury Rand left $40,000 to his cat, Buster, cutting off his relatives without a penny due to their "cruelty to my cat." Buster died in 1945, intestate.

THE WORLD'S 7 WEALTHIEST DOGS

"I desire my sister, Marie Bluteau, and my niece, Madame Calonge, to look to my cats. If both cats should survive me, thirty sous a week must be laid out upon them, in order that they may live well. They are to be served daily, in a clean and proper manner, with two meals of meat soup, the same as we eat ourselves, but it is to be given to them separately in two soup plates. The bread is not to be cut up into the soup, but must be broken into squares the size of a nut, otherwise they will refuse to eat it. A ration of meat, finely minced, is to be added to it; the whole is then to be mildly seasoned, put into a clean pan, covered close, and carefully simmered before it is dished up. If only one cat should survive, half the sum mentioned will suffice."
–from the will of Mme. Dupuis, a famous French harpist of the seventeenth century

1 Countess Karlotta Libenstein of Germany left approximately $106 million to her Alsatian, Gunther III, when she died in 1992. Her trustees invested the money and tripled the fortune for Gunther's own heir, Gunther IV, making him the wealthiest dog in the world, with a treasure in the neighborhood of $318 million.

2 Toby Rimes inherited about $80 million from New York owner Ella Wendel.

3 Frankie was endowed with $5.3 million dollars. He currently resides in a mansion in San Diego, California.

"Money will buy you a pretty good dog, but it won't buy the wag of his tail."
—Henry Wheeler Shaw

4 Moose, the Jack Russell terrier that starred as Eddie on the TV show *Frasier*, was worth approximately $3.2 million. He earned more than $10,000 per episode.

5 Heiress Diana Myburgh rescued her dog Jasper from a shelter and endowed him with nearly $700,000.

6 In 2002, actress Drew Barrymore followed through on her promise to reward her life-saving pooch, Flossie, with a new dog house. She placed her entire Beverly Hills home, valued at $3 million, in trust with her yellow Lab mutt.

7 Eighty-nine-year-old spinster Norah Hardwell, who passed away in July of 2004, left more than half of her £800,000 estate to her two collie-cross dogs, Tina and Kate. She also left a portion of her estate to the Animal Health Trust in England.

In 2007, a dog named Pepper ate $750 in cash that belonged to the mother of his owner, Debbie Hulleman, of Oakdale, Minnesota. Happily, $647 was recovered from Pepper's poop and vomit, and the bills were exchanged for clean ones at a bank.

9 RICH PARENTS WHO AREN'T LEAVING THEIR MONEY

TO THE KIDS

Most parents want to leave their kids with a safety net. And for some, that net could be several million (or billion) dollars strong. But a growing number of rich-and-famous parents, afraid inherited wealth could damage their children, are planning to away give most of their fortunes to charity instead.

1. WARREN BUFFETT

Warren Buffett may currently be on the list of richest Americans, but don't congratulate his three children. The savvy investor, who built Berkshire Hathaway into a multi-billion-dollar juggernaut, has promised to give away most of his fortune because, he has said, "a rich person should leave his kids enough to do anything but not enough to do nothing." In fact, the Omaha, Nebraska, native has already started. In 2006, he promised a majority of his Berkshire shares to charity, with a good chunk going to his good pals' Bill & Melinda Gates Foundation, which as has so far received $6 billion worth of shares.

> "Let parents bequeath to their children not riches, but the spirit of reverence."
> —Plato

2. ANDREW CARNEGIE

The steel magnate has been dead for nearly ninety years but his legacy lives on. Perhaps his most lasting and influential contribution has been his belief that after you've accumulated your fortune, you must give it away rather than leaving it to your descendants. By the time he died in 1919, he had given away billions of dollars to build thousands of public libraries, Carnegie Mellon University, Carnegie Hall in New York City, and a pension fund for workers now known as TIAA-CREF. For his family, he left behind a modest trust.

3. BILL GATES

Bill Gates has promised to give away most of his Microsoft billions. He and wife Melinda established a foundation in 1994 and have been giving away truckloads of money ever since. Gates said that he thinks inherited wealth creates a distorted view of "how you measure yourself, how your friends think about you, and how they do things with you. And it's also bad for society. We're picking the grandchildren of the people whose skill and luck accumulated the money and saying to them that they should have this vast control of society's resources. I just don't think that's a great way to run a society."

> "All heiresses are beautiful."
> —John Dryden (1631–1700), British poet, dramatist, and critic

4. LEONA HELMSLEY

When the real estate mogul died in August 2007 at the age of eighty-seven, she bequeathed two of her grandchildren $10 million each as long as they visited their father's grave at least once a year. The other two grandchildren were disinherited "for reasons which are known to them." But the bulk of her estate went to the dogs, literally. Her will established a $12 million trust for the care of her dog, Trouble, and the rest, estimated to be worth nearly $8 billion, went to the Leona M. and Harry B. Helmsley

Charitable Trust, whose sole aim is the care of dogs.

5. WILLIAM BARRON HILTON

Paris Hilton's grandfather, hotel magnate William Barron Hilton, made headlines when he announced in late 2007 that he had bequeathed nearly all of his $2.3 billion fortune to a foundation started by his father, Conrad. "My father left 97 percent of his wealth to the Conrad N. Hilton Foundation, and I am proud to follow my father's example," he said. He didn't mention that about twenty years earlier, he had sued his father's estate after being left only a small portion. Years of legal wrangling ensued, but he ultimately scored 60 percent of the income from his father's estate for life, with the other 40 percent going to the foundation. Bummer for Paris.

6. NIGELLA LAWSON

The domestic goddess has declared that she did not plan to leave her two children from her first husband, deceased journalist John Diamond, with much of her cookbook and TV show fortune. Lawson, an heiress to the J. Lyons and Co. food empire in England and wife of a super wealthy ad guy, said that she was "determined that my children should have no financial security. It ruins people not having to earn money." After the ensuing outcry, she added she "had no intention of leaving my children destitute, but I believe you have to work in order to learn the value of money."

7. ANITA RODDICK

Anita Roddick's two daughters knew since they were teenagers that their mom wanted to give away her Body Shop fortune to charity. So when she died at the age of sixty-four in 2007, some $76 million flowed into the Roddick Foundation. Said daughter Sam, "If my mum had said to me, 'I'm not leaving the money to you but I've decided to give it all to a distant cousin,' then I would have found that offensive. But giving it all to charity is different. You can't argue about someone giving their money away, can you?" She added, "They've already given us everything in terms of love and support."

8. GENE SIMMONS

Gene Simmons of the rock group Kiss doesn't want his two kids to end up like a lot of rock 'n' roll progeny: broke with no idea of how to support themselves. So he's cutting them off—sort of. In 2007, he said his children with longtime partner Shannon Tweed "are gonna be taken care of, but they will never be rich off my money. Because every year they should be forced to get up out of bed and go out and work and make their own way." How's he going to do it? They'll receive a yearly allowance covering basics like rent and food but "if you want riches, you should do that yourself."

9. SIR ANDREW LLOYD WEBBER

Sir Andrew Lloyd Webber doesn't believe in spoiling his kids. The Brit, who gained fame and fortune from such hits as *Phantom of the Opera* and *Cats*, has said his five kids from two different wives shouldn't expect much of a free ride. "I am not in favor of children suddenly finding a lot of money coming their way because then they have no incentive to work," said Webber, who is estimated to be worth some $1 billion. "So I will give them a start in life but they ain't going to end up owning [his company] the Really Useful Group."

"Never say you know a man until you have divided an inheritance with him."
—Johann Kaspar Lavater (1741–1801), Swiss poet and physiognomist

8 FAMOUS INHERITANCES

1 Upon the death of Howard Hughes in 1976, his $2.5 billion fortune was shared by his twenty-two cousins. Melvin Dummar, a gas station owner who once helped Hughes out of a jam, claimed that Hughes had promised him $156 million. The claim proved to be fraudulent.

2 Despite claims by Anna Nicole Smith that her eighty-nine-year-old husband, J. Howard Marshall II, planned to leave her half of his $1.6 billion estate, the courts awarded her the sum of only $88 million. Marshall passed away in 1995.

3 In 1924, Doris Duke, the daughter of tobacco magnate James Buchanan Duke, inherited approximately $100 million–$1 billion in today's dollars. She was only twelve years old at the time.

4 Charlene de Carvalho-Heineken became the richest woman in the Netherlands when her father, Alfred Heineken, died in 2003. The Heineken beer company she inherited was worth more than $7 billion.

5 On her eighteenth birthday, Allegra Versace inherited more than $700 million after her uncle, Gianni Versace, the famed Italian fashion designer, passed away in 1997.

6 On her twenty-fifth birthday, Lisa Marie Presley, the daughter of Elvis, inherited an estimated $100 million.

7 Philanthropist Brooke Astor, who passed away in 2007 at the age of 105, left most of her $198 million estate to her only son, Anthony Marshall. But Marshall and his attorney, Francis X. Morrissey Jr., were subsequently indicted on charges that they swindled her out of millions after they took control of her charitable foundation in the 1990s. On December 21, 1999, Marshall, convicted of first-degree grand larceny and thirteen other charges, was sentenced to one to three years in prison, and Morrissey received the same sentence. Their cases are on appeal at the time of this writing.

8 After the death of her father, television mogul Aaron Spelling, in 2006, daughter Tori expected to share her father's $500 million estate with her brother, Randy, but each received a mere $800,000.

> "a louse i used to know told me that millionaires and bums tasted about the same to him"
> —Don Marquis

SPENDING HABITS OF THE ULTRA-WEALTHY

Traditionally, the wealthy comprised the ranks of self-made entrepreneurs, doctors, accountants, and lawyers, but these professions bring pauper's paychecks when compared to the hedge fund manager, whose wealth is reaching stratospheric heights.

According to *Fortune* magazine, this trend is leading to some resentment among the "merely rich," who have worked just as hard and if not harder for their wealth and find it unfathomable that people who haven't followed the same rules are making ten times as much as they are. The "merely wealthy" are finding themselves shut out of co-chairmanships for nonprofits and are finding it hard to compete for private school slots for their kids.

It seems crazy that people who are in the 99th percentile of the wealth bracket are bickering among themselves, while middle class incomes are stagnating and the general income gap between rich and poor appears to be widening.

Prince & Associates, a market research firm that tracks the spending habits of people who have money to burn, polled the buying habits of 294 hedge fund managers with a median net worth of $61.7 million.

According to the survey, these managers each spent the following average amounts in the year 2005:

FINE ART
$3.99 million

HOTELS & RESORTS
$304,900

TRADITIONAL SPA SERVICES
$124,000

WINE & SPIRITS FOR THE HOME
$48,900

YACHT CHARTERS
$429,700

WATCHES
$271,300

ELECTRONICS
$99,300

JEWELRY
$376,400

FASHION & ACCESSORIES
$204,200

ENTERTAINING FRIENDS
$76,700

7 FAMOUS MISERS

In July 2007, the *Austin American-Statesman* ran a front-page story about Gene Burd, a seventy-six-year-old journalism professor at the University of Texas who lives in a tiny apartment, does not own a car, and wears shoes he found in the trash. His modest salary, handled with extreme frugality, had resulted in a small fortune. Call them what you will—misers, Scrooges, cheapskates, skinflints—these people all learned the hard way that you can't take it with you.

1 Hetty Green died in New York City on July 3, 1916, at the age of eighty and earned immortality as a longstanding "World's Greatest Miser" entry in the *Guinness Book of World Records*. Despite the fact that she had an inherited net worth of $7.5 million, she became infamous for her stinginess, spurning heat and hot water and limiting herself to only one dress and set of undergarments, replacing them only when they wore out. She died, appropriately, of apoplexy while arguing with a maid.

2 In the 1950s, a man named Charles Huffman was found dead on a Brooklyn, New York street with no money in his pockets. Not surprisingly, he was traced to a $7-a-week room in a boarding house. Surprisingly, that room was filled with bank books and more than $500,000 in stock certificates.

3 Andrew Carnegie (1835–1919), the Scottish-born American industrialist, businessman, and a major philanthropist with special interests in business, education, and world peace, was known to be a lousy tipper.

"A miser grows rich by seeming poor; an extravagant man grows poor by seeming rich." —William Shenstone (1714–1763), English poet

4 Homer Lusk Collyer (1881–1947) and Langley Collyer (1885–1947) were two miserly, reclusive brothers who, in life, were known to be obsessive collectors of newspapers, furniture, musical instruments, and God knows what else. But no one could have predicted the hundred tons of rubbish that was discovered in their Fifth Avenue home in Harlem, New York, once they both died (Langley's body was discovered beneath tons of rubbish, where he had died of starvation). In addition to the piles of garbage and debris resulting from the deterioration of the building, police also found:

» baby carriages
» rusted bicycles
» a collection of guns
» glass chandeliers
» bowling balls
» camera equipment
» the folding top of a horse-drawn carriage
» a sawhorse
» three dressmaking dummies
» countless paintings and art objects
» rusted bed springs
» a kerosene stove
» countless pieces of furniture
» more than 25,000 books
» human organs pickled in jars
» eight live cats
» the chassis of a Model T

- » hundreds of yards of silks and fabric
- » fourteen pianos
- » a clavichord
- » bundles of newspapers and magazines
- » outdated phone books
- » a horse's jawbone
- » an early X-ray machine

5 British Parliamentarian John Elwes (1714–1789) was born into a respectable English family, was well educated, and enjoyed a fine social standing. Yet the influence of a favorite penurious uncle transformed Elwes into one of the most famous misers in England.

SPITZ & NATHANSON PRESENT

WHEN WOMEN LOVE A PLAY TRUE TO LIFE.

THE MISER.

He wore ragged clothes that others had discarded and walked in the rain rather than spending money on a carriage. He ate rancid meat, treated his own illnesses to save money on physicians, and possessed only one suit. He lived on £50 a year, yet left half a million pounds to his sons when he died.

"Money is like manure. If you spread it around, it does a lot of good, but if you pile it up in one place, it stinks like hell." —Clint W. Murchison, financier

6 Englishman Daniel Dancer (1716–1794) was as mean as he was cheap. Coming from a long line of cheapskates, Dancer inherited a small fortune—£3,000 was a lot in the eighteenth century—upon his father's death, yet he spent most of his life hoarding money. He bathed and washed his clothes rarely, wearing them until they literally fell to shreds. He ate food that even poor peasants would spurn; he was once known to have found a partly decomposed sheep and to have dined on it for two weeks. His only indulgence was a pet dog, but fearing a lawsuit if the dog attacked the neighbors, he had its teeth removed. After he died, authorities uncovered money caches everywhere on his property; £2,500 was found in a dung heap.

7 John Camden Neild (1780–1852), son of a prosperous English goldsmith, inherited £250,000 at the age of thirty-four and spent the rest of his life trying to avoid spending any of it. He wore rags, argued with everyone about the smallest expenditures, and mooched meals and lodgings whenever he could. Oddly enough, upon his death, Neild left most of his money to Queen Victoria, who increased the meager amounts of money he had left to his executors and servants. England's *Dictionary of National Biography* mercifully lists him only as "an eccentric."

12 SELF-PROCLAIMED FRUGAL CELEBRITIES

1. TYRA BANKS

Despite a fortune estimated at $75 million, this thirty-four-year-old is an avowed penny pincher. "I am frugal," she said in a June 1, 2008, *New York Times Magazine* profile. "I've always been this way. When I was young, my mom would give me my allowance, and I'd peel off a little each week and have some to spare. Banks's culinary tastes run toward the Cheesecake Factory, and she is known to stock up on hotel soap.

2. HALLE BERRY

Halle Berry can make a fashion designer millions simply by wearing a gown on a red carpet. After all, she's one of the world's most photographed women. Still, this fashion icon would sooner hit the sales racks than fly to Paris for a couture fitting. Berry, whose mom struggled to raise her and her older sister after their father walked out when she was four, is an unabashed saver. "I am pretty frugal," say the twice-divorced Oscar winner and new mom. "I save a lot because I'm always worried about when this trip is going to stop. So I'm saving for that day so I can have a life that is secure and comfortable."

3. LEONARDO DICAPRIO

Other than shelling out $2.5 million for an island near Belize in 2005, the actor and environmental activist tends to live on the cheap. "I don't pay lavish expenses," he has said. "I don't fly private jets. I still have only one car, and that's a Toyota Prius. I don't spend money on a lot. Money is very important to me because it allows me the freedom to choose what I want to do as an actor and most importantly because I want to accumulate enough so that one day I can do something really great and beneficial for other people, for the environment, or for children."

4. SARAH MICHELLE GELLAR

Growing up, money was tight at Sarah Michelle Gellar's house, especially after her dad walked out when she was just six. Now after soap opera and movie fame, the New York native remains careful about her money. "I take my reusable bag to Whole Foods so I get a discount," Sarah told *Self* magazine in 2007. "I go to Bloomingdale's on double reward days. And I always print my dry cleaning coupons before I go. The main thing I want to do is make sure that I can take care of myself and my mother," she said in 2000.

5. DAVE GROHL

This ex-Nirvana drummer who formed the Foo Fighters lives the typical life of a suburban dad. "You can't take your lifestyle for granted," this jeans-and-t-shirt-wearing thirty-nine-year-old said in a 2003 interview. "I've got tons of money, but I'm afraid to spend it. Knowing I don't even have a high school diploma to fall back on, I'm going to be really careful with what I've got." So while he has a large L.A. house with a recording studio, Grohl is not likely to end up bankrupt like some of his musical brethren.

6. TERI HATCHER

This divorced single mom credits her childhood for her frugalness. "I feel like your value system is created when you're a child and I am not sure it ever really changes," she said in 2005. That same year, she told *People* magazine, "I drive my cars for ten years until they have 100,000 miles on them." Her one indulgence: travel. "The only thing I really did was take a fantastic trip to Africa with my daughter."

7. MICK JAGGER

Jagger reportedly pulled out of buying a painting by bandmate Ron Wood because the $140,000 price tag "scared him off." His ex-wife, model Jerry Hall, complained, "He always wanted me to pay for everything to do with the house and the children. He's generous with gifts and presents, but yeah, he's pretty tight with the day-to-day stuff." He explains that he was taught as a child to be frugal: "We don't like to throw computers away as soon as they don't work—apart from out of the window in frustration. We like cars to be repaired instead of junked."

8. JAY LENO

Despite his huge fortune, the only flashy thing about Leno is his collection of cars and motorcycles. "When I was a kid . . . I had one job for which the money went in the bank and the other job that I lived off of," he said in 2004. "I still do that to this day. I have yet to touch a dime of my *Tonight Show* salary. I live off the money I make as a comedian . . . Maybe it comes from having parents who grew up during the Depression." While Conan O'Brian offered to cover the salaries of pink-slipped staffers during the writers' strike, Leno only did so after being shamed by a lot of bad press.

9. EVA LONGORIA

Her wedding in 2007 reportedly cost $1.5 million, but this *Desperate Housewives* star still scored a lot of freebies to give to her two hundred guests: Van Cleef & Arpel 18K yellow-gold charm bracelets, and L'Oreal, Cole Haan, and Bebe products were a few. She says the frugal gene runs in her family, explaining that her dad would take her and her three siblings camping with no food. "He would tell us that we could live off the land. I can skin a deer, a pig, a snake . . ."

10. PAUL MCCARTNEY

Paul McCartney is worth more than $1 billion, but he's not likely to advertise

it. At a birthday party for his ex-wife, he made the guests pay for their drinks. Even his fashion designer daughter, Stella, reportedly called him "a tight bastard" for sending her and her three siblings to local state schools rather than posh private ones.

11. TOBEY MAGUIRE

Even after his price jumped up to $26 million a picture thanks to three *Spider-Man* mega-hits, Maguire is usually photographed wearing lived-in t-shirts and jeans. "You know those Lotto winners, who win big and blow through all that money? [Yes, we do! See page 238.] That would never happen to me," says Maguire, who credits his poverty-stricken childhood as the impetus for his quest for financial security. "I just never wanted to put myself in the position where my spending was so huge that I had to keep making movie after movie."

12. SARAH JESSICA PARKER

Contrary to Parker's character in *Sex and the City*, the forty-three-year-old isn't such a slave to fashion. In fact, she used to get sick from buyer's remorse and return items the next day. Explaining that her family went through a time when they were on welfare, Parker says of her son, "Just because Mommy and Daddy are rich and famous, that doesn't mean he should ride the gravy train through life. . . . I want [James] to be normal."

TRUMP TRIVIA

He's one of the most flamboyant characters in the history of money. His name is plastered on some of the most expensive real estate in the country, and he's known as a billion-dollar deal-maker who once filed a $5-billion libel suit against biographer Timothy L. O'Brien and publisher Warner Books for claiming that he was only a millionaire with a personal worth of somewhere between $150 million and $250 million and not a billionaire. He has numerous books, a TV show, and a board game to his credit. He has funny hair and is a known germophobic. Can we ever get enough of The Donald?

1 Donald Trump is a longtime friend of WWF owner Vince McMahon, and a longtime fan of the World Wrestling Federation. The Donald hosted Wrestlemania IV and V at Trump Plaza, and appeared in a ringside seat at a few others. He has also appeared on WWF TV shows and participated in WWF story-lines.

2 He was among the guests at Usher Raymond's 26th birthday party.

3 In his first book, *The Art Of The Deal*, he wrote that he briefly thought of attending the University of Southern California (USC), with the idea of becoming a film producer or studio executive. He eventually changed his mind when he decided that the real estate business was more lucrative.

4 Trump became a first-time grandfather when his son, Donald Trump Jr., and his son's wife, Vanessa Haydon, became the parents of a girl named Kai Madison on May 12, 2007, just a year after his own son Barron William Trump, was born on March 20, 2006.

5 He has a sister who is a judge.

6 Though he owns labels that market it, he doesn't drink alcohol.

7 He was awarded a Star on the Hollywood Walk of Fame in January 2007.

8 He threw out the opening pitch to game 2 of the Red Sox/Yankees double-header on 8/18/06. It was the Jimmy Fund fund-raiser day, where he, the Boston Red Sox, and many other donors gave nearly three million dollars for cancer research. The Red Sox lost that game 14 to 11.

9 The Donald is half German and half Scottish.

10 He doesn't carry a briefcase and possesses a morbid fear of shaking hands.

11 He was voted the class "Ladies Man" by classmates in New York Military Academy's class of 1964 at Cornwall-on-Hudson, NY.

12 He is a graduate of the University of Pennsylvania.

13 Donald Trump's father, Fred Christ Trump (1905–1999), was a multi-millionaire developer son of German parents.

Simon Cowell, Russell Simmons and Kimora Lee Simmons, Matt Lauer, Rudolph Giuliani, Kelly Ripa, Chris Matthews, Don King, Katie Couric, Regis Philbin, Heidi Klum, Pat O'Brien, Mark Burnett, Billy Bush, and others.

18 His biggest yacht, a $29 million, five-deck, 282-foot craft, is named Trump Princess.

19 In 2004, Trump filed a trademark application for the phrase "You're fired," which he had popularized on his TV show *The Apprentice*.

20 He owns his own bottled water company, Trump Ice, which has one of the highest bottled water prices in the country at $2.00 per bottle.

21 Trump owns two beauty pageants: the Miss Universe pageant and the Miss USA pageant.

22 He is an appointed ambassador for Scotland.

23 His nicknames include The Don, The Donald, The Trumpster, and DJT.

24 His show *The Apprentice* was nominated for Emmy awards in 2004 and 2005 in the Outstanding Reality-Competition Program category.

14 In 2007, a Florida zoning board fined Donald Trump $1,250 a day for flying a supersized American flag atop an 80-foot flagpole that violates several of the town's codes and ordinances.

15 When Trump was in college, he read federal foreclosure listings for fun. Before he graduated, he bought his first housing project.

16 He appeared briefly in *Home Alone 2: Lost In New York*. Kevin asks him where the main lobby is. Trump says, "Down the hall and to the left."

17 Guests at Trump's wedding to Melania Knauss included: Bill and Hillary Clinton, Kathie Lee and Frank Gifford, Star Jones, Shaquille O'Neal, Barbara Walters, Billy Joel, Tony Bennett,

THE WORLD ACCORDING TO DONALD

"I like thinking big. If you're going to be thinking anything, you might as well think big."

"I have made the tough decisions, always with an eye toward the bottom line. Perhaps it's time America was run like a business."

"You can't know it all. No matter how smart you are, no matter how comprehensive your education, no matter how wide ranging your experience, there is simply no way to acquire all the wisdom you need to make your business thrive."

"Watch, listen, and learn. You can't know it all yourself . . . anyone who thinks they do is destined for mediocrity."

"It's tangible, it's solid, it's beautiful. It's artistic, from my standpoint, and I just love real estate."

"I'm not running for office. I don't have to be politically correct. I don't have to be a nice person. Like I watch some of these weak-kneed politicians, it's disgusting. I don't have to be that way."

ABOVE, LEFT: Donald Trump in better hair days

FAMOUS PEOPLE WHO HAVE DECLARED BANKRUPTCY

OR TRIED TO AVOID TAXES

It's hard to believe that America was a country founded by people looking for ways to avoid high taxes. The IRS (or "theirs" if you leave out the space between those two words) has forever been a fly in the ointment of prosperity. Here are some well-known—and surprising—bankrupts and tax evaders:

PHINEAS TAYLOR BARNUM

The greatest American showman filed for bankruptcy in 1871 due to losses he incurred in unwise business ventures. After bankruptcy, he organized his famous circus, "The Greatest Show On Earth." In 1881, he merged his circus with one belonging to his most successful competitor, James A. Bailey, under the name of Barnum and Bailey Circus.

CHUCK BERRY

In 1979, the rock legend admitted to the IRS that he had neglected to pay taxes on much of the cash income he earned in the 1970s. He was ordered to perform a thousand hours of benefit shows and to serve four months in prison.

MATHEW BRADY

The distinguished Civil War photographer filed for bankruptcy in 1872 because after the Civil War people just lost interest in his work and he became unable to pay his business debts. Three years after he filed for bankruptcy, the United States War Department agreed to purchase part of his photography collection for $25,000. He reopened his gallery and went on to success.

AL CAPONE

The notorious gangster is said to have once remarked that tax laws were a joke because "the government can't collect legal taxes on illegal money." Actually, they could. In 1931, he was slapped with eleven years in jail and an $80,000 bill from the IRS.

WALT DISNEY

The cartoon creator filed for bankruptcy in 1920 after the main client of his new business filed bankruptcy. In 1923, he formed a new company with a loan from his parents and his brother. In 1928, he created "Mickey Mouse" and went on to world-renowned success.

HEIDI FLEISS

The "Hollywood Madam" apparently failed to report her ill-gotten income to the IRS and was convicted in 1997 for pandering, tax evasion, and money laundering. She spent three years in prison.

HENRY FORD

The famous automobile manufacturer owned two automobile manufacturing companies that failed. The first company filed for bankruptcy and the second ended because of a disagreement with his business partner. In June 1903, at the age of forty, he created a third company, the Ford Motor Company, with a cash investment of $28,000. By July of 1903, the bank balance had dwindled to $223.65, but by then Ford had sold its first car, and it was all uphill from there.

RICHARD HATCH

He won $1 million in prize money for being the last man standing on TV's *Survivor*, but he later claimed that it was his understanding that CBS had agreed to pay his taxes. The judge didn't buy it, and in 2006, Hatch was sentenced to fifty-one months in prison and three years of supervised release to follow.

HENRY JOHN HEINZ

The famous condiment manufacturer started his company in 1869 selling horseradish, pickles, sauerkraut, and vinegar. In 1875, the company filed for bankruptcy due to an unexpected bumper harvest that the company was not able to process. He immediately started a new company and introduced a new condiment, tomato ketchup, to the market. The rest is condiment success.

LEONA HELMSLEY

The Queen of Mean spent four years in prison after being found guilty of some $2.6 million in tax fraud in 1992. Her famous defense: "We don't pay taxes. Only the little people pay taxes."

MILTON SNAVELY HERSHEY

The founder of Hershey's chocolate started four candy companies that failed, and filed bankruptcy before starting what is now Hershey's Foods Corporation. Mr. Hershey had only a fourth grade education, but was certain he could make a good product that the public would want to purchase. His fifth attempt was clearly successful.

MARTIN LUTHER KING, JR.

In 1960, a warrant was issued for Dr. King's arrest on charges he had falsified his 1956 and 1958 Alabama state income tax returns. Such charges were typical of the ways in which the government harassed civil rights leaders at the time. King was acquitted by an all-white jury.

SOPHIA LOREN

The sultry actress made headlines in 1982 when she served an eighteen-day sentence in an Italian prison for tax evasion.

LUCIANO PAVAROTTI

The world-famous Italian opera singer was accused of owing back taxes in 1999, and was ordered to pay nearly $11 million to the Italian government.

REMBRANDT VAN RIJN

The famous Dutch painter accumulated more debts than he could repay and filed for bankruptcy at the age of fifty in 1656. Many of Rembrandt's paintings and his house were sold at an auction. After the bankruptcy, he continued to paint but was not allowed to sell his works directly to customers. He was able to circumvent this law by having his son take over his business.

WILLIE NELSON

In 1990, the IRS sent the country music legend a tax bill for $16.7 million. Many of his dedicated fans purchased Nelson's assets, which the IRS auctioned off, and returned them to the singer. Nelson later poked fun at his tax problems in ads for H&R Block.

JOSEPH NUNAN

While Nunan's name may not be as celebrated as others listed here, it's notable that in 1952 he was charged with failing to pay taxes on an $1,800 bet that he'd made that Harry Truman would win the presidential election. He had been, after all, the IRS commissioner from 1944 to 1947.

O. J. SIMPSON

In 2008, Simpson, already suffering from other legal woes, was ordered to pay some $1.4 million in back taxes. Repayment is unlikely given Simpson's current residence in Nevada prison for his conviction for kidnapping and armed robbery.

DONALD TRUMP

The celebrated businessman filed Chapter 11 bankruptcy cases for his casino empire twice—once in 1992 and then again in 2004.

MARK TWAIN (SAMUEL LANGHORNE CLEMENS)

Our pre-eminent author lost most of his money investing in a worthless machine called the Paige Compositor, an automatic typesetting machine. He filed for bankruptcy in 1894 and discharged all his debts, but repaid them all when he finally became successful. He also wrote several of his more famous books after filing bankruptcy, including *Pudd'nhead Wilson* and *Following the Equator*.

OSCAR WILDE

The acclaimed poet and author was forced into bankruptcy in 1895. He had earlier been convicted of homosexual activity, which in England was illegal at that time, and was sentenced to two years in prison at hard labor. He was declared bankrupt on November 12, 1895, and his property was auctioned off. After being released from prison, he published his poem about the experience, *The Ballad of Reading Gaol*.

100 HIGH-PROFILE ENTERTAINERS

There wasn't a dry eye in the house when Percy Sledge sang "When a Man Loves a Woman" at the wedding of rocker Steven Van Zandt to Maureen Santoro on New Year's Eve of 1982. The legendary Sledge has since retired, but if music soothes your soul and you have money to burn, here are (or were, in the case of the deceased or retired) the performance fees for one hundred entertainers, all of whom have been known to play private parties. Note that these prices represent the *artist fee only*, and do not include costs for all the ancillary expenses necessary to stage a performance—stage, sound, lights, stagehands, backline (equipment), artist catering, air, hotel and grounds, etc. Often, these associated costs can run much higher than the artist fee.

$15,000
Count Basie Orchestra
Duke Ellington Orchestra
Martha Reeves & the Vandellas
Staple Singers

$20,000–$30,000
Buckwheat Zydeco

$25,000
Chubby Checker
Jose Feliciano
Richie Havens
Sha Na Na

$25,000–$30,000
Dr. John

$30,000
Blood, Sweat & Tears
Aaron Neville

$35,000
Four Tops
Village People

$45,000–$50,000
Marvin Hamlisch

$50,000
Burt Bacharach
John Hiatt
Chaka Khan
Manhattan Transfer
Neville Brothers
The O'Jays
Pointer Sisters
Booker T and the MGs
Richard Thompson

$65,000
Smash Mouth

$70,000
Smokey Robinson

$75,000
Jerry Lee Lewis
Dionne Warwick

$75,000–$100,000
Billy Ray Cyrus
Emmylou Harris
The Monkees
Kellie Pickler
Lucinda Williams
Dwight Yoakam

$100,000
Beach Boys
Tracy Chapman
Gipsy Kings
Alison Krauss & Union Station
Yo-Yo Ma

$125,000
Allman Brothers
Aretha Franklin

$125,000–$150,000
Wynton Marsalis
Willie Nelson

$140,000
Macy Gray

$150,000
Tori Amos
Patti Labelle
Wayne Newton
Trisha Yearwood

$150,000–$200,000
Fantasia Barrino

$185,000
Diana Ross

$200,000
Al Green
Vince Gill

$250,000
Clay Aiken
Tony Bennett
Mary J. Blige
Brooks & Dunn
Elvis Costello
Crosby, Stills & Nash
Bob Dylan
Norah Jones
Journey
Reba McIntire
Bonnie Raitt

$300,000
Kelly Clarkson

$350,000
Sheryl Crow
Carly Simon
Usher

$400,000
Steely Dan

$500,000
Alabama
Josh Groban
Alicia Keys
Barry Manilow
James Taylor
ZZ Top

$500,000–$600,000
Paul Simon

$700,000
Gloria Estefan

$750,000
Sarah MacLachlan
Santana
Rod Stewart

$750,000–$1,000,000
Justin Timberlake

$900,000
Janet Jackson

$1,000,000
Cher
Kenny Chesney
Neil Diamond
Eagles
Billy Joel
Dave Matthews Band
Bette Midler
Sting
Van Halen
Stevie Wonder

$1,500,000
Elton John
Prince

$3,000,000
Eric Clapton
Céline Dion
Madonna
Barbara Streisand
U2

$3,000,000 +
Paul McCartney
Rolling Stones

WHO HAVE INSURED THEIR BODY PARTS

The tradition of celebrity insurance for body parts can be traced back to the 1920s, when silent film star Ben Turpin, famous for his crossed eyes, took out a $20,000 insurance policy lest they become uncrossed. The practice soon became common among those with special assets. In 1934, yo-yo champion Harvey Lowe had his hands insured for $150,000, and a male stripper named Frankie Jakeman insured his penis for $1.6 million. In Britain, a performer known as Mr. Methane was denied coverage for his talent, which consisted of performing songs such as "Twinkle, Twinkle, Little Star" using his naturally produced gases. Here are some policies that were approved.

WHO?	WHICH PART?	HOW MUCH?
Fred Astaire	legs	$150,000
David Beckham	legs and feet	$70 million
Mariah Carey	legs	$1 billion
Jamie Lee Curtis	legs	$1 million
Bette Davis	waistline	$28,000
Angie Dickinson	legs	$1 million
Marlene Dietrich	voice	$1 million
Jimmy Durante	nose	$50,000
America Ferrera	teeth	$10 million
Michael Flatley	feet	$39 million
Betty Grable	legs	$1 million
Mary Hart	legs	$1 million
Angelina Jolie	body	$1 million
Tom Jones	chest hair	$7 million
Heidi Klum	legs*	$2.2 million
Jennifer Lopez	derrière	$27 million

WHO?	WHICH PART?	HOW MUCH?
Dolly Parton	breasts	$600,000
Keith Richards	middle finger of left hand	$1.6 million
Rihanna	legs	$1 million
Egon Ronay	taste buds	$400,000
Claudia Schiffer	face	$5 million
Brooke Shields	legs	undisclosed
Bruce Springsteen	voice	$6 million
Rod Stewart	voice	$6 million
Tina Turner	legs	$3.2 million

* One of Heidi's legs is insured for $200,000 less than the other due to a small scar.

CELEBRITY VICTIMS OF IDENTITY THEFT

When one hears of identity theft, it is easy to imagine that a thief would want a lesser-known name that would not attract too much attention. But, in fact, many criminals target celebrities and other well-known individuals, counting on the fact that they have larger assets to plunder. Here, according to Identity Protection Services, is proof that not even the rich and famous are immune to identity theft:

WILL SMITH

Identity thief Carlos Lomax opened fourteen credit accounts using Will Smith's legal name, Willard C. Smith. More than $30,000 was charged to these bogus accounts. Lomax had a prior conviction for using the identity of Atlanta Hawks basketball player Steve Smith to rack up $81,000 worth of charges on a credit card account.

TIGER WOODS

Con man Anthony Lemar Taylor fleeced golf great Tiger Woods for $50,000 worth of goods using nearly a dozen different lines of credit with different department stores. Though he did not resemble Woods in any way, the thief was able to carry out his crimes by using the athlete's legal first name of Eldrick rather than Tiger.

BARRY BONDS

The big league baseball player had his identity stolen by Jason Keys, an individual working as an employee of a company that shreds sensitive information and documents for celebrities, medical offices, and government organizations. Keys then applied for a credit card using Bonds's name and social security number.

According to UPI, Gregory Mortel, a twenty-three-year-old New Yorker, managed to obtain credit cards issued to him using the names of famous people, including Dallas Mavericks owner Mark Cuban, clothing mogul Tommy Hilfiger, and George Hornig, the chief operating officer of investment bank Credit Suisse First Boston.

MICHAEL BLOOMBERG

The New York City mayor found himself the victim of identity theft when Odalis Bostic attempted to rob him of $420,000. Mr. Bostic created the Laderman Development Company in Elizabeth, N.J., and set up accounts in the company's name at two banks, PNC and Sovereign Bank. He then deposited two forged checks, drawn from Bloomberg's personal account, into each of these banks.

RUBEN STUDDARD

Ronald W. Edwards, Studdard's ex-manager and public relations director, used the singer's name and personal information to take out credit cards, later maxing them to the tune of well over $100,000. Another $150,000 worth of checks was written for goods and services. Additional stolen checks in the amount of $25,000 were also deposited into Edwards's bank account.

1 Henry Budd died in 1862 leaving a £200,000 trust fund for his sons on the condition that neither of them would ever grow a mustache.

2 Eleanor E. Ritchey, the heir to the Quaker State Refining Corporation, left $4.5 million to her dogs—all 150 of them—in 1968. Not surprisingly, the family contested the will, and by the time it was settled, the value of the bequest had grown to $14 million. The dogs got $9 million and the family got the rest. When the last dog died in 1984, the remainder of the money was donated for research into animal diseases.

> "I owe much; I have nothing; the rest I leave to the poor."
> —François Rabelais

3 Sameul Bratt's wife didn't let him smoke, so he used his will to get even with her. He left her £330,000 on the condition that she smoked five cigars a day.

4 In 1955, Juan Potomachi left more than $50,000 to the Teatro Dramatico in Buenos Aires on the condition that his skull be used as a prop in at least one performance of *Hamlet*.

5 In 1983, the family of Tom Goodson was instructed, upon his death, to present everyone who attended his funeral with an envelope containing a £1 note and a card that read, "Have a smoke, crack a joke. Thanks for coming."

6 When Mark Schwartz and his wife, Christina Marie Petrowski-Schwartz, were slain in their home in 2008, it was difficult for their families to grieve, as their will made no bones about where they stood. The will was lengthy, with rambling tirades and impractical provisions. Leaving her mother, father, and siblings one dollar each, she stipulated that the money be donated to "their precious church to whom they had a greater allegiance than to their child and sister." Mark asked to be laid out in scuba gear for a burial at sea—"perhaps a beach party with strippers," he suggested. Mark also left $25,000 to each of his two best friends, advising them not to tell their wives.

7 In Denmark, an eighty-three-year-old woman died, leaving $60,000 to six chimpanzees housed in a Copenhagen zoo.

> "To kill a relative of whom you are tired is something. But to inherit his property afterwards, that is genuine pleasure."
> —Honoré de Balzac

8 A French doctor stipulated that his estate be used to award an annual prize to the man or woman with the "finest nose." The competition was open to all nationalities except Russian. Each contestant had to have red hair or black eyebrows.

9 In his will, the Prince of Islington stated that four days after his death, surgeons should be hired to operate on him to make sure he was dead.

10 T. M. Zink, a lawyer from Iowa, asked to have his estate used to build the Zink Womanless Library, where there would be no books by female authors, no magazines with articles penned by women, and no "feminine decorations." The words "No Women Admitted" were to be carved above the door. Luckily, his $100,000 wasn't even

enough to pay for the foundation of the library.

"No matter how rich you become, how famous or powerful, when you die the size of your funeral will still pretty much depend on the weather."
—Michael Pritchard

11 William H. Jackson of Athens, Georgia, was the author of *A Tree Deed*. He was so fond of a particular oak tree that grew on his land, that when he died in 1850, he left a will giving full possession of his land to the tree.

12 A wealthy New Yorker left the following will: "To my wife I leave one dollar and the knowledge that I wasn't the fool she thought I was. To my son, I leave the pleasure of earning a living which he had not done since thirty-five years. To my daughter, I leave one thousand dollars. She will need it. The only good piece of business her husband ever did was to marry her. To my valet I leave the clothes he has been stealing from me regularly for the past ten years. Also my fur coat that he wore last winter when I was in Palm Beach. To my chauffeur, I leave my cars. He almost ruined them and I want him to have the satisfaction of finishing the job. To my partner, I leave the suggestion that he take some clever man with him at once if he expects to do any business."

13 In 1948, George Harris was pinned underneath his tractor, and he had a terrible feeling that he was about to buy the farm. Nine hours later, he died. A few days later, someone noticed some writing scratched into the fender of the tractor. It read: "In case I die in this mess, I leave all to my wife. –Cecil George Harris." The fender was removed from the tractor and was admitted to probate and filed with the registrar of wills as Harris's last will and testament.

14 James Kidd's safe deposit box wasn't discovered until eight years after he died. It was then discovered that he had left a sum of $174,065.69, stating that the money should go "in a research or some scientific proof of the soul of a human body which leaves at death I think in time their can be a Photograph of soul leaving the human at death" [*sic*]. More than a hundred petitions were filed with the court, each claiming they had proof of the human soul. In 1971, the money was divided between the American Society for Psychical Research and the Psychical Research Foundation.

15 Abdel Nahas left $2 million to a dead mouse that he had had mummified the year before he died.

16 A Portuguese aristocrat with no family to speak of left his fortune to seventy names that he picked at random from the phone book.

17 A Canadian attorney left $568,106 to the mother who gave birth to the most babies following his death in 1928. A "baby derby" ensued, and two mothers who each gave birth to nine babies split the prize.

18 George Bernard Shaw, the Irish playwright, left his fortune to the person who could create a new English alphabet. The money was ultimately shared among five people who created phonetic alphabets.

19 Comic book writer Mark Gruenwald provided in his will that his cremated ashes be mixed with ink and used in a comic book.

20 *Star Trek* creator Gene Roddenberry's ashes were flown into space and shot out as the satellite orbited the earth.

FAMOUS PHILANTHROPISTS

In addition to donating portions of their earnings to various charitable efforts, celebrities are able to raise awareness about issues around the world, and indeed, millions of their dollars have benefited a wide range of causes. Whether the donations are made for altruistic reasons or tax deductions, they have improved the lives of millions. Here are just some of their efforts.

ATHLETES

ANDRE AGASSI

Andre Agassi created the Andre Agassi Charitable Foundation to provide recreational and educational opportunities for at-risk boys and girls. The Foundation funds a combination of emotional, physical, and academic programs designed to enhance a child's character, self-esteem, and career possibilities.

TROY AIKMAN

Troy Aikman established the Troy Aikman Foundation in 1992 with the mission of providing financial support for the physical, psychological, social, and educational needs of children.

LANCE ARMSTRONG

Lance Armstrong founded the Lance Armstrong Foundation to enhance the quality of life for those living with, through, and beyond cancer.

DAVID BECKHAM

The soccer legend and his wife, Victoria, founded The Victoria and David Beckham Charitable Trust to assist children and people with special needs worldwide.

BRANDON BURLSWORTH

Brandon Burlsworth, the former All-American offensive lineman for the Arkansas Razorbacks, was killed in an automobile accident in 1999 shortly after being drafted by the Indianapolis Colts. The Brandon Burlsworth Foundation, established in his memory, strives to make opportunities available to needy children.

JOEY CHEEK

The U.S. speed skater received $40,000 for winning two medals at the 2006 Olympics and donated all of his winnings to Right to Play, a Toronto-based humanitarian organization, to help Sudanese refugee children in Chad. His challenge to Olympic sponsors to match his pledge has resulted in more than $300,000 in donations.

DOMINIQUE DAWES

The Olympic gold medal–winning gymnast is the new president of the Women's Sports Foundation, which recently launched its three-year, $10 million GoGirlGo! initiative to fight the emotional and physical health risks that result from physical inactivity.

CHRIS EVERT

Chris Evert Charities, Inc. raises funds in support of innovative programs designed to encourage positive youth development, strengthen families, and prevent substance abuse.

ROGER FEDERER

The Swiss tennis champion's foundation funds projects that benefit disadvantaged children, especially in South Africa, and programs that promote tennis and other sports for young people around the world.

DOUG FLUTIE

Doug Flutie and his wife, Laurie, started Dougie's Team in 1998 to honor their son Doug, Jr., who has autism, and to help other families facing childhood autism through support and education.

KEVIN GARNETT
The NBA All-Star forward launched 4XL "For Excellence in Leadership®" in early 2002 to connect minority high school and college students with business leaders and Internet-based guidance while preparing them for business-related careers and entrepreneurship.

JEFF GORDON
The four-time NASCAR Cup Series champion established his foundation in 1999 to help organizations that support children with serious and chronic illnesses and their families.

MIA HAMM
Soccer star Mia Hamm's eponymous foundation is focused on providing support for two important causes: raising funds and awareness for bone marrow diseases and continuing the growth in opportunities for young women in sports.

LEBRON JAMES
In 2005, the Cleveland Cavaliers forward and his mother established the James Family Foundation, a charitable organization that sponsors events to raise money for programs that benefit youth in Akron, Ohio.

DEREK JETER
The New York Yankee founded his Turn 2 Foundation to support and create programs and activities that motivate

youth to choose healthy lifestyles and "turn away" from substances such as drugs and alcohol.

MAGIC JOHNSON
Magic Johnson started his foundation in 1991 as a single-disease organization that worked to raise funds for community-based organizations dealing with HIV/AIDS education and prevention programs.

NANCY KERRIGAN FOUNDATION
Nancy Kerrigan established a foundation to support those with visual impairment in honor of her mother, who is legally blind.

JOHANN KOSS
This former Norwegian speed skater, who won three gold medals in the 1994 Olympics, is now the CEO and President of Right to Play, a Toronto-based, athlete-driven, international humanitarian organization that uses sport and play as a tool for the development of children and youth in the most disadvantaged areas of the world.

PEYTON MANNING
The Indiana Colts' quarterback founded the PeyBack Foundation, which funds agencies and organizations that actively advance the welfare of disadvantaged children, especially in Indiana, Tennessee, and New Orleans, Louisiana.

MARK MCGWIRE
Mark McGwire founded the Mark McGwire Foundation for Children in an effort to expand our knowledge

about the complex issues surrounding child abuse.

SCOTT MELLANBY
St. Louis Blues hockey player Scott Mellanby and his wife, Susan, established the Mellanby Autism Foundation in honor of their son, Carter. The foundation funds autism research, special autism programs, and support for parents of autistic children.

PHIL MICKELSON
With his wife, Amy, the PGA golfer donates money for each birdie or eagle he makes to efforts to adapt or build accessible homes for soldiers returning to the States with serious injuries or disabilities. The couple also partners with ExxonMobil to offer a five-day Teachers Academy for two hundred third- to fifth-grade educators to improve their skills in motivating students and in teaching math and science.

BODE MILLER
In 2005, Olympic medalist and World Cup champion skier Bode Miller and his family established the Turtle Ridge Foundation, which is dedicated to supporting health, diversity, and sustainable living in our local communities. His foundation also supports organic farming and organizations that protect nature's precious resources.

ALONZO MOURNING
The NBA basketball player created Zo's Fund for Life to raise money for Columbia University's Glomerular Institute, one of the leading centers

in the United States for research and clinical studies on kidney disease. His charity also raises funds for nonprofits serving at-risk children and youth.

SHAQUILLE O'NEAL

The basketball star frequently donates time and money to charitable causes, including $1 million to the Boys & Girls Clubs of America to create technology centers in Clubs nationwide, in partnership with Microsoft Corporation.

JORGE POSADA

Jorge Posada, catcher for the New York Yankees, established the foundation that bears his name to support athletic programs for children in New York and Puerto Rico, and organizations that work with children who suffer from craniosynostosis.

ALBERT PUJOLS

The first baseman for the St. Louis Cardinals started his own family foundation in 2005 to support charities for children with Downs Syndrome and assist impoverished families in the Dominican Republic, his native country.

CAL RIPKEN, JR.

Inspired by their father's teachings, work ethic, and love for baseball, Cal Ripken, Jr., and Bill Ripken intend to use the Cal Ripken, Sr. Foundation, started in 2001, to reach out to millions of underprivileged kids. The Foundation is dedicated to "building character through baseball the Ripken Way."

ALEX RODRIGUEZ

The New York Yankees' star hitter and third baseman works extensively with the Boys & Girls Clubs of Miami. In 2002, he donated $3.9 million to the University of Miami to fund an annual scholarship to a Boys & Girls Club member and to build a baseball stadium.

JALEN ROSE

The Jalen Rose Foundation was established to show Jalen's appreciation for the communities where he has lived and played basketball. Grants are distributed in Detroit, Chicago, and Indianapolis.

MAX STARKS

Steelers offensive tackle Max Starks established a fund at the Pittsburgh Foundation in 2005 to promote childhood literacy and education. At twenty-three, he is one of the youngest donors to create such a fund.

GRANT WISTROM

Seattle Seahawks defensive end Grant Wistrom created a grantmaking public charity in 2002 to positively affect the lives of children, especially those with cancer, through fun and recreational activities.

TIGER WOODS

Tiger Woods and his foundation actively promote parental responsibility and involvement in the lives of children.

WORLD SPORTS HUMANITARIAN HALL OF FAME

This museum on the campus of Boise State University in Idaho celebrates all that is good in sport and honors athletes who have given back to their communities.

KRISTI YAMAGUCHI

The Olympic gold medal–winning figure skater established the Always Dream Foundation in 1996 to fund programs "designed to inspire and embrace the hopes and dreams of children and adolescents."

SINGERS AND MUSICIANS

GARTH BROOKS

Garth Brooks's Teammates For Kids Foundation was set up in 1999 to engage baseball and hockey players and others in supporting programs for kids.

CHER

Perhaps inspired by her role in *Mask*, the singer and actress is the national spokesperson and major donor for the Children's Craniofacial Association, whose mission is "to empower and give hope to facially disfigured children and their families." She also supports and promotes Get A-Head, which aims to improve the quality of life for people with head and neck diseases.

MARIAH CAREY

Mariah Carey works with the Make-A-Wish Foundation and the Fresh

Air Fund, and supports a variety of other charities.

DAVE MATTHEWS BAND

In addition to performing at benefit concerts, the musicians established the Bama Works Fund to carry out their commitment to charitable works, both close to home and worldwide. With his sister, Jane, Dave Matthews also created the Horton Foundation, a private foundation that focuses on small organizations working on specific humanitarian, educational, and environmental projects here and abroad.

RICK DELLARATTA

The jazz artist and founder of Jazz for Peace promotes music education in schools and donates musical instruments to underprivileged children around the world.

FARM AID

Dave Matthews, Willie Nelson, and many other artists sing in these annual concerts to raise awareness about the loss of family farms and to raise funds to keep farm families on their land.

PETER GABRIEL

Peter Gabriel cofounded Witness, an international human rights organization that provides equipment, training, and support to local groups to produce and use video in their human rights advocacy campaigns.

ELTON JOHN

Since 1992, the Elton John AIDS Foundation has distributed more than

$30 million internationally to support HIV/AIDS prevention, the elimination of prejudice and discrimination against HIV/AIDS-affected individuals, and direct services to those living with HIV/AIDS.

QUINCY JONES

The Quincy Jones Foundation (formerly Listen Up) supports programs that meet the healthcare and educational needs of children, and works to bridge the gap between privilege and poverty for young people around the world, especially in South Africa. The man who put together We Are the World ($60 million in charitable funds), along with Bono, met with Pope John Paul II in 1999, resulting in $27.5 billion in debt relief for impoverished nations.

BRIAN LITTRELL

After struggling with his own heart-related illnesses, Brian Littrell, from the Backstreet Boys, established a club to encourage pediatric heart health. The Brian Littrell Healthy Heart Club for Kids offers education, exercise, nutrition, and counseling to children ages eight to twelve who suffer from a heart condition or have a strong disposition toward developing heart disease.

MADONNA

The singer founded the Ray of Light Foundation, which gives primarily to Kabbalah Centers but also to medical research and health associations, particularly those for musicians who are facing health problems.

SARAH MCLACHLAN

Singer/songwriter Sarah McLachlan's foundation is "dedicated to the advancement of music education and, in particular, to the musical education and appreciation of disadvantaged youth" in Canada.

RUSSELL SIMMONS

Hip-hop and entertainment leader Russell Simmons, cofounder of Def Jam Records and Phat Farm Clothing, established the Rush Philanthropic Arts Foundation and Hip-Hop Summit Action Network, nonprofits for youths to get involved in arts and social causes.

BRITNEY SPEARS

The foundation started by Britney Spears is focused on helping children in need. The philosophy behind the foundation is that music and entertainment have a healing quality that can truly benefit these kids.

STING AND TRUDIE STYLER

The mission of the Rainforest Foundation started by Sting and his wife, Trudie, is to support indigenous peoples and traditional populations of the rainforest in their efforts to protect their environment and fulfill their rights.

U2 AND BONO

U2 and Bono have been involved in many issues throughout the years and they support the work of Greenpeace, War Child, and Amnesty International. Most recently, Bono has worked with Jubilee Plus to erase third world debt to wealthy countries.

ACTORS, DIRECTORS, TV CELEBRITIES, AND AUTHORS

TYRA BANKS

In response to the many letters she receives from girls seeking advice, Tyra Banks created T-Zone, a summer camp designed to build the self-esteem of young women.

PIERCE BROSNAN

The Irish TV and film actor supports and promotes environmental and children's organizations from around the world.

JACKIE CHAN

The martial arts movie star is a Goodwill Ambassador for UNAIDS and UNICEF to help arrest the spread of HIV/AIDS.

GEORGE CLOONEY

The film actor/producer leverages his celebrity and donates money for disaster relief and other causes, including The One Campaign To Fight Global AIDS and Poverty.

BILL COSBY

To honor the memory of their son, Cosby and his wife, Camille, formed the Hello Friend/Ennis William Cosby Foundation to support programs that educate young children with learning differences.

KATIE COURIC

Katie Couric's National Colorectal Cancer Research Alliance (NCCRA) is dedicated to the eradication of colon cancer by harnessing the power of celebrity to promote education, fund-raising, research, and early medical screening.

LEONARDO DICAPRIO

Established in 1998, the movie actor's eponymous foundation has actively fostered awareness of environmental issues, placing particular emphasis on the issues of global warming, alternative and renewable energy sources, and the preservation of the planet's amazing biodiversity.

CLINT EASTWOOD

The longtime actor, director, and one-time mayor of Carmel, California, is also a major supporter of film preservation and archives.

JANE FONDA

The actor and political activist supports reproductive health and education. To honor her contributions and efforts, Emory University named their adolescent reproductive health center after her, and she founded the Georgia Campaign for Adolescent Pregnancy Prevention in 1995, where she remains an active donor and board member.

MICHAEL J. FOX

Michael J. Fox created the Foundation for Parkinson's Research, which is dedicated to ensuring the development of a cure for Parkinson's disease through an aggressively funded research agenda.

RICHARD GERE

Richard Gere's foundation primarily contributes directly to His Holiness the Dalai Lama and the Tibetan community-in-exile to aid in the cultural, religious, health and educational survival of the Tibetan people

MEL GIBSON

The film actor, director, and producer donated $10 million in October 2004 to two Los Angeles hospitals to provide care for needy children from foreign countries. Since 2000, his family has given $17 million to Healing the Children, a nonprofit that serves young people with serious yet correctable medical problems.

TOM HANKS

The Oscar-winning actor has favored the James Fund for Neuroblastoma Research at Sick Kids and serves as the American ambassador for the Freeplay Foundation, which provides wind-up radios to the world's poorest populations, especially children living on their own.

AUDREY HEPBURN

After her death in 1993, the Audrey Hepburn Children's Fund was created to continue Audrey's international appeals on behalf of ill-treated and suffering children around the world.

ANGELINA JOLIE

The film actress and Goodwill Ambassador for the United Nations High Commissioner for Refugees (UNHCR) uses her fame and fortune to raise awareness and funds for UNHCR's programs, which currently assist 20 million refugees in approximately 120 countries.

JENNY JONES
Former national talk show host Jenny Jones is empowering individuals to make a lasting impact on their community. Through her foundation, Jenny is giving away $2 million of her own money. Her Jenny's Heroes program awards grants of up to $25,000 to individuals who submit the best ideas for tangible, lasting community projects chosen for their significant long-term benefits.

DAVID LETTERMAN
In 1993, the late night talk show host started his foundation, which was called the DL Foundation. Now called the American Foundation for Courtesy and Grooming, it gives primarily to children's services and education.

"He had learned over the years that poor people did not feel so poor when allowed to give occasionally."
—Lawana Blackwell, *The Courtship of the Vicar's Daughter,* 1998

JACK LORD
The star of the sixties police drama *Hawaii Five-0*, who died in 1998, and his wife, Marie, who passed away in 2005, bequeathed $40 million to a dozen Hawaiian nonprofit organizations. The bequest will create the Jack and Marie Lord Fund at the Hawaii Community Foundation, which will generate an estimated $1.6 million to $2 million a year to be divided among the twelve organizations.

PAUL NEWMAN
Paul Newman donated 100 percent of his after-tax profits from the sale of Newman's Own products for educational and charitable purposes.

ED NORTON
After high school, the stage and screen actor worked for his late grandfather's Enterprise Foundation, a national nonprofit that provides affordable housing for low-income people in large cities. Norton now serves as a trustee for the organization in which his grandmother, a cofounder, still serves as vice president and secretary.

ROSIE O'DONNELL
Rosie O'Donnell established her For All Kids Foundation, Inc. in 1997 to provide financial support to nonprofit programs serving economically disadvantaged and at-risk children and their families.

HAROLD PINTER
The British playwright, director, actor, poet, and political activist, who received the 2005 Nobel Prize in Literature, supports and promotes several human rights and social justice organizations.

VANESSA REDGRAVE
The veteran film and stage actor supports human rights causes. With her brother, Colin, she formed the Peace & Progress Party, a British political party to campaign for human rights.

CHRISTOPHER REEVE
Christopher Reeve's Paralysis Foundation is committed to funding research that develops treatments and cures for paralysis caused by spinal cord injury and other central nervous system disorders.

J. K. ROWLING
The British children's author was recently named president of One Parent Families, a U.K. nonprofit that supports, educates, and advocates for single parents. Rowling, once a single parent herself, has been one of the organization's major supporters and ambassadors since 2000.

MARTIN SCORSESE
Since he formed it in 1990, Martin Scorsese's Film Foundation has been committed to fostering greater awareness of the urgent need to preserve motion picture history.

ANDREW SHUE
With his friend Michael Sanchez, the TV/film actor founded Do Something, a nonprofit online community site to help young people change the world.

STEVEN SPIELBERG
In 1994, after filming *Schindler's List*, Steven Spielberg established Survivors of the Shoah Visual History

Foundation with an urgent mission: to videotape and preserve the testimonies of Holocaust survivors and witnesses.

SHARON STONE

Sharon Stone's foundation, Planet Hope, is involved in sponsoring many diverse activities for children of all ages and cultures.

MONTEL WILLIAMS

The goals and scope of Montel's MS Foundation are far-reaching: to provide financial assistance to select organizations and institutions conducting research, to raise national awareness, and to educate the public about multiple sclerosis.

ROBIN WILLIAMS

The actor and comic supports numerous social causes. Efforts include performing in Comic Relief to raise money for the homeless, and starting the Windfall Foundation with former wife Marsha Garces to support arts, education, and social services.

BRUCE WILLIS

The movie actor supports youth causes through his private foundation. He also actively supports the Screen Actors Guild Foundation to encourage interest in acting.

OPRAH WINFREY

Oprah Winfrey announced Oprah's Angel Network on September 18, 1997, to inspire people to use their lives to reap the truest rewards that come from giving to others.

WEALTHY INDIVIDUALS

MICHAEL BLOOMBERG

The mayor of New York City and founder of Bloomberg L.P., a global financial news service, also is one of the country's most generous philanthropists, giving millions to arts, education, healthcare, and social services.

BILL GATES

The foundation started by Bill and Melinda Gates is dedicated to improving people's lives by sharing advances in health and learning with the global community.

GEORGE SOROS

George Soros has been active as a philanthropist since 1979, when he began providing funds to help black students attend the University of Cape Town in apartheid South Africa. Today he is chairman of the Open Society Institute and the founder of a network of philanthropic organizations that are active in more than fifty countries.

"There is a natural law, a Divine law, that obliges you and me to relieve the suffering, the distressed, and the destitute."
—Conrad Hilton

"What's a soup kitchen?"
—Paris Hilton

e won't even try to tell you how to go about getting rich. Thousands of books address themselves to the subject, offering advice on everything from budgeting, investing, and estate planning to debt and tax issues. And, of course, there's no shortage of books—by charlatans and experts alike—claiming to contain the secrets to "guaranteed" wealth. So we steer this chapter in a different direction entirely, focusing instead on holding onto what we have by acting responsibly in all of our money interactions.

Knowing how to protect yourself against identity theft, asking for a raise, and avoiding overspending are just a few of the defensive measures you'll find here. Looking at the advice of the best money columnists and bloggers can give even a beginner the confidence to face up to money issues that most of us avoid, and our lists of recession-proof jobs and the secrets of self-made millionaires can help plan futures. If recent years have taught us anything about money, it's the fact that we need to be better prepared in a fast-changing world. The resources we offer here are, in essence, survival tactics.

Yet there is a vast difference between making a living and making a life, and knowing which is which can make the difference between happiness and misery. So while we acknowledge the fact that more money is usually better than the alternative, we're hoping that the tools offered here can take some of the stress out of the subject of money and also remind us that wealth and abundance lie not in our bank accounts but in our hearts.

THE URGE TO SPLURGE: 14 REASONS WE OVERSPEND

You've written a budget and you've memorized it. Yet somehow, you still arrive home from a shopping trip with six pairs of slipper socks in assorted sizes (they were on sale!). What goes on in your brain when you splurge on items you don't need and can't afford? It's basically a battle between your thoughts and emotions. You know you can't afford it but you want it anyway.

Here are fourteen reasons we spend money we don't have:

ABOVE: The way to a woman's heart, c.1910

1 Spending money can make you feel rich, especially when you're in the market for a luxury. You know you don't have the money, but you can't resist that temporary escape to a life in which money is no object.

2 You think the item will make you happy. Despite what the ads tell you, happiness doesn't come in a blisterpack. But if you're feeling as though something in your life is missing, it's sometimes hard not to wonder if slipper socks won't do it.

3 You hate shopping. You hate it so much that you just don't have the patience to deal with it. So you go to the stores picking up whatever is available, finding out too late that you still don't have what you need.

4 You feel guilty. So you take a friend out to dinner or buy the kids a couple of DVDs or send flowers to Mom. Kids especially are great at eliciting these feelings. Remember that sometimes a sincere conversation can go a long way.

5 You're looking for love. Showering people with gifts won't buy love or friendship, but we often go overboard with such overtures.

6 We forget how much money we really have. Too often, budgets don't take into account the unexpected expenses that come up (the new carburetor; that roof repair that no one saw coming), so while it may seem like that trip to Bermuda is affordable, your next bank statement tells you otherwise.

7 You're keeping up with the Joneses. They're spending money on things you don't need, but hey, if they can afford a 96-inch flat screen TV, you can too. After all, you have more money than they do. Do you? Perhaps they mowed their own lawns for a year to afford that TV. The worst part of all this is that the Joneses are most likely trying to keep up with you.

8 It doesn't seem like real money if you can charge it. Besides, you can always just make the minimum payment on the card. True, and that's just what the credit card companies want you to think. The result? Billions of dollars of credit debt at unconscionable interest rates.

9 You feel entitled. You work hard. You work overtime. You clip coupons. You should be able to afford something luxurious once in a while.

10 You're trying to maintain a previous lifestyle. A financial downturn or the loss of a spouse can completely change your situation. Denial does not help.

11 You feel rich on payday. Somehow, you can't bring yourself to look ahead. That money is burning a hole in your pocket!

12 You constantly think about buying things and you keep a running wish list of "stuff." But your list never seems to get shorter. As soon as you acquire an item, you add two more to the list.

13 You haven't figured out the difference between *wanting* something and *needing* something. When you walk into a store, the child inside of you screams "Gimme!"

14 You don't really understand how money works. You know that you can get away with paying the minimum on your credit account, and you're a little fuzzy on the subject of budgeting and future needs. You avoid balancing your checkbook every month, assuming you'll hear about it soon enough if money starts to run out. You're not quite sure how much money you have in the bank.

A successful lawyer was getting out of his brand-new Lexus when a truck sped past and completely tore off the door on the driver's side. A crowd gathered and someone dialed 911. A policeman approached the lawyer, who was screaming hysterically about the fact that his luxury car had just been destroyed and that it could never be fixed properly. The policeman, amazed, said, "How can you be that materialistic? Don't you even notice that your left arm is missing from the elbow down?"

"Oh my god!" screamed the lawyer. "Where's my Rolex?"

WHY WE BUY: THE PSYCHOLOGY OF SPENDING

It's not always your fault. There are forces at work out there that are cleverly implemented for one goal only: getting you to part with as much money as possible. Being aware of them can help keep you out of debt.

ADVERTISING

Countless dollars are being spent to understand your buying habits and create a psychological connection between you and a product. Advertisers use "psychographics"—the study of lifestyle, ambitions, and worldview—to help marketers focus in to specific psychological triggers. And once those ads tap a deep psychological level, it becomes difficult to remain rational.

SHOPPING AS EXPERIENCE

Shopping is not just about purchasing what you need and then going home. It is entertainment and social involvement. Shopping malls have become "experiential." They are vast, complex, and complete. Studies have shown that most actual purchases occur in the third hour of shopping, thus malls are designed to keep a shopper there for at least that long, with winding architecture, appealing music, and pleasing aromas.

THE MEDIA

Popular television shows and movies display images of "the good life," yet the lifestyles they depict are often way out of line with reality. These projected images deeply influence the way we see our personal level of success.

THE PROLIFERATION OF CONSUMER GOODS

There is simply so much to buy! Walk into any large children's toy store and count the types of dolls alone. Or an electronics store—the variety of stereos and DVD players is staggering. Goods and services that used to be luxury items are now more in the financial range of most consumers. This leads to increased spending because everything is "so affordable."

SOCIETY

What is "success"? Walk into a financial institution to request a home loan when you are wearing an expensive watch, designer clothes, and stylish accessories. Walk into the same place wearing rags and see if you get equal treatment. Society defines success by what we look like, how much money we make, and what we own. There is no doubt that we have more clout when we convey an air of "success."

It is not surprising that we are often tempted to buy things that will make us appear wealthier.

FRIENDS AND FAMILY

Pressure from friends and family members can be overwhelming. You may feel a strong sense of expectation from them, believing that they deserve to live with certain things and in a particular way. You may not want to disappoint them or cause conflict so you spend to their desires. Saying "no" to the people you love is an extremely difficult thing to do—and many people don't.

EASY CREDIT

It is easier than ever to borrow money for the things we want but can't really afford. Go into any department store in America and more than likely you will be asked if you would like to apply for their store credit card. It is also easier to obtain credit even when you have a "bad" credit history, so those already deep in debt can continue to plunge further. Cash advances, "instant checks," payday loans, and high credit limits all contribute to the temptation to overspend.

15 WAYS TO AVOID OVERSPENDING

According to researchers, the middle class is most guilty of overspending. In the 1990s, they spent money as soon as they had it. Today they spend money they don't even have. The media doesn't help: Ads are designed to scare us into believing that if we don't buy their products, we do so at our own peril. Further, even the TV shows we watch encourage us to spend. In real life, *Sex and the City*'s Carrie could never afford her lifestyle on her journalist's salary. Here are some tips for curbing your enthusiasm the next time you shop:

1 Admit you have a problem overspending and face it. You need a budget. You need a mantra. You need common sense.

2 Allow yourself a cooling-off period before you make a purchase. That portable treadmill looked mighty nifty in the store, but given a few days, you may decide that you don't really have room for it, and the gym is a more social experience.

3 Pay with cash or debit cards instead of credit cards. Feeling the pinch sooner will remind you that you are not made out of money.

4 Shop around. The Internet leaves no excuse for overpaying. Research an item online before you purchase to make sure you're getting the lowest price around.

5 Beware of phony "bargains." Buying a discount card to, say, Barnes and Noble, only makes sense if you shop there often. A 5-pound can of coffee may sound like a great bargain at $10, but if most of it will be old and stale by the time you get around to using it; it's not a bargain at all. When shopping at wholesale stores such as Costco and Sam's Club, make sure the items you buy are really cheaper there. Some of them aren't. Don't forget to take into account the cost of your membership when calculating your savings.

6 Know when salespeople and advertisers are working against you. Read Paco Underhill's classic *The Science of Shopping* to learn more about your being manipulated as a consumer. (Did you know that since most shoppers are right-handed, expensive items are placed on the right as you enter a store; or that mirrors, a known distraction, are strategically placed throughout stores to keep you there longer?)

7 Keep the tags on new items until it's time to wear them. You might find, after a month, that the garment really doesn't fit your lifestyle after all.

8 Keep track of your spending. List every purchase you make. You need to know where your money is going (see "Top 10 Money Wasters," page 276).

9 Know that money—and its trappings—does not determine your worth in the world.

10 When you need to buy things, buy them all at once so that you don't spend time wandering around stores. Once you know you have what you need, you don't have to enter a store at all.

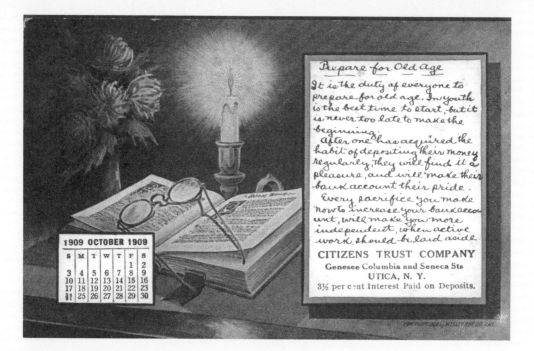

Within the postcard image:

Prepare for Old Age

It is the duty of everyone to prepare for old age. In youth is the best time to start, but it is never too late to make the beginning.

After one has acquired the habit of depositing their money regularly, they will find it a pleasure, and will make their bank account their pride.

Every sacrifice you make now to increase your bank account, will make you more independent, when active work should be laid aside.

CITIZENS TRUST COMPANY
Genesee Columbia and Seneca Sts
UTICA, N. Y.
3½ per cent Interest Paid on Deposits.

1909 OCTOBER 1909

S	M	T	W	T	F	S
					1	2
3	4	5	6	7	8	9
10	11	12	13	14	15	16
17	18	19	20	21	22	23
31	25	26	27	28	29	30

11 Don't shop online when you're tired. That's how slipper socks happen. On the other hand, shopping on the Internet means less time in stores, which is a good thing. Check out return policies before you buy.

12 Don't go food shopping when you're hungry.

13 Know when and how to haggle (see "How to Bargain Like a Pro," page 302).

14 Don't borrow money from friends or relatives. Ever.

15 Don't shop when you are in a bad mood. In a study conducted at Harvard's John F. Kennedy School of Government, participants were asked how much they'd be willing to spend on a sporty water bottle. Then they were shown a sad movie (*The Champ*, in which a little boy cries upon the death of his father). Those prices went up almost 300 percent!

ABOVE: A 1909 calendar postcard from the Citizen Trust Company in Utica, New York, offers sound advice.

23 SIGNS THAT YOU ARE REALLY BROKE

American Express calls and says, "Leave home without it!"

You receive CARE packages from Europe.

Consumer Credit Counseling services said "No."

You've been using the pilot light in your stove for mood lighting.

Your bologna has no first name.

Your idea of a seven-course meal is taking a deep breath outside a fine restaurant.

You visit a Coinstar daily.

At Communion, you go back for seconds.

You rob Peter . . . and then rob Paul.

You've been buying creamed kale—in bulk.

You have to save up to qualify as poor.

You're formulating a plan to rob the food bank.

You finally clean your house, hoping to find change.

You drip dry.

Cutting your hair doesn't seem so bad after all.

Long distance companies no longer call you to switch.

You think of a lottery ticket as an investment.

You go trick-or-treating even when it's not Halloween.

Sally Struthers sends you food.

You give blood every day—for the orange juice.

You got married for the rice.

Your credit card companies raised the rates from 6.9 to 24.9 percent.

All your kitchen condiments come from McDonald's.

TOP 10 MONEY WASTERS

Even if you have your major expenses under control, it's easy to overspend on a day-to-day basis. Here, according to www.BankRate.com, are the top money drains to which we are all susceptible:

1. COFFEE

The average cup of coffee costs $1.38, Starbucks notwithstanding. If you buy coffee on weekdays, you're spending more than $360 on coffee annually.

2. CIGARETTES

The Campaign for Tobacco Free Kids reports that the average price for a pack of cigarettes in the United States is $4.54. Pack-a-day smokers fork out $1,660 a year. Weekend smoker? Buying a pack once a week adds up, too: $236.

3. ALCOHOL

Two beers per day, with a tip included, can add up to $3,650 per year. It's twice that for two mixed drinks a day at the local bar. Note that wine by the glass, at about $8, often comes from a bottle that costs just that: $8.

4. BOTTLED WATER FROM CONVENIENCE STORES

A 20-ounce bottle of Aquafina bottled water costs about $1, more for the fancy stuff. That's $365 a year if you go through a bottle a day.

5. MANICURES

The average cost of a manicure is $20.53. A weekly manicure costs you about $1,068 per year.

6. CAR WASHES

According to www.CostHelper.com, the average cost for a basic auto detailing package is $58. Getting your car detailed every two months costs $348 per year. Even a simple $8 car wash comes to $416 a year.

7. WEEKDAY LUNCHES OUT

These can cost an average of $10. Eating out on weekdays comes to about $2,600 a year. On the other hand, if you pack a lunch, at a cost of about $4, you can save more than $1,500 annually.

8. VENDING MACHINE SNACKS

The average vending machine snack costs $1. If you buy a pack of cookies every afternoon at work, you're spending $260 per year. Better to buy a box and keep it in a drawer.

9. INTEREST CHARGES ON CREDIT CARD BILLS

According to a survey released at the end of May 2007, the median amount of credit card debt carried by Americans is $6,600. Assuming an interest rate of 13.44 percent, which is far lower than most companies charge, and assuming you make the minimum payment each month, it will take 250 months (almost twenty-one years) to pay off the debt, and you will have paid $4,868 in interest.

10. UNUSED MEMBERSHIPS

On average, gym memberships cost about $480 per year.

THE CHEAPSKATE HALL OF FAME

We're not suggesting you take any of these measures. Then again, when things get tough, the tough start saving. All of these are actual postings on www.walletpop.com.

1 "My uncle was so cheap that before he went to bed he removed the battery of his watch and put it back in the morning to save battery life."

2 "My friend brings library books, CDs, tapes, and movies to parties as gifts. Then he expects the recipient to return them to his town library by the date due. He lives far away, and the recipient has to mail the items back to his local library on time, or to pay the late fees."

3 "Someone I know actually charged me for text messaging him, believe it or not."

4 "I know someone who would go to the cemetery, get the flowers off the graves, and make a bouquet of flowers for his wife at different occasions. This went on for a couple of years until she found out."

5 "My grandma was so cheap that she would only bathe on holidays, to save on soap and water. Boy, did my grandpa love Christmas and New Year's, because her baths were a week apart."

6 "For the four years he worked at a national park, my stepson dressed in clothing from the park's lost and found pile."

7 "My father-in-law recently came to live with us; he told us that he sleeps on one side of the bed one week and the other side of the bed the next week just so he is not washing a clean side of the sheets and wasting money."

8 "I caught my boss running out into the rain to wipe down his Audi. He admitted he was doing it to save the price of a car wash."

9 "My dad's uncle is so cheap he uses a teabag and then dries it and uses it again."

10 "A guy I work with lunches on samples at food stores and just drinks water."

11 "I have a friend who goes to a fast-food joint and orders a senior coffee to go. He then fills the bag with creamers, sugar, and napkins to last a month. All for just 49 cents."

12 "My mom would buy two-ply toilet paper and split it in half to make one-ply paper."

13 "My friend's Dad used to put the person he wanted his mail to go to in the return address area, and purposely forget postage. When it was returned, it wasn't returned to him; it was brought to the person he wanted to send it to!"

14 "One person at my office would have a totally free lunch every day composed of many packets of ketchup, salt and pepper, hot water, several packets of saltine crackers, and a glass of cold water."

15 "My ex-boss used to water down the Windex bottle and hang up the paper towels to dry and reuse them on the glass."

16 "When his grandmother passed away my friend refused the funeral home's charges for the hearse. He rented a black minivan instead to transport his grandmother's casket to the cemetery."

17 "My ex-husband bought me candy and flowers for Valentine's Day. He said I could look at the flowers for about an hour and have one piece of the candy and then he took the candy and the flowers to his mother and his sister for their Valentine's gifts."

18 "My hubby and I were at the store the night before Valentine's Day picking up kids' treats. We were in the card lane and he handed me a sweet mushy card and said, 'Here, read this so I can put it back. It's $2.79.'"

19 "I know a woman who refused to buy a refrigerator with an ice maker. She would put her lunch in a plastic cooler and take it to work. At work, she would go to the canteen and fill her cooler with the 'free' ice."

20 "I've got a golfing buddy that is so cheap (and he's a millionaire) that he saves his dental floss and re-uses it. He puts the floss on a nail in his garage, and saves it, to be used again once it's dried out."

21 "I have a friend who used to come for Thanksgiving and Christmas dinners armed with a paper sack full of empty Tupperware containers (and nothing else). At the end of the meal, he would scoff up the leftovers to take home!"

22 "I have an aunt who doesn't even use toilet paper, she uses a hand towel and rewashes it. Now that's what I call cheap."

23 "My wife's friend and her mother have a collection of restaurant cups that they take back and get free drinks on return trips. Hopefully they will be caught someday and arrested."

24 "My boss recycles her bathwater. She uses it to wash her car, wash her hair, clean the house, water the flowers, mop the floors. And get this, she puts a little bleach in it and uses it to wash her dishes."

25 "I took a friend out to dinner for his birthday, I paid for the meal and left a tip. The cheapskate returned to the table and took the tip, and said he could use the money to purchase cigarettes."

"The only reason a great many American families don't own an elephant is that they have never been offered an elephant for a dollar down and easy weekly payments."
—*Mad Magazine*

MONEY ETIQUETTE

It's easy to squabble about money but rarely worth it. Here are some awkward moments—and tips for handling them—from Peggy Post, director of the Emily Post Institute and author of *Emily Post's Etiquette*:

Someone takes you out for a meal at a nice restaurant but leaves a horrible tip. The service wasn't great, but not bad either. Can you add cash to the table?

It depends on whom you're with. If your host is a close friend or relative, you can say, "Would you mind if I put down a few dollars? You probably didn't notice, but our server was extra helpful to me." With someone you don't know well, however, it's better to just let it go. You wouldn't want to seem like an ungrateful or judgmental guest.

Your coworkers are collecting money for someone's baby gift. You are pretty low on the totem pole—do you have to ante up as much as the senior staff?

Not at all. Chip in what you can; a few bucks is fine. Office celebrations can be so frequent that contributing might get burdensome. One solution: Suggest that your group try a collection pool. Pick a month to start and have everyone contribute an agreed-upon amount. The resulting fund pays for parties and gifts for the next year—no more collections, no more pressure.

Your niece is always asking you to sponsor her school by buying popcorn, magazines, etc. You don't let your kids collect from relatives this often. How do you stop the cycle?

Just say no. You've become your niece's best customer—why would she stop soliciting for more? The next time she calls, let her know that you'll be cutting back: "Danielle, I'll be happy to buy some cookies, but you should know that this is the only fundraiser of yours that I can give to this year. I'm getting a lot more requests recently, so I've decided to participate in just one for each niece and nephew each year.

At a tag sale, a friend spots something fabulous but pricey—and she has only $10. She borrows $50 and promises to repay right away . . . but a week goes by, and then two, with no word. What should you do?

There's no need to drop hints or mince words; simply ask for your money back. She probably just forgot and would appreciate a reminder. The next time you're on the phone, casually say, "Do you have that $50 I spotted you?" But if she really is dodging, don't let her put you off any longer. Tell her you need the money that day, and you'll swing by her house to get it.

Your aunt wants to buy a stroller for your baby, so you show her the one you'd like, which costs $200. She gets it but later emails you that she paid only $50 for a stroller when her own daughter was born. Now you feel bad. How should you respond?

Your aunt is obviously annoyed, but whatever she's feeling, it's tacky for her to point out the price difference. (And if the last stroller she bought was for her own child—who's presumably all grown up now—she may also be out-of-date on current price tags.) If she had a cost limit in mind, she should have let you know in advance rather than complain afterward. However, you can learn from the experience. In this situation, it would have been safer to say: "This is the stroller I have my heart set on. It's kind of expensive. If it fits your budget, that would be terrific . . . but if not, there are lots of other things I'd love to have." Mention a few other lower-priced items on your wish list so the giver will have choices.

You live on a cul-de-sac that ends in a large grass-covered patch, which the neighbors take turns mowing all summer. Now some people (including you) want to hire a lawn service, but others are balking at the cost. What now?

Unless you have a neighborhood association where the majority rules, you can't force dissenters to pay. Instead, graciously accept everyone's decision—then designate which weeks the service will mow and which weeks the nonpaying households will take their turns.

Your father is having a milestone birthday, so you and your three siblings are chipping in for an expensive group gift. Two of you are married; the other two are single. Should the gift be divided evenly, with each sib paying 25 percent, or should those with spouses put in more?

Split the bill four ways. Your father has four kids, and they're the ones who should be springing for the present (although it is only courteous to have husbands and wives sign the card). If this turns into a major argument, avoid the situation in the future by having each family member find his or her own gift.

Make it clear if you're treating.

You can invite friends to a restaurant without picking up the tab, but use language that makes it clear. Say, "John, would you and Ellen like to meet us at Jackson's Grill on Saturday? If you're up for it, I'll make the reservation." If you do want to pay for everyone's dinner, you'd phrase it differently: "We're hosting a dinner at Ronin's and would like you to be our guests." A written invitation also says that you are treating.

Avoid haggling.

When you go out to dinner with a group of people, you should assume that the check will be split equally rather than calculated down to the penny. It's easiest for everyone, so plan accordingly. But if you think you'll be ordering just a light salad with no cocktails and want to pay appropriately, ask for separate bills before you order. (Most restaurants will comply.) Or, when plans are being made, say, "I'd really like to come, but I'm strapped for cash this month. I hope you won't mind if I get a separate bill." You won't overpay, and the arrangement doesn't have to be discussed at the table.

Don't skip tips.

If your experience was less than stellar, it's okay to leave 10 percent (or 8 percent if it was poor). Leaving nothing is harsh and ambiguous—the server may think you forgot. Decide if the waiter really caused the problems (it might have been the kitchen's fault that the food was so slow in coming out). And don't wait until you're leaving to express dissatisfaction. Mention it as soon as you can so the waiter has a chance to make you happy.

THE TEN COMMANDMENTS OF MONEY

These commandments appear nowhere in Scripture, nor are they endorsed by any religious bodies we can think of. But they are the most oft-repeated pieces of advice where financial stability and personal well-being are concerned.

I Thou Shalt Not Worship Money: Too many people make the accumulation of money their sole activity in life. Money exists to facilitate living. Life does not exist to accumulate money.

II Thou Shalt Not Murder: Murder is inexcusable. Money is valuable, but it is never worth a life.

III Thou Shalt Not Steal: It is wrong to take what is not yours, or what you did not earn.

IV Thou Shalt Not Commit Fraud: Money fraud is essentially the same as stealing, but deserves its own commandment. Fraud and identity theft have no place in a civil world.

V Thou Shalt Not Keep Up with the Joneses: Keeping up with the Joneses is a big reason many people get into debt. If you desire something, set realistic goals and work toward them.

Remember that your neighbor may have gone into debt to buy the same thing that you desire!

VI An Emergency Savings Account Will Help You Deal with Unforeseen Events: Saving money for a rainy day ensures you are prepared for an emergency and will not have to break the Tenth Commandment of Money.

VII Be Charitable and Help Your Neighbor in Need: Many people tithe, which is giving a set percentage of their income to the church. If you do not believe in tithing, or do not feel you can afford to tithe a set percentage of your income, there are other ways to be responsible toward others. Some ideas include donating what you feel you can afford, donating items to charities, or donating your time, energies, or skills.

VIII Money Shalt Not Be for You an Expression of Power and Domination and an Occasion of Sin: Having money does not equal power, nor does it give you the right to sin. Likewise, a lack of money does not equal weakness. You are not your money, nor your belongings.

IX Thou Shalt Have Insurance: Auto insurance is a requirement in all states, but you should have other insurance as well. Life, homeowner's or renter's, medical, dental, and other forms of insurance are vital parts of maintaining a healthy financial well-being.

X Thou Shalt Not Have Excessive Debt: Debt is sometimes necessary, even though it can lead to hardship later in life. Mortgages, medical bills, educational costs, and a *reliable* (not excessive) means of transportation are legitimate reasons to go into debt. Excessive debt for consumer goods should be avoided at all costs.

8 STEPS ON THE PATH TO ABUNDANCE

FENG SHUI FOR PROSPERITY

Do you know where your financial "power spots" are? The contemporary methods of feng shui associate prosperity issues with the back left corner of any space. Stand at your front door facing into the house; your wealth area is at the back of the house on the left-hand side. There's also a wealth area within each room: Facing in from the doorway, it's the corner area in the back of the room on the left-hand side. Where are the wealth areas within your office, living room, kitchen, and bedroom? Now that you've identified your money power spots, here are some quick and easy ways to apply feng shui to these spaces.

Note that a true experience of prosperity is determined not by how much money you have, but by how well you notice and enjoy what is already present in your life. The formal name for the wealth area is "fortunate blessings." As you de-clutter, repair, and accessorize your money power spots keep this broader meaning in mind. When you celebrate being rich in friends and family, or rich with laughter, or the richness of your spiritual life, or even being rich in air and sunshine if nothing else seems to be going well for you today, material blessings will come to you more readily as well.

1 Clear out any clutter from these important areas. Clutter is a sign of stagnant energy, and clutter in your money power spots can clog up your cash flow. Getting rid of clutter is one of the most powerful ways to shift the energy of your power spots into high gear.

2 Fix things that are broken. Anything that doesn't work as it should is a sign of something wrong in the area of your life that corresponds to that part of your space. Examine each of your money power spots to look for anything that needs repair. It's time to do something about that loose doorknob, nonworking light switch, stuck file drawer, or clock that doesn't keep correct time, to name just a few possible examples. Remove items like these from your power spots or fix them so they work properly.

3 Enhance your power spots with symbols of prosperity, such as a bowl of coins (add your loose change to it every day), a "lucky bamboo" plant, or anything that symbolizes success and prosperity to you. There are lots of Chinese luck symbols available, but you don't have to use them unless you want to. A picture of your dream house, or a model of that luxury car you long for, is an effective money symbol because it has personal meaning for you.

4 Accent your money areas with the colors green and purple. Green symbolizes vitality and growth, and purple is the color of wealth. Place a bowl of green and purple grapes (real or artificial) in the wealth area of your kitchen, to symbolize abundance filling your home. If you use real grapes, it's okay to eat them, just add more from time to time so the grapes remain fresh and the bowl is always more than half full.

7 Live generously. Money is a form of energy, and it needs to flow through your life, not just into it. Hoarding and scrimping work against more coming in, while giving generously within your means makes space for even greater abundance. If you don't yet have ample money to share, give as generously as you can of your time, energy, compassion, and appreciation.

8 Take a few moments every evening to think about all the good things that happened to you that day and to express your gratitude for what you have received. Small things count, too, so it's okay if there's little of the spectacular on your list most of the time. It's not what happened that's important, it's getting in the habit of focusing on the positive side of things every day that matters. The more you notice, appreciate, and express gratitude for blessings received, no matter how small, the more good things will come your way, including money.

5 Pay attention to how you handle money every day. Do you keep paper money neatly sorted in your wallet or money clip, or is it jammed in there any old way, or crumpled up at the bottom of your pocket? Clean the clutter out of your purse and wallet, and start handling your money as though you value it.

6 If you neglect your money, it will neglect you, so be sure to balance your checkbook regularly and pay your bills on time. Put your checkbook in an attractive cover (choose green, purple, red, blue, or black) and keep it in the wealth area of your desk—again, that's the rear left corner—or in the wealth area of your office.

9 SIGNS THAT YOU WILL SOON BE RECEIVING MONEY

According to superstition:

1 If the palm of your right hand is itchy

2 If you find money and don't spend it

3 If you find a brown spider in your house

4 If you see a brown grasshopper in your house

5 If bird poop falls on your head

6 If it rains on your wedding day

7 If you pick up burnt matches

8 If you throw a penny into a well or a pond

9 If a spider crawls into your pocket

11 SIGNS THAT YOU ARE ABOUT TO LOSE MONEY

1 If the palm of your left hand is itchy

2 If you receive a wallet as a gift and it does not contain some token money

3 If you kill a snake

4 If you put your handbag on the floor

5 If you pick up money that you have found on a road

6 If your front door directly faces your back door

7 If you see a green grasshopper in your house

8 If you are winning at a gambling table and get up to wash your hands

9 If you gamble against a pregnant woman

10 If the color red exists anywhere on the southeast wall of any room of your house

11 If you pay back a loan on New Year's Day

7 SPELLS TO BRING MONEY AND WEALTH

All of these are recommended by various faiths and disciplines; we guarantee the effectiveness of none.

SPELL #1
You will need:
» your business card » a pen » cotton wool » a short length of red ribbon » a glass bottle with a stopper » honey

This spell should be performed on a waxing moon.

Visualize yourself happy and working and say: "My life and accounts shall soon be in balance."

Draw a bee on the back of your business card, buzzing from flower to flower. Lay it on the cotton wool.

Roll it into a cylinder and wrap the ribbon around it saying: "My life and accounts shall soon be in balance."

Place the scroll in the bottle, fill it with honey, replace the stopper, saying: "My life and accounts shall soon be in balance."

Place the bottle in a freezer. Every evening in the waxing moon turn the bottle clockwise.

SPELL #2
You will need:
» a 7-day green candle » cinnamon oil » an unpaid bill » patchouli incense

This spell requires good visualization. Take the candle and anoint it with the cinnamon oil. Take the bill you owe and place it under the candle. Hold your hands over the candle and say: "This candle burns to light the way for the money I need to pay this bill in a way that harms no one."

Light the candle and burn patchouli incense. Meditate for about five minutes as the candle burns. Visualize yourself paying the bill. Burn the candle every day around the same time for seven days, fifteen minutes at a time. Burn patchouli incense each time you do this. On the last day, burn the bill* with the flame from the candle and let the candle burn completely out.
* Make a copy first!

SPELL #3
You will need:
» one or more dollar bills » a permanent marker

Take one or more one-dollar bills and write a blessing on it with a permanent marker. (Better yet, do it in pencil or on a Post-it, as defacing currency is against federal law and shortens the life of the bill.) For instance: "May You Be Blessed with Health, Wealth, and Love." Then take the bills out into the world and hide them in places where people will find them. Do not just drop them on the ground; they must be purposefully hidden. You may slip one inside a newspaper (in the Help Wanted section, for instance), among the lettuce heads at the supermarket, inside the paper roll in a public restroom, or anywhere that would serve as a delightful place to find money. Never hang around to see who picks up your bill.

SPELL #4

You will need:
» a piece of paper   » a pen that writes in green   » two green candles

This spell should be performed on a full moon at around 10 p.m. Write the names of five people in green ink on the paper. Light two green candles, then burn the paper while chanting: "Take these names and do them no harm. Instead bring them luck, money, and charm. So might it be."

SPELL #5

You will need:
» fresh gingerroot   » cinnamon sticks
» 1 bunch fresh basil   » a washcloth or potpourri pouch

This ritual is performed in the bath. Wrap all ingredients in the washcloth or pouch and hang it on the spigot as you run the bathwater. Once you are in the bath, close your eyes and dunk your head three times. Promptly leave the bath.

SPELL #6

You will need:
» two black candles

Begin this spell on a Sunday, Thursday, or Friday.

Etch your name and the words "money," "wealth," "riches," and any other things you desire along the sides of the candles. Then light the candles and grasp them firmly in your hands until you feel your pulse

throbbing beneath your fingers, a sign that your intentions are becoming firmly grounded in the candles. Think about what you want, while chanting: "These candles bring me wealth and riches. In no way will this spell cause me to suffer any adverse effects."

Extinguish the flames with a spoon, candle snuffer, or your fingers (not your breath, which will change the spell).

Re-light the candles every night until they are completely burned down. Daily repetition will increase the spell's effectiveness.

SPELL #7

You will need:
» a green candle   » green paint
» a rock that is nearly square in shape

Begin this spell during the waxing moon.

Charge the green candle with money-attracting energy by visualizing yourself enjoying the money that you need. Then light the candle. In the glow of the candle flame, paint symbols for money such as the dollar sign (or any other symbol that makes you think of money) on the rock. As you do this, concentrate on how this rock will bring needed money into your life. After seven minutes, snuff the candle. Light the candle every day for 7 minutes until it is completely burned down.

9 MORE TALISMANS FOR WEALTH

1. Keep a piece of snakeskin in your wallet. (Snakes are a symbol of wealth in Japan.)
2. Place a piece of cornbread near your money.
3. Wear a jade ring on your pinky finger.
4. Cut a length of green cotton string and wrap it around your little finger in a clockwise direction. (Males should do this on their left hands; women on their right.) Then make a knot and wear the string throughout the day. If the string gets wet, discard it and start with a new string.
5. Every morning before you leave your house, use a red pen to make a dollar sign in your right palm. Do this every morning for fifteen days beginning with the first day of a new moon.
6. Keep a small amount of sea salt in a plastic bag in your wallet. Or place small containers of sea salt in all the corners of your house. Similarly, a bag of sea salt hung on the center of a main door will attract wealth. In all cases, the salt should be changed once a month, as it loses its potency.
7. Eat collard greens on New Year's Eve.
8. Turn your wallet or purse by the light of a waxing crescent moon three times to draw money to you. Make sure you first spy the full moon outdoors.
9. Lucky charms come in a variety of forms, from shamrocks and horseshoes to rabbits' feet and lucky pennies and may be carried for the hope of wealth and good fortune.

17 MONEY DREAMS AND WHAT THEY REALLY MEAN

All of these are popular theories according to one discipline or another:

1 If you dream that you are giving money away, you are looking forward to a period of financial stability.

2 Dreaming that you are losing money signifies temporary unhappiness or a setback in personal affairs. You may be feeling weak, vulnerable, as if your life is out of control.

3 If you dream of spending money, you are looking for love.

4 Seeing others giving money away suggests that you are feeling ignored or neglected.

5 Hogging or hoarding money indicates insecurity or selfishness.

6 A dream about having no money signifies a fear of losing one's place in the world or a feeling that one lacks the abilities needed to achieve some desired goal. It can also represent a feeling of being ignored or neglected by others.

7 Dreaming that you steal money may mean that you are finally pursuing those things that you associate with value.

8 If you dream that your wallet is stolen, it could mean that you are unwilling to share your wealth with others.

9 If you dream of finding money, you may be unhappy or dealing with some form of anxiety or disappointment.

10 Coins can represent a number of things in a dream, including energy, your heart and circulatory system, intuition, and hands-on healing. The value of the coin or indeed the quantity of coins can also be the significant symbol in the dream.

11 Dreaming of copper coins denotes despair and physical burdens.

12 Gold coins in dreams represent success and wealth.

13 Silver coins represent spirituality, intuition, values, your sense of self-worth, and your feminine side.

14 Stacked coins in your dream symbolize masculine power, dominance, and energy.

15 Dreaming that you are flipping a coin means you have a casual attitude about making some decision or ignoring a responsibility. It can also refer to your own irrational thoughts.

16 Dreams of dealings with a bank or financial institution could warn you of a sudden monetary loss. If the bank seems empty with no one available to help you, business losses are possible.

17 To see or win money in your dream indicates that success and prosperity are within your reach.

21 SECRETS OF SELF-MADE MILLIONAIRES

Self-made millionaires come in all shapes and sizes, and the sources of their money are just as varied. But there are some things they have in common—their values, for instance. Here are some guidelines on which they all seem to agree:

1 Dream big dreams. Thinking big will change your life.

2 Create a specific picture of exactly what it is you wish to accomplish. The more specific you are, the more likely you are to get there.

3 Think and act like you're the owner of a business, the business of everything you do. Even if you work for someone else, your attitude will plant seeds for your future success.

4 Love whatever you are doing now. If you don't love it, leave it. Find something that you love doing and do it well.

5 Create a mastermind group. Have regular meetings with others who are committed to building great lives. Share your experiences, learn from them, and support each other.

6 Establish a healthy work ethic. Make taking action your best friend.

"After a certain point money is meaningless. It ceases to be the goal. The game is what counts."
—Aristotle Onassis

7 Commit to constant, never-ending improvement. Make it a point to learn something new each and every day.

8 See your work as a service. Helping others will grow your business.

9 Know your business from top to bottom. That's your job.

10 Prepare for opportunity. It will knock, so be ready when it does.

11 Stay physically fit. Strong minds create strong bodies. Weak bodies are the result of weak minds. Your physical and mental health are the core of your success in life.

12 Prioritize your life. Do what's most important first.

13 Deliver more than your customer expects. This builds loyalty and repeat business and is in itself rewarding.

14 Discipline yourself. Fill your life with activities and people that make you grow. Discard activities and people that have negative results in your life.

15 Pay yourself first. This is the first rule of the wealthy. Put money into savings before you pay bills. And don't touch it.

16 Make time to be alone. This time is for planning and listening to what's inside you. Give your creativity time and give silence a chance to speak to you.

17 Go for greatness. Value the best and don't settle for less.

"There are two times in a man's life when he should not speculate: when he can't afford it, and when he can."
—Mark Twain

18 Honesty is the best policy. Know who you are and what you want. Express this with integrity at all times.

19 Be prepared to make decisions quickly and slow to change them.

20 Failure is not an option. If your mindset is focused on success, you will have success.

21 Be determined to attain your goals. Tenacious persistence builds confidence and this will lead to success.

THE RICH MAN

The rich man has his motor car,
His country and his town estate.
He smokes a fifty-cent cigar,
And jeers at Fate.

He frivols through the livelong day,
He knows not Poverty her pinch.
His lot seems light, his heart seems gay,
He has a cinch.

Yet though my lamp burns low and dim,
Though I must slave for livelihood—
Think you that I would change with him?
You bet I would.

—Franklin P. Adams

17 THINGS MILLIONAIRES WON'T ADMIT THEY DO

According to Dr. Thomas Stanley's exhaustive research while writing *The Millionaire Next Door* and *The Millionaire Mind,* first-generation millionaires tend to do the following:

1 Have shoes resoled or repaired. Millionaires know that if they purchase expensive shoes, and occasionally get the shoes resoled, then the cost per wear is much less than having to buy a new pair.

2 They have their furniture reupholstered or refinished instead of buying new. It's so much easier to pick out new fabric for an existing couch than spending endless hours shopping for a new one.

3 They have their clothes mended or altered instead of buying new.

4 They raise the thermostat setting on their air conditioners during daytime hours.

5 They switch long distance companies.

6 They take out loans to avoid high-interest credit-card debt.

7 They never buy anything through telephone solicitations.

8 They write a shopping list before grocery shopping and stick to it.

9 They use discount coupons when buying groceries.

10 They buy appliances and motor vehicles that have been "top-rated" by *Consumer Reports*.

11 They leave a department store as soon as they have purchased what they came for.

12 They buy household supplies in bulk at warehouse stores, i.e., Sam's Club and Costco, and they shop at Wal-Mart.

13 They use discount brokerage firms when investing.

14 They shield their wealth in tax shelters, trusts, and similar mechanisms. (Lost income from foreign tax shelters costs the U.S. government anywhere from $20 to $40 billion annually.)

15 They're not really that smart: According to *The Millionaire Mind*, the average college grade point average for millionaires is 2.9 and the average SAT score is 1190.

16 They often rent and lease expensive goods instead of buying them. Luxury cars, clothing, handbags, furniture, jewelry, art, and antiques are all eligible for what is known as "fractional ownership."

17 They're happy, according to a study conducted by the Wharton School of Business. Most millionaires reported that money helped them to create happiness by affording them more choices and freedom. Millionaires laugh and smile more often, reported the study.

ALL ABOUT IDENTITY THEFT

Valuable advice from the Federal Trade Commission (FTC):

Identity theft occurs when someone uses your personally identifying information—like your name, Social Security number, or credit card number—without your permission, to commit fraud or other crimes.

The FTC estimates that as many as nine million Americans have their identities stolen each year. The crime takes many forms. Identity thieves may rent an apartment, obtain a credit card, or establish a telephone account in your name. You may not find out about the theft until you review your credit report or a credit card statement and notice charges you didn't make—or until you're contacted by a debt collector.

Identity theft is very serious. While some identity theft victims can resolve their problems quickly, others spend enormous amounts of time and money repairing damage to their good name and credit record. Some victims lose out on job opportunities or are denied loans. In rare cases, they may even be arrested for crimes they did not commit.

For identity thieves, your personally identifying information or other financial account information is as good as gold. Skilled thieves use a variety of methods to obtain your information, including:

DUMPSTER DIVING

They rummage through trash looking for bills or other paper with your personal information on it.

SKIMMING

They steal credit/debit card numbers by using a special storage device when processing your card.

PHISHING

They pretend to be financial institutions or companies and send spam or pop-up messages to get you to reveal your personal information.

CHANGING YOUR ADDRESS

They divert your billing statements to another location by completing a change of address form.

OLD-FASHIONED STEALING

They steal wallets and purses; mail, including bank and credit card statements; pre-approved credit offers; and new checks or tax information. They steal personnel records, or bribe employees who have access.

PRETEXTING

They use false pretenses to obtain your personal information from financial institutions, telephone companies, and other sources.

Once they have your personal information, identity thieves use it in a variety of ways.

CREDIT CARD FRAUD

They may open new credit card accounts in your name. When they use the cards and don't pay the bills, the delinquent accounts appear on your credit report.

They may change the billing address on your credit card so that you no longer receive bills, and then run up charges on your account. Because your bills are now sent to a different address, it may be some time before you realize there's a problem.

PHONE OR UTILITIES FRAUD

They may open a new phone or wireless account in your name, or run up charges on your existing account.

They may use your name to get utility services like electricity, heating, or cable TV.

BANK/FINANCE FRAUD

They may create counterfeit checks using your name or account number.

They may open a bank account in your name and write bad checks.

They may clone your ATM or debit card and make electronic withdrawals in your name, draining your accounts.

They may take out a loan in your name.

GOVERNMENT DOCUMENTS FRAUD

They may get a driver's license or official ID card issued in your name but with their picture.

They may use your name and Social Security number to get government benefits.

They may file a fraudulent tax return using your information.

OTHER FRAUD

They may get a job using your Social Security number.

They may rent a house or get medical services using your name.

They may give your personal information to police during an arrest. If they don't show up for their court date, a warrant for arrest is issued in your name.

The best way to find out if your identity has been stolen is to monitor your accounts and bank statements each month, and check your credit report on a regular basis in order to limit the damage.

Unfortunately, many consumers learn that their identity has been stolen after some damage has been done.

You may find out when bill collection agencies contact you for overdue debts you never incurred.

You may find out when you apply for a mortgage or car loan and learn that problems with your credit history are holding up the loan.

You may find out when you get something in the mail about an apartment you never rented, a house you never bought, or a job you never held.

Checking your credit reports, notifying creditors, and disputing any unauthorized transactions are some of the steps you must take immediately to restore your good name. To learn more about these procedures or to file a

complaint, visit the Federal Trade Commission at FTC.gov.

It's also important to file an Identity Theft Report, which entitles you to certain legal rights when it is provided to the three major credit reporting agencies or to companies where the thief misused your information. An Identity Theft Report can be used to permanently block fraudulent information that results from identity theft. Identity Theft Reports can prevent a company from continuing to collect debts that result from identity theft, or selling them to others for collection.

HOW LONG CAN THE EFFECTS OF IDENTITY THEFT LAST?

It's difficult to predict how long the effects of identity theft may linger. That's because it depends on many factors including the type of theft, whether the thief sold or passed your information on to other thieves, whether the thief is caught, and problems related to correcting your credit report.

Victims of identity theft should monitor financial records for several months after they discover the crime. Don't delay in correcting your records and contacting all companies that opened fraudulent accounts. Make the initial contact by phone, even though you will normally need to follow up in writing. The longer the inaccurate information goes uncorrected, the longer it will take to resolve the problem.

PROS AND CONS OF ONLINE BANKING

When people use the Internet, they expect convenience, speed, and efficiency. The same expectations apply to online banking. Consumers view online banking as a quick way to pay bills and check their finances. But there are a few drawbacks to online banking if it's used incorrectly. Here are some pros and cons that can help you avoid pitfalls:

PROS

CONVENIENCE: Unlike your corner bank, online banking sites never close; they're available 24 hours a day, seven days a week, and they're only a mouse click away.

UBIQUITY: If a money problem arises while you're out of state or out of the country, you can log on instantly to your online bank and take care of business—24/7.

TRANSACTION SPEED: Online banking sites generally execute and confirm transactions at or quicker than ATM processing speeds.

EFFICIENCY: You can access and manage all of your accounts, including Individual Retirement Accounts, CDs, even securities, from one secure site.

EFFECTIVENESS: Many online banking sites offer sophisticated tools, including account aggregation, stock quotes, rate alerts, and portfolio managing programs to help you manage all of your assets more effectively. Most are also compatible with money managing programs.

CONS

IT MAY TAKE TIME TO GET STARTED: If you're new to online banking, it might take time to register for your bank's online program—it may be easier to physically fill out a form at your local branch. If you and your spouse wish to view and manage your assets together online, one of you may have to sign a durable power of attorney before the bank will display all of your holdings together.

LEARNING CURVE: Some banking sites can be difficult to navigate. Plan to invest some time and/or read the tutorials in order to become comfortable in your own virtual lobby.

BANKING SITE CHANGES: Even the largest banks periodically upgrade their online programs, adding new features in unfamiliar places. In some cases, you may have to re-enter account information.

TRUST: Trusting an online banking system is an issue for two main reasons: identity theft and operator error. If you use a non-secure wireless Internet connection, it might not be a good idea to use online banking. It's too easy for a savvy ID thief to view your personal information. In regard to operator error, some users worry that they might have clicked the transfer button too many or too few times. The best solution to this problem is to always print the transaction receipt and keep it with your bank records until it shows up on your personal site and/or your bank statement.

10 WAYS TO GO GREEN AND SAVE MONEY

AT THE SAME TIME

Want to help the environment, but not too keen on all of the expensive suggestions floating around out there? Here are ten frugal ways to incorporate green living into your life without throwing your budget to the wind.

1. SAFETY RAZORS

Giving up disposable razors for the old-fashioned safety razor is a great way to save money and the environment. The multi-packs of flat razor blades are not only inexpensive, they come without all of the extra plastic housing that ultimately ends up in landfills. An added bonus: You don't have to carve out extra storage in the cabinets when you stock up. Flat packs of blades store very efficiently in a minimal amount of space.

2. MINERAL SALT DEODORANT STICKS

You can find these at nearly any health food or natural living store. They last an incredibly long time, don't contain any harmful ingredients, and as with the safety razor idea listed above, don't come with a ton of obnoxious plastic packaging to toss in the landfill once the product has been used up. It also takes up minimal space, making it excellent for travel.

3. REUSABLE COFFEE FILTERS

Just imagine never having to buy or run out of these little babies again!

4. GIVE UP PAPER TOWELS

This isn't easy, at least in the beginning. Create a simple, workable system for having clean rags on hand. Hang a bag of them where you normally keep paper towels. When you need to reach for something to wipe up a spill or do a quick cleanup, reach for a washable cleaning rag instead of a paper towel.

5. RECYCLE OLD ATHLETIC SOCKS

Cut each old sock off just slightly above the ankle, and below the ribbed leg section. The leftover foot portion can be used instead of those expensive disposable dusting mittens. These things are great for getting around stair banister railings or gripping table and chair legs to dust. The other ribbed section, particularly if it is ribbed the entire length of the piece, is great to slice up one side and use for a moisture-holding dish rag. The ridges give you extra scrubbing power, too.

6. SHOPPING FOR SECONDHAND GOODS

Anything you are comfortable buying secondhand keeps that same item from ending up in a garbage dump. This applies to furniture, clothing, toys, kitchenware, and to a certain extent, automobiles. This effort goes a long way in helping out the planet and your pocketbook at the same time.

7. THINK BEFORE YOU PRINT

Save money on ink and paper by checking to see if you really need a paper copy of a particular document before hitting the print button. Still think you really need it? Check out the econo mode for printing, which will at least use less ink and save you money in the long run on those refilled cartridges.

8. CELEBRATE THE POWER OF TIE-DYE

This is a great affordable way to give lightly stained, lighter-colored linens and clothing items a second shelf life. Some ideas? Old sheets, curtains, pillowcases, socks, and T-shirts to name a few.

9. FIND A SECOND USE FOR THOSE PLASTIC GROCERY BAGS

These things really can help out a time or two more after making it home from the grocery store. Use them to line small trash cans (one less item to buy), to pick up after your dog, or instead of Styrofoam "popcorn" to provide extra cushioning in holiday postal packages.

10. CONSIDER A PERSONAL FILTER FOR YOUR KITCHEN FAUCET

This will enable you to skip the extra packaging that comes with large cases of bottled water and carve some extra cash out of your personal budget at the same time.

THE HIGH COST OF RAISING KIDS

Since 1960, the U.S. Department of Agriculture has provided estimates of expenditures on children from birth through age seventeen. The following data is for the year 2007. Budget components are provided by age of child and family income.

Housing expenses include shelter (mortgage interest, property taxes or rent, maintenance and repairs, and insurance), utilities (gas, electricity, fuel, telephone, and water), and house furnishings and equipment (furniture, floor coverings,

small and major appliances). Health care expenses include all medical and dental services, prescription drugs, and medical supplies not covered by insurance. Childcare and education expenses include daycare tuition and supplies, babysitting, and elementary and high school tuition, books, and supplies. It does not include the cost of a college education.

Miscellaneous expenses include personal care items, entertainment, and reading materials.

BEFORE-TAX INCOME: LESS THAN $45,800 (average = $28,600)

AGE OF CHILD	TOTAL	HOUSING	FOOD	TRANS-PORTATION	CLOTHING	HEALTH CARE	EDUCA-TION	MISC
0–2	$7,830	$2,970	$1,070	$930	$340	$600	$1,220	$700
3–5	8,020	2,930	1,190	900	340	570	1,370	720
6–8	8,000	2,830	1,530	1,050	370	650	810	760
9–11	7,950	2,560	1,830	1,140	420	710	490	800
12–14	8,830	2,850	1,930	1,290	700	720	340	1,000
15–17	8,810	2,300	2,080	1,730	620	770	580	730

BEFORE-TAX INCOME: $45,800 TO $77,100 (average = $61,000)

AGE OF CHILD	TOTAL	HOUSING	FOOD	TRANS-PORTATION	CLOTHING	HEALTH CARE	EDUCA-TION	MISC
0–2	$10,960	$4,010	$1,280	$1,390	$410	$780	$2,000	$1,090
3–5	11,280	3,980	1,470	1,360	400	750	2,210	1,110
6–8	11,130	3,880	1,880	1,510	440	850	1,420	1,150
9–11	10,930	3,600	2,210	1,600	480	920	930	1,190
12–14	11,690	3,900	2,230	1,740	820	930	680	1,390
15–17	12,030	3,350	2,480	2,200	730	980	1,170	1,120

BEFORE-TAX INCOME: MORE THAN $77,100 (average = $115,400)

AGE OF CHILD	TOTAL	HOUSING	FOOD	TRANS-PORTATION	CLOTHING	HEALTH CARE	EDUCA-TION	MISC
0–2	$16,290	$6,380	$1,690	$1,950	$530	$900	$3,020	$1,820
3–5	16,670	6,340	1,910	1,910	520	860	3,290	1,840
6–8	16,310	6,240	2,310	2,060	570	990	2,260	1,880
9–11	15,980	5,970	2,680	2,150	620	1,060	1,580	1,920
12–14	16,810	6,260	2,820	2,300	1,030	1,070	1,210	2,120
15–17	17,500	5,710	2,970	2,780	940	1,120	2,120	1,860

Estimates are based on 1990–92 Consumer Expenditure Survey data updated to 2007 dollars using the Consumer Price Index. For each age category, the expense estimates represent average child-rearing expenditures for each age (e.g., the expense for the three–five age category, on average, applies to the three-year-old, the four-year-old, or the five-year-old). The figures represent estimated expenses on the younger child in a two-child family. Estimates are about the same for the older child, so to calculate expenses for two children, figures should be summed for the appropriate age categories. To estimate expenses for an only child, multiply the total expense for the appropriate age category by 1.24. To estimate expenses for each child in a family with three or more children, multiply the total expense for each appropriate age category by 0.77. For expenses on all children in a family, these totals should be summed.

ESTIMATED ANNUAL EXPENDITURES* on children born in 2007, by income group, overall United States

YEAR	AGE	INCOME GROUP		
		lowest	middle	highest
2007	1	$7,830	$10,960	$16,290
2008	1	8,070	11,300	16,790
2009	2	8,320	11,650	17,320
2010	3	8,790	12,360	18,270
2011	4	9,060	12,750	18,840
2012	5	9,340	13,140	19,420
2013	6	9,610	13,370	19,590
2014	7	9,910	13,780	20,200
2015	8	10,210	14,210	20,820
2016	9	10,460	14,390	21,030
2017	10	10,790	14,830	21,690
2018	11	11,120	15,290	22,360
2019	12	12,740	16,860	24,250
2020	13	13,130	17,390	25,000
2021	14	13,540	17,920	25,770
2022	15	13,930	19,020	27,660
2023	16	14,360	19,610	28,520
2024	17	14,800	20,210	29,410
Total		**$196,010**	**$269,040**	**$393,230**

* Estimates are for the younger child in husband-wife families with two children.

6 GUIDING PRINCIPLES

People with financial difficulties all have one thing in common: They want to see their children avoid some of the mistakes they have made.

Here are some basic ideas to help parents break the cycle of debt and raise their children to be wise about their financial lives:

1. START EARLY
Many parents make the mistake of waiting to teach their kids about money. We've met people who think even their teenage kids are too young to be bothered with such concerns. That's far too late; most experts agree that kids should start learning about money as soon as possible. Depending upon the individual child and his/her aptitude, three years old is not too early to begin teaching about the value of money and using it wisely.

2. USE AN ALLOWANCE
An allowance is the first, best tool for teaching your kids about money. Giving them a regular income will help train them for their working life. We believe it's important to tie the allowance to household chores and tasks that are the child's responsibility. This will teach them an invaluable lesson about the relationship between work and income.

3. HELP THEM ESTABLISH A BANK ACCOUNT
After you've given your child his/her allowance, make sure it is deposited in a financial institution. Teach your children that the best place for their savings is in the bank or credit union, not under the mattress. Find a local bank or credit union that will set up custodial accounts for children. Wise financial institutions know that these kinds of accounts will help them create lifelong relationships with their banking customers.

4. INVOLVE THEM IN THE HOUSEHOLD FINANCES
It's crucial that you teach your children the value of money, and the value of purchases. They need to learn how far their allowance, savings, and eventually their paycheck will go. A great way to help them learn these lessons is by including them in part of the monthly bill-paying ritual. If they understand the costs associated with running a household, from mortgage payments to utilities, then they'll be less likely to take them for granted.

5. LET THEM GET A SUMMER JOB
Many parents don't think their teenagers should have to work. Consequently, many teens grow into adults who don't think they should have to work. The best way you can prepare your kids for their adult lives is to let them start early with part-time or summer work. This will help them evolve from the allowance you set up in their childhood into the adult world of work. Good early experiences in a real workplace, even a minimum-wage fast-food job, will teach them how to handle themselves as part of the grown-up workforce.

6. LEAD BY EXAMPLE
Children learn everything from observing the world around them. This especially applies to the way their parents conduct themselves. Every time you go through a checkout line with your kids in tow, they are watching you and learning. That means it's prudent to avoid impulse buys and frivolous purchases in front of the kids. You can't expect your kids to be good stewards of their money if you don't manage yours well.

16 GREAT WEB SITES FOR BARTERING

Why buy when you can barter? You can get exactly what you want on a tight budget. It takes a little more effort—but it's fun and creative, and it's been popular for thousands of years. Revived by the Internet, bartering is becoming more and more popular as pocketbooks shrink. Where to start? Here are 20 Web sites that will help you click your way to a new wardrobe, a bookshelf, or even four walls and a ceiling.

1. BOOKMOOCH.COM
What's traded: All sorts of used books
Here you earn and spend "mooch points" by offering and acquiring books. There's also an option that allows you to donate books to charities. It's a win-win proposition—and since books fit nicely into small parcels, it operates worldwide.

2. BOOKCROSSING.COM
What's traded: Books
But in the most fun way possible. You register your book onto the site on its own profile, and then you write the book's individual Book Crossing identifier and associated Web address on the book's inside cover, along with a message asking anyone holding the book to go online and register where and how they got it. Then you take it somewhere fun, and leave it there. You update the profile to say where you left it. And you watch. With a bit of luck, it's the start of an amazing journey! Meanwhile, you check what books have been "freed" in your local area, and you go in search of them. Awesome fun.

3. CRAIGSLIST.ORG
What's traded: Absolutely everything
This is the daddy of all bulletin board sites. It's been the subject of a documentary, and it's permanently busy (20 billion page views a month). Search hard enough and you'll find just about anything you can possibly be looking for.

4. FREECYCLE.ORG
What's traded: There is nothing that isn't offered on Freecycle
It's life in miniature. This is a colossal (4,000+ groups, 6 million+ people) network of nonprofit recycling hubs, operating as online bulletin boards. Everything is given away free. You log on at key points during the day, scan down the list of offers, spot something you need, and leap to the phone, hoping nobody beats you to it. Even an iBook was posted here—apparently snapped up in about ten seconds.

5. FRUGALREADER.COM
What's traded: Books . . . and book-related gossip
It's not just a site for swapping books. It's also a reading community, with reviews, discussion forums, and all sorts of lines of communication at work. A standout from its competitors.

6. HOUSE4TRADE.COM
What's traded: Your house
This site is all about permanent house trading and is fairly sophisticated. The backbone of the site is a very real Real Estate Network.

7. MAKEUPALLEY.COM/ SWAP/
What's traded: Used makeup (no kidding)
You browse the items on offer—you find something of your own that the swapper would be willing to accept in return—and off you go. The FAQ notes that all swapped items should be cleaned with alcohol before swapping, and only unused mascara should be

swapped, but even so, there will be some people who will flinch. There's a feedback system that provides an element of accountability.

8. PAPERBACKSWAP.COM
What's traded: Paperback books
When you successfully send away a requested book for trade, your account swells by one credit (or two if it's an audio book). You use your credits to get books. You can put in a standing order for a book that's not yet available—which is unlikely, as there are more than 3 million titles in there.

9. REHASHCLOTHES.COM
What's traded: Clothes and books
When you "rehash" (i.e., put up for swap) an item, it's listed as a page in the site's Trading Post hub, and people make offers that you can flick through and weigh. Once you've confirmed a mutually acceptable deal, the mechanics of getting the item to the new owner are left completely up to you.

10. SWAPACE.COM
What's traded: Everything under the sun
If you crave the push and pull of a negotiated deal, this site is for you, because you don't swap based on existing predetermined values—you decide how much your swap is worth by haggling (using their fancy electronic negotiation system). When you both see eye to eye, the swap can take place—and you get the quiet satisfaction of knowing you gave it your best shot.

11. SWAPCOVE.COM
What's traded: Everything
There are no points, no credits here; it's all about how much you think your swappable item is worth. You use this San Francisco–based site to come to an arrangement on your terms only. The site has plenty of great features (you can find deals within so many miles of your home) but is relatively new at the time of this writing. One to watch.

12. SWAPSTYLE.COM
What's traded: Glam—clothes, accessories, cosmetics, shoes
You build up your swapping potential by gaining a positive feedback score, so that other people can see you're a trustworthy recipient of their fashion triumphs. You can also go for Address Verification status, which is a physical letter containing a code that, once entered, confirms you're where you say you are. Once you're trusted and verified, you never have to wear the same thing twice.

13. SWAPTREE.COM
What's traded: Books, music, film and television DVDs, and video games
It's all about the barcode. Input the UPC or the ISBN from the back of the item you have, and the fancymajiggery behind the scenes at Swaptree will find what items are offered for trade in return, and display them Amazon-style down the screen. What's more, it'll keep searching while you're logged off, meaning you're faced with a new list of potential swaps every time you log

on. Specific to entertainment media— but brilliant at what it does.

14. TRADEAWAY.COM
What's traded: Things from the very, very small to the astoundingly large
This one claims to be the "World's Largest Online Barter Exchange Auction Site." There's plenty to see here. Listings range from the so-brief-they-must-be-spam all the way to exhaustively detailed multimillion-dollar property offers, but the theme is bartering. This is where hugely expensive real estate gets swapped.

15. U-EXCHANGE.COM
What's traded: Items big and small, including vehicles and homes
How does it work? It's up to you: This site puts you in touch with a wide range of bartering services and provides you with a profile. Less a specific service, more a gateway to lots of them.

16. WHATSMINEISYOURS. COM
What's traded: Fashion
How does it work? This site is based in Britain but most items seem to have overseas delivery as an option. As a trader, you put up a detailed ad, attach a price to it for comparative purposes, and mention what items you're interested in acquiring in return. Then you wait for an offer, tailored to the price or your item (or perhaps attempting to haggle a bit). You can also set up your own boutique, much like a shop in eBay. Handbags are the most popular trading item here.

HOW TO BARGAIN LIKE A PRO

1 Know when to haggle—at flea markets, large electronics shops (over things such as TVs and computers—not for CDs and accessories), mom and pop stores, any service-oriented business.

2 Nothing is set in stone. Even if "everyone pays that much" or "there are no substitutions on our packages," don't be shy about proposing a deal on your own terms. The worst that can happen is that you'll be turned down.

3 Start low. Never feel guilty offering what seems to be a ridiculously low price, as many merchants automatically quote prices that are several times more than they actually expect to get. Your starting price should be no more than one-third to one-half the asking price.

4 Use your poker face. The less your face betrays your interest in the item or the service, the better. Coming back again and again to admire an item is a good way to ensure that you'll overpay. Stay cool, and don't be afraid to point out flaws in whatever is being offered to you.

5 Do your homework. Find out before you go shopping how much the item is actually worth.

Have a target price in mind before you begin haggling, and think in terms of a maximum price, to keep from going over budget.

6 Be prepared to commit to the purchase once your target price is approved. Have your checkbook ready; don't give the vendor too much time to rethink his position.

7 Play "good cop/bad cop." Bring a friend with you and ask that person to appear to discourage you from the purchase. If you seem reluctant, the price might go down. Try to bring someone who has experience shopping for this particular item.

8 Refuse any vendor who bargains rudely or who doesn't seem to respect your position. His tactics may be indicative of the kind of service he delivers.

9 Let them know you have options. Make it clear that you're shopping around and that you have every intention of staying within your budget. Get competing estimates in writing and bring these with you when you shop.

10 Just say no. If the vendor isn't budging, be prepared to walk. Thank her for her

time and walk away. The price may plummet at that point.

11 Don't haggle just for the fun of it. Once you engage in bargaining, be prepared to make the purchase once your terms have been met. Declining an item after you have finally gotten your way is considered rude.

12 Keep cool at all times. The second you become angry or lose your composure, you've lost.

13 Let them know that, if you get a good price, you will shop there again and recommend the store to your friends.

14 Cash works wonders—if you cannot agree on a price, offer cash.

15 Shop just before a store is about to close at the end of the day; their resistance will be lowest.

SCAMOLOGY

Some of these are decades old but continue to haunt us, presumably because they get results. Some of us never learn. Yet guarding your home, your belongings, and your identity isn't really rocket science. If something seems too good to be true, it's just that. Use logic in all your money transactions. Don't deal with companies whose integrity you haven't researched, and make sure you leave a paper trail where money dealings are concerned. Use the Internet and the Better Business Bureau to learn all you can about companies and parties lest you fall victim to any one of these common scams.

ADVANCE FEE FRAUD

The most common of these is the Nigerian letter, in which a supposed "relative" of a senior government official in mainly African countries writes asking for assistance in getting funds out of his country. He offers a percentage of the sizable amount of money to you as a reward for using your bank account to clear the funds. Another form is the estate-type scams that often originate out of the United Kingdom and claim to be an estate company trying to track down beneficiaries of an estate. They usually ask for money to be sent to cover the legal fees associated with lodging a claim and then disappear from contact, with your money. Bogus credit and loan companies also ask for upfront fees for credit cards and loans that never materialize.

AFFINITY FRAUD

Affinity fraudsters prey on people who trust each other, particularly members of religious, social, or cultural groups. They use the trust that exists within these groups to help steal money. Targeted groups can include the elderly, ethnic groups, and religions. Perpetrators present themselves as trusted members of the group and then proceed to engage in everything from phony land deals to pyramid schemes.

ASTROLOGY AND PSYCHIC SCAMS

These promotions advise that you could come into a fortune if only you send funds to mail boxes for talismans, golden eggs, or fortune-telling guides to personal wealth. The material is normally bulk mailed from overseas, though it appears to be specifically written to you (thousands of others may have been mailed the same material).

BANKING SCAMS

Banking scams use technology to steal consumer information that can then be used to access money in people's bank accounts. Common variants include "phishing," where scammers appear to be authentic banks or Web sites such as eBay that ask for confirmation of customer details such as social security and account numbers. Such information may also be obtained using "skimming" devices that are fitted into ATM machines.

CHECK OVERPAYMENT

This scam usually occurs in association with online auctions. A fake bidder offers to buy a product over the Internet and sends a check for more than the agreed amount. The bidder then contacts the seller and asks for the additional money to be refunded by money order. Once the seller sends the overpayment, the bidder then cancels the original check leaving the seller out of pocket.

DRUG AND PHARMACEUTICAL SCAMS

These scammers offer items that are too good to be true–a new form of Viagra, creams that can melt wrinkles in minutes, or diet pills that really work. You get an initial supply for free or for a nominal payment. All you do is pay the postage (which is not nominal). You get a 30-day money-back guarantee. The trick here is that if you don't return the merch after the guarantee period, you are sent another supply each month–at exorbitant cost.

EMPLOYMENT SCAMS

These scams often appear in the classified ads. They offer ways to make large amounts of money by simply stuffing envelopes from home or by assembling products from pieces, such as toys and dolls. The problem is that you have to pay up front for supplies. By the time you've done that, you've lost contact with the company. Another employment scam involves calling you and telling you that you got whatever job it is you applied for and asking you for personal information for their human resources records. This information is used to steal your identity.

FALSE CHARITIES

These scams usually follow a major international disaster and pose as a charity raising funds for victims of the disaster.

IDENTITY THEFT

Identity theft is the takeover of a person's identity by utilizing stolen personal information, or fraudulently obtained, forged, or stolen identity documents.

Identity theft often results in the takeover of a victim's existing bank accounts or by the fraudulent operation of new accounts opened by the perpetrator in the victim's name. See page 291 for further details.

INTERNET SCAMS

Where does one begin? The most common Internet scams involve phony investments in work-at-home schemes and pyramid selling schemes.

The Internet makes it easy for high-tech touts to hide, shut down, or move on. Clever Web sites may look legitimate and be more convincing than newspaper advertisements. Online auctions can also be filled with dangerous procedures, such as asking customers to make untraceable payments (such as cash or money orders). Also, when buying something online, make sure that you communicate with the seller. Some hackers access sales transactions and then step in as the seller, giving you a different set of instructions for making payment. The real seller has no idea that this is taking place.

INVESTMENT SCAMS

This promotion offers a unique investment opportunity with high returns for very little risk. It is often only available to "a very few investors" and it demands consumers make very quick decisions.

These investments frequently don't exist at all and investors lose all their money. In another scenario, investors see early modest dividends that lull them into a false sense of security. Unfortunately, those are the only returns they ever see.

PRIZE AND LOTTERY SCAMS

These scams claim that the recipient has won a major international lottery. To release the money, the person must send through a payment to cover administration costs, and they must supply personal information so the money can be transferred. This money then disappears, and no further contact can be made.

PYRAMID SCHEMES

In a typical pyramid, or "Ponzi," scheme a potential member is asked to pay to join the association. The only way to advance is to recruit others, who also pay to join. As long as enough people join, the pyramid grows, but that soon ends. These schemes are illegal yet they continue to thrive among the naïve. See page 220.

TELEPHONE SCAMS

Most commonly, you are asked to donate to a charity, and yes, they can charge it to your credit card!

12 MONEY-SAVING TIPS FOR THE TRULY DESPERATE

1

Don't eat on Mondays.

2

Don't shop in stores that are smaller than football stadiums. You may have to rent space to store that flat of pickled mushrooms, but you'll save in the long run.

3

Can't afford contact lenses? Simply cut out small circles of plastic wrap and press them into your eyes.

4

Save money on vanity license plates by changing your name to match your existing plate.

5

Don't waste money buying expensive binoculars. Just stand closer to the object you wish to view.

6

Go back to VHS.

7

Skip the brand names: Why pay more just for the name? A Romex watch tells the right time most of the day, and for a fraction of the cost of its well-known counterpart.

8

Go to Mexico for vacations. There's a 50 percent chance that it won't be a scam.

9

Move to a less expensive house. You may think you want a certain quality of life, like being the only family in your home, but you could save hundreds by splitting the rent with five or six other families.

10

Go to the bathroom at your friend's house. If you can get away with it, shower there, too.

11

It's always darkest before dawn. So if you're going to steal your neighbor's newspaper, that's the time to do it.

12

Dump all your friends just before Christmas and then apologize after the gift-giving season is over.

HOW TO OVERCOME CHROMETOPHOBIA

Do you break out in a sweat when you think about money? Does shopping make you anxious and uncomfortable? Do you feel stressed out when paying your bills, even if you have enough money to pay them? You may be suffering from a condition known as *chrometophobia* (or *chrematophobia*)—the fear of money.

It's not surprising that many people fall into the category. We live in a consumerist society that urges us to spend more than we can afford. Jobs seem scarce, and it seems that the economic landscape will never look as appealing as it did a decade ago. Yet money is part of daily life, and there is no way to escape it. Happily, most problems that people have with money are based on emotions and not facts, and there are measures you can take to get over the condition:

You can conquer your fear of money by following these steps. You don't have to like money, but you don't have to fear it either.

1 Understand why you fear money. The first step in overcoming your fears is to recognize your fear and understand why you fear it. It could be the fear of not having enough, the burden of debt, or other reasons. Think about why money causes you fear or stress.

2 Learn more about money. We fear things we do not understand. Learn about money by talking about it with your spouse or friends; read books, magazines, or Web sites; or watch financial shows on TV. The more you know about money, the less you have to fear.

3 Address your fears. Just like a spider, you should respect money, but not fear it. If living paycheck to paycheck is causing you anxiety, try saving up enough money to get ahead one paycheck. If you feel crushed by debt, build a repayment plan to pay your debt off more quickly. The more quickly you address your fear of money, the more quickly you can overcome your fears.

4 Control money, don't let money control you. Setting up a budget is a good way to get control of your financial situation. Start by tracking your income and expenses for a month, then try to begin making a plan. You can use a simple spreadsheet or a budgeting program to make the job easier.

5 Seek professional help. Sometimes working on a problem by yourself is not enough. If you have tried multiple fixes and still haven't found a cure for your fear of money, then you may need to seek professional help.

TOP CELEBRITY MONEY MISTAKES

Behind the fancy clothes and retouched photos, celebrities are just people who, like us regular Joes, make serious money mistakes. Here are some that have made the news:

NO. 1: NOT SIGNING A PRE-NUP

You don't need to be filthy rich to need a pre-nup. If you bring assets to your partnership that you want to be sure you keep if things don't work out, it's essential to get a prenuptial agreement before you are married. Madonna made this mistake, and so did Paul McCartney, who was ordered to pay his ex, Heather Mills, a whopping $48.7 million.

NO. 2: OUT-OF-DATE WILLS

We all get busy, but be sure you update your will to address any major life event, such as marriage, divorce, or the birth of a child or grandchild. Actor Heath Ledger's tragic death was compounded by the fact that neither his girlfriend, Michelle Williams, nor their daughter, Matilda, was included in his will. That wasn't a slight; Ledger just hadn't updated his will since 2003, well before either person was in his life.

NO. 3: LOSING HOMES TO FORECLOSURE

Losing one's home to foreclosure usually indicates a purchase that never should have been made in the first place. Ed McMahon, Aretha Franklin, José Canseco, Stephen Baldwin, and LaToya Jackson have all suffered the ordeal.

NO. 4: OOPS! I SPENT IT AGAIN

According to court papers from her custody battle, Britney Spears never saved one penny of her $737,000 monthly income. Michael Jackson, once worth $500 million, almost lost Neverland to his debtors. They're not alone. Save early, save often, and avoid the fate of celebs who put their financial future at risk with reckless spending.

NO. 5: FALLING FOR INVESTING SCAM

Every year, millions of people are hurt by investing scams. And stars aren't immune. Talk show host Larry King admitted to having been the victim of an unscrupulous insurance agent, and the list of Bernie Madoff's victims (see page 222) is star-studded. If it sounds too good to be true, it is.

NO. 6: RUNNING UP GAMBLING DEBTS

Basketball great and TNT analyst Charles Barkley admitted that he has lost about $10 million gambling. Golfer John Daly claims to have lost an unbelievable $50 to 60 million, and basketball superstar Michael Jordan once lost $1 million on one round of golf. The super-rich often feel immune to the laws of nature, especially the one about what goes up. It's not bad to try your hand at the blackjack table or hit a slot machine or two *for fun* once in a while, but never play with more than you can comfortably afford to lose.

NO. 7: HAVING IRRESPONSIBLE HEIRS

You think you've been embarrassed by family members? Poor Barron Hilton, patriarch of the Hilton family—yes, those Hiltons—was so mortified by his granddaughter Paris Hilton's outrageous behavior that he left his money to charity instead. We can't help wonder if Paris's partying and wild antics were worth the $60 million it cost her.

ADVICE FROM RICH PEOPLE

APPLE CEO STEVE JOBS:

"Stay hungry. Stay foolish."

AMAZON CEO JEFF BEZOS:

"Successful folks focus in on what they love and they wait for the world to come to them."

WORLD'S WEALTHIEST AUTHOR, J. K. ROWLING:

"It is impossible to live without failing at something, unless you live so cautiously that you might as well not have lived at all—in which case, you fail by default."

MICROSOFT COFOUNDER BILL GATES:

"Humanity's greatest advances are not in its discoveries—but in how those discoveries are applied to reduce inequity."

GOOGLE COFOUNDER LARRY PAGE:

"Families brought you here, and you brought them here. Please keep them close and remember: They are what really matters in life."

GOOGLE CEO ERIC SCHMIDT:

"It's possible to spend your life inside the computer. Life is the people around you."

VIACOM CHAIRMAN SUMNER REDSTONE:

"It's not about the money—it's about winning."

GOOGLE "BUSINESS FOUNDER" OMID KORDESTANI:

"Think and act like an immigrant."

WHY WOMEN (ESPECIALLY) SHOULD EMBRACE

PERSONAL FINANCE

1 Women generally earn less than men and therefore need to know how to maximize their money and its growth.

2 Women have babies and therefore lose money and promotion opportunities when they are out of the workplace. They must know how to get and keep the jobs that offer the best pay and benefits.

3 Women need independence. Given the divorce rate (around 50 percent), and the fact that women live longer than men, it's likely that a woman will at some point be required to fly solo. She needs to be prepared.

"Woman's ability to earn money is a better protection against the tyranny and brutality of man than her ability to vote." —Victoria Clayton Woodhull (1838–1927), women's rights activist

4 Women teach children. Those who are financially savvy will be able to pass on what they've learned to their children and also set a good example for girls especially.

5 Women manage households. Knowing how to budget and shop wisely is important for women, who for the most part control household spending. They also play a big role in the purchase of big ticket items like appliances, cars, and real estate.

6 Women need financial identity. Having bank accounts, credit cards, and money in one's own name gives a woman an identity in the eyes of government and commerce. It also gives a woman a sense of safety and identity. Women should participate in all family business transactions including loans, car ownership, and mortgages.

7 Woman have jobs and therefore need to be able to negotiate salaries, bonuses, and benefits. Knowing that you can achieve success through career development gives a woman a strong sense of worth.

8 Women tend to put others first. But as flight attendants tell us, you can't help others if you haven't saved yourself. Women who help themselves by embracing and mastering their personal finances will be in a position to advise and empower others.

"Whatever you fear most has no power . . . it is your fear that has the power."
— Oprah Winfrey

CREDIT CARD STATISTICS

There were 984 million bank-issued Visa and MasterCard credit card and debit card accounts in the United States in 2006.

The top ten credit card issuers controlled approximately 88 percent of the credit card market at the end of 2006, based on credit card receivables outstanding.

Visa cardholders in the United States alone conduct more than $1 trillion in annual volume.

Consumers carry more than one billion Visa cards worldwide. More than 450 million of those cards are in the United States.

Seventy-eight percent of American households—about 91.1 million—had one or more credit cards at the end of 2008.

Seventy-six percent of undergraduates have credit cards, and the average undergrad has $2,200 in credit card debt. Additionally, they will amass almost $20,000 in student debt.

On average, today's consumer has a total of thirteen credit obligations on record at a credit bureau. These include credit cards (such as department store charge cards, gas cards, and bank cards) and installment loans (auto loans, mortgage loans, student loans, etc.). Not included are savings and checking accounts (typically not reported to a credit bureau). Of these thirteen credit obligations, nine are likely to be credit cards and four are likely to be installment loans.

Average credit card debt per household—regardless of whether they have a credit card or not—was $8,329 at the end of 2008.

The average outstanding credit card debt for households that have a credit card was $10,679 at the end of 2008.

Total U.S. consumer debt (which includes credit card debt and non–credit card debt but not mortgage debt) reached $2.56 trillion at the end of 2008.

The typical consumer has access to approximately $19,000 on all of his or her credit cards combined. More than half of all people with credit cards are using less than 30 percent of their total credit card limit. More than one in seven is using 80 percent or more.

Anchorage, Alaska, has the highest per capita credit card debt.

Lincoln, Nebraska, has the lowest per capita credit card debt.

One in six families with credit cards pays only the minimum due every month.

Ninety-three percent of cards allow the issuer to raise any interest rate at any time by changing the account agreement.

Today, credit cards are responsible for more than $2.5 trillion in transactions a year and are accepted at more than 24 million locations in more than 200 countries and territories.

It is estimated that there are 10,000 payment card transactions made every second around the world.

Credit and debit card fraud is the No. 1 fear of Americans in the midst of the global financial crisis. Concern about fraud supersedes that of terrorism, computer and health viruses, and personal safety.

MOST UNUSUAL CREDIT CARD DEALS

There are more than 900 million debit and credit cards in circulation today, and lenders are scrambling for ways to draw attention and snag new customers. Visa and MasterCard now offer snazzy cards bearing images of everything from Batman and Hello Kitty to Garfield and Looney Tunes characters. If you're tired of standard zero-APR-no-annual-fee-cash-back-rewards-program plastics, consider the offers below: They provide innovative features and unique rewards. (Note that these cards may only be made available during company promotions.)

1. CREDIT CARDS THAT SMELL

Commerzbank AG, one of Germany's major banks, has launched a range of Visa and MasterCard branded credit cards in four aromas: coffee, mint, cinnamon, and orange. Marketing gurus suggest that scented cards contain the benefits of aromatherapy.
Yeah, right.

2. FINANCE YOUR PLASTIC SURGERY!

Plastic surgery procedures such as breast augmentation and rhinoplasty (a "nose job") have become as common as teeth whitening. So it's no wonder that a credit card designed for plastic-surgery patients is being issued by GE Money Company. CreditCare is targeted at consumers who want to finance various medical procedures typically not covered by insurance. They include dental treatments, cosmetic surgery, cosmetic treatments, vision care and laser eye surgery, hearing aids, and even veterinary medicine for your pets.

3. THE AMERICAN DREAM

If you like playing the lottery, you can now do it every time you use your credit card. American DreamCard™ MasterCard® issued by HSBC Bank Nevada, N.A. offers sweepstake entries just for making day-to-day purchases. Participants earn one entry for each dollar spent. Monthly winners receive 50 percent of the total amount of dollars spent by all American DreamCard holders during each drawing period. Thus the monthly sweepstakes jackpot depends on the number of credit card users and the amount of money they spend.

As this list proves, the IRS gets you—coming and going.

SEX SALES TAX: Sin got pricier in Utah when owners of sexually explicit businesses where "nude or partially nude individuals perform any service" began paying a 10 percent sales-and-use tax. The measure didn't raise much money: Only one or two businesses in staid Utah are actually wild enough to be subjected to the tax.

FLUSH TAX: In 2004, Maryland began charging homeowners and businesses for producing wastewater. The funds are used to help protect Chesapeake Bay.

JOCK TAX: This is a tax on income earned by athletes, entertainers (not just jocks), and their various entourages, including non-athletic or non-performer employees. Generally, any money a player or performer earns while playing in that particular city or state gets taxed. California levied the first jock tax in 1991, on athletes from Chicago, right after the Chicago Bulls beat the L.A. Lakers. (Chicago quickly responded in kind.) Today, most states with a professional sports team impose a jock tax.

BLUEBERRY TAX: Like fresh, wild blueberries? If they come from Maine, you may be paying a bit of a premium.

Anyone who grows, purchases, sells, handles, or processes the fruit in the state is subject to a penny-and-a-half-per-pound tax.

Dear IRS: I'm sending you this money because I cheated on my income tax and my conscience has been bothering me. If it doesn't stop, I'll send you the rest.

WAGERING TAX: Illinois forces casinos to charge a $2 admission price, which is remitted to the city and state.

FUR CLOTHING TAX: Keeping comfy during Minnesota winters can cost you. Businesses in the state must pay a 6.5 percent tax on the total amount received for the sale, shipping, and finance charges associated with the purchase of clothing in which fur accounts for three times more of the garment than the next most valuable material.

FOUNTAIN SODA DRINK TAX: If you buy a fountain soda drink in Chicago, you'll pay a 9 percent tax.

If you buy the same soda in a bottle or a can, you'll only pay 3 percent.

AMUSEMENT TAX: Most states, including Massachusetts, Virginia, and Maryland, and cities like New Orleans, have amusement taxes on tickets sold at any venue with more than 750 to 1,000 seats.

TATTOO TAX: Anyone in Arkansas wanting to get an eagle etched on their abs or a nose ring notched in their nostrils has to pay an additional 6 percent sales tax.

IRS CALLING

"Hello, is this Father O'Malley?"
"It is."
"This is the IRS. Can you help us?"
"I can."
"Do you know a Ted Houlihan?"
"I do."
"Is he a member of your congregation?"
"He is."
"Did he donate $10,000 to the church?"
"He will!"

32 GREAT HIDING PLACES FOR MONEY

Just as putting all your eggs in one basket can get dangerous, so, too, when hiding money at home, it's important not to hide it all in one place. Burglars are motivated to steal your valuables and then vacate the place as soon as possible. Finding a small stash of money (say $100) may convince them that that's all there is.

It's also dangerous to leave valuables inside something valuable, like a jewelry box or a treasured vase. Those are the first places burglars will look. They'll also target dresser drawers, drawers near phones, desks, closets, a safe (if not bolted down), boxes, and purses.

Be forewarned, however, that you *must* inform any and all people you live with or who conceivably have access to these places (such as a cleaning service) that these items are not what they seem!

Here are some ideas:

1 The underside of trash cans

2 Inside laundry detergent

3 Inside false packaging (but make sure the package is camouflaged among real packages)

4 At the bottom of a hamper filled with soiled clothing

5 In an envelope taped to the bottom of a kitchen shelf

6 In a watertight plastic bottle or jar in the tank on the back of your toilet

7 In an envelope at the bottom of your child's toy box

8 In a plastic baggie in the freezer

9 In a medicine bottle kept in the medicine cabinet

10 In the pocket of a particular shirt in your closet

11 In a "random" folder in your filing cabinet

12 In an envelope taped to the bottom of your cat's litter box

13 In an envelope taped to the back of a wall decoration

14 Between several pages in a random book or two on your bookshelf

15 Buried in a jar in the back yard

16 Underneath a potted plant (or even buried in a small jar in the soil)

17 In an envelope taped to the bottom of a dresser drawer (reachable from the drawer below)

18 Inside a big coffee cup in the back of a cupboard

19 Inside your Christmas decorations box

20 Inside an empty beer bottle in the back of the fridge with the cap seemingly in place

21 In a plastic baggie inside a flour or coffee container or in any food container

22 In an envelope inside of a DVD case

23 In a false wall that you've built in a discreet area of your home

24 Somewhere in the crawl space of your house

25 Underneath a tacked-down carpet inside a closet or underneath a piece of furniture

26 Folded in a towel at the back of the linen closet

27 In a sack of dog food

28 In a phone book

29 In a box clearly marked "Clothing for Charity"

30 Inside an empty lipstick tube

31 Inside an unplugged toaster

32 In the bank!

A woman in Israel who had stashed some $1 million in cash in American dollars and Israeli shekels in her mattress was horrified to wake up in the middle of the night only to realize that she had thrown out the mattress. The women spent the following weeks sorting through tons of garbage at the dump where her trash had been taken. As the woman searched, security at the dump was increased to deter treasure-hunters. The money was never recovered.

HOW TO ASK FOR A RAISE

If you think you are underpaid and undervalued, you owe it to yourself to address the matter in a professional, well-prepared, and objective way. Asking for a raise can be a traumatic experience, but if you proceed with confidence, you are more likely to be perceived as an asset to your company.

1 Know when to make your move. If the standard practice is to review salaries only annually, there's no point in asking. But if the rules have been broken on occasion and you have a good case, go for it.

2 Know what you're worth. Do the research to find out just how much you are being underpaid, if that's the case. If you're already making more than the average in your position, you'll need lots of ammo. Network with others in similar jobs to determine your marketability. Professional associations often provide salary surveys.

3 Make a list of your assets, accomplishments, and any other conditions that would suggest you should be paid more. Have your responsibilities recently changed? Have you been working overtime? Any special projects in the works? You may be worth more than you think. When you present your case, start with the most recent and work your way backwards.

4 Be straightforward in addressing your request for a pay raise to your supervisor. Schedule an appointment and indicate the nature of the meeting. She may need time to research the subject.

5 Start the meeting by letting your boss know how much you like working at the company and how rewarding your job has been. Keep things amicable. Smile a lot.

6 Tell your boss the specific pay raise you'd like to see. Be prepared to present the research that supports your request for a pay raise.

7 Indicate that it's not just money you're after—you're also hoping for more responsibility and advancement.

8 Anticipate the counterarguments you are likely to hear and be prepared with responses.

9 Don't talk or think in terms of "I want" or "I need." This is about your performance and what you deserve. Do not raise issues of personal hardship. Don't whine.

10 Remember that it's not always just salary that's at stake. Be prepared to discuss benefits, titles, and modifications to your responsibilities, management, or assignments.

11 Keep the discussion focused on your work, and avoid personal issues, including the failings of other workers.

12 If you give your boss an ultimatum, be prepared to walk. Be sure you have a plan B—another job—waiting.

13 If you are turned down, ask if perhaps he or she would like some more time to think the matter over. Ask what you can do to make yourself eligible for a raise as soon as possible. Show that you are willing to work for it.

13 RECESSION-PROOF JOBS

When the going gets tough, these careers get going.

1. ACCOUNTING
Bad times increase businesses' and individuals' desire to wisely account for every last dollar.

2. EDUCATION
Even in the recent tough times, our political leaders are calling for increased education spending, and voters continue to pass education bonds.

3. ENTERTAINMENT
During the Great Depression, the movie industry boomed as people with tons of time on their hands craved escapism. Today the film, videogame, sports, and creative arts industries remain viable.

4. UTILITY COMPANIES
Even in the worst times, the need for utilities does not subside.

5. REPAIRERS
In a bad economy, people generally repair instead of replace.

6. NUCLEAR ENERGY
Despite all the media attention to solar power, the nuclear industry may, over the next decade, create the most jobs.

7. HEALTH CARE
As the population grows, so too does its need for registered nurses, physician assistants, internal medicine physicians, dentists, optometrists, pharmacists, and physical therapy assistants. Many government jobs in accounting, actuarial science, information systems, and management will undoubtedly result from health care reforms.

8. SENIOR SERVICES
An increasingly aging population will increase the need for housing, home retrofitting, geriatric care management, and healthcare.

9. LAW ENFORCEMENT
Crime doesn't take a break in tough times. In fact, it tends to increase.

10. "SIN" INDUSTRIES
Jobs related to the liquor and sex industries have always thrived, in good times and bad.

11. THE CLERGY
People seek spiritual support in tough times.

12. REPOSSESSION, FORECLOSURE, AND DEBT COLLECTION INDUSTRIES
Someone will have to repossess all those big SUVs from owners who knew they couldn't afford them but took advantage of no-qualification loans all the same.

13. GOVERNMENT WORK
The Obama presidency is creating government jobs across the board but especially in homeland security, healthcare, accounting/auditing, information technology, and the IRS. The government has the power to collect taxes in good times and bad, and is thus impervious to economic declines.

"To force myself to earn more money, I determined to spend more."
—James Agate (1877–1947), British author

THE 10 WORST JOBS YOU CAN GET TODAY

(NOT BASED ON SALARY)

It's not always about the money. In researching two hundred jobs, JobsRated.com took into account the stress levels associated with various vocations in order to determine the worst and best careers. The results were surprising. Many jobs that seem like "easy money" are anything but. Taxi drivers get to sit all day, but they also have to deal with the constant stress of traffic. Workers who maintain oil rigs deal with intense physical demands in a dangerous environment. If you are considering a career change, here are some terrible choices. The stress levels you see are based on a 1 to 100 scale, 100 being the most stressful:

1. TAXI DRIVER
Hours per week: 47.5
Annual income: $21,127
Stress level: 100

2. LUMBERJACK
Hours per week: 45
Annual income: $32,124
Stress level: 67.6

3. EMERGENCY MEDICAL TECHNICIAN
Hours per week: 40
Annual income: $26,158
Stress level: 67.1

4. LABORER
Hours per week: 50
Annual income: $29,140
Stress level: 65.6

5. DAIRY FARMER
Hours per week: 52.5
Annual income: $33,109
Stress level: 64.5

6. SEAMAN
Hours per week: 50
Annual income: $34,160
Stress level: 51.3

7. IRONWORKER
Hours per week: 45
Annual income: $32,129
Stress level: 50.9

8. WELDER
Hours per week: 45
Annual income: $33,127
Stress level: 47.7

9. ROOFER
Hours per week: 42.5
Annual income: $34,164
Stress level: 46.6

10. GARBAGE COLLECTOR
Hours per week: 42.5
Annual income: $30,189
Stress level: 42.8

Reaching the end of a job interview, the interviewer asked the young MBA fresh out of MIT, "And what starting salary were you looking for?" The candidate said, "In the neighborhood of $125,000 a year, depending on the benefits package."

The interviewer said, "Well, what would you say to a package of five weeks vacation, fourteen paid holidays, full medical and dental, a company-matching retirement fund up to 50 percent of salary, and a company car leased every two years—say, a red Corvette?" The young engineer sat up straight and said, "Wow!!! Are you kidding?" The interviewer replied, "Certainly, but you started it."

THE 10 BEST JOBS YOU CAN GET TODAY

(NOT BASED ON SALARY)

According to JobsRated.com. Criteria were stress, physical demands, hiring outlook, compensation, and work environment.

1. ACTUARY
Hours per week: 45
Annual income: $88,146
Stress level: 20.2

2. MATHEMATICIAN
Hours per week: 45
Annual income: $94,160
Stress level: 24.7

3. SOFTWARE ENGINEER
Hours per week: 50
Annual income: $86,139
Stress level: 25.0

4. COMPUTER SYSTEMS ANALYST
Hours per week: 45
Annual income: $75,160
Stress level: 25.0

5. BIOLOGIST
Hours per week: 45
Annual income: $74,273
Stress level: 27.0

6. STATISTICIAN
Hours per week: 45
Annual income: $72,197
Stress level: 28.0

7. HISTORIAN
Hours per week: 45
Annual income: $61,209
Stress level: 28.4

8. ACCOUNTANT
Hours per week: 45
Annual income: $59,173
Stress level: 31.1

9. INDUSTRIAL DESIGNER
Hours per week: 45
Annual income: $58,206
Stress level: 32.1

10. SOCIOLOGIST
Hours per week: 45
Annual income: $63,195
Stress level: 34.1

HUMANS FOR SALE

Have you been thinking about putting yourself up for sale lately? Ever wonder how much money you could get on the open human market? Go to Humanfor-sale.com and take their fun quiz, which will attempt to place a value on your life using a variety of criteria in four basic facets of life. Among the criteria used are athletic ability, education level, income, amount of exercise, weight, and sense of humor. This is obviously a very subjective survey and is not intended and does not claim to be scientifically accurate. The more honestly you answer the questions, the more realistic the dollar value returned will be.

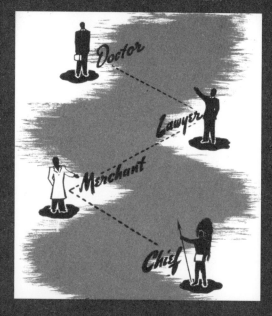

10 ORIGINAL IDEAS FOR ONLINE BUSINESSES

THAT WORKED BIG TIME

1 Make a home page with a million pixels. Charge a dollar per pixel. That's perhaps the dumbest idea for an online business anyone could have possibly come up with. Still, Alex Tew, a twenty-one-year-old university student in Britain who came up with the idea in 2005, is now a millionaire. The Web site, www.milliondollar homepage.com, became an Internet phenomenon. On January 1, 2006, the final 1,000 pixels were put up for auction on eBay. The auction closed on January 11 with a winning bid of $38,100 that brought the final tally to $1,037,100 in gross income. In the meantime, copycats abound.

2 Get a postal address in North Pole, Alaska, pretend you are Santa Claus, and charge parents ten bucks for every letter you send to their kids. Byron Reese has sent more than 200,000 letters since the start of the business (www.SantaMail.org) in 2001, making him a couple of million dollars richer.

3 LaserMonks.com is a for-profit subsidiary of the Cistercian Abbey of Our Lady of Spring Bank, an eight-monk monastery in the hills of Monroe County, ninety miles northwest of Madison. When they're not communing with the Lord, they refill used printer cartridges and resell them online. Hallelujah! Their 2005 sales were $2.5 million! Praise the Lord.

4 Jason Wall made his millions selling cute smiley-face tennis balls that you stick on your car antennae. After selling four million balls through local gas stations and convenience stores, Wall landed some major national accounts, including Wal-Mart. He had sales of $1.15 million in 1999, one year after he started his business.

5 Create a deck of cards featuring exercise routines, and sell it online for $18.95. Sounds like a disastrous idea, but former Navy SEAL and fitness instructor Phil Black reported 2005 sales of $4.7 million.

6 Faux-suede padded covers for game controllers and gel thumb pads for analog joysticks? These products proved to be so popular, they got picked up by Target and Wal-Mart's online stores, and annual sales now exceed half a million dollars.

7 Who in the world needs *fake plastic* wishbones? A lot of people, it turns out. Now producing 30,000 wishbones daily (they retail for three bucks a pop) Ken Ahroni's sales have reached $1 million.

8 Teenager Ashley Qualls, who had a flair for the creative, set up a site to offer layouts for MySpace and free tutorials. The idea took off, and she now gets around seven million visitors to her Web site, www.WhateverLife.com, every month. She's managed to land some major advertising contracts and has received offers to buy her site that have exceeded $1.5 million.

9 If there is one thing dogs don't need, it's a pair of goggles, but this idea—doggles—which got its start online, has made millions of dollars. The original idea of UV-protective doggles was eventually expanded, and the product line now includes jewelry.

10 Two teens had a simple idea: Why not create an online yearbook for people? The idea turned into a social networking site called MyYearbook.com and they've been able to raise more than $4 million in venture capital. The company has forty-five employees, three million members, and some heavy-duty advertisers.

FINANCIAL JOB DESCRIPTIONS

ACCOUNTANT
Someone who knows the cost of everything and the value of nothing.

ACTUARY
Someone who brings a fake bomb on a plane, because that decreases the chances that there will be another bomb on the plane.
(Laurence J. Peter)

AUDITOR
Someone who arrives after the battle, and bayonets all the wounded.

BANKER
A fellow who lends you his umbrella when the sun is shining and wants it back the minute it begins to rain.
(Mark Twain)

ECONOMIST
An expert who will know tomorrow why the things he predicted yesterday didn't happen today.

STATISTICIAN
Someone who is good with numbers but lacks the personality to be an accountant.

Workers earn it,
Spendthrifts burn it,
Bankers lend it,
Women spend it,
Forgers fake it,
Taxes take it,
Dying leaves it,
Heirs receive it,
Thrifty save it,
Misers crave it,
Robbers seize it,
Rich increase it,
Gamblers lose it,
I could use it.
—Richard Armour

A growing body of research finds that taller people make more money.

A study conducted in Australia revealed that men who are six feet tall earn approximately $1,000 a year more than their shorter counterparts. "Taller people are perceived to be more intelligent and powerful," claims the study, which was published in Australia's *Economic Record*. "Our estimates suggest that if the average man of about five feet ten inches gains an additional two inches in height, he would be able to earn an extra $950 per year, which is approximately equal to the wage gain from one extra year of labor market experience," said study co-author Andrew Leigh, an economist at the Australian National University.

Other studies in the United States and Britain put the extra earnings at nearly that much per inch.

"The truth is, tall people do make more money. They make $789 more per inch per year," says Arianne Cohen, author of *The Tall Book*.

Being tall may boost self-confidence, helping to make a person more successful and also prompting people to ascribe more status and respect to him or her, says Timothy Judge, a management professor at the University of Florida and a member of the U.S. research team.

Judge concludes that the advantages of height today are rooted in our evolutionary decision-making regarding who was most powerful. "When humans evolved as a species and still lived in the jungles or on the plain, they ascribed leader-like qualities to tall people because they thought they would be better able to protect them," Judge said. "Some of those old patterns still operate in our perceptions today."

Here are your best career choices, according to Natalie Josef of DivineCaroline.com:

Were you born to be rich? A 2008 Career Builder.com survey of close to 9,000 workers determined that those born under Scorpio, Leo, Taurus, or Cancer are the most likely to earn more than $100,000 per year. Sorry, Capricorn and Aquarius, you folks are most likely to earn less than $35,000 per year. We won't all be rich, but we can find satisfaction in our jobs, especially if we seek out ones that are congruent with our zodiac signs.

ARIES

Aries is the youngest sign in the zodiac. There is a reason the sign is represented by a ram—Aries are strong (and strong-willed), vibrant, enthusiastic, and competitive. They thrive in commission-based jobs, especially if there is a bonus involved. Due to their bravery (and their impulsivity), they are the heroes of our lives—the police officers and firefighters. They are excellent promoters and may find that the world of advertising and public relations appeals to their outgoing nature. Best jobs: entrepreneur, soldier, rescue worker; they work well in the fields of government and politics, television, and recreation.

TAURUS

One of the things a Taurus enjoys most is stability. They will work very hard for certain guarantees—good benefits, vacation time, salary, job security. Determined, patient, honest, and methodical, they are excellent team members and extremely dependable. Taurians have a fondness for beautiful things and love working with flowers, food, jewelry, and luxury items. They are also known for their clear, strong voices and do well as announcers, public speakers, or receptionists. Best jobs: accountant, educator, engineer, lawyer, designer, landscaper, chef.

GEMINI

Want to make a Gemini happy? Give him or her plenty to do and make it intellectually stimulating. Remember that Geminis are twins, which means you have to engage two people, so they need to have a lot going on and like fast-paced, pressured environments. They won't survive long doing tedious or repetitive work. Jobs that require travel are perfect, as are jobs that require social networking. Geminis are optimistic and full of energy—they should be encouraged to let go and express themselves rather than be confined to traditional rules. Best jobs: stockbroker, switchboard operator, technical support, teacher, architect, machine operator, rescue worker.

CANCER

Cancer is the mother of the zodiac (Capricorn is the father), so these sensitive types do well in jobs that require nurturing or taking care of things.

However, this isn't just about working with children or puppies; Cancerians make excellent executives, much like a multitasking mom who's in charge. Cancerians give great advice and are very protective. They handle responsibility with ease and are imaginative problem solvers. Best jobs: gardener, social worker, childcare worker, human resources person, lawyer, teacher, CEO, soldier.

LEO

Nothing like a mighty lion to lead your company into success and high profits. Fearless, inspiring, and independent, Leos work best when they are in the spotlight, and love jobs that bring status and power. They can be high-maintenance and disruptive to a team environment, but their charm usually wins everyone over in the end. Not to be micro-managed, Leos possess spontaneity and ingenuity and do well when encouraged to lead instead of follow. Best jobs: CEO, performer, tour guide, real estate agent, interior decorator, fashion designer, government, salesperson.

VIRGO

Virgos are known for their perfectionism and do very well in detailed-oriented professions. They remember things, excel at abstract thinking, and are very tidy and neat. Many Virgos do well in service-type jobs—you would be very happy with a Virgo manicurist or server (plus Virgos tend to make more money when working for tips). Writing, research, and statistics come easy to the meticulous Virgo brain. They are also easy to get along with as they are generally very cheerful. Many Virgos have a knack for languages. Best jobs: editor/writer, teacher, critic, technician, translator, detective, statistician.

LIBRA

Libras—what would we do without them? They are good-looking and charming, gracious and entertaining. Their cooperative nature makes them excellent ambassadors and team leaders. If you ever have to deal with customer service over the phone, it will go much smoother if the operator is a Libra. More so than any sign, Libras are people people. They are not the type to slave away in some dark room; they thrive in buzzing, social environments. Many Libras gravitate toward the arts and will most likely be the lead singer of a band, interacting with the audience, rather than being a brooding songwriter. Best jobs: diplomat, dancer, salesperson, host, negotiator, travel agent, supervisor.

SCORPIO

Intense—that's what they are. Need a bomb diffused? How about complicated brain surgery? Trust me, you want a Scorpio for the job. Scorpios are able to block out distractions, concentrate, and focus like a laser beam. They are curious and are often drawn to mysteries—you would never want to be cross-examined or interrogated by a Scorpio, for they are not only intimidating, but also very intuitive. Scorpios are also drawn to the abnormal and they like to know what makes things tick (think Fox Mulder on *The X-Files*). Just don't hover around them—they need their independence and their employer's trust. Best jobs: detective, lawyer, educator, scientist, surgeon, physicist.

SAGITTARIUS

Sagittarians are ethical, full of energy, and rather philosophical. They are excellent decision-makers and make fair and easygoing bosses. Many Sagittarians are spiritual, which can translate well into careers involving the environment, animals, and counseling, as well as religion. They also love to travel and be outdoors. Outgoing and fun-loving, they are likable and witty coworkers who can defuse tense situations with humor and tact. They will not be tied down or bothered with the little details. Routine kills their spirit. Best jobs: minister, animal trainer, editor, public relations professional, coach, and anything having to do with travel.

CAPRICORN

Capricorns are very ambitious and need challenges to be happy. Just as the mountain goat climbs on the tiniest crags to get to the top, Capricorns are determined and persistent—they will do what whatever it takes. Most are responsible and conscientious; many enjoy power. They run a tight ship—and will enforce rules and keep everyone on schedule. If you need something done right (and to exact standards), look no further than a Capricorn. They also tend to be workaholics. Best jobs: manager, administrator, editor, banker, and anything science-related.

AQUARIUS

The quality that sets Aquarians apart from everyone else is their humanitarian nature (it's also why they are flighty in matters of the heart, but that's another story). They love to explore avant-garde ideas, and have a curious and adventurous nature. They are the most likely to have an unconventional job, maybe even one of their making. They will rebel against corporate environments, needing freedom of thought and movement. They will not be satisfied doing things the same way they have always been done. If you need a fresh

approach, an Aquarius will not let you down. Best jobs: scientist (if they can explore new theories), inventor, organic farmer, aviator, designer, musician.

PISCES

Pisces is the oldest sign in the zodiac and many Pisceans have that "old soul" feel about them. The key words here are creative and passionate. They excel in the traditional arts (music, dance, photography). Pisceans are also highly intuitive. If your stylist is a Pisces, she will not only give you a modern and unique haircut, she will also give you the haircut that fits *you* best. Many astrologers and tarot practitioners are Pisces. Their intuition also helps in fields that require compassion. Best jobs: artist, nurse, physical therapist, philanthropist, veterinarian, psychologist.

39 THINGS MONEY CAN'T BUY

The smile of a child	A peaceful heart	A hand to help you when you least expect it	Spiritual fulfillment
The changing of the seasons	Good manners	The ability to laugh	A good reputation
A perfect rose	Forgiveness	Talent	Clouds
The sound of laughter	Clean air everywhere	Creativity	Lost time
A fond memory	A good night's sleep	Intelligence	Happiness
The welcoming arms of a loved one	Wisdom	Street smarts	Love
A friend who truly cares	Self-reliance	The loyalty of a pet	A gorgeous sunset
The respect of a colleague	Job satisfaction	A sense of humor	Loving parents
Perfect health	The love of family	A sunny day	Great memories
	The sound of rain against a windowpane	Courage	Forgiveness

"The day, water, sun, moon, night . . . I do not have to purchase these things with money."
—Plautus (c. 254–c. 184 B.C.), Roman playwright

We are grateful to the following individuals for their contributions and expertise:

AOL Food and Walletpop.com for "9 Rich Parents Who Aren't Leaving Their Money to Their Kids." (Walletpop is a trademark of AOL LLC.)

Hannah S. Grove and Russ Prince for "Spending Habits of the Ultra-Wealthy." Taken from The Sky's the Limit (Charter Financial Publishing Network, 2007). Reprinted with permission.

Allan Halprin and Walletpop.com for "12 Self-Proclaimed Frugal Celebrities" and "The Cheapskate Hall of Fame"

Joseph Kenny for "Celebrity Victims of Identity Theft"

Diana Lai and The Foundation Center (FoundationCenter.Org) for "Famous Philanthropists"

Jeannine Moore and BalancePro.Net for "Why We Buy: The Psychology of Spending"

Ryan Patrick Guina and CashMoney Life.com for "The Ten Commandments of Money"

Stephanie Roberts Serrano of Fast FengShui.com for "Feng Shui for Prosperity"

Myscha Theriault, co-author of 10,001 Ways to Live Large on a Small Budget (Skyhorse, 2009) and blogs at Wisebread.com and TrekHound.com, for "10 Ways to Go Green and Save Money at the Same Time"

Melinda Oppenhemier and credit.org for "Teaching Your Children About Money: 6 Guiding Principles"

EcoSalon.com for "Trading Places: 16 great Websites for Bartering"

Andrew Lawrence, author of Discover Your Life Purpose in 30 Minutes (CreateSpace, 2008) and The Happiness Transformation (CreateSpace 2009) and other books, for "How to Overcome Chrometophobia"

Ecommerce-Journal.com for "Most Unusual Credit Card Deals" Natalie Josef (author) of Divine Caroline.com for "Best Careers for Your Zodiac Sign"

PHOTO CREDITS

p. 15: CoinCoin.com, Library of Congress
p. 16: Library of Congress
p. 17: Library of Congress
p. 19: Library of Congress
p. 20: HeritageAuctions.com
p. 25: CoinCoin.com
p. 29: Library of Congress
p. 30: Library of Congress, Sandra Stanton (right)
p. 31: Library of Congress
p. 37: Library of Congress
p. 38: Netvision
p. 40: Library of Congress
p. 45: Library of Congress
p. 52: Library of Congress
p. 63: Library of Congress

p. 65: Chad Price, Ella Shaffer
p. 66: Richard Park
p. 69: Library of Congress
p. 70: Authors' collection
p. 76: Library of Congress
p. 77: Library of Congress
p. 79: Scripophily
p. 82: Library of Congress
p. 85–86: banknotes.com
p. 91: Library of Congress
p. 97: Authors' collection
p. 102: Library of Congress
p. 107: Library of Congress
p. 113: Library of Congress
p. 116: Authors' collection
p. 128: Library of Congress
p. 129: Library of Congress

p. 131: Library of Congress
p. 137: Phil Skinner
p. 139: PanAm World Airways, Inc., autotransportdirect.com
p. 147: Library of Congress
p. 151–152: Library of Congress
p. 156: Library of Congress
p. 157: pr@cafepress.com
p. 158: Luxurycarts.com
p. 159: Clive.com
p. 172: JoelsCoins.com
p. 174: Library of Congress
p. 175: Stacks.com
p. 188: LittletonCoin.com
p. 197: Library of Congress
p. 199: Library of Congress

p. 201: Lyn Knight Auctions
p. 217: Library of Congress
p. 221: Kosmas Ballis
p. 252: David M. Beach
p. 270: Authors' collection
p. 283: CreativeSlush.com
p. 318: Library of Congress

INDEX

SELECTED BIBLIOGRAPHY

Bowers, Q. David and David M. Sundman. *100 Greatest American Currency Notes*. Racine, Wis.: Whitman, 2005

Bowersock, Glen W. *Edward Gibbon and the Decline and Fall of the Roman Empire*. Boston: Harvard University Press, 1977

Davies, Glyn. *A History of Money*. Cardiff, Wales: University of Wales Press, 2002

Eagleton, Catherine. *Money: A History*. Buffalo, New York: Firefly Books, 2007

Ferguson, Niall. *The Ascent of Money*. New York: Penguin, 2009

Isaacson, Walter. *Benjamin Franklin: An American Life*. New York: Simon & Schuster, 2004

Nass, Herbert E. *Wills of the Rich and Famous*. New York: Warner Books, 1991

Niven, David. *Up! A Pragmatic Look at the Direction of Life: 365 Ways Today Is the Best Time to Be Alive*. Carlsbad, California: Hay House, 2010

Standish, David. *The Art of Money*. San Francisco: Chronicle Books, 2000

Weatherford, Jack. *The History of Money*. New York: Three Rivers, 1998

Weschler, Lawrence. *Boggs: A Comedy of Values*. Chicago: University of Chicago Press, 2000

USEFUL WEB SITES

ABA.com
Absoluteastronomy.com
AtoZinvestments.com
Aviewoncities.com
CFO.com
China.org
CNBC.com
CNN.com
Coinfacts.com
Daviddfriedman.com
Economictheories.org
Encyclopedia.com
Explorenorth.com
Factolex.com
Familyinnewyork.com
FDIC.gov
Forbes.com
Freesian.com
Globalsecurity.org
Fordham.edu
Freemaninstitute.com
IMF.org
Investopedia.com
Jasonzhao.hotpng.com
Judaism.about.com
Kidsmoney.org
Mastercard.com
Money.cnn.com
Moneyfactory.com
Moneyreformparty.org.uk
Myfico.com
Newsweek.com
Onlygold.com
People.com
Projects.exeter.ac.uk
Rateitall.com
Retireat21.com
Secretservice.gov

Stock-exchange-history.com
Stockmarketstory.com
Thelastbestwest.com
Thepeoplehistory.com
Time.com
Unisyssecurityindex.com
USNews.com
Visa.com